DEVELOPING APPLICATIONS WITH
VISUAL BASIC AND UML

The Addison-Wesley Object Technology Series

Grady Booch, Ivar Jacobson, and James Rumbaugh, Series Editors

For more information check out the series web site [http://www.awl.com /cseng/otseries/] as well as the pages on each book [http://www.awl.com/cseng/I-S-B-N/] (I-S-B-N represents the actual ISBN, including dashes).

David Bellin and Susan Suchman Simone, *The CRC Card Book*, ISBN 0-201-89535-8

Robert V. Binder, *Testing Object-Oriented Systems: Models, Patterns, and Tools*, ISBN 0-201-80938-9

Bob Blakley, *CORBA Security: An Introduction to Safe Computing with Objects*, ISBN 0-201-32565-9

Grady Booch, *Object Solutions: Managing the Object-Oriented Project*, ISBN 0-8053-0594-7

Grady Booch, *Object-Oriented Analysis and Design with Applications, Second Edition*, ISBN 0-8053-5340-2

Grady Booch, James Rumbaugh, and Ivar Jacobson, *The Unified Modeling Language User Guide*, ISBN 0-201-57168-4

Don Box, *Essential COM*, ISBN 0-201-63446-5

Don Box, Keith Brown, Tim Ewald, and Chris Sells, *Effective COM: 50 Ways to Improve Your COM and MTS-based Applications*, ISBN 0-201-37968-6

Alistair Cockburn, *Surviving Object-Oriented Projects: A Manager's Guide*, ISBN 0-201-49834-0

Dave Collins, *Designing Object-Oriented User Interfaces*, ISBN 0-8053-5350-X

Jim Conallen, *Building Web Applications with UML*, ISBN 0-201-61577-0

Bruce Powel Douglass, *Doing Hard Time: Designing and Implementing Embedded Systems with UML*, ISBN 0-201-49837-5

Bruce Powel Douglass, *Real-Time UML, Second Edition: Developing Efficient Objects for Embedded Systems*, ISBN 0-201-65784-8

Desmond F. D'Souza and Alan Cameron Wills, *Objects, Components, and Frameworks with UML: The Catalysis Approach*, ISBN 0-201-31012-0

Martin Fowler, *Analysis Patterns: Reusable Object Models*, ISBN 0-201-89542-0

Martin Fowler, *Refactoring: Improving the Design of Existing Code*, ISBN 0-201-48567-2

Martin Fowler with Kendall Scott, *UML Distilled, Second Edition: Applying the Standard Object Modeling Language*, ISBN 0-201-65783 X

Ian Gorton, *Enterprise Transaction Processing Systems: Putting the CORBA OTS, Encina++ and OrbixOTM to Work*, ISBN 0-201-39859-1

Peter Heinckiens, *Building Scalable Database Applications: Object-Oriented Design, Architectures, and Implementations*, ISBN 0-201-31013-9

Christine Hofmeister, Robert Nord, Soni Dilip, *Applied Software Architecture*, ISBN 0-201-32571-3

Ivar Jacobson, Grady Booch, and James Rumbaugh, *The Unified Software Development Process*, ISBN 0-201-57169-2

Ivar Jacobson, Magnus Christerson, Patrik Jonsson, and Gunnar Overgaard, *Object-Oriented Software Engineering: A Use Case Driven Approach*, ISBN 0-201-54435-0

Ivar Jacobson, Maria Ericsson, and Agneta Jacobson, *The Object Advantage: Business Process Reengineering with Object Technology*, ISBN 0-201-42289-1

Ivar Jacobson, Martin Griss, and Patrik Jonsson, *Software Reuse: Architecture, Process and Organization for Business Success*, ISBN 0-201-92476-5

David Jordan, *C++ Object Databases: Programming with the ODMG Standard*, ISBN 0-201-63488-0

Philippe Kruchten, *The Rational Unified Process, Second Edition: An Introduction*, ISBN 0-201-70710-1

Wilf LaLonde, *Discovering Smalltalk*, ISBN 0-8053-2720-7

Dean Leffingwell and Don Widrig, *Managing Software Requirements: A Unified Approach*, ISBN 0-201-61593-2

Chris Marshall, *Enterprise Modeling with UML: Designing Successful Software through Business Analysis*, ISBN 0-201-43313-3

Lockheed Martin Advanced Concepts Center and Rational Software Corporation, *Succeeding with the Booch and OMT Methods: A Practical Approach*, ISBN 0-8053-2279-5

Thomas Mowbray and William Ruh, *Inside CORBA: Distributed Object Standards and Applications*, ISBN 0-201-89540-4

Bernd Oestereich, *Developing Software with UML: Object-Oriented Analysis and Design in Practice*, ISBN 0-201-39826-5

Meilir Page-Jones, *Fundamentals of Object-Oriented Design in UML*, ISBN 0-201-69946-X

Ira Pohl, *Object-Oriented Programming Using C++, Second Edition*, ISBN 0-201-89550-1

Rob Pooley and Perdita Stevens, *Using UML: Software Engineering with Objects and Components*, ISBN 0-201-36067-5

Terry Quatrani, *Visual Modeling with Rational Rose 2000 and UML*, ISBN 0-201-69961-3

Brent E. Rector and Chris Sells, *ATL Internals*, ISBN 0-201-69589-8

Paul R. Reed, Jr., *Developing Applications with Visual Basic and UML*, ISBN 0-201-61579-7

Doug Rosenberg with Kendall Scott, *Use Case Driven Object Modeling with UML: A Practical Approach*, ISBN 0-201-43289-7

Walker Royce, *Software Project Management: A Unified Framework*, ISBN 0-201-30958-0

William Ruh, Thomas Herron, and Paul Klinker, *IIOP Complete: Middleware Interoperability and Distributed Object Standards*, ISBN 0-201-37925-2

James Rumbaugh, Ivar Jacobson, and Grady Booch, *The Unified Modeling Language Reference Manual*, ISBN 0-201-30998-X

Geri Schneider and Jason P. Winters, *Applying Use Cases: A Practical Guide*, ISBN 0-201-30981-5

Yen-Ping Shan and Ralph H. Earle, *Enterprise Computing with Objects: From Client/Server Environments to the Internet*, ISBN 0-201-32566-7

David N. Smith, *IBM Smalltalk: The Language*, ISBN 0-8053-0908-X

Daniel Tkach, Walter Fang, and Andrew So, *Visual Modeling Technique: Object Technology Using Visual Programming*, ISBN 0-8053-2574-3

Daniel Tkach and Richard Puttick, *Object Technology in Application Development, Second Edition*, ISBN 0-201-49833-2

Jos Warmer and Anneke Kleppe, *The Object Constraint Language: Precise Modeling with UML*, ISBN 0-201-37940-6

DEVELOPING APPLICATIONS WITH VISUAL BASIC AND UML

Paul R. Reed, Jr.

ADDISON-WESLEY

An imprint of Addison Wesley Longman, Inc.

Reading, Massachusetts • Harlow, England • Menlo Park, California
Berkeley, California • Don Mills, Ontario • Sydney
Bonn • Amsterdam • Tokyo • Mexico City

Executive Editor: J. Carter Shanklin
Project Editor: Krysia Bebick
Editorial Assistant: Kristin Erickson
Production Coordination: Diane Freed Publishing Services, Inc.
Cover Design: Simone R. Payment
Compositor: Stratford Publishing Services

Many of the designations used by manufacturers and sellers to distinguish their products are claimed as trademarks. Where those designations appear in this book and Addison Wesley Longman, Inc., was aware of a trademark claim, the designations have been printed in initial caps or all caps.

The author and publisher have taken care in the preparation of this book, but make no expressed or implied warranty of any kind and assume no responsibility for errors or omissions. No liability is assumed for incidental or consequential damages in connection with or arising out of the use of the information or programs contained herein.

The publisher offers discounts on this book when ordered in quantity for special sales. For more information, please contact:

AWL Direct Sales
Addison Wesley Longman, Inc.
One Jacob Way
Reading, Massachusetts 01867
(781) 944-3700

Visit AW on the Web: www.awl.com/cseng/

Library of Congress Cataloging-in-Publication Data

Reed, Paul R.
    Developing applications with Visual Basic and UML / Paul R. Reed, Jr.
        p.   cm.—(Addison-Wesley object technology series)
    Includes bibliographical references.
    ISBN 0-201-61579-7 (alk. paper)
    1. Application software—Development. 2. Microsoft Visual BASIC.
    3. UML (Computer science) I. Title. II. Series.
    QA76.76.A65R44   1999
    005.1—dc21   99-42512
                                                                       CIP

ISBN 0-201-61579-7

Text printed on recycled and acid-free paper.

ISBN 0201615797

2 3 4 5 6 7   CRS   03 02 01 00

2nd Printing   March 2000

To my parents, Paul and Jan, who showed me an honorable path.

To my wife, Jeanette, who so graciously shares her path with mine.

To my children, Micaela and Connor,
for whose paths I hope to set a most admirable example.

Also, thank you, Grady Booch, Jim Rumbaugh, and Ivar Jacobson
for giving us the UML.

Contents

CHAPTER 8   *The Technology Landscape   183*

CHAPTER 9   *Data Persistence: Storing the Objects   207*

CHAPTER 14   *Alternative Interfaces: The Internet   421*

APPENDIX A   *Estimating Projects Using Use Cases   441*

APPENDIX B   *Adding Additional Functionality to Rational Rose Data
Definition Language Capability   451*

Foreword
by Grady Booch

At first you may say, "But Visual Basic isn't object-oriented!" Well, to be
excruciatingly precise, Visual Basic is an object-based, not an object-
oriented, programming language. (Visual Basic lacks true inheritance,
such as is found in C++ and Java.) That said, the object-oriented principles of abstraction, encapsulation, and information hiding apply
directly to Visual Basic. Furthermore, as you move to systems of scale,
the architectural principles of the separation of concerns and a bal-
anced distribution of responsibilities apply as well. That's where Paul's
book comes in. He shows you the principles, processes, and pragmatics
of using Visual Basic to develop and deploy quality systems using
object-oriented concepts.

Visual Basic as it exists today is a far cry from the original Basic
developed at Dartmouth in the early 1960s. While at Microsoft, Alan
Cooper, considered the father of Visual Basic, developed a program
called Ruby, a prototype that demonstrated a metaphor for visual
development. Around 1989, Ruby was bolted to a product called
QuickBasic, thus forming the first version of Visual Basic. Since then,
Visual Basic has grown mightily. Visual Basic can be used to build Web-
centric systems, coupled with technologies such as Microsoft Transaction Server, Active Server Pages, and Structured Query Language.
Indeed, by many reports, Visual Basic is the most widely used programming language in the world, exceeding the number of developers
who use COBOL, C++, and Java. Perhaps the reason for its being so

ubiquitous is that Visual Basic (and its relative, VBScript) is often used as the glue to tie together heterogeneous systems built around Microsoft technologies.

However, one of the challenges in building systems using Visual Basic is that it's very easy to build simple things quickly. That's both good (especially in the presence of rapid development schedules) and bad (as the initial system grows based on its early successes, it quickly reaches a point where it becomes brittle and difficult to change, so it ultimately collapses under its own weight). Developing Visual Basic systems using object-oriented principles mitigates that risk of failure. Furthermore, using the Unified Modeling Language lets you develop blueprints for the system that reconcile the viewpoints of different stakeholders and help you guide the project as it grows over time.

In this book, Paul will show you how to apply Visual Basic in an object-oriented context, using the Unified Modeling Language as the language for the blueprints of a system. He shows you how to apply the principles of abstraction, encapsulation, and information hiding to Visual Basic and how to architect systems of scale. What I particularly like about Paul's book is its pragmatism. Not only does he address these principles, but he also shows you how to build executable systems on top of technologies such as Microsoft Transaction Server, Active Server Pages, and Structured Query Language.

Grady Booch
Chief Scientist
Rational Software Corporation

Foreword
by Francesco Balena

Not long ago, many programmers regarded Visual Basic as a "toy language" or, in the best cases, as a "glue language," good only to keep together different technologies, such as ActiveX controls, Data Access Object, and Component Object Model.

To be honest, the first versions of Visual Basic probably deserved this treatment. Visual Basic v1 wasn't even able to deal with databases, and Visual Basic v2 could do it only through Open Database Connectivity (ODBC) API functions, which isn't precisely the simplest way to access data. Visual Basic v3 added some limited database capabilities, but they weren't enough to make it a robust environment for enterprise-wide projects.

Things changed when Microsoft entered the client/server arena with the release of Visual Basic v4, a competitive and powerful product capable of building complete N-tier applications. Not only could Visual Basic programmers develop Component Object Model components, they were even able to experiment with Remote Automation, the precursor of Distributed COM, and spread their executables over the network. Doing distributed computing had never been so easy. Since then, Visual Basic has continued its evolution at a fast pace: Visual Basic v5 included a compiler and the capability to create ActiveX controls and various Internet features, and Visual Basic v6 added better support for Active Data Objects, Internet Information Server, and Dynamic HTML. Combine all this with other products such as SQL

Server 7, Microsoft Transaction Server, and Microsoft Message Queue, and you'll realize what powerful applications you can build with Visual Basic.

However, my impression, based on my seminars and consulting jobs in Europe and in the United States and on feedback from readers of my articles and books, is that many still use the language mainly as a Rapid Application Development (RAD) tool. The (incorrect) assumption is that the user interface is what really makes a successful application. While this attitude is adequate for small utilities and could sometimes be tolerated for simple, medium-sized database applications, it is simply unacceptable for larger client/server systems. Nevertheless, many ambitious enterprise projects are started without a serious design phase, preliminary documentation, risk estimation, class modeling, and all the steps that should be undertaken before writing the very first line of code. It shouldn't surprise anyone that so many projects don't meet their deadlines and produce applications that don't perform adequately or that are difficult to maintain and extend.

This is where *Developing Applications with Visual Basic and UML* fits in. There are many reasons why I really like this book, and I am so glad I had the opportunity to write a foreword for it. One reason is that although there are many books on the Unified Modeling Language and object-oriented analysis and design, this is one of the few that looks at those topics from the perspective of Visual Basic programmers in a convincing way. Paul has plenty of experience in both fields and can therefore effectively mediate between object-oriented programming purists and Visual Basic aficionados. As proof, read Chapter 2 for the most intelligent analysis of Visual Basic's object-oriented capabilities.

Instead of offering a reference guide for the entire Unified Modeling Language, Paul correctly and cleverly decided to focus on the features that are indispensable for building great Visual Basic N-tier applications. At the same time, he provides enough information, as well as an accurate bibliography, about what he doesn't cover exhaustively, so curious readers know where to look to refine their expertise.

I am sure that all Visual Basic programmers will appreciate the practical approach that permeates these pages. It was a joy seeing how you can combine theory with technologies such as ActiveX, Active Data Objects, Internet Information Server, Component Object Model, and the Distributed Internet Architecture. The thorough discussion of the many techniques for marshaling data between Windows applications is a great example of the compromises that sometimes must be made when moving from pure theory to real-world practice. Similarly, the description of how to write code that works with and without Microsoft Transaction Server demonstrates how much the author cares for those tiny but essential details that greatly contribute to a successful application.

Let me conclude with a little piece of advice. Don't rush from cover to cover, and stay clear from the Visual Basic code editor for a while. Rather, read everything carefully, digest the many notions offered in each chapter, and take your time to build your classes and databases, using a modeling tool if possible. Only then will you realize that Unified Modeling Language combined with a sound, well-thought-out design phase can save you days, weeks, and even months on larger projects.

Francesco Balena
www.vb2themax.com
Editor-in-Chief, *Visual Basic Journal*, Italy
Contributing Editor, *Visual Basic Programmer's Journal*
Author, *Programming Microsoft Visual Basic 6* (Microsoft Press)

Preface

Why Buy This Book?

Most software projects undertaken today don't come close to meeting their original goals or their estimated completion dates. My reasoning for this is that most project teams don't have a clue about what a development process is or how to customize one for a project's unique characteristics. In addition, most projects have little in the way of analysis and design artifacts to show how they got where they are. That is, projects traditionally lack traceability.

With this said, most authors of books on VB never consider it in "the large." Instead, they focus on the small view, filling the pages with nifty routines to load list boxes and call native Windows API functions. Although this view, too, is necessary, unfortunately no one seems to touch on project planning, software process, and the methodology for building enterprise-status VB applications. This is because it is a much more difficult topic to explore and present.

This book focuses on the most powerful approach available today to model and build industrial-strength applications: the Unified Modeling Language (UML) adopted in 1997 by the Object Management Group (OMG) as the standard for modeling object-based applications. With the UML, and a sound development life cycle (which I introduce as the Synergy process in this book), VB projects can move closer toward predictable success, as opposed to the less desirable, luck-of-the-draw chances. In addition, although this book's focus is on VB, almost all of the concepts presented can be applied to any programming language (C++, Java) when coupled with the UML.

The Sad Truth

My career with computers began in 1979 when I began working on large IBM mainframe applications using technologies such as IBM's IMS and later DB2, what many of you today would call "legacy" applications. However, I prefer "heritage" or "senior" systems to "legacy." Not only did I learn about and work with some really great tools and super sharp people, I also learned the value of project planning and establishing a clear architecture and design of the target application. I saw this pay back in a big way as a sound process established a clear line of communication for the project team. More important, it provided the stepping stones for completing a successful project.

In 1990, I worked on a first-generation client/server application using Smalltalk on the OS/2 platform. This was the start of a new career path for me, and I was shocked by the "process" used to build "production" applications in the client/server environment. The planning was cavalier, as was the delivery of analysis and design artifacts (something that showed why we built what we built).

This pattern of "shooting from the hip" software development continued with my use of PowerBuilder and later VB. The applications delivered with these products worked, but they were fragile. I think today many applications that wear the "client/server" moniker are just as much legacy applications as some of their mainframe counterparts, if not more so. Even worse, these became legacy applications a month or two after they went into production. The fault wasn't with the tool. Rather, it was with the lack of a sound process model and methodology that ensured that what got built was what the users actually wanted and that what got designed didn't fall apart the first time it was changed.

Slowly, I began to apply my own opinions about process and methodology to the applications built in the client/server environment. This worked quite well. The applications were more resilient and accepted change more easily, and the users typically had smiles on their faces once the project was completed.

This book combines all of my experience building client/server applications with the UML, which I feel is the best artifact repository for documenting the analysis and design of an application today. I hope that you will enjoy reading this book as much as I enjoyed writing it.

Who Should Read This Book

This book is for anyone who wants to successfully build VB applications that can stand up over time. It provides an accurate road map for anyone to achieve the following goals.

- Establish a sound project plan (presented in-depth in Appendix E).

- Estimate projects with confidence, rather than with a hit-and-miss approach (presented in-depth in Appendix A).

- Understand and describe the requirements of the application using the models supported by the UML.

- Create a sound design based on the models supported by the UML and the architectures supported by the organization.

- Use the power of Microsoft's Distributed Internet Architecture (DNA) strategy to build location transparency into the application.

- Use a visual modeling tool such as Rational Rose by Rational Software, or Visual Modeler by Microsoft, not only to create and track UML artifacts but also to generate skeletons for the component code. (Note: Visual Modeler is a subset of Rational Rose offered by Microsoft. With the exception of creating dynamic models, Visual Modeler can be used in place of Rational Rose in this book.)

- Effectively use the latest Microsoft technologies, such as Distributed Component Object Model (DCOM), Microsoft Transaction Server (MTS) and the Internet via Active Server Pages (ASP), VBScript, and JavaScript.

Anyone building VB applications today needs this book.

What You Need to Know to Use This Book

Maybe it's best to start out with what you don't need to know to benefit from this book.

First, you don't need to know anything about the UML. I present the essential aspects of the UML and, more important, how they relate to VB deliverables. Although the UML is expressed with nine separate diagrams, you will benefit the most from a core set.

Second, you don't need a formal background in object-oriented concepts. I discuss standard object constructs in the text and review many of these in Appendix C.

Third, you don't need to know COM or DCOM. I use both extensively throughout the book and cover some of the "plumbing" issues involved in Appendix D.

Finally, you don't need a formal understanding of the key technologies that surround MTS and the World Wide Web (Web). Each receives detailed treatment in the book.

This book does assume that you have a working knowledge of VB. Both the new and the experienced VB programmer will benefit. However, I don't cover the basics of simple VB constructs, assuming that you already know these. If you have had no exposure to VB, buy this book anyway and open it after you have had some initial training in that programming language.

This book also assumes that you have experience with Structured Query Language (SQL) and with relational databases. Some exposure to Active Data Objects (ADO) and Open Database Connectivity (ODBC) would also help. The project used as a model in the book uses ADO exclusively with ODBC drivers.

Structure of the Book

Following is a summary of the book's chapters and contents.

Chapter 1: The Project Dilemma

This chapter reviews the current state of software development and my reasoning regarding why it's in the shape that it is today. It also reviews the concept of iterative and incremental software development and provides an overview of my Synergy methodology used as the guide in the book. It also touches on the primary components of the UML that will be covered in more depth later in the book.

Chapter 2: Visual Basic, Object-Oriented, and the UML

This chapter covers some of the benefits that result from the adoption of VB as a development environment. It presents these in the context of VB's implementation of encapsulation, inheritance, and polymorphism. It then maps the UML to various VB deliverables. Highlights include mapping the UML class to VB class modules; mapping use case pathways to VB entity, interface, and controller types of classes; and mapping component diagrams to VB executables and DLLs and optionally to MTS.

Chapter 3: Getting the Project Started

This chapter explores the case study used in the book, Remulak Productions. This fictional company sells musical equipment and needs a new order entry system. It introduces a project charter, along with a tool, called the event table, to help quickly solidify the application's features. Further, the chapter maps events to the first UML model, the use case.

Chapter 4: Use Cases

This chapter reviews the use case, one of the central UML diagrams. Included is a template to document the use case. Actors and their roles in the use cases are defined. The chapter reviews the concept of use case pathways, as well as the project's preliminary implementation architecture. Also reviewed is an approach to estimating projects that are built by using the use case approach.

Chapter 5: Classes

This chapter explores the UML class diagram, the king of UML diagrams. It offers tips on identifying good class selections and defines the various types of associations. It also covers business rule categorization and how these rules can be translated into both operations and attributes of the class. Finally, it discusses the utilization of the visual modeling tool, Rational Rose, as a means to better manage all UML artifacts.

Chapter 6: Building an Early Prototype

This chapter reviews unique user interface requirements of each use case. It develops an early prototype flow and an eventual graphical prototype. Finally, it maps what was learned during the prototype to the UML artifacts.

Chapter 7: The Dynamic Elements of the Application

This chapter discusses the dynamic models supported by the UML, exploring in depth the two key diagrams, often referred to as the interaction diagrams, sequence and collaboration. These are then directly tied back to the pathways found in the use cases. Other dynamic diagrams discussed include the state and activity diagrams.

Chapter 8: The Technology Landscape

This chapter covers the importance of separating logical services that are compliant with DNA. It explores technology solutions specific to the Remulak Productions case study, including distributed solutions using DCOM, MTS, and the Internet using HTML forms and ASP. Two scripting languages are used for the Internet portion of the applications, VBScript and JavaScript.

Chapter 9: Data Persistence: Storing the Objects

This chapter explores the steps necessary to translate the class diagram into a relational design to be supported by both Microsoft SQL Server and Oracle databases. It offers rules-of-thumb suggestions regarding how to handle class inheritance and the resulting possible design alternatives when translating the class diagram to an RDMBS. It also explores VB's support for data-aware classes, as well as the importance of a separate Data Translation Services layer that contains the SQL logic related to each class.

Chapter 10: Applying the Infrastructure

This chapter finalizes the design necessary to implement the various layers of the application. It also presents the communication mechanism utilized between the layers and possible alternatives. Each class is delegated to one of three types: entity, interface, or control. These are used as the basis for the design implementation and as the solution to providing alternative deployment strategies.

Chapter 11: Generating Code from the UML Class Diagram (Part 1)

This chapter explores the issues of generating VB code directly from the class diagram, again using Rational Rose. It reviews the setup steps necessary to make the process go smoothly and discusses the importance of the entire process of round-trip reengineering, along with a process to ensure that it happens.

Chapter 12: Generating Code from the UML Class Diagram (Part 2)

This chapter fills in the body of the VB class stubs generated in the previous chapter, focusing on a single pathway through a use case. It also presents all of the code necessary to make it a reality, from the user interface to the back-end.

Chapter 13: Creating a Distributed Implementation: DCOM and MTS

This chapter uses the solutions built in Chapters 12 and 13 to explore the necessary steps to deploy it on various server configurations. It covers all of the tasks necessary to ensure a successful DCOM implementation, including using the deployment wizard and using various utilities to ensure that both the client and server are correctly set up.

Chapter 14: Alternative Interfaces: The Internet

This chapter covers one of the hottest areas today: the Internet. This is where all of the design work covered in the previous chapters really pays off. In the chapter, an HTML form-based front-end to the order entry inquiry function is created. ASP is used as the interface between the browser and the layers of the VB application. The chapter explores VBScript as the primary scripting language on the Web server and JavaScript as used on the browser. Microsoft's Visual InterDev is used as the development tool for this part of the project.

Updates and Information

I have the good fortune to work with top companies and organizations not only in the United States, but also in Europe, Asia, and South America. In my many travels, I am always coming across inventive ideas regarding how to use and apply the UML to build more-resilient applications that use not only VB but also C++ and Java. Please visit my Web site at *www.jacksonreed.com,* where you can get the latest on the training and consulting services that I offer, as well as all of the source code presented in this book. I welcome your input and encourage you to contact me at *prreed@jacksonreed.com.*

Acknowledgments

Anyone today can trace their perceived success through the company they keep. I owe my good fortune to the many people that shaped my career over the years.

I would like to thank Coby Sparks, Dale McElroy, Richard Dagit, Mike Richardson, John Peiffer, Kurt Herman, Steve Symonds, Dave Remy, David Neustadt, Selena Wilson, John Girt, Robert Folie, Terry Lelievre, Bill Carson, Larry Deniston, Jeff Kluth (a.k.a. Jeffery Homes of this book, a hell of guitar player, backpacking buddy, and the owner of the real Remulak, a DB2 consulting firm). Thanks also to Ellen Gottesdiener of EBG Consulting (*www.ebgconsulting.com*) for her wonderful assistance on project charters, use cases, and business rules.

I have the benefit of working with some great clients in both the United States and abroad. A special thanks goes to Rick Cassidy and Kevin Boettcher of Lockheed-Martin's Advanced Concepts Center (ACC) for providing me with the occasional interesting object-oriented assignment. I would also like to thank the folks at Manatron, Inc. (*www.manatron.com*) whose bold efforts provided me with many insights into using Visual Basic (VB) in an enterprise manner. In particular, at Manatron I want to thank Larry Deniston, John Gumpper, Mark Murphy, Dilawar Jaulikar, and Gina Riggs. I would also like to thank Vicki Cerda at Florida Power and Light, Jones Wu and Daniel Yee at Pacific Gas and Electric, Daryl Kulak at CBSI, Inc., all my friends at Ford Motor Company, Mansoor Osmani at IIT House (Saudi Arabia),

Lawrence Lim at LK Solutions (Singapore, Malaysia, and United Arab Emirates—*www.lks.com.my*), Tony Shaw at Technology Transfer Institute (USA), Jeremy Hall at Technology Transfer Institute, LTD. (London), and Ricardo Quintero at the Panama Canal Commission.

My special thoughts go out to my wife, Jeanette, who gladly gave up her most successful career as an MVS/DB2 systems programmer and Oracle DBA to raise our most precious assets, Micaela and Connor. It was also Jeanette, together with my very good friend Mike Richardson, who looked me in the eye in 1992 and asked, "Why are you working for someone else?" That led to Jackson-Reed, Inc., and I have never looked back.

I want to give a very special thanks to my special friend Steve Jackson. Steve is "Consultant Emeritus" of Jackson-Reed, Inc. (*www.jacksonreed.com*). He, together with his partner Bryan Foertsch, founded the successful mergers and acquisitions firm Omni International (*www.omninow.com*) in 1998. Steve taught me two very important lessons I will never forget. The first was how to do "the deal." The second, and more important, was to make sure that when everyone walks away from the deal, their smiles are bigger than when they sat down.

Lastly, special thanks goes to J. Carter Shanklin of Addison-Wesley for having the foresight to give a VB/UML topic serious consideration. Thanks to Krysia Bebick for showing me the ropes of publishing and to Kristin Erickson for the continuous support she provided to me and the reviewers of this book. A really big thank you also goes to Diane Freed of Diane Freed Publishing Services, Inc., who kept me from going crazy during the production process for this book. And a special thank you to my agent, Margo Maley of Waterside Productions, who made the occasional bumpy ride much smoother.

Now, the real heroes of this project are the reviewers who slugged their way through my early drafts and weren't shy at all to cast darts when necessary. They are Larry Deniston, Director of Software Research and Development, Manatron, Inc.; Jim Conallen, Rational Software, Inc.; Matt A. Arnold, Intelligent Algorithms Enterprises, Ltd.; Gary Cernosek; John Moody; and Steve Nordmeyer. Finally, thanks to Francesco Balena for some last-minute technical tweaks.

CHAPTER 1

The Project Dilemma

I have run across more projects after the fact that missed their initial goals than met them. This is because most project teams had no clue about what a development process was or how to customize one for a project's unique characteristics. It also is because most projects had little in the way of analysis and design artifacts to show how they got where they were. The whole endeavor lacked the ability to be tracked; that is, it lacked traceability.

This chapter lays the groundwork for a software process called Synergy. The **Synergy** *process is based on my extensive analysis, design, and construction experience building client/server applications, as well as many mainframe-based applications. It uses the Unified Modeling Language (UML) as its primary artifact trail. This process, along with the UML, can ensure that your next Visual Basic (VB) project has all of the muscle it needs to succeed. More important, these projects will stand the test of time. They will be able to flex and bend with shifts in both the underlying businesses they support and the technology framework upon which they were built. They won't be declared legacy applications before they reach production status.*

GOALS

⇨ Review the dilemma that projects face.

⇨ Explore the nature of an iterative, incremental, risk-based software development process.

1

⇨ Get acquainted with the software process model used in this book, called Synergy.

⇨ Examine how the project team can market the use of the Synergy process to project sponsors.

⇨ Review the UML and its artifacts and how it serves as the primary modeling tool for the Synergy process.

The Project Dilemma

Few projects proceed totally as planned. Most start out with much enthusiasm but often end in a mad rush to get something out the door. The deliverable is often hobbled with inaccuracies or, worse, invokes unrepeatable responses from the project sponsors. Figure 1-1 shows a timeline/effort comparison of person-hour expenditures for most projects that don't meet their commitments.

You know the drill: The project plants a stake in the ground, with a big-bang deliverable two and half years away. And then you plod along, making adjustments and adding functionality, until, toward the end, you realize, "we aren't going to make it." You are so far off the mark that you start adding more pounds of flesh to the effort. Before long, you begin to jettison functionality, for example reporting, archiving, security, and auditing functionality activities. You end up with a poor deliverable that adds to the black eye of the Information

FIGURE 1-1   *Timeline with exponential increase in hours.*

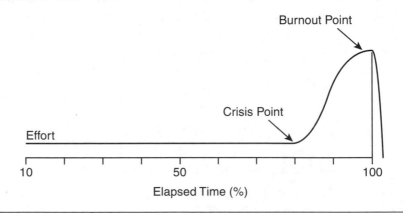

Technology (IT) department and further confirms to the project sponsors that you can't develop software at all, let alone on time and within budget.

Unfortunately, like lemmings racing to the sea, companies repeat this saga again and again and again.

Iterative and Incremental Software Development

This dilemma stems from the unwillingness of both the IT department and the project sponsors to take a learn-as-you-go approach to software development, more formally known as **iterative and incremental software development**.

In the context of a software project, many people confuse the terms *iterative* and *incremental*. The American Heritage Dictionary, Second College Edition, defines these terms as follows.

> Iterative 3 . . . procedure to produce a desired result by replication of a series of operations that successively better approximates the desired result.

> Incremental—1. An increase in number, size, or extent. 2. Something added or gained. 4. One of a series of regular additions or contributions.

Let's give these academic definitions a bit of a software flavor.

> **Iterative**: The application of tasks in a repetitive fashion that works towards bettering an interim or final product

> **Incremental**: The creation of interim deliverables such that each one adds significant value to the overall project, stands on its own or operates within a well-defined interface, or might take part as a subcomponent of some final product

As an example, suppose you are constructing a wooden play set for children. You begin by simplifying the project by breaking it up into two incremental parts: (1) tower and attached slide chute and (2) swing and trapeze frame. You realize the project by iterating through the building of each increment. The iterations might be first to create a detailed drawing, then to buy, measure, and cut the wood, next to bolt together the pieces, and finally to stain the wood. Each iteration betters the goal of producing a product that stands on its own. This approach is powerful because many of the same iterative tasks (that is, drawing, sawing, bolting, and staining) are going to be applied to each increment (that is, tower/slide and swing/trapeze).

The challenge, however, is to ensure that the first increment will bolt (interface) onto subsequent increments. This requires that you learn enough about all of the increments so that you can approximate how they will work together as an integrated product. See Figure 1-2 for a sample timeline for a project using an iterative, incremental approach.

Through years of applying these concepts to many different types of projects, using many different tools and languages, I have no doubt that this is the only way that software can be successfully developed today and in the future.

Risk-Based Development

Experience has taught me to always be a silent pessimist when I approach any new project. This stems from the repeated observation that something is always lurking nearby that will shift the project's course toward eventual disaster. While this attitude might seem like a negative way to look at project development, it has saved many projects from disaster.

The project team must always be on the lookout for risks. Risks must be brought to the surface early and often. One way to do this is to

FIGURE 1-2   *Timeline with iterative/incremental flow.*

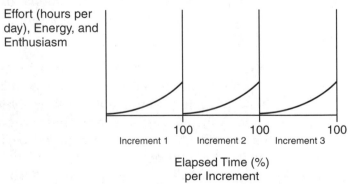

extend the project development philosophy from being iterative and incremental to being also risk-based. In Appendix E, a sample project plan representing the Synergy process is presented. You will easily see that the task "assess and mitigate risks" occurs often. Figure 1-3 shows a visual representation of how an iterative, incremental project framework founded on a risk-based approach might look.

One very positive side-effect of this approach is the continual improvement of the end product. In addition, risks are addressed promptly because those project components that present the greatest risk are staged first.

The Iterative Software Process Model

It helps to visualize what combining the notion of iterative and incremental development might look like graphically. Figure 1-4 provides a view of an iterative and incremental process model.

FIGURE 1-3   *Iterative, incremental project framework with risk mitigation.*

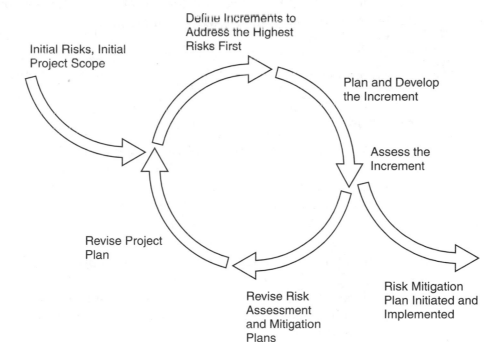

FIGURE 1-4   *Iterative and incremental process model: one-dimensional.*

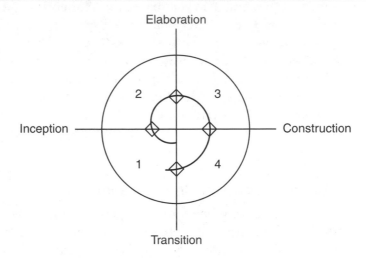

This framework is sometimes called the **Spiral process model** and has been popularized by many practitioners. Each of the four quadrants shown in the figure are labeled as a phase:

- Inception
- Elaboration
- Construction
- Transition

These four phases parallel the terminology used by the Rational Unified Process (RUP) from Rational Software. Rational's Unified Process has as its roots the Objectory Process, created by Ivar Jacobson in the 1980's. What you label them doesn't really matter as long as the labels reflect the evolutionary nature of a software project.

In the Inception phase, the project begins. This is a discovery phase, a time for solidifying the project charter and incorporating a clear understanding of what features the project will implement.

In the Elaboration phase, early requirements identified in the Inception phase are solidified and more rigor is added to the process. This phase also details the dynamic nature of the application and attempts to model the actual uses of the system that are anticipated by the project sponsors.

In the Construction phase, both the static and dynamic perspectives of the application are realized in the form of a language (for example, VB) and a form of persistent storage (for example, Oracle).

In the Transition phase, components produced in the Construction phase are packaged into deployable units. This phase also details the support issues that surround the application and how the project will be maintained in a production environment.

Within each phase, multiple iterations will typically take place. The Synergy process introduced in this book has a minimum of three unique iterations for each phase, as illustrated in Figure 1-5.

The number of iterations within each phase might vary, depending on the project's unique requirements. For projects with a higher risk factor or more unknown elements, more time will be spent learning and discovering. The resulting knowledge will have to be translated to other deliverables in a layered fashion.

To make the project even more interesting, the activities traditionally associated with any one phase may be performed in early or later

FIGURE 1-5   *Iterations within phases.*

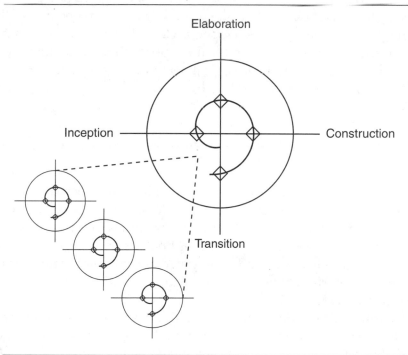

phases. For example, if the project has a strong, unique visual component or is breaking new ground, you might need to simulate a prototype during inception just to generate ideas and solidify the proof-of-concept going forward.

Nothing about the Synergy process says that you must do a task in a given order. However, for most applications, a predominant process order does exist. In addition, a related artifact trail, using UML diagrams, will be fairly common across most projects.

Combining Iterative with Incremental: Multidimensional View

Given that an iterative process is beneficial, next we envision the previous flow imposed upon an incremental delivery schedule. Figure 1-6 illustrates the iterative nature of typical software development projects and shows that different increments will be in different stages of the lifecycle.

Notice that each increment (the three upper spirals) is in a different phase of its evolution. Each phase (for example, Inception) might also be in its own iteration cycle. At first glance, you might think that this all seems overly complex. From the project manager's perspective, more balls do need to be juggled. However, from the perspectives of the user, analyst, designer, and developer, a clear demarcation exists between each increment. The reason for this approach is, once again, to lessen risk by disassembling the logical seams of the application and then attacking each increment individually.

The Synergy Process Model

The Synergy process, which is based on iterative, incremental software development, combines with an implementation project plan that is your road map pinpointing the stepping stones that you must follow to ensure your project's success. As this book unfolds, the Synergy process model will be revisited and highlighted and the supporting project plan will also resurface as we review each task to be performed, as well as the sample deliverables.

Figure 1-7 provides a preview of the Synergy process model. The boxes (for example, Release Cycle and Project Scope) represent categories of activities or processes. They are linked via a sample flow of order,

FIGURE 1-6   *Iterative and incremental process model.*

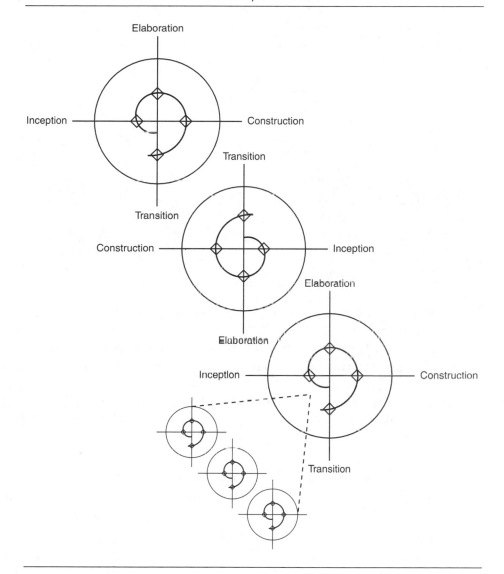

although recall that some tasks might be performed earlier or later depending on a project's needs.

The vertical bars labeled Inception, Elaboration, Construction, and Transition represent the project's phases. Notice that the Inception bar slices through the Use Case Analysis and

FIGURE 1-7   *Synergy process model.*

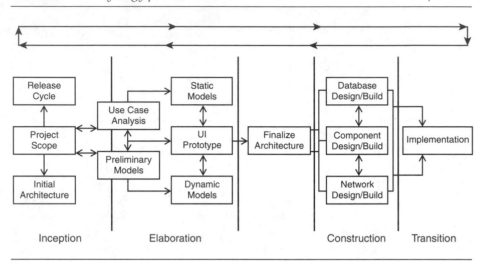

Preliminary Models boxes. This depicts graphically that early in the project's lifecycle, we will "fly-by," or iterate through, some of these activities so as to estimate the duration and cost of our project.

The Synergy process model is explained in detail as you move through the book. You will see that a sound software process model, combined with a detailed project plan and the UML's ability to depict the real-world nature of a project through its nine diagrams, will prove to be a very powerful combination.

Selling the Idea of a Software Process to the Business

To sell an iterative, incremental, risk-based software development approach, we all must become better marketers. At first glance, the business community probably won't like the idea of this approach. Why? When project sponsors are told that their solution will be delivered in multiple increments, their reaction, from their past experience, tells them that phase II never happens. Projects get cancelled, resources get drawn away to other efforts, priorities shift. So, as a rule, they will strive to put everything possible into that first increment. Thus the biggest challenge is selling the idea to project sponsors.

Here are some of the top benefits of a software process that must be worked into your marketing plan.

- The business gets useful increments in a staged fashion that continually build toward the final product.

- Each increment delivers value-added benefits, while increasing confidence that the project can be flexible enough to adjust to continually evolving business needs. The business doesn't stay static, so how can the software be expected to?

- Each increment is relatively short in duration, 3 to 9 months, so the possibility of the project's becoming a "runaway train" is lessened dramatically.

- Any problems with the design or the technology surface early, not 90% into the project timeline.

- Users, analysts, designers, and developers stay very focused on each increment. They can celebrate successes much sooner. The team confidence that this builds is priceless.

This book stresses following a sound project plan, using a proven development process as the guide. To facilitate communication and to drive out both the requirements and design of the system, a common modeling language is applied: the UML.

The Unified Modeling Language

The Object Management Group (OMG) adopted the UML v1.0 in November 1997. This was a remarkable, never before seen event, as it marked the acceptance of a standard modeling language based on the best current practices for the analysis, design, and development of object-oriented software.

The UML sprang from the combined efforts of the "three amigos": Grady Booch with his Booch method, James Rumbaugh with his Object Modeling Technique (OMT), and Ivar Jacobson with his Object-Oriented Software Engineering (OOSE) method. As mentioned earlier, some of the terminology and philosophy found in the Synergy process is based on Jacobson's Objectory Process.

Beginning in 1994, under the auspices of Rational Software, the UML began to take shape. Although the UML clearly reflects the three amigos' combined approaches, it also includes the best practices from such organizations as Hewlett Packard, IBM, and Microsoft, as well as other industry practitioners such as Shlaer/Mellor, Coad/Yourdon, and Martin/Odell. The UML was also submitted as a formal response to the OMG's Request for Proposal for a standard object-oriented modeling notation.

The ramifications of the OMG's adoption of the UML cannot be overestimated. Those of us who grew up in the Structured Analysis and Structured Design (SA/SD) world had numerous diagramming notations from which to choose and several software process models to apply. Wouldn't it have been wonderful if the likes of Ed Yourdon, James Martin, and Tom DeMarco, to name a few, had sat down one day in the late 70s and agreed to put aside any and all egos and to adopt one notation for the SA/SD approach to software development? Had there been only one way to express the application domain, many organizations would have benefited significantly. Not only would all of the organization's models have been similar, but an individual moving from company to company or application domain to application domain would have had a common notation as a baseline.

The UML then is the first notation that has garnered consensus among most practitioners, software vendors, and academics as the de facto standard for expressing a business domain of the accompanying software solution.

The UML and Its Place in the Software Process

The UML is not a software process model or a systems development methodology; it is a notation, a mechanism to "pen the problem" in such a way as to uncover the essence of an application domain. The combination of the UML with a sound process model (Rational's Unified Process, Ernst and Young's Fusion, or the Synergy process used in this book) results in a powerful combination for building successful applications.

The UML's goal is twofold. One is to provide consistency in giving feedback to the project sponsor that the problem domain is well understood. The other is to provide a consistent model for proper software implementation. However, if you attempt to use the UML without a sound process model and project plan (discussed throughout this book and fully presented in Appendix E), your project will fail.

All of the artifacts that the UML delivers are *traceable*. If done in conjunction with a sound process model, the models can build on one another. This element of traceability is key to the project. With the UML, the project will not only produce fewer useless and "go nowhere" deliverables, but will serve as a checkpoint of the previous model's soundness. Since the UML models are interlocked in their creation, identifying when a component is missing or potentially incorrect is easier.

Some artifacts used in the Synergy process model are not UML diagrams. As is explored later in the book, the UML doesn't directly address some aspects of a project, including these:

- Graphical user interface (GUI)
- Process distribution
- Data distribution

In all cases, though, the information needed from these vital areas is based on knowledge gained from the UML diagrams. For example, one artifact useful in distributed systems is the Object/Location matrix. This matrix details geographically interested locations in the domain and assesses the kind of usage that they perceive for the objects in the system. Its input are the classes identified on the class diagram and the locations uncovered in the use cases. Again, all artifacts are traceable; otherwise, they aren't worth creating.

The Essence of Modeling

A key benefit of modeling is that it provides a communication pipeline for project team members. Without sound models, team members learn their knowledge of the system from their own perspectives. A project can't tolerate individualized perspectives of, for example, requirements. If it did, then the project would end up not meeting "perceived" requirements. And regardless of what the project charter says, the project team would still be blamed for not meeting someone else's agenda.

Grady Booch says that modeling should accomplish the following four goals:

1. Assist the project team to visualize a system as it is or as it is intended to be.
2. Assist in specifying the system's structure or behavior.
3. Provide a template which guides in constructing the system.
4. Document the decisions that the project development team has made.

All of these goals echo the common theme of maintaining good communication. Without good communication, the project will fail. The UML meets these goals, and more.

The UML Diagrams

The UML consists of nine different, interlocking diagrams of a system:

- Activity
- Class
- Collaboration
- Component
- Deployment
- Object
- Use case
- Sequence
- State

The package diagram is another often-used model that can contain all the other nine.

The diagrams are evolutionary in their construction. Nevertheless, they are merely different views of the domain. Because people have different backgrounds in modeling, categorizing the diagrams along multiple perspectives can be helpful. The nine diagrams are divided into three categories: static, dynamic, and architectural.

A **static diagram** depicts the system's structure and responsibilities. Static diagrams are similar to the building contractor's "as-built" drawings, which depict multiple subsystems, all interacting within the framework of the physical structure. Following are the static diagrams:

- Use case
- Class
- Object

A **dynamic diagram** depicts the live interactions that the system supports. Dynamic diagrams detail the interaction between structural artifacts from the static diagrams (classes). These dynamic interactions are discovered in the use cases as pathways performed in response to some external system stimulus. Dynamic diagrams also provide a much clearer picture of the intended, realized behavior of the system. Following are the dynamic diagrams:

- Activity
- Collaboration
- Sequence
- State
- Use case

An **architectural diagram** depicts the realization of the system into running and executable components. Architectural diagrams also distinguish the physical location of execution and storage nodes and a framework within which they can interact. They often are produced very early in the project (for example, during project scoping) to indicate the intended physical architecture. They are further detailed during the Construction and Transition phases to clarify early assumptions that are going to be physically implemented. Following are the architectural diagrams:

- Component
- Deployment

The Unified Modeling Language and the "4+1" View of Architecture

An interesting perspective of a project's architecture and the UML modeling artifacts used to describe the system comes from the "4+1" view of software architecture. This view involves, in fact, five different views, as illustrated in Figure 1-8:

- Use case
- Logical
- Implementation
- Process
- Deployment

FIGURE 1-8   *"4+1" view of software architecture.*

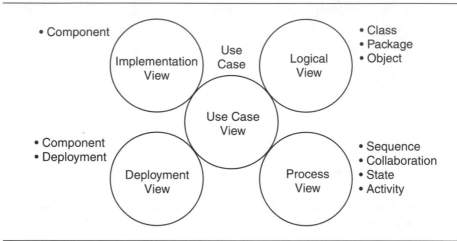

The Use Case view describes the functionality that the system should deliver as perceived by the external "actors" and the requirements of the system. Intended for users, analysts, designers, developers, and testers, the use case view is central because its contents drive the development of the other views. The use case should be technology-neutral, contain no object-speak, and focus on the *what*, not the *how*, of the system solution.

The Logical view describes how the system functionality is provided. Intended mainly for designers and developers, it looks inside of the system, in contrast to the more macro Use Case view. It describes both the static structure (classes, objects, and relationships) and the dynamic collaborations that occur when objects send messages in response to some external or internal event.

The Implementation View describes the implementation modules and their dependencies. The modules can provide for crosschecks back to the other deliverables to ensure that all requirements are eventually actualized into code. It is mainly for developers and consists of the component diagram.

The Process View (also called the Concurrency view) describes the division of the system into processes and processors. This division allows for efficient resource usage, parallel execution, and the handling of asynchronous events. Intended for developers and integrators, it consists of dynamic diagrams, state, sequence, collaboration, and activity, as well as component and deployment diagrams.

The Deployment View describes the physical deployment of the system via the component and deployment diagrams. Developers, integrators, and testers utilize this view.

Using the UML Diagrams in Context

While nine diagrams might seem a bit overwhelming, not every project will use all of them. For example, many projects might not require state or activity diagrams. A state diagram is used to model the lifecycle of instances of one class, and then only when that class exhibits complex or interesting dynamic behavior. Such classes are prevalent in embedded real-time applications but are not as common in business-oriented applications. Activity diagrams are useful for modeling complex steps within a use case or an operation found in a class.

Other diagrams offer complementary views of the same thing, such as those found in the sequence and collaboration diagrams. Actually, many visual modeling tools allow you to create the collaboration from the sequence diagram.

In practice, projects will always produce the following diagrams at a minimum:

- Use case
- Class
- Sequence

Projects also should produce component and deployment diagrams. In my consulting work, I have encountered the recurring problem of the project team not taking enough time to visualize and model the design's physical realization. They assume a cavalier attitude toward component assembly and, more important, the assignment of components to actual processors. Often, the requirements are realized and the design is elegant, but response times are poor or ongoing issues of component distribution impact the application's supportability. Many of these issues can be resolved by using the rich and expressive syntax of the component and deployment diagrams.

This book offers a number of hints regarding when to apply which diagrams. It also stresses the importance of traceability between the diagrams. Early in my career, success as an analyst or designer depended on the weight and thickness of the requirements and design documents. I would like to think that after finishing this book, you will better know when to use which artifact diagrams and will end up with project documentation that is as light as possible and yet complete.

Checkpoint

Where We Have Been

1. Successful software development requires that complex problems be broken down into smaller, more comprehensible and manageable tasks.

2. By iteratively applying sound approaches to construct each increment, the project team manages risk while producing a quality deliverable.

3. Successful projects require a sound software process model; the process model used in this book is called Synergy.

4. The project team must effectively market the benefits of an iterative, incremental, risk-based approach to software development.

5. The UML consists of nine different, semantically rich, interlocked diagrams. These diagrams, when used in conjunction with a sound software process, enable deliverables to be traceable throughout the project's lifecycle.

6. Not all of the UML diagrams need to be used in every project. At a minimum, all projects will produce use case, class, and sequence diagrams.

7. Some other diagrams aren't included in the UML (e.g., graphical user interface, distribution) but add additional relevance to the picture of the application domain.

8. A project, using the UML in a vacuum, without a sound software process and accompanying project plan, will fail.

Where We Are Going Next

In the next chapter, we:

1. Explore why VB is one of today's most commonly used integrated development environments.

2. Discuss VB's capabilities to build sound, object-oriented applications.

3. Cover why VB lends itself to utilizing a sound software process in conjunction with the UML so as to improve a project's results.

CHAPTER 2 | *Visual Basic, Object-Oriented, and the UML*

As mentioned in Chapter 1, for software development to be successful in today's ever-changing business climate, it must follow an approach that is different from the big-bang approach. The big-bang approach, or waterfall model, offers little risk aversion or support for modification of requirements during development. The waterfall model forces the project team to accept insurmountable risks and create software that usually doesn't approximate the original vision of the project sponsors.

This chapter looks at VB as an enterprise solution for constructing and implementing industrial-strength applications that will better approximate what the sponsors intended. Although VB has many strong object-oriented capabilities, it is not considered a true object-oriented language. This chapter deals with this by reviewing VB's object strengths and weaknesses.

The UML is object-oriented, and its diagrams lend themselves to being implemented in software that is object-oriented. This chapter examines how the UML, coupled with a sound software process model such as Synergy, can produce applications that not only meet the project sponsor's goals but also are adaptive to the ever-changing needs of the business.

GOALS

⇨ Review VB's object capabilities.

⇨ Explore VB and its relationship to the UML.

⇨ Review UML diagram to VB mappings.

Visual Basic as an Industrial Strength Development Tool

Microsoft's Visual Basic has undergone six major releases since its introduction to the marketplace, the latest being v6.0, released in October 1998. By early 1999, the unofficial number of VB licenses on the street had reached 3 million. By 2003, that number is expected to climb to 6.8 million, according to a survey by International Data Corporation, or 25.6% of the programming language market. By contrast, languages such as C /C++ and Java are expected to capture only 17.9% and 15.1% respectively (with COBOL capturing 5.2%).

VB has come a long way since its early days. Not long ago, many practitioners considered it a toy and really practical for only very small desktop applications. "Prototype in VB; build the production version in C" was an often-heard mantra. Not so today.

Microsoft, with each successive release, has added more and more capabilities and features, many of which die-hard VB'ers have been awaiting for years. These include object-oriented capabilities, native code compilation, and middle-tier support of business logic.

The maturation and acceptance of VB has been advanced by several events.

- The introduction of the Component Object Model (COM) as the technology infrastructure to develop both distributed and object-oriented applications. All of Microsoft's applications, as well as scores of third-party products, have COM as their messaging infrastructure.

- Support of advanced communication and resource management technology in the form of Microsoft Transaction Server (MTS) and Microsoft Message Queue (MSMQ) services.

- A rich, third-party marketplace for snap-in components (based on COM) that extend VB's reach and functionality. These components range from fancy grid controls to controls that interface with native Internet services such as File Transfer Protocol (FTP) and Simple Mail Transfer Protocol (SMTP).

- The utilization of VB for Applications (VBA), a subset of VB, as Microsoft's primary macro language. VBA is supported in many of Microsoft's desktop applications (for example, Word, Excel, and PowerPoint). Now, organizations can leverage their VB skills outside of VB's integrated development environment (IDE).

- The licensing of VBA to third-party software vendors for use as their own native macro language (for example, Corel, Visio, and AutoCAD).

- The utilization of VBScript, a derivative of VBA, as both a client-side and server-side scripting language for Internet and Intranet applications. The existing VB skill sets can be extended into other areas.

- Microsoft's introduction of the Distributed interNet Applications Architecture (DNA) as a vehicle to tie all of the application layers together, while also providing rich support for Intranet, Internet, and extranet application functionality.

- The increased presence of Microsoft in the corporate environment coupled with increasing numbers of companies moving to distributed client/server development. These organizations need a development environment to which they can easily transition their existing staff (many of whom are mainframe COBOL programmers) and which lessens their need for yet another vendor relationship.

- Offering three different versions of VB with a commensurate increase in both functionality and price.

This last point is particularly interesting. Price exerts a huge influence psychologically on the typical IT manager. For example, in 1992, the chief information officer of a large Fortune 100 company told me that VB would have been his company's choice, except for one consideration—the conviction that any product that sells for 10 times *less* than its closest competitor can't be industrial strength. Since that meeting,

VB's Enterprise version has sold for three times the price of its 1992 version. Although the capabilities of the version available then and the version available now have grown immensely and so account for part of this increase, this example demonstrates how the perceived ability of a product can be judged solely by its price.

Visual Basic and the Concept of Object-Oriented

VB is an IDE that has several object-oriented features. Many in the industry call products like VB object-*based* versus object-*oriented*. Others argue that the only true object-oriented languages are Smalltalk and Eiffel and that all of the others have "morphed" themselves with object-oriented features.

To appease those that live and die by language comparisons, let's put VB under the scrutiny of what constitutes an object-oriented language. For those not familiar with what object-oriented is, first read the object-oriented primer in Appendix C.

No definitive definition of what makes a language object-oriented is globally accepted. However, a commonly accepted set of criteria can be used to assess whether it is, or is not. Specifically, an object-oriented language must support the following:

- Classes
- Complex types
- Message-passing
- Encapsulation
- Inheritance
- Polymorphism

These are discussed in the next subsections.

Visual Basic and Classes

VB allows classes to be defined. A **class** is a static template that contains the defined structure (attributes) and behavior (operations) of some entity in the application domain. At runtime, the class **instantiates**, or brings to life, an **object** born in the image of itself.

In VB, you can create a class in three ways. One is by using VB's Class Builder Wizard (see Figure 2-1), and a second is by natively coding the class in the development environment (see Figure 2-2). Classes also can be built dynamically through the VB programming model (this is how products such as Rational Rose generate classes into VB). However, a discussion of this technique is outside the scope of this book.

VB exposes the class to potential outside users through its public interface. A **public interface** consists of the signatures of the public operations supported by the class. A **signature** is the operation name and its input and return attributes (if any).

An operation in VB can be one of three forms:

- **Property**: Sets or returns an attribute value.

- **Subroutine**: Performs a set of statements and returns no value.

- **Function**: Performs a set of statements and returns a value.

Good programming practice encourages developers to declare all attributes as private and allow access to them only via operations.

FIGURE 2-1   *Creating a class using the Class Builder Wizard.*

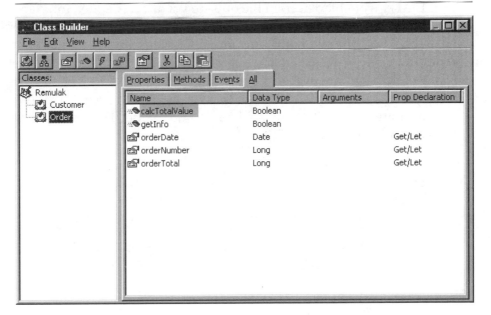

FIGURE 2-2   *Creating a class in the Code window.*

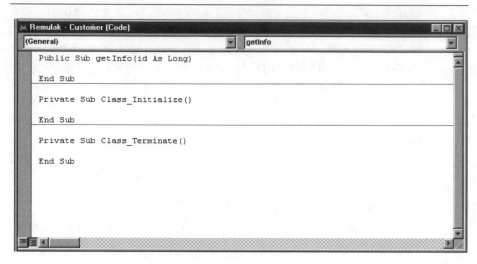

However, as with most languages, this is not totally enforced in VB. Figure 2-3 outlines the concept of a class and its interface.

The figure uses a common metaphor of the eggshell to describe the concept of the interface as well as encapsulation. The internal details of the class are hidden from the outside via a well-defined interface. In this case, only four operations are exposed in the interface (Operation_ A,B,C,D). The other attributes and operations are protected from the outside world. Actually, to the outside world, it's as if they don't even exist.

Suppose you want to create an `Order` class in VB that has three attributes—`orderNumber`, `orderDate`, and `orderTotal`—and two operations—`calcTotalValue` and `getInfo`. The resulting class definition would look as follows.

```
'Class Order
Private morderDate As Date 'local copy
Private morderNumber As Long 'local copy
Private morderTotal As Long 'local copy

Public Function getInfo() As Boolean
End Function

Public Function calcTotalValue() As Long
End Function
```

FIGURE 2-3 *A class's public interface.*

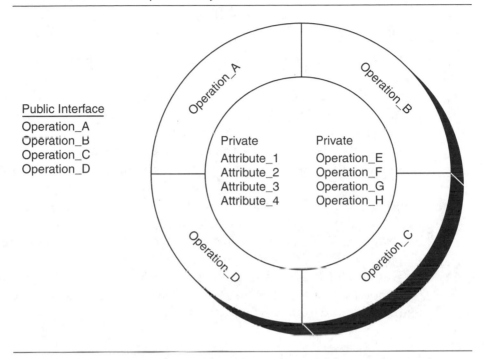

Public Interface
Operation_A
Operation_B
Operation_C
Operation_D

```
Public Property Let orderTotal(ByVal vData As Long)
    morderTotal = vData
End Property

Public Property Get orderTotal() As Long
    orderTotal = morderTotal
End Property

Public Property Let orderNumber(ByVal vData As Long)
    morderNumber = vData
End Property

Public Property Get orderNumber() As Long
    orderNumber = morderNumber
End Property

Public Property Let orderDate(ByVal vData As Date)
    morderDate = vData
End Property
```

```
Public Property Get orderDate() As Date
    orderDate = morderDate
End Property
```

A class can also have what are called *class-level operations* and *attributes*. VB does not support these. The closest it comes to these are the `class_initialize` and `class_terminate` operations. (In C++ and Java, these called static operations and attributes.) Class-level operations are typically, but not always, needed in order to invoke either a service of the class before any real instances of that class are instantiated or a service that doesn't directly apply to any of the instances. An example is an operation that retrieves a list of `Customer` instances based on some search criteria. A class-level attribute can be used to store information that all instances of that class may access. This attribute might be, for example, a count of the number of objects currently instantiated or a global value that all instances might need to reference.

The lack of these features poses no real problem for applications developed using VB; it is just a nuisance. Later in this book, you will read about how to simulate these features in VB.

Visual Basic and Complex Types

A **complex type** allows variables typed as something other than simple base types (for example, String and Boolean) to be declared. In object-oriented systems, variables that are "of" a particular class such as `Order`, `Customer`, or `Invoice` must be defined. Taking it a step further, `Order` could then consist of other classes such as `OrderHeader` and `OrderLine`.

In VB, you can define different variables that are references to runtime objects of a particular class type, as shown next.

```
Public myOrder As Order
Public myCustomer As Customer
Public myInvoice as Invoice
```

Such variables can then be used to create actual object instances and subsequently to serve as recipients' messages. In the previous code fragment, the variable `myOrder` is an `Order`. After the `myOrder` object is created, messages can be sent to it and `myOrder` will respond, provided that the operation is supported by `myOrder`'s interface.

Visual Basic and Message-Passing

Central to any object-oriented language is the ability to pass messages between objects. In later chapters, you will see that work gets done in a system only by objects that collaborate (by sending messages) to accomplish some goal (which is specified in a use case) of the system.

It would be simpler if the language allowed us to have only classes, related operations, and attributes—no stray functions floating around that are not attached to some class. This is the case in some object-oriented languages such as Smalltalk and Java, in which all work must be done by an operation attached to a class. VB, similar to C++, has no requirement that there be classes. Even in many well-built VB systems—those using sound, object-oriented concepts—some stray code will still be floating around in the form of BAS modules. This is partly due to the nature of VB's programming model. Error-handling code is typically the most common VB component living outside of a class. However, internally to VB, "Err" is an object.

VB supports message-passing, which is central to using VB's object-oriented features. The format closely resembles the syntax of other languages such as C++ and Java. In the following code fragment, assume that a variable is declared called `myCustomer` that is of type `Customer` and an operation is defined for `Customer` called `calcTotalValue`. Then a message `calcTotalValue` being sent to the `myCustomer` object in VB would look like this:

```
myCustomer.calcTotalValue
```

Many feel that, in any other structured language, this is just a fancy way of calling a procedure. Calling a procedure and sending a message are similar in that, once invoked, both implement a set of well-defined steps. However, a message differs in two ways.

1. There is a designated receiver, the object. Procedures have no designated receiver.

2. The interpretation of the message, that is, the "how-to" code (called the *method*) used to respond to the message, can vary with different receivers. This point will become more important later in the chapter when polymorphism is reviewed.

The concepts presented in this book rely heavily on classes and the messaging that takes place between their instances, or objects.

Visual Basic and Encapsulation

Recall that a class exposes itself to the outside world via its public interface and that this should be done by exposing operations only, and not attributes. VB supports encapsulation via its ability to declare both attributes and operations as either *public* or *private.*

Using the previous Order example code, suppose you want to set the value of the orderDate attribute. In this case, you should do so with an operation. An operation that gets or sets values is usually called a *getter* or a *setter.* The local copy of the order date, morderDate, is declared private. (Note the use of the lowercase "m" in morderDate. The "m" refers to *member variable* and reflects a standard naming convention in the object community.) Actually, all attributes of a class should be declared as private. Then they would be accessible only via operations that were exposed as public to the outside world.

Encapsulation provides some powerful capabilities. To the outside world, VB can hide how it derives its attribute values. If the orderTotal attribute is stored in the Order object as morderTotal, then the corresponding Get property defined previously looks like this.

```
Public Property Get orderTotal() As Long
        orderTotal = morderTotal
End Property
```

This would be invoked if the following code was executed by an interested client.

```
Dim localTotal as Long
Dim localOrder as New Order
localTotal = localOrder.orderTotal
```

However, suppose the attribute orderTotal isn't actually kept as a local value of the Order class but rather derived via some other mechanism (perhaps messaging to its OrderLine objects). If Order contains OrderLine objects (declared as a collection of OrderLines called myOrderLines) and OrderLine knows how to obtain its line totals via the message orderLineTotal, then the corresponding Get property for orderTotal within Order will look as follows.

```
Public Property Get orderTotal() As Long
        Dim lTotal as Long
```

```
              Dim iIndex as Integer
              For iIndex = 1 To myOrderLines.Count
                    lTotal = lTotal + _
                    myOrderLines(iIndex).orderLineTotal
              Next iIndex
              Let orderTotal = lTotal
       End Property
```

This code cycles through the `myOrderLines` collection, sending the `orderLineTotal` message to each of `Order`'s `OrderLine` objects until no more objects remain in the collection. It will be invoked if the following code is executed by an interested client.

```
    Dim localTotal as Long
    Dim localOrder as Order
    localTotal = localOrder.orderTotal
```

Notice that the "client" code didn't change. To the outside world, the class still has an `orderTotal` attribute. However, you have hidden, or *encapsulated*, just how the value was obtained. This allows the class's interface to remain the same (hey, I have an `orderTotal` that you can ask me about), while the class retains the flexibility to change its implementation in the future (sorry, how we do business has changed and now how we derive `orderTotal` must be done like this). This kind of resiliency is one of the compelling business reasons to use an object-oriented programming language.

Visual Basic and Inheritance

The inclusion of inheritance is often the most cited reason for granting a language object-oriented status. There are actually two kinds of inheritance: *interface* and *implementation*. Figure 2-4 gives an example of interface inheritance, and Figure 2-5 gives an example of implementation inheritance.

Interface inheritance declares that a class that is inheriting an interface will be responsible for implementing all of the method code of each operation defined in that interface. Only the signatures of the inherited class are actually inherited; no method code is inherited.

Implementation inheritance declares that a class that is inheriting an interface may, at its option, use the method code implementation

FIGURE 2-4   *Interface inheritance.*

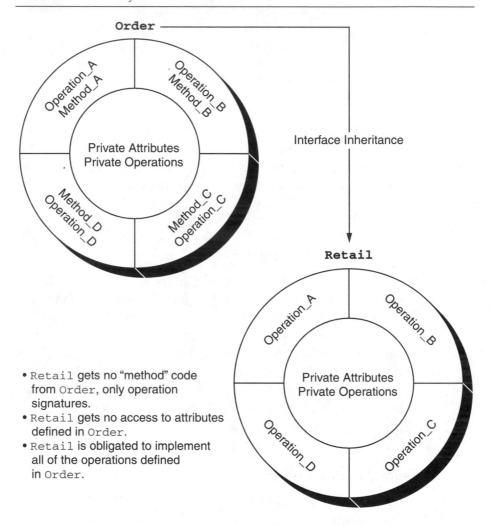

- Retail gets no "method" code from Order, only operation signatures.
- Retail gets no access to attributes defined in Order.
- Retail is obligated to implement all of the operations defined in Order.

already established for the interface. Alternatively, it may choose to implement its own version of the interface. In addition, the class inheriting the interface may extend that interface by adding its own operations and attributes.

Sometimes, interface inheritance should be used rather than implementation inheritance and vice versa. Interface inheritance is best used when the following are true.

FIGURE 2-5   *Implementation inheritance.*

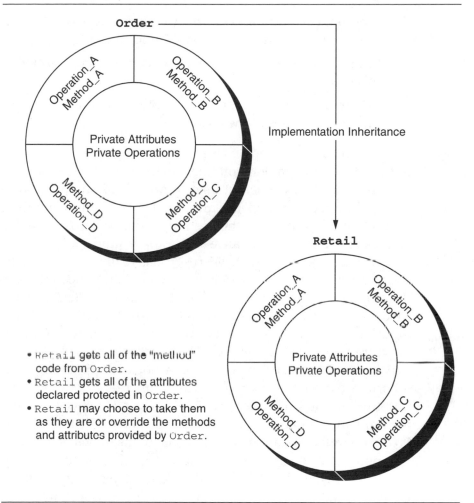

- Retail gets all of the "method" code from Order.
- Retail gets all of the attributes declared protected in Order.
- Retail may choose to take them as they are or override the methods and attributes provided by Order.

- The base class presents a generic facility, such as a table lookup, or a derivation of system-specific information, such as operating system semantics or unique algorithms.

- The number of operations is small.

- The base class has few, if any, attributes.

- Classes realizing or implementing the interface are diverse, with little or no common code.

Implementation inheritance is best used when the following are true.

- The class in question is an entity class that is of primary interest to the application (that is, not a utility or controller class).

- The implementation is complex, with a large number of operations.

- Many attributes and operations are common across specialized implementations of the base class.

Now for the bad news. VB supports only interface inheritance; it does not support implementation inheritance. If VB ever had a black eye, this is certainly where it takes it on the chin time and time again. We explore later how to get around this by using containment and delegation. However, this shortcoming requires you to do more coding and leads to more maintenance as the application evolves.

This is one area in which Microsoft has really missed satisfying one of its most sought-after extensions, especially since VB is the only development environment it offers that doesn't support this feature. Visual C++, Visual J++, and Visual FoxPro all support implementation inheritance. So do VB's largest competitors—Inprise's Delphi, Sybase's PowerBuilder, and Centura's SQLWindows.

Microsoft has justified its decision not to support implementation inheritance by stating that this form of inheritance can get applications into trouble and lead to less-flexible designs. However, just try removing implementation inheritance from Visual C++, Visual J++, and Visual FoxPro—and then stand back and listen to the howls of the wolves.

Apparently, incorporating implementation inheritance into VB would be technically difficult because of its existing architecture and its tight binding to COM. COM does not support implementation inheritance. This is because two key COM interfaces, `IUnknown` and `Idispatch`, would have to be automatically incorporated into classes that want to inherit method code from a base class. This in turn would conflict with adding a new vtable entry to an implemented interface, and the developer then would have to juggle interleaved vtables—not pretty. Many in the industry suspect that COM+, Microsoft's future version of COM, will address these issues. For a primer on COM and COM+, see Appendix D.

My last thought on the issue of implementation versus interface inheritance is this; let me, the designer and developer, have the option to use whichever form of inheritance is most appropriate for the task at hand. If that choice, as Microsoft seems to think, leads to a brittle solution, so be it. But at least the implementer was able to choose between two popular and industry-accepted forms of inheritance.

Visual Basic and Interface Inheritance

VB supports interface inheritance with the `Implements` keyword. A class wanting to realize a given interface (actually being responsible for the method code) simply adds an `Implements ClassName` statement to its class definition. To continue the previous example, suppose that you have two different types of orders that each warrants its own class: `Commercial` and `Retail`. You would still have an `Order` class (which isn't instantiated directly and which is called abstract). The previous fragment showed the code for the `Order` class. Following is the code for the `Commercial` class.

```
'Class Commercial which Implements the Order Interface
Implements Order

Public Function calcVariance() As Long
End Function

Private Function Order_getInfo() As Boolean
End Function

Private Function Order_calcTotalValue() As Long
End Function

Private Property Let Order_orderDate(ByVal RHS As Date)
End Property

Private Property Get Order_orderDate() As Date
End Property

Private Property Let Order_orderNumber(ByVal RHS As
Long)
End Property

Private Property Get Order_orderNumber() As Long
End Property
```

```
Private Property Let Order_orderTotal(ByVal RHS As Long)
End Property

Private Property Get Order_orderTotal() As Long
End Property
```

Here is the code for the Retail class.

```
'Class Retail which Implements the Order Interface
Implements Order

Public Function calcDiscount() As Long
End Function

Private Function Order_getInfo() As Boolean
End Function

Private Function Order_calcTotalValue() As Long
End Function

Private Property Let Order_orderDate(ByVal RHS As Date)
End Property

Private Property Get Order_orderDate() As Date
End Property

Private Property Let Order_orderNumber(ByVal RHS As Long)
End Property

Private Property Get Order_orderNumber() As Long
End Property

Private Property Let Order_orderTotal(ByVal RHS As Long)
End Property

Private Property Get Order_orderTotal() As Long
End Property
```

Notice that when an interface is implemented, the property, function, and subroutine signatures for the interface (the implemented class) get copied into the class that is implementing the interface. The class appends on the front of the property the name of the interface, in this case Order. So the operation within Commercial called Order_calcTotalValue is the signature of the operation defined in Order, but no method code is available (because only interface inheritance is available).

If you try to implement an interface and remove any of the interface's operations, your new class will not compile. Even if you don't want to implement any method code for some of the operations, you still must have them defined in your class, as empty skeletons. The VB IDE will copy all of these into your class for you, so you don't have to worry about copying and pasting code between classes. Simply select the "object" drop-down in the Code window and select Order. Then select the subroutine drop-down and pick each operation defined for Order. The skeletons will appear.

One very powerful aspect of interface inheritance is that a class can implement many interfaces, all at once. For example, a class could easily implement both the Commercial and Retail interfaces. It needs only an Implements ClassName statement for each class, or interface, being implemented.

Visual Basic's Alternative to Implementation Inheritance

Later in the book we will cover how to construct the example Order application for Remulak Productions. At that time, we will deal with a relatively simple, although not ideal, method to simulate implementation inheritance by using *containment* and *delegation* (this is how COM handles implementation inheritance).

As a sneak preview, though, for you curious types, the class that wants the method code of an interface, such as Commercial, will keep an instance variable locally for the class that has the method code that you want to reuse (such as Order). This is called *containment*. Now, when a message is sent to the Commercial class and a property of Order is invoked, you simply forward that message on to the local copy of the Order class. This will invoke the method code for that operation from Order. This is called *delegation*. Figure 2-6 provides a perspective of how this works behind the scenes in VB. We use this technique later in the implementation of the Remulak Productions solution.

Visual Basic and Polymorphism

Polymorphism is one of those fifty-dollar words that dazzles the uninformed and sounds really impressive. In fact, polymorphism is one of the most powerful features of any object-oriented language.

FIGURE 2-6   *Containment and delegation.*

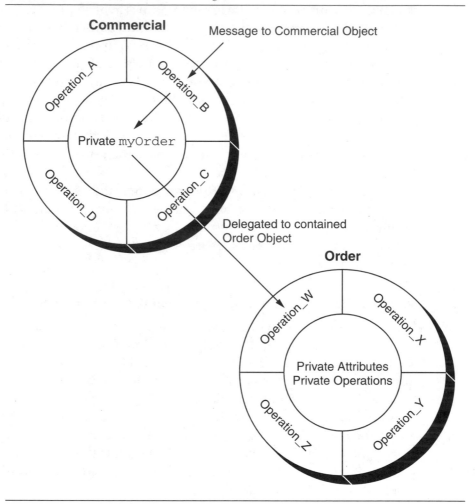

Roget's II Thesaurus cross-references the term *polymorphism* to the main entry of *variety*. That will do for starters. Variety is the key to polymorphism. The Latin root for polymorphism is simply "many forms." Polymorphism applies to operations in the object-oriented context. So, by combining these two thoughts, you could say that operations are *polymorphic* if they are identical (not just in name but also in signatures) but offer variety in their implementations. On the surface, polymorphism is the ability of two different classes to each have an operation that has the same signature, while having two very different forms of method code for the operation.

In languages such as COBOL and FORTRAN, defining a routine to have the same name as another routine will cause a compile error. In object-oriented languages such as VB, C++, and Java, several operations commonly might have the same signature. This is in fact encouraged because of the power and flexibility it brings to the design.

VB supports polymorphism well. As mentioned previously, the `Implements` keyword lets the application take advantage of polymorphism. Recall that the order system for Remulak Productions deals with two types of `Orders`: `Commercial` and `Retail`. Suppose, then, that differences exist in the fundamental algorithms used to value the profitability (whether commercial or retail) that the specific `Order` brings to Remulak. Also, Remulak wants to be able to value all of the `Orders` that a given customer has with the company at any time, which can be a combination of many `Commercial` and `Retail` `Orders`. Since both `Commercial` and `Retail` implement the `Order` interface, an application can actually treat instances of these classes the same.

A key concept behind polymorphism can be drawn from this maxim: *A class implementing an interface can be treated as an instance of the interface class.* For example, assume that there is a collection of `Orders` defined as a property of the `Customer` class. That class could support a `calcTotalValue` operation, which simply iterates over its collection of `Orders` so as to individually get its unique value.

```
'Class Customer
Private mcolOrder As Collection 'local collection
'of Order Objects

Public Function getInfo(id As Long) As Boolean
End Function

'Iterate over all the Customers Orders and send
'the calcTotalValue message to each of them
Public Function calcTotalValue() As Long
    Dim oObjOrder As Order
    Dim lTotalValue As Long
    For Each oObjOrder In mcolOrder
        lTotalValue = lTotalValue + oObjOrder. _
        calcTotalValue
```

```
        Next
        calcTotalValue = lTotalValue
    End Function
```

Since a `Customer` may have many different `Orders` (each will be either a `Retail` or `Commercial Order`), VB will make sure that the correct `calcTotalValue` operation gets called. Later, if you add a new type of `Order`, say, `Web`, it will be totally transparent to the `Customer` class. That class will still have a collection of `Orders`, except that it will have three different ones instead of two, each of which will have its own unique implementation of the `calcTotalValue` operation.

This is polymorphism at its best. At runtime, the class related to the object in question will be identified and the correct "variety" of the operation will be invoked. Polymorphism provides powerful extensibility features to the application by letting future unknown classes implement a predictable and well-conceived interface without affecting how other classes deal with that interface.

Why the UML and Visual Basic?

When modeling elements, our goal is to sketch the application's framework with a keen eye toward using sound object-oriented principles. For this reason, the UML, as an object-oriented notation, is a nice fit for any project using VB as its implementation language. VB has more than enough of the "object plumbing" to benefit from the design elements of UML models. More important, when UML is combined with a sound software process such as Synergy, the chances for the project's success increase dramatically.

Jim Rumbaugh once said, "You can't expect a method to tell you everything to do. Writing software is a creative process, like painting, writing, or architectural design. There are principals of painting, for example, that give guidelines on composition, color selection, and perspective, but they won't make you a Picasso." You will see what he means when later in the book, the UML elements are presented in a workable context during the development of an application using VB. At that time, artifacts will be chosen that add the most value to the problem. We will still need a sound process in order to be successful, however—and a little luck wouldn't hurt, either.

All of the UML artifacts used in this book will cumulatively lead to better-built VB applications. However, some of the UML deliverables will have a much closer counterpart to the actual VB code produced. For example, use cases are technology-neutral. Actually, using use cases would benefit any project regardless of the technology employed because they capture the application's essential requirements. All subsequent UML deliverables will derive from the foundations built in the use cases.

For core business and commercial applications, four UML diagrams most heavily impact the VB deliverable: class, sequence (or collaboration), component, and deployment. Now, I run the risk of having you think the other diagrams are never used; they are, depending on a project's characteristics and requirements. Yes, the project may also benefit, based on its unique characteristics, from other diagrams such as State and Activity diagrams. However, in my experience, the previously mentioned four diagrams are the pivotal models that will be most heavily used. Table 2-1 provides a cross reference of UML diagrams to VB mappings.

Class Diagram

The king of UML diagrams is the class diagram. This diagram is used to generate VB code using a visual modeling tool (in this book, Rational Rose). In addition, everything learned from all of the other diagrams will in one way or another influence this diagram. For example, the key class diagram components are represented in VB as follows.

- **Classes**: The classes identified will end up as automatically generated class modules in the VB IDE.

- **Attributes**: The attributes identified in the class will be generated as private (optionally public) member variables in the class module. Each attribute will have Public Property procedures of the type Get, Set, and Let (optional) created in the class module.

- **Interface**: Through the messaging patterns uncovered in the sequence diagrams, the interface of the class, or its public operations, will begin to take shape as operations are added to the class.

- **Operations**: Every operation defined for a class will end up as either Public Subroutines (no value returned) or Public Functions (value returned) within the class. The operations initially will be

TABLE 2-1   *UML Diagram to VB Mappings*

UML Diagram	Specific Element	VB Counterpart
Package	Instance of	Depending on usage, but can relate to componentizing strategy
Use case	Instance of	User Interface Artifacts (downplayed early on) Pathways which will become sequence diagrams
Class	Operations	Property, subroutine, function declarations
	Attributes	Property declarations
	Associations	Properties of type ClassName to support messaging outlined in the sequence diagram
Sequence	Instance of	Pathways through the application
	Message target	Operation in the receiving class
Collaboration	Instance of	Pathways through the application
	Message target	Operation in the receiving class
State	Actions/Activities	Operations in the class being lifecycled
	Events	Operations in the class being lifecycled or in another collaborating class
	State Variables	Attributes in the class being lifecycled
Activity	Action States	Method code to implement a complex operation
Component	Components	EXE, DLL (in-process, out-of-process)
Deployment	Nodes	Physical, deployable install sets destined for client and/or server hosting MTS packages

without the complete signature specification (operation name only) but eventually will contain fully specified signatures.

- **Associations**: The associations identified between classes will end up as attributes of the classes so as to enable messaging patterns as detailed by sequence diagrams.

- **Finalized classes**: Finalized classes will be used to generate first-cut database schemas (assuming a relational database as the persistence store) in the form of a DDL.

The UML class diagram and its VB counterpart, the class module, are the core of what drives the application's implementation.

Sequence Diagram

The tasks required to satisfy an application's goals are specified as *pathways* through a use case. In most cases, each major pathway will have a sequence diagram created for it. Each, although logically stated in the use case, will eventually end up as a dynamic collaboration between runtime objects, all sending messages to one another.

For example, when the `Customer` object wants each of its `Order` objects to perform the operation `calcTotalValue`, it sends a message. Each message requires the receiver object (the `Order`) to have an operation defined to honor the request. Operations all end up in a class somewhere. These classes eventually are used to generate code into the VB environment.

The project team uses the sequence diagram to "walk" the application. Once it gets comfortable with the UML, and the accompanying Synergy process used in this book, it will no longer need to walk code. Once the sequence diagram passes inspection, actual implementation of the method level coding can occur.

Eventually, the sequence diagram walk-thrus will be the primary confirmation of whether a use case pathway is correct. Visual modeling tools, at present, do not generate VB code from the message patterns outlined in the sequence diagram. However, I contend this wouldn't be difficult to do, and the next version of these products likely will support this ability. Having it would certainly differentiate competitors.

Component Diagram

The fully developed classes are assigned to components in the visual modeling tool's component diagrams. Many will fit a variety of possible physical manifestations.

- Graphical forms (standard.exe's)
- Business-level rule components (standard.exe's, activex.exe's, or activex.dll's)
- Transaction or persistence components (standard.exe's, activex.exe's, or activex.dll's)

These component choices will impact the actual "make" process that VB will go through to generate the application.

Deployment Diagram

Components defined in the visual modeling tool are deployed on nodes specified in the deployment diagrams. These diagrams depict the physical machines that will house the components specified previously. These configurations may be traditional client-centric control or more flexible multitier solutions.

Visual Modeling Tool Support

The UML and VB fit together well. The value that UML adds is enhanced by the use of a visual modeling tool that supports both forward and reverse engineering (creating code from models and creating models from code). The use of a visual modeling tool also aids traceability and cross-checking the model components.

A project that combines an effective software process model and a robust modeling language such as the UML nevertheless will be hindered if it lacks a visual modeling tool. Without such a tool, it will produce paper models that won't get updated or, worse, that will be lost in the shuffle of day-to-day project activity. Many excellent products are available, and they continue to evolve. Pick a tool, and make it part of your process.

Checkpoint

Where We Have Been

1. Once considered a small fish in the big pond of integrated development tools, VB has come a long way to take a front-seat in this market.

2. VB has grown in acceptance for many reasons, including its support of COM, MTS, and MSMQ and the existence of a rich third-party marketplace for add-on products.

3. VB does not support implementation inheritance. This can be simulated, however, by using the COM concept of containment and delegation.

4. VB is greatly influenced by the work done in four UML diagrams: class, sequence, component, and deployment. The use case diagram is the starting point for all artifacts produced by the project.

Where We Are Going Next

In this chapter, we:

1. Explore the project plan for the Synergy process model.
2. Review the importance of project scoping, and look at deliverables from that effort.
3. Get acquainted with the book's continuing project, Remulak Productions.
4. Produce an event list as a precursor to use case analysis.

CHAPTER 3   *Getting the Project Started*

This chapter sets the groundwork for how to start a project by creating a project charter. It shouldn't be surprising that this is where most projects make their first wrong turn. The project charter sets the stage for the project's Inception phase. As the first artifact to be produced, its importance cannot be under-estimated.

A project charter is driven by the following five key inputs:

- *The features that the system must support*

- *The stakeholders who will fund and/or oversee the system's use*

- *The actors who will actually interface with the system*

- *The events that the system must be aware of and respond to*

- *The constraints and risks placed on the project*

The project charter also must put into place the administrative plumbing necessary for managing the project. This, too, is key to the project's success. Change control, risk assessment, and training are just as meaningful as requirements. Many project teams take these housekeeping chores too lightly and end up being the victims of scope creep, risky choices, and a staff with skills that are inadequate to enable them to perform their assigned tasks. The project charter sets out the stepping stones toward successfully using the Synergy process model introduced in Chapter 1. Following its activities and observing its dependencies will move us closer to our goal of building quality, object-oriented, VB applications.

This chapter takes you through Iteration One of creating the project charter. In the next chapter, the project charter deliverable will be completed.

GOALS

- Introduce Remulak Productions, the project specimen for the book.

- Introduce the process model activities pertinent to the Inception phase.

- Review the project charter template.

- Define and introduce the actors and their roles in the project.

- Explore the event table and its components and how it forms the basis for identifying use cases.

Establishing the Project Charter

Remulak Productions is the subject of the sample project that will unfold throughout the remaining chapters. A very small company located in Newport Hills, Washington, a suburb of Seattle, Remulak specializes in finding hard-to-locate musical instruments, in particular guitars, ranging from traditional instruments to ancient varieties no longer produced. It also sells rare and in-demand sheet music. Further, it is considering adding to its product line other products that are not as unique as its instruments, including recording and mixing technology, microphones, and recordable compact disk (CD) players. Remulak is a very ambitious company; it hopes to open a second order processing location on the East Coast within a year.

Although some of its sales come from third-party commercial organizations, most orders are taken in-house by its order entry clerks. Remulak's founder, owner, and president, Jeffery Homes, realizes that he cannot effectively run his company with its current antiquated order-entry and billing system. The challenge that you and I must meet is to design and implement a system that not only meets the company's immediate needs but that is also flexible enough to support other types of products in the future.

Our first step is to uncover the features that the application needs and to scope the project. The charter will define the boundaries of the project and limit the possible features, as well as implement the house-keeping framework that will guide the project forward. Appendix E contains the complete project plan (produced by using Microsoft Project) that we will follow for Remulak Productions. Before beginning, however, let's re-orient ourselves to the Synergy, the software process model introduced in Chapter 1.

The Process Model

Recall that the Synergy process model is our guide to performing activities in a predictable order. Figure 3-1 shows the Synergy process model from Chapter 1, this time highlighting the activity categories that we will focus on in the Inception phase.

Working Template of the Project Charter

The project charter is the key deliverable of the Inception phase. It is much more than a superficial document that merely mentions objectives and desires. It lists the events, use cases, and architectural components that the project will support. And it is a vital step toward understanding the requirements of the application.

We can best describe the project charter by outlining a proposed template that covers, at a minimum, the topics listed in Table 3-1.

FIGURE 3-1 *Synergy process model and the Inception phase.*

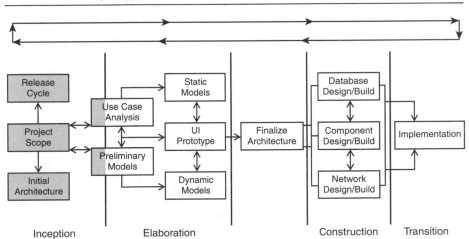

TABLE 3-1   *Proposed Project Charter Template*

Topic	Purpose
Business Purpose	The business reason why this project is being undertaken.
Business Objectives	The business objectives of the project. What are the bottom line benefits that the project will bring to the organization (for example, remain competitive, profitable, leading edge, reactive)?
Desired Features	A list of features that the project must support (for example, order tracking and control, expedient billing, management of inventory, one-day turnaround on special orders).
Critical Success Factors	The key factors that will make the project a success (for example, deliver products on time and within budget, hire talented project manager, pull skilled analysts and developers from existing projects, obtain full-time user commitment).
Constraints	Constraints from a time, cost, and functionality perspective (for example, the project must be completed by year's end, provide a payback within two years, implement a minimum of usable functionality before going into production).
Risks	The clear risks of the project (for example, the project team has never used VB let alone object-oriented programming techniques and the UML, the existing system will prove difficult to convert due to its antiquated design, the executive sponsor is giving only lip service to full-time user involvement).
Roles and Responsibilities	The logical functions that will be performed and by whom (for example, Executive Sponsor: Jeffery Homes, Lead Analyst: Rene Becnel, Lead User: Dan Fruge, Lead Designer: Todd Klock, Lead Architect: Jose Aponte).
Locations of Interest	The geographical areas (if any) that will be expected to use the applications (for example, New Orleans, Denver, Seattle).
Actors	Usually human beings, who stimulate the system in one form or another. However, they might also be other systems, timers or clocks, or hardware devices (for example, order clerk, billing clerk, shipper, accounting system, bar-code reader).

TABLE 3-1   *(continued)*

Topic	Purpose
Event List/Event Table	Outline of the essential events of which the system must be aware and which will provoke some perceived system response. Also might want to specify location, frequency of arrival, and arrival pattern (for example, customer places order, customer inquires about order status, order is shipped, order is billed, order is back-ordered).
Use Cases	Grouped, related events identified in the event table. Use cases are used to categorize major groupings of functionality (for example, process order, maintain order, ship order, manage inventory, bill for order).
Use Case Course of Events	Pathways through the use cases that depict real-life instances of an event identified in the event table. Every event will be satisfied by a use case in the form of a pathway through that use case. (For example, process order: customer calls in an order for an in-stock item and provides a P. O. number for billing, process order: customer calls in an order for an out-of-stock item and wants to pay with a VISA card.)
Preliminary Execution Architecture	The architecture that is initially envisioned for the construction and production maintenance of the application (for example, VB over a TCP/IP Wide Area Network (WAN) using an N-tier design approach). The database will initially be Microsoft SQL Server, but all data access will be made via OLE-DB providers so as to allow the application to migrate to a different RDBMS in the future. Visual Source Safe will be used for source control, and Microsoft's Systems Management Server (SMS) will be used to distribute software components to remote locations.
Project Infrastructure	Details how change control and risk assessments will be made (for example, all changes will be tied back to the original event table and any changes not defined within that event table will have to go through a change control procedure).
Project Release Strategy	Planned release strategy for the project, indicating the increments, duration of each, and anticipated implementation schedule (for example, there will be three increments for the project: (1) order entry and maintenance, (2) billing, and (3) inventory management).

To provide some of the artifacts identified in the charter, we need to explore deeper what comprises the essence of the application: actors, event lists, and event tables.

The Actors

Actors are key to obtaining several artifacts in the project. *Actor* is a term coined by Ivar Jacobson in his OOSE approach to software development (originally called Objectory Process and now called the Rational Unified Process). Actors are essential in the project. Identifying them gives us better insight into the events that the system must support.

Actors are usually thought of as human beings, but they also may be other systems, timers and clocks, or hardware devices. Actors stimulate the system and are the initiators of events; they also can receive stimuli from the system and in this case are considered passive. They are discussed in more detail in Chapter 4 on use cases. For now, they are represented as they are identified in the UML, as stick figures, as shown in Figure 3-2. However, they may also be rendered graphically in other ways that more directly illustrate the specific domain of the application.

Too often people attempt to get their hands around the project by producing reams of paper describing what the system will support. This is a wasted exercise that can be remedied by first focusing on the actors, that is, the users, involved in the system. To find the actors, ask the following questions.

- Who/what will be interested in the system?
- Who/what will want to change the data in the system?

FIGURE 3-2 *Examples of the actors of a project.*

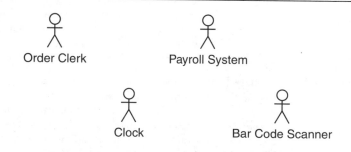

- Who/what will want to interface with the system?
- Who/what will want information from the system?

Be careful to focus specifically on the role that each actor will play. This is very important because a given person might play more than one role. As we uncover more information about how the actor interfaces with the system, clumping all of these roles together and treating them as the roles of one actor could be a mistake, since that actor might not always play those multiple roles.

Logically, the role that the actor plays might require different interface skills, knowledge of the system, and comprehension levels. We would err by manifesting the interface based on an assumption that the actor is super-human and can cover lots of bases. Rather, we should analyze the role that the actor plays in the system. This will certainly make the system more pliable if the actor's responsibilities change. Table 3-2 lists the proposed actors for Remulak.

Now that we have identified the actors, we'll explore the events that they are responsible for generating.

Event List and Event Table

The **event list** is the catalyst that flushes out use cases; we do that in Chapter 4. Use cases are not always intuitive, however. Events, on the

TABLE 3-2 *Proposed Actors for Remulak's Application.*

Actor	Definition
Customer	Places orders for products.
Supplier	Supplies products to the company for resale.
Accounting System	Gets accounting information from the system.
Billing Clerk	Coordinates and tracks all sales from a financial perspective.
Shipping Clerk	Coordinates the routing of fulfilled product orders.
Packaging Clerk	Prepares the product for shipment.
Order Clerk	Takes orders and maintains existing orders.
Customer Service Clerk	Services customers and their demographic information.
Manager	Requests reports on the status of the company's orders.

other hand, are easy to brainstorm and are very much on the project sponsors' minds. Once the events are identified, the definition of use cases is easier.

The event list can be brainstormed separately from the event table, but one leads to the other. The system must be aware of many types of events. Typically, events fall into two categories: external and internal.

External events are the easiest to find. They are any stimuli to the system that originates from outside of its boundaries (for example, a customer places an order). To find them, focus on the event and ask the question, who or what is stimulating the event? Most events that we will identify are external.

Internal events are more diverse. One type, and the only one that we will identify now, is the clock or timer event. I view this type of internal event as "that big timer in the sky that goes off, causing the system to do something." Internal timer events are very common in most systems, across all types of domains. Examples of an event that is stimulated by an internal timer are "produce backorder reports nightly" and "interface with the general ledger system every two days." Again, focus on the event and ask the question, who or what is stimulating the event.

Other types of internal events, which we don't focus on now, are those generated by the system. These typically fall into the category of certain limits being reached or entities being created or deleted. For example, consider the following criterion: "If a customer's credit is exceeded, we need a supervisor's approval to complete the sale." That the credit is exceeded is an event; however, this type of event will be specified in a later chapter as a *business rule* that is owned by a class in the domain.

Sometimes, project teams struggle with which external events to include in the project's scope. To help get around this, ask if the system would be stable if you chose not to respond to the event. For example, the event "customer places referral order" might be a valid event; however, it is out of the scope of this project. An event that is critical to the integrity of a system, such as keeping creditworthy customers, isn't something that could be implemented optionally.

One last point on external events that might be out of scope: Don't exclude them during this initial brainstorming session. You would be surprised how many times you will revisit the list later, and you might resurrect some events that previously were deemed out of scope. It is a good idea not to cloud the session with premature assumptions about boundaries. Remember: Ask for the sky, prioritize, and then simplify.

We can begin brainstorming the events. Think of an event as following this general form:

Subject + Verb + Object

Where:

Subject is an Actor defined earlier in the process, for example, Customer and Shipping Clerk.

Verb shows the action, such as places, sends, buys, and changes.

Object is the focus of the action defined in the *Verb*.

Here are some examples:

Customer + Places + Order
Shipping Clerk + Sends + Order Items
Customer + Buys + Warranty
Order Clerk + Changes + Order

It can be helpful to brainstorm events in one session and then, in another session, focus on adding additional information and placing the events in an events table. The goal is to get the events into the event table quickly, as it is one of the first key artifacts produced as part of the project charter effort.

The event table identifies additional information that will provide important input to other areas of the organization (operations, network support). Table 3-3 sets out a proposed format for the event table.

The arrival pattern might be more or less important, depending on the application domains. Following are typical values for it:

Periodic: Events are defined by the period in which they arrive.

Episodic: No known arrival pattern; unpredictable.

Eventually, we will want to be even more specific regarding the granularity of the arrival pattern (peak hour frequency), as this will be vitally important to the network and operations staff. For example, 1,000 *Customer Places Order* events in a given day might not concern the network staff, but 900 occurring between 8 A.M. and 9 A.M. definitely will. At this point in the project, we might not know this level of detail; regardless, we still must take a stab at predicting the arrival pattern. Also, if the locations are known now, the frequency cell in the table should outline those and their unique frequencies.

TABLE 3-3 *Proposed Format of an Event Table*

Subject	Verb	Object	Frequency	Arrival Pattern	Response
Customer	Places	Order	1,000/day	Episodic	Order is edited and saved in the system.
Shipping Clerk	Sends	Order	700/day	Episodic	Order is packaged and shipped according to the shipping terms.
Customer	Buys	Warranty	60/day	Episodic	Order is validated as to terms and then recorded.
Customer	Changes	Order	5/day	Episodic	Order is edited to make the change and then recorded.
Supplier	Sends	Inventory	5-10/day	Episodic	New inventory is checked in.
Customer	Cancels	Order	1/week	Episodic	Order is removed from the system.
Time	Produces	Backorder Report	3/week	Episodic	Report is produced.
Time	Produces	Accounting Interface	1/week	Episodic	Interface to system.
Customer ServiceClerk	Changes	Address	5/week	Episodic	Address is changed.
Packaging Clerk	Prepares	Order	100/day	Episodic	Package is readied for shipment.
Manager	Inquires	Orders	5/day	Episodic	Request is honored.
Billing Clerk	Inquires Past Due	Invoice	10/day	Episodic	Past-due report is produced.

The anticipated responses are somewhat high level at this point. However, anticipated responses is an important component of the event table because they are the expectations of the actors, many of whom are probably members of the project team. These responses will be realized as design components and actual code later in the project.

Project Charter: Iteration One

In Iteration One of the project charter, the project team must agree on the template's basic components (features, critical success factors), the actors, and the events to be supported. Although accomplishing this effort can be done in any of several different ways, a facilitated session works best, preferably supervised by a disinterested third party skilled in facilitating and keeping things on track.

For very large projects, the project team should consider breaking up the sessions by logical subsystem, for example, accounting, billing, and order entry. Whether you do this depends on the size of the project. For example, I once worked with a large automobile company that was attempting to integrate state-of-the-art human interaction technology into the automobile. We broke up the project team into six separate teams and gave each a week to come up with its part of the project charter.

Iteration One Complete

We have now completed Iteration One. In Chapter 4, we proceed to the final two iterations. We will assign events to use cases. We also will add detail to some parts of the use cases before attempting to estimate the project's release cycles (increments) and timeframes—we need to know more about the project before we estimate the effort. This is where the Synergy process differs from many other processes. (An approach to estimating use cases is covered in a later chapter as well as in Appendix A.) It is wise to remember that regardless of the caveats you put on an estimate, people later will recall only the estimate itself.

Checkpoint

Where We Have Been

1. Projects need boundaries and a way to express those boundaries coherently. The project charter provides this.

2. The actors and their roles need to be defined based on information available about the application domain.

3. The events are the embryo of what the system must support. It is the nucleus of the requirements of the system and will be satisfied by use cases defined in the next chapter.

4. Providing estimates too early damages credibility. Typically, more information is needed before workable release cycles (increments) and estimates can be provided.

Where We Are Going Next

In the next chapter, we:

1. Explore Iterations Two and Three of the Inception phase.
2. Review the concept of the use case and its modeling components.
3. Assign events to use cases.
4. Identify the primary, alternate, and exception pathways through the use cases.
5. Detail some of the pathways through the use cases.
6. Prioritize and package the use cases.
7. Estimate release cycles (increments).
8. Define preliminary software architecture.

CHAPTER 4

Use Cases

Having defined the project charter components, the actors, and the events of interest in the system, we next move to assigning the events to use cases. The **use case** is the one UML artifact that focuses on what the system will be contracted to do, not how it will do it. Use cases are the hub from which all requirements are derived.

Every event identified in Iteration One of the Inception phase must be satisfied by a use case. One use case can be responsible for satisfying many events. As a result, a use case may have more than one pathway through it. This chapter examines how to identify those pathways, as well as details the primary pathway through each use case.

The Inception phase also details a preliminary software architecture. This architecture is based on what is known about the application's execution domain and is represented by the UML component and deployment diagrams.

This phase will also produce an estimate of both the number of increments in which the system will be realized and the time/cost estimates for deliverables. This grouping of functionality is visualized with the UML package diagram.

GOALS

↩ Add to our information about Remulak Productions, especially pertaining to preliminary technology needs and goals.

↪ Explore the concept of the use case and the use case diagram.

↪ Review a sample use case template.

↪ Define the various pathways through the use case: primary, alternate, and exception.

↪ Learn how to detail the most common pathway through a use case.

↪ Discuss a preliminary software and hardware architecture.

↪ Review the planned increments and implementation schedule.

The Sample Project

Recall from Chapter 3 that Remulak, which specializes in locating hard-to-find musical instruments, primarily guitars, wants to replace its legacy order-entry application. Company founder, owner, and president Jeffery Homes has contacted us regarding his concern about his company's ability to keep up with technology.

Since Jeffery is not an IT expert, he knows that success depends on the solution being extensible into the future. His initial concern is the Internet and its applicability to his business. Jeffery wants to minimize cost outlays regarding the technology that is used while maintaining flexibility to change platforms later. Jeffery makes the following observations about the company.

- Many of its products are very expensive and require quite a bit of handholding and selling by the order clerk.

- Many, if not all, of its customers want to be able to get information on orders that have been placed and shipped without interacting with a company representative.

- Many of its customers want to order other products from Remulak that are not as unique as its instruments, including recording and mixing technology, microphones, and recordable CD players.

From this, he decides that an Internet-based inquiry ability could benefit Remulak. However, the need remains in some cases for customized, personal interaction, at least initially to get the order into the system. So it appears that all but the more complicated orders could utilize an Internet-based order solution. These facts are crucial to consider as we devise our initial software architecture for Remulak.

The Process Model

Once again, the Synergy process model is spotlighted, with the emphasis on the Inception phase (Figure 4-1).

Use Cases

The project's success depends largely on defining requirements in a manner that is intuitive to both the IT staff and the project sponsors. The requirements documentation not only serves as a key artifact, but also must be a living artifact. Requirements cannot be expected to remain stable throughout the entire project effort, so they must be in a format that can be easily assimilated by the current project team, as well as new team members.

The concept of the use case sprang from Jacobson's early work on large telecommunications switching systems at Ericsson. This was his primary contribution to the UML. As mentioned in earlier chapters, his

FIGURE 4-1   *Synergy process model and the Inception phase.*

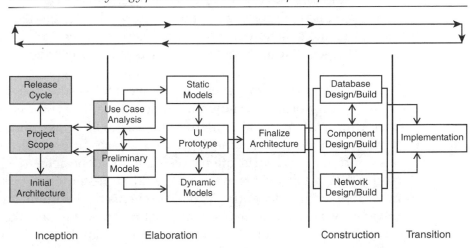

Objectory Process was transformed into Rational Software's popular process model, Rational Unified Process (RUP).

Use cases are goal-oriented and serve as containers of sorts for the interactions that they satisfy. Jacobson's definition of a use case will serve as a baseline as we begin our exploration of this key UML artifact:

> A behaviorally related sequence of interactions performed by an actor in a dialogue with the system to provide some measurable value to the actor.

Let's examine this in more detail.

1. "Behaviorally related" means that the interactions should, as a group, comprise a self-contained unit that is an end in itself, with no intervening time delays imposed by the business.

2. The use case must be initiated by an actor and seen through to completion by an actor.

3. "Measurable value" means that the use case must achieve some business goal. If we cannot find a business-related objective for the use case, then we should rethink it.

4. The use case must leave the system in a stable state; it cannot be half done.

Use cases are goal-oriented. Remembering this is key to using them effectively. They represent the *what* of the system, not the *how*. Use cases are also technology-neutral, so they can apply to any application architecture or process. Even if you were to chuck all that the UML offers and use only use cases, a project's requirements would still be defined in a much clearer and coherent fashion than if use cases were not used.

Figure 4-2 sets out the sequence that we follow to arrive at the use cases.

When readdressing the event table, we make sure the table is grouped in actor order, as shown in Table 4-1, as this will assist us in brainstorming the use cases. Often, a use case will be associated with only one actor. However, some types of use cases, those that provide information such as reports, often have more than one actor.

Notice that certain events in the table tend to cluster together, such as those dealing with order entry. Also some events deal with maintaining an order as well as inquiring about an existing order. We take these natural groupings and write a short (one or two words) descriptive phrase for each, asking these questions.

FIGURE 4-2   *Getting to use cases.*

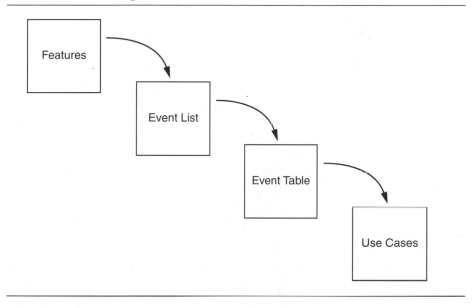

- What do these events have in common?
- Do these events have the same ultimate goal? If so, what is it?

Next, we place these descriptive phrases next to an oval, along with the associated actors to produce our first attempt at a use case diagram, shown in Figure 4-3.

The actors are connected to the use cases via an *association*. Notice the *Accounting System* actor. This actor, being an external system and nonhuman, is rendered using the *interface stereotype* and drawn as a box. Stereotypes are discussed in more detail later in the chapter. For now, think of a stereotype as a categorization or grouping mechanism. Using stereotypes is optional; there is nothing semantically incorrect by representing this actor as a stick figure. I consulted on a project whose management took a dim view of stick figures as part of the deliverables, so we went with the box notation. You can probably guess that this organization had quite a few other hurdles to clear before it became successful at using the UML.

Notice also the line with the large triangle arrow connecting *Customer Service Clerk* to *Order Clerk*. This means that a *Customer Service Clerk* "is an" *Order Clerk*. This denotes a *generalization relationship*. That

TABLE 4-1 *Event Table with Events Grouped by Actor*

Actor	Verb	Object	Frequency	Arrival Pattern	Response
Customer	Places	Order	1,000/day	Episodic	Order is edited and saved in the system.
Customer	Buys	Warranty	60/day	Episodic	Order is validated as to terms and then recorded.
Customer	Changes	Order	5/day	Episodic	Order is edited to make the change and then recorded.
Customer	Cancels	Order	1/week	Episodic	Order is removed from the system.
Customer	Inquires	Order	200/day	Episodic	
Customer	Changes	Address	5/week	Episodic	Address is changed.
Shipping Clerk	Sends	Order	700/day	Episodic	Order is packaged and shipped according to the shipping terms.
Supplier	Sends	Inventory	5- 10/day	Episodic	New inventory is checked in.
Time	Produce	Backorder Report	3/week	Episodic	Report is produced.
Time	Produce	Accounting Interface	1/week	Episodic	Interface to Accounting system.
Customer Service Clerk	Changes	Address	5/week	Episodic	Address changed
Packaging Clerk	Prepares	Order	100/day	Episodic	Package is readied for shipment.
Manager	Inquires	Orders	5/day	Episodic	Request is honored.
Billing Clerk	Inquires Past Due	Invoice	10/day	Episodic	Past-due report is produced.

is, the two actors can be substituted for the same thing and that they actually perform the same logical function but happen to be physically one person (recall from Chapter 3 that we are supposed to focus on the role and not on the person).

FIGURE 4-3   *The Remulak Productions use case diagram.*

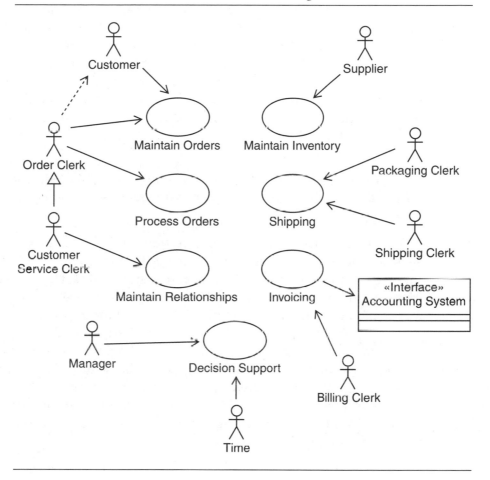

One last feature to notice is the dashed line from *Order Clerk* to *Customer*. This denotes a *dependency association* relationship. That is, one actor depends on the other, in this case the *Order Clerk* depends on the *Customer*, as shown by the arrow pointing from the *Order Clerk* to the *Customer* (rather than vice versa). Many practitioners would say that the actor involved in processing an order is the *Customer*. This is debatable, as the user interface will be geared toward the *Order Clerk*, not the *Customer*. However, the *Order Clerk* is useless without the *Customer*'s input.

As a consistency check, we determine whether any events identified during Iteration One have not found a home in a use case. Any that haven't are either out-of-scope or worded incorrectly or are missing a use case. As a good practice, we add a column to the event table in which to record which use case is satisfying each event.

This is a good time to talk about **scope creep**. Every project suffers from it. If you haven't experienced it yet, then you have had the luxury of wonderful project sponsors or you aren't telling the truth in order to protect the guilty. Keep the following bit of wisdom close at all times.

> All requirements originate with the events to be satisfied and the use cases that satisfy them. If it isn't defined as an event and satisfied by a use case, then it is a change request that requires some form of change control action.

This doesn't mean that the project won't accept changes. Rather it says that to keep your schedule true to the increments to be implemented, changes must be tracked and assigned to a later-scheduled increment that will satisfy them. Do you need to update the event table and related use case documentation? You bet. If the event table and use cases are not kept up-to-date, then you will lose all traceability.

We have now completed the first UML diagram, the use case diagram (although it is subject to change). This is the most important diagram, from the perspectives of the project sponsors, because it represents their domain. It represents the boundaries of the project scope from a high-level perspective and is the basis for dividing the project into multiple increments.

Finding the Pathways through the Use Case

Before we can complete the project charter, we need to do more work: We need to find the various pathways through each use case. We will identify three levels of pathways: primary, alternate, and exception.

We have assigned events to use cases. Recall that use cases are goal-oriented and serve as containers for the interactions that they satisfy. Also recall that, as mentioned earlier in this chapter, ". . . the interactions should, as a group, be a self-contained unit that is an end in itself." To better document the use cases, we employ a use case template, as follows, that we apply to all use cases.

Use Case Template

Use Case Name	(a short, concise name for the use case; two or three words)
Use Case Description	(a short description of the use case, stated as a goal)
Use Case Authors	(the authors of the use case)
Actors	(the actors involved in this use case)
Locations	(the locations that will perform this use case; typically based on a geographical location but may be departments or divisions)
Status	(the stage that the use case is in: initial pathways defined and completed)
Priority	(the priority of the use case; ranked on an ordinal basis, with 1 being the highest)
Assumptions	(what is assumed to be true, or false, about this use case)
Preconditions	(facts that must be true before this use case and its internal pathways can be initiated; sometimes called the *required system state for execution*)
Postconditions	(facts that must be true when this use case ends; sometimes called the *required system state upon completion*)
Primary Pathway	(the name of the primary pathway)
Alternate Pathways	(alternate pathways through the use case)
Exception Pathways	(exception pathways or error conditions)

This is the beginning of the use case template. Later in the chapter, it is presented in its entirety using one of the Remulak Productions use cases.

We need to know more about the interactions stimulated by events and now assigned to use cases. Specifically, we need more information about what happens when a use case responds to an event. We learn this by setting out the individual steps within a pathway that a use case takes in response to an event.

Finding the Happy Path

The use case template is initially used to define the primary pathway, called the **happy path**, or, more formally, the Basic Course of Events (BCOE). The happy path, or as one of my seminar attendees called it, the "sunny-day path," is the most commonly occurring pathway through the use case. It is usually one that depicts the perfect world, in which nothing goes wrong. If a use case has a lot of happy paths, then we arbitrarily pick one as *the* happy path. However, I contend that with a little work, we'll likely find that one of these potential happy paths either happens more often than the others or is more interesting to the project sponsor.

We want to identify the happy path for every use case we have at this point. Table 4-2 does that for Remulak Productions.

Finding the Alternate Pathways

Having identified the happy path for each use case, we next tackle finding the alternate pathways. An **alternate pathway** is a pathway that is still considered a good citizen pathway; it's just not the most heavily traveled one. Another term often used for this type of pathway is Alternate Course of Events (ACOE). Table 4-3 sets out the alternate pathways for the Remulak Productions use cases.

TABLE 4-2   *Happy Paths for the Remulak Productions Use Cases*

Use Case	Happy Path
Maintain Orders	A customer calls in to inquire about an order's status.
Maintain Inventory	The products arrive at the warehouse with a copy of the P. O. attached.
Process Orders	A customer calls in and orders a guitar and supplies and pays with a credit card.
Shipping	An entire order is shipped from stock on hand to a customer.
Invoicing	An order is invoiced and sent to the customer, indicating that payment was satisfied via credit card billing.
Maintain Relationships	A customer calls in to change its mailing address.
Decision Support	The manager requests backorder status report.

TABLE 4-3   *Alternate Pathways for the Remulak Productions Use Cases*

Use Case	Alternate Pathway
Maintain Orders	A customer calls in to change a product quantity for one order item on the order.
	A customer calls to cancel an order.
	A customer calls to add a new item to an order.
	A customer calls to delete an item from an order.
	A customer calls to change the shipping terms of an order.
	A customer buys an extended warranty on an item.
	A customer calls to change the billing method.
Maintain Inventory	The product arrives at the warehouse with a P. O. attached but incomplete as to the products ordered.
	The product is ordered to replenish stock on hand.
	The product is ordered to fill a special order.
	The product is ordered to fill a backorder.
	Products are accounted for through a physical inventory count.
Process Orders	A customer calls in and orders a guitar and does not have a P. O.
	A customer calls in and orders a guitar and uses the Remulak easy finance plan to pay.
	A customer calls in and orders an organ and pays with a credit card.
	A customer calls in and orders an organ and uses a P. O.
Shipping	A partial order is shipped from stock on hand to a customer. An entire order is shipped to a customer sourced directly from a third-party supplier.
Invoicing	An overdue notice is sent to a customer for a past-due account.
	Interface of subledger transactions to the accounting system.
Maintain Relationships	A customer calls in to change its default payment terms and payment method.
	A new customer is added to the system.
	A prospective customer is added to the system.
	A new supplier is added to the system.
	A supplier calls in to change its billing address.
Decision Support	Time to print the backorder report.

Finding the Exception Pathways

Things don't always go as planned. An **exception pathway** is intended to capture an "unhappy" pathway. An **exception** is an error condition that is important enough to the application to capture. In some application domains (such as failure analysis applications), the error conditions are more important than the success-oriented happy path. Some use cases, however, might not have exceptions that are interesting enough to capture; don't be concerned about those. Table 4-4 details the exceptions for Remulak.

One last thought on events, pathways, and use cases. If a use case has only one pathway, then the granularity of the use case is much too fine. The effort has probably produced a functional decomposition of the domain. For example, while on a consulting assignment at an international banking organization, I was introduced to its use case diagram. I was awestruck to learn that they had identified almost 300 use

TABLE 4-4   *Exception Pathways for the Remulak Productions Use Cases*

Use Case	Exception Pathway
Maintain Orders	A customer calls in to cancel an order that isn't found in the system.
	A customer calls to add a warranty that is no longer valid for the time that the product has been owned.
	A customer calls to change an order, and the product to be added is not found in the system.
Maintain Inventory	A product arrives with no P. O. or bill of lading.
Process Orders	A customer calls in to place an order using a credit card and the card is invalid.
	A customer calls in with a P. O. and has not been approved to use the P. O. method.
	A customer calls in to place an order, and the items desired are not in stock.
Shipping	Order is ready to ship and has no shipping address.
Invoicing	None.
Maintain Relationships	None.
Decision Support	None.

cases. Closer examination revealed, however, that they had elevated what were simple pathways to the rank of use case. After a little work, we ended up with 17 use cases. Now that's more like it.

Shadow Use Cases

Traditionally, use cases are viewed from the eyes of the business, that is, the user. However, in many application domains some use cases usually are never properly accounted for. These represent areas of functionality that meet all of the criteria of use cases but that often have more meaning to the IT staff, which is their "user." The business sponsor might acknowledge them but often underestimates their impact on the application and the estimated time to completion. These use cases often end up being budget busters.

I call these **shadow use cases** because they are never given their due respect in most applications. Figure 4-4 shows the most common shadow use cases found across all application domains: security, audit, archiving, and architecture infrastructure.

Often, both security and audit will show up in "includes" relationships to other use cases (*Process Orders "includes" Security*). However, both are usually much more complicated than just logging onto a system (for example, maintaining users and profiles, application functionality, value-level security, and field-level security). Both should be represented on the business view of the use case diagram. I worked on one project whose security package alone contained 15 distinct classes and consumed about 500 person hours of effort. This all grew from an innocuous statement found in a use case pathway: "clerk is validated by the system."

Archiving also belongs on the business view of the use case diagram, but it typically is given little consideration. Archiving is not as easy as just backing something up and deleting objects. For example, for a project that is complicated by effective dating schemes, what and when to archive something isn't all that straightforward.

Architecture infrastructure relates to the necessary plumbing that must be in place to allow the layers of the application to communicate, for example the components that allow a user interface to communicate to the business rules of the application (COM, DCOM, or CORBA). The same applies from the business rules to the data management

FIGURE 4-4   *Shadow use cases.*

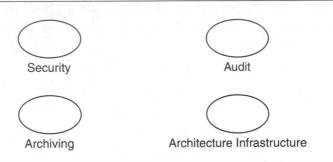

component (DAO, RDO or ADO). This use case should not be on the business view of the use case diagram but rather on a use case specifically for the IT staff.

Although some might argue that these are simply "functional requirements" and not use cases, the estimates made after completing the project scope will be off. In practice, if these facts are brought to the surface and treated as first-class use cases, they will be given the attention that they demand and deserve.

Detailing the Happy Path

Now we have our use cases defined, along with their primary, alternate, and exception pathways. For the Inception phase, we have one more task to do regarding use cases: Detail the happy path. We detail the happy path (or any pathway) by outlining the necessary steps to implement the pathway's functionality. These derive from a *what* perspective and not *how*.

Detailing is necessary so that we can better understand the complexity that might be involved in realizing the use cases. We also need this level of understanding in order to estimate both the incremental release strategy and the accompanying time/cost component. The detailed steps of the happy path for the use case *Process Orders: (Customer calls in and orders a guitar and supplies and pays with a credit card)* are set out as follows.

1. Customer supplies customer number.
2. Customer is acknowledged as current.

3. For each product that the customer desires:

    3.1 Request product ID or description.

    3.2 Resolve description to ID if necessary.

    3.3 Request quantity.

    3.4 Calculate item price.

4. Calculate extended order total.

5. Apply tax.

6. Apply shipping charges.

7. Supply extended price to the customer.

8. Customer supplies credit card number.

9. Validate customer credit card.

10. Reduce inventory.

11. Finalize and complete the sale.

The detailed steps for the pathway are meant to be somewhat high level. Notice that there are no specific references to technology in the form of, for example, "buttons clicks" and "scanning." How we detail the happy path will be determined both by the features identified in the charter and any assumptions made about the use case. We will consider these when the project later produces more design-oriented artifacts. Appendix F has a complete listing of the detailed steps for each use case's happy path.

Completed Process Orders Use Case

Now that we have completed most of the framework for the use cases, a sample of a completed template is in order. Following is the use case template for *Process Orders*.

Use Case Template

Use Case Name: Process Orders

Use Case Description: This use case starts when an order is either initiated or inquired about. It handles all aspects of the initial definition and authorization of an order. It ends when the order clerk completes a session with a customer.

Use Case Authors:	Rene Becnel
Actors:	Order clerk
Locations:	New Port Hills, Washington
Status:	Pathways defined
Priority:	1
Assumptions	Orders are taken by the order clerk until such time that the customer base is comfortable with the specialized services being provided now.
Preconditions:	Order clerk has logged onto the system.
Postconditions:	- Order is placed. - Inventory is reduced.
Primary Path:	Customer calls in and orders a guitar and supplies and pays with a credit card.
Alternate Path(s):	- Customer calls in and orders a guitar and uses a P. O. - Customer calls in and orders a guitar and uses the Remulak easy finance plan. - Customer calls in and orders an organ and pays with a credit card. - Customer calls in and orders an organ and uses a P. O.
Exception Path(s):	- Customer calls in to place an order using a credit card and the card is invalid. - Customer calls in with a P.O. but has not been approved to use the P. O. method. - Customer calls in to place an order, and the items desired are not in stock.

The detailed use case pathways are then specified for all of the individual pathways in each category (primary, alternate, and exception).

Preparing the Preliminary Architecture

We now know a lot more about Remulak Productions's requirements, as well as some of its technology needs and desires. The last artifact we will create to complete the project charter and to allow us to estimate the project better is the preliminary architecture of the order taking application. Table 4-5 lists the technology components of the architecture.

To better depict this architecture, we use two different UML diagrams, which we combine to show both the software realization (component diagram) and hardware hosts (deployment diagram). Remember that this is a preliminary architecture. It is a point-in-time snapshot based on what is known at this juncture of the project. Figure 4-5 shows the preliminary architecture model rendered in a hybrid UML component within the deployment diagram format.

For scalability reasons, the architecture must be able to enable various layers of the application to run on a processor other than the client.

TABLE 4-5 *Preliminary Architecture of the Remulak Productions Order Processing Application*

Component	Implementation
Hardware: Client	166-MHz Pentium-based clients with 128MB of RAM and an 8GB hard disk
Hardware: Server	Dual CPU 400-MHz Pentium-based server with 256MB of RAM and RAID-5 I/O subsystem supporting 60GB of storage
Software: Operating System (server)	Windows/NT 4.0
Software: Operating System (client)	Windows 95
Software: Application (client)	Visual Basic 6.0 Enterprise Edition
Software: Database (server)	Microsoft SQL Server 7.0
Software: Transaction (server)	Microsoft Transaction Server
Software: WEB (server)	Microsoft Internet Information Server
Software: WEB interface (server)	Active Server Pages
Software: Visual Modeling	Rational Rose (Enterprise Edition)
Protocol: Network	TCP/IP
Protocol: Database	ADO using OLE/DB provider

FIGURE 4-5   *Preliminary architecture with UML component and deployment diagrams.*

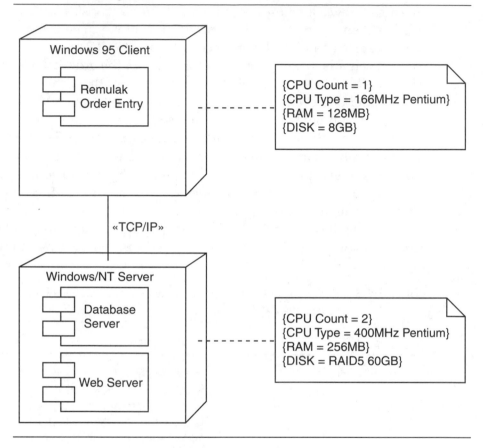

In addition, we will want to take advantage of MTS to coordinate all of the various resources of the application. We will explore these and other technical considerations as the application evolves.

Project Charter: Increments and Estimates

Increments

So far, our mantra has been to approach any application development effort with an eye towards incremental releases. Recall from Chapter 1 that risk is reduced exponentially by tackling the project in stages. Also beneficial is focusing first on the highest-risk requirements. Toward that end, we propose the following release cycles as the staged increments for Remulak Productions.

1. Increment One
   1.1 Process Orders
   1.2 Maintain Orders
   1.3 Maintain Relationships (customer Pathways only)
   1.4 Application Infrastructure
2. Increment Two
   2.1 Maintain Inventory
   2.2 Shipping
   2.3 Invoicing
   2.4 Maintain Relationships (remaining pathways)
3. Increment Three
   3.1 Decision Support
   3.2 Security
   3.3 Audit
   3.4 Archiving

Estimates

For years, analysts and designers have been told in classroom settings to never provide estimates until all of the requirements are known. With the Synergy process, and any other process that is iterative and incremental, we use the learn-as-you-go approach. Our bases are somewhat covered because we have done a fly-by of all of the events, use cases, and pathways and detailed the happy paths. However, we still don't know all of the supporting detail behind the requirements. Yet the project sponsors need an estimate; they can't say go or don't go without it.

Varying levels of success have been realized with structured approaches to project estimating. Estimating still is a combination of mystic art, the school of hard knocks, and plain luck. However, some very interesting research has been done at Rational Software by Gustav Karner (initially begun while at Objectory AB, later purchased by

FIGURE 4-6 *The Remulak Productions increments.*

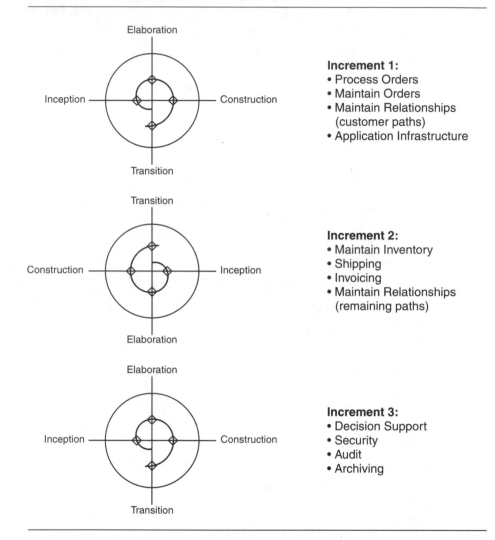

Increment 1:
• Process Orders
• Maintain Orders
• Maintain Relationships
  (customer paths)
• Application Infrastructure

Increment 2:
• Maintain Inventory
• Shipping
• Invoicing
• Maintain Relationships
  (remaining paths)

Increment 3:
• Decision Support
• Security
• Audit
• Archiving

Rational Software). The result is a modification of work originally done by Albrecht on estimating by using function point analysis. Appendix A provides an overview of that estimating technique, as well as how the estimates were arrived at for Remulak Productions.

Remulak Productions's deliverable will be realized by implementing three different increments, staged as three different release cycles. This will enable Remulak to manage the risk of the project as well as

FIGURE 4-7   *The Remulak Productions package diagram.*

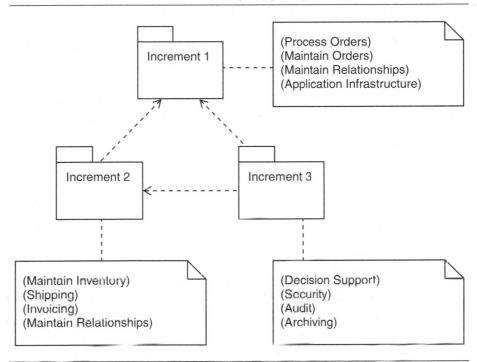

ease it into the new millennium without too much new-system shock. The estimates for each increment are as follows.

Increment One: 670 person hours

Increment Two: 950 person hours

Increment Three: 950 person hours

Figure 4-6 depicts what the project looks like with all of the increments in-flight. It does a good job showing the iterative, incremental approach we will take for the Remulak Productions application. The middle spiral is flipped to indicate that many increments or deliverables can be active at any one time, each in its own phase.

The UML package diagram can depict the same thing, while hiding much of the detail. Figure 4-7 is a package diagram reflecting the incremental deliverables.

The Inception phase is now complete. Our road is laid out for us, clearly and concisely. The diagrams produced, together with the project charter, are collectively called the **requirements model**. Our next step is to create a project plan that reflects the decision to implement three increments. The basis for that plan is referenced in Chapter 3 and presented in Appendix E.

The remainder of this book will explore the details of the analysis, design, and implementation of the first increment for Remulak Productions.

Checkpoint

Where We Have Been

1. Use cases are technology-neutral and applicable to any process or methodology used by a project team.

2. Use cases are a behaviorally related sequence of interactions performed by an actor in a dialogue with the system to provide some measurable value to the actor. They are goal-oriented and are significant to the business.

3. The primary pathway, or Basic Course of Events, is considered the most common pathway through a use case. It is also called the "happy path."

4. Alternate pathways are also "good" pathways, but they are not as often traveled.

5. Detailing the pathway chronicles the steps that must be undertaken to satisfy the originating event. The steps should avoid, if possible, reference to how it is actually being performed.

6. The documentation produced up to this point, including the UML diagrams, are collectively called the requirements model.

Where We Are Going Next

In the next chapter, we:

1. Identify more detail about the use cases in Increment One.

2. Explore how to derive classes from the use cases.

3. Explore how to derive associations.

4. Review various UML diagramming constructs for various types of associations (generalization, composition, and aggregation) and how they relate to the Remulak Productions solution.

5. Create a complete class diagram for Remulak Productions.

6. Begin to identify attributes and operations for Remulak Productions' classes.

CHAPTER 5 *Classes*

The project is taking shape. Chapters 1 through 3 culminated in the completion of the project's Inception phase in Chapter 4. Some key deliverables were produced, including a requirements model consisting of several UML diagrams and the project charter. In the next phase, Elaboration, we expand the boundaries placed by the requirements model.

During the Inception phase, we took a fly-by across the entire application. This produced a list of in-scope use cases and all of their individual paths (primary, alternate, and exception), as well as detailing for their happy pathways. This was done to gain enough knowledge about the project so as to plan implementation increments and estimate required resources.

Among the most important deliverables produced thus far, from the project sponsors' viewpoints, are the incremental delivery schedule and the supported functionality. The functionality was expressed in the form of use cases and project estimates accompanying each of the three delivery increments.

From an IT viewpoint, a key deliverable was the use cases. These provided a clear, easy-to-understand format for sketching out the application's preliminary requirements. They were created in conjunction with the project sponsors and framed in their terminology.

This chapter covers the Elaboration phase of the project. This phase further fleshes out the application's requirements, as well as proposes a design for the solution. It also explores the additional static and dynamic components through the use of more UML diagrams. It identifies, refines, *and adopts a collection of interesting application entities, called classes. Then it explores the associations that are explicitly and implicitly found in the use cases.*

We will use the class diagram to build the skeleton of the application's design and the sequence diagram as the arteries of the application, representing the flow of messages between the skeletal components, or classes.

GOALS

⮌ Detail all of the alternate and exception pathways for Increment One of the Remulak Productions project.

⮌ Learn to identify and categorize business rules.

⮌ Examine the notion of classes and how to identify them.

⮌ Explore ways to refine the class list by applying some common class filtering rules.

⮌ Define the concept of associations and how to identify them from components in the use cases.

⮌ Explain how and when to use an object diagram, a runtime version of the class diagram.

⮌ Review the class diagram for Remulak Productions.

⮌ Begin to identify both attributes and operations for the classes identified for Remulak Productions.

Elaboration Phase

Before completing the pathway detail for all of the Increment One use cases, let's review the Synergy process model and the project plan for the Elaboration phase of the project. Figure 5-1 shows the process model, with the focus of the project at this point highlighted.

The Elaboration phase focuses on several areas, as shown in the figure. In this chapter, we place our attention on the following.

• The "Use Case Analysis" block, when we deal with further detailing of the use cases that are part of Increment One

FIGURE 5-1 *Synergy process model and the Elaboration phase.*

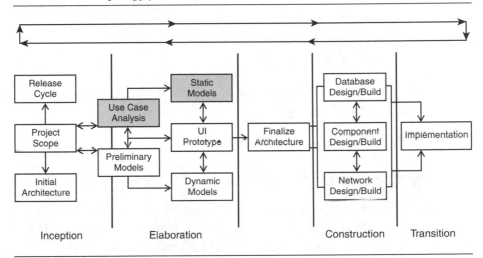

- The "Static Models" block, when we deal with a first cut of the class diagram for the project

In subsequent chapters, the other Elaboration phase blocks will get similar attention.

Detailing Pathways

The first goal of the project will be to further flesh out the detailed pathways for all the alternate and exception pathways in the use cases. The use cases referred to here are only those that will be implemented in the first increment. Remember from the previous chapter that pathway detail was already completed for each use case's happy path (for all the increments). In that chapter, we detailed the happy path *(Customer calls in and orders a guitar and supplies and pays with a credit card)* for the use case *Process Orders*.

Remember that the detailed pathway shows the tasks necessary to satisfy that course of the use case. Now all the pathways for all the use cases in Increment One need to be detailed. The use cases in Increment One are:

- Process Orders
- Maintain Orders
- Maintain Relationships (customer pathways only)
- Application Infrastructure

We use the examples produced in Chapter 4 and set out in Appendix F to detail the alternate and exception pathways.

Identifying and Categorizing Business Rules

The term *business rule* got quite a bit of attention in the 90s. Seminars were devoted entirely to the subject. Many practitioners did considerable work in this area, most notably Ronald Ross.

Our goal is to categorize rules about the business that naturally arise during the Inception phase and that continue into the Elaboration phase. This book so far has not addressed business rules because the focus of the Inception phase needed to be more strategic and less tactical. However, business rules are some of the building blocks of the project.

Business rules can be categorized as follows.

Structural Fact: Requires certain facts or conditions to be true; for example:

each order must have an order-taken date

each customer must have approved credit

Action Restricting: Prohibits one or more actions based on its condition; for example:

add a new business customer if and only if that customer has a D&B rating

Action Triggering: Instigates one or more actions when its condition becomes true; for example

when an invoice is not paid by the due date, then assess a 1% penalty

Inference: States that if certain facts are true, a conclusion is inferred or new knowledge is known; for example:

if a customer incorporates, then it changes to being a business customer

Derivation: Performs computations and calculations; for example:

total value is the sum of all past orders plus the additional amount derived from the current order

These categories are not hard and fast, but they do provide a good baseline to frame business rules. You can add additional categories to provide more granularity.

We add a business rules section to the use case template in which to note each use case's rules that we uncover. Later sections of the chapter, during the design modeling process, offer some ideas about to what a rule might map, from an implementation perspective (attributes/operations). Following is the use case template for *Process Orders*, with the addition of the business rules section.

Use Case Template

Use Case Name:	Process Orders
Use Case Description:	This use case starts when an order is either initiated or inquired about. It handles all aspects of the initial definition and authorization of an order. It ends when the order clerk completes a session with a customer.
Use Case Authors:	Rene Becnel
Actors:	Order clerk
Locations:	New Port Hills, Washington
Status:	Pathways defined
Priority:	1
Assumptions:	The order clerk takes orders until the customer base becomes comfortable with the new specialized services.
Preconditions:	Order clerk has logged onto the system.
Postconditions:	- Order is placed.
	- Inventory is reduced.

Primary Path:	Customer calls in and orders a guitar and supplies and pays with a credit card.
Alternate Path(s):	- Customer calls in and orders a guitar and uses a P. O.
	- Customer calls in and orders a guitar and uses the Remulak easy finance plan.
	- Customer calls in and orders an organ and pays with a credit card.
	- Customer calls in and orders an organ and uses a P. O.
Exception Path(s):	- Customer calls in to place an order using a credit card and the card is invalid.
	- Customer calls in with a P.O. but has not been approved to use the P. O. method.
	- Customer calls in to place an order, and the items desired are not in stock.
Business Rules:	- Action Restricting: Customer cannot place an order unless it has either an accepted means of payment or approved credit.
	- Action Triggering: If customer's current order amount plus its outstanding balance from a prior order exceeds its credit limit, then supervisor authority is necessary to finalize the sale.

If the business rules are specific to a particular pathway (for example, purchase by credit card versus a P. O.), then you can note that in the business rules section. Too often, these building blocks are lost or provided no formality in their structure or categorization. Now, however, the project has a means to capture them and allocate them to the business view of the system as expressed by the use cases. As you will see later, some of these rules will map to attributes, operations, or associations between classes or to combinations of all three of these UML constructs.

Uncovering Classes

Iteration 1: Role of the UML Class Diagram

The class diagram will eventually become the most important UML artifact we produce. By eventually, it is meant that initially it will be somewhat sparse and lacking in anything of real significant value. However, with each iteration, as we learn more about the static and dynamic features of the application, it will begin to evolve into the pivotal diagram from which all else going forward is derived. Even the UML component and deployment diagrams depict how classes will be packaged and ultimately delivered in runtime form.

Chapter 4 noted that the majority of visual modeling tools today generate their code structures directly from the class diagram. Tools that support reverse engineering derive their diagrammatic elements from the classes built by the specific language environment (for example, header files in C++). In the case of VB, even a form is reverse engineered as a class.

What Makes a Good Class?

Selecting classes requires skill; it can be difficult and tricky at times. The next several sections provide guidelines to help you learn how. With a little practice, you will see that there is a methodology to the madness of selecting classes.

The class is the key entity in the application domain. It represents an interesting abstraction of something that contains structure (attributes), as well as behavior (operations). Often, project teams, depending on the level of its familiarity with an application domain, initially brainstorm the classes just by using facilitated sessions to produce a list of entities.

Another, more methodical approach that has its roots in the relational modeling world is to visit the source of the requirements produced thus far and simply extract the nouns. In the context of the UML, the source for this noun-extraction exercise is the completed use cases. In a very quick and unstructured manner, you simply scan the use cases and pull out all of the nouns. As you get better at the exercise, you should begin to apply some noun filtering so as to eliminate nouns that obviously will not make good classes. The most common nouns filtered out are those that represent domain attributes, which are characteristics of some other class in the application.

For instance, with Remulak Productions, the detailing of the use cases produced the noun *credit card number*. Although this is undoubtedly a noun, ask yourself if it is something that will have both structure and behavior. Probably not. It is an attribute of some other class (noun) that might not have been identified yet (perhaps it is an attribute of `Order` or `Customer` or both).

My rule of thumb is not to filter anything on the first iteration of the exercise. I just create a list. Some practitioners like to put each noun on a self-sticking note to allow for easier shuffling and resurrection of filtered nouns.

A third mechanism to discover classes is to hold a *CRC session*, where CRC stands for Classes, Responsibilities, Collaborations. CRC is a role-playing exercise used to discover classes and their individual roles in an application's life. See, for example, *The CRC Card Book* by Bellin and Simone, whose full reference is given in the Suggested Readings. I use CRC sessions as an ice breaker for people new to object-oriented techniques. However, my only concern with CRC sessions is that they do require a strong facilitator and the team must be agreeable to role-playing. For really complex interactions, CRC sessions sometimes can get really out of hand.

Applying Filter Rules

Once we have completed the initial list of nouns, we apply simple filtering rules to winnow it down. Seven different filters can be applied to the domain of nouns. We remove any candidate classes that have any of the following characteristics.

1. **Redundant**: Two nouns that represent the same thing are redundant. *Order* and *Product Order* are really the same thing. Settle on *Order*, as it is more succinct and represents what is actually being modeled.

2. **Irrelevant**: Nouns that have nothing to do with the problem domain are irrelevant. They might be valid classes but not within the scope of the current project. *Employee Performance Rating* is a noun, but Remulak Productions's system isn't going to measure or track performance, so it is irrelevant for this project. Any temptation to include it might be an indication of scope creep. If anyone debates the exclusion of a class that appears to be out of

scope, perhaps they need to reaffirm what was agreed upon in the prior deliverable.

3. **An attribute**: Nouns that are really describing the structure of some other class are attributes. This is the most common filter applied in most domains. Be careful not to completely remove these, however, as they will end up as an attribute in some class. *Credit card number* is a noun that is describing something else in the system. However, it is not a class.

    Be careful with attribute recognition versus class recognition, especially in the context of the application domain. For example, a common noun, *ZIP code*, is usually thought of as an attribute of an address class. However, depending on the domain, it might be a class. For example, to the postal service, ZIP code is a class because it contains both attributes (geographical location, census, rate structures, and shipping information), as well as behavior (routing and scheduling of deliveries).

    As another test to apply to attributes, ask if the noun stands on its own or does it prompt you to ask "<noun> of what?".

4. **An operation**: A noun that is describing a responsibility of some other class is not a class in its own right; it is an operation. *Tax calculations* is a responsibility of some other class (perhaps an algorithm class) but in and of itself is not a class.

5. **A role**: A noun that is describing the state of some entity or its classification is likely not a class; it is a role. *Preferred customer* is the state of a customer at a given time. Customer is actually the class, and the fact that a customer is *preferred* is probably indicated by some attribute within Customer (status).

    A word of caution when dealing with roles: Often, roles that are removed return later when the concept of class generalization and specialization (a.k.a. inheritance) is reviewed. If it is known up-front that the role has unique structural and behavioral elements that the domain is interested in tracking, then don't be too hasty to remove the role. However, if it is removed, it will be addressed later as the class diagram is iteratively refined.

6. **An event**: Nouns that describe some time frequency are usually depicting some dynamic element that the domain must support. *Print invoices once a week* is a timer-oriented event that the system must support. *Week* is not a candidate class.

In some real-time, embedded applications, events are, in fact, classes. If an event has some interesting structural elements or behavior that is important to the domain, then it might be a class.

7. **An implementation construct**: A noun that is depicting a hardware element (*Printer*) or some algorithm (*Compound Interest*) is best dealt with by being removed and assigned as an operation of some other class.

In many real-time, embedded applications, hardware components are classes (controller, servo). They have attributes (current position, head) and behavior (seek, set position) that meet all of the criteria of a class. The act of creating a class out of an inanimate object and prescribing structure and behavior to it is called *reification*.

When selecting the final name for a class, always use clear and concise names. Favor the singular tense (Customer, Order) over the plural (Customers, Orders). Also, note that class names are always capitalized when used on diagrams or in other documentation.

Types of Classes

Many people confuse classes with database entities. Database entities have the sole mission of recording only structural (persistent) elements of the application. Classes are very similar. In fact, they are a superset of what is provided by the database entity. However, classes also have behavioral characteristics that entities don't. The project is very concerned about the data attributes, and that is where traditional entity data modeling ends—capturing the data structures.

Classes bring much more to the understanding of the application in the form of behavior (operations) that the class is responsible for implementing. As mentioned in the previous chapter, the operations represent the services that the class is committed to carrying out when requested by other classes in the application domain. From a relational perspective, entities have been said to have no *class* and do not know how to *behave*.

In object systems, and through our modeling efforts, classes must be categorized into groups. Jacobson groups classes into three groups, or what the UML refers to as **stereotypes**.

1. **Entity**: These classes represent the core of the application domain (Customer, Order). They are meant to keep information about

the persistent application entities over time, as well as capture the services that drive the majority of interactions in the application. Don't confuse the term *entity* as used here with the more traditional use of the word when describing a relational entity. An entity class may not become a relational entity. Some practitioners use the term domain class to provide a better distinction.

2. **Interface**: These classes serve as a boundary between the external actors wishing to interact with the application and the entity classes. Typically, interface classes are meant as a shield, or go-between of sorts, that segregates much of the interaction details regarding how to reach services offered by the application. Most interface classes are user interface components, which take the shape of forms and screens used to interact with the application. Interface classes can also be found when messaging to external application systems or as wrappers around existing legacy components.

3. **Control**: These classes are coordinators of activity in the application domain. Control classes (sometimes called *controllers*) are repositories of both structure and behavior that aren't easily placed in either of the other two types of classes. Typically, a control class can play any of several roles:

   - As transaction-related behavior
   - As a control sequence that is specific to one or a few use cases (or pathways through a use case)
   - As a service that separates the entity objects from the interface objects

Categorizing the classes into these three types makes the application less fragile to change. These changes may result from the business evolving in a dynamic marketplace or because individuals want to view information in the application differently. Figure 5-2 shows the three types of classes in action. Then the following subsections discuss each in more detail.

Entity Classes

For Remulak Productions, Table 5-1 lists the potential entity classes (with filters applied) for the application. It covers all of the use cases documented so far (all of Increment One's use cases and the happy paths from the remaining use cases).

FIGURE 5-2 *Entity, interface, and control types of classes.*

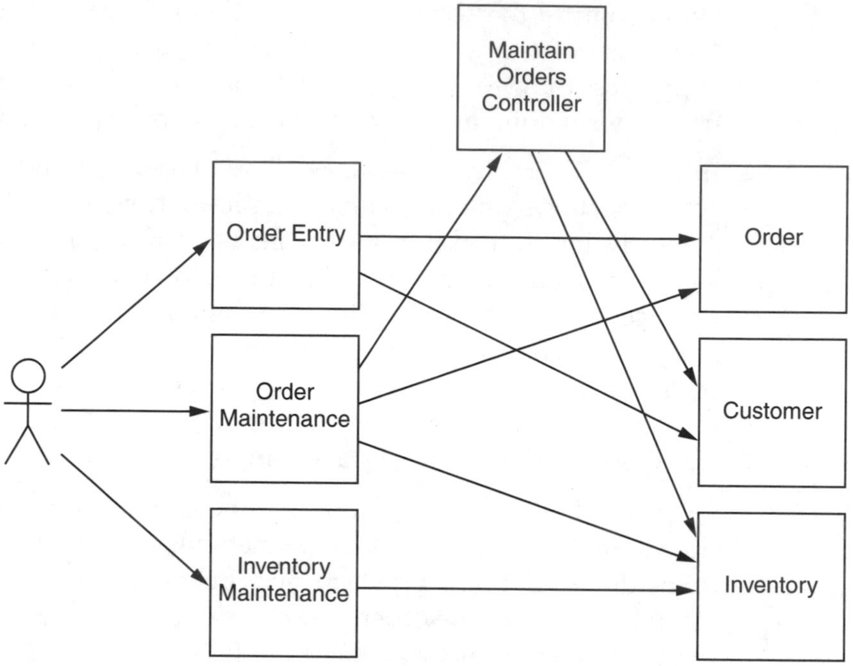

TABLE 5-1 *Potential Entity Classes for Remulak Productions*

Address	Customer	Order
Invoice	Order Header	Order Line
Order Summary	Payment	Product
Shipment	Guitar	Sheet Music
Supplies		

Entity objects usually have some very specific services they provide, typically operations that do any of the following:

- Store and Retrieve entity attributes.
- Create and remove the entity.
- Provide behavior that may need to change as the entity changes over time.

Most visual modeling tools generate these class structures for you. Entity classes are also used to derive the first cut at the implementation for the physical database. If the persistent storage mechanism is going to be a relational database, then these may not end up being a one-to-one mapping.

Interface Classes

Interface classes are the "viewport" into the application, as well as insulators to the outside. Consider the Order class. It likely won't change much over time—it might undergo some behavioral changes (for example, how pricing discounts are applied) but probably not many structural changes (attributes). What will change is likely the following.

1. How people (actors) want to place orders (via telephone response systems, via the Internet)

2. How other systems (actors) want to interface with the order application and how the order application will be expected to interface with other systems (actors)

3. How people (actors) want to view information from a reporting and decision support perspective

To better facilitate these trends and to insulate the business entity classes, you should place any and all behavior relating to interfaces into interface classes. Also place in interface classes all functionality that is specified in the use case descriptions and that is directly dependent on the system environment.

The easiest way to brainstorm interface classes is to focus on the actors in the system. Each actor will need its own interface into the system. The classes can be further refined from information found in the use case description and the use case pathway details. An interface class will exist for each screen-oriented form and each report, as well as for each system interface (for example, accounting, billing, and credit card authorization). Table 5-2 shows a first cut at the interface classes for Remulak Productions.

Control Classes

Control classes tie together courses of events and thus carry on communication with other objects in the application domain. They are

TABLE 5-2   *Potential Interface Classes for Remulak Productions*

Maintain Order Panel	Inquire Order Panel	Process Order Panel
Maintain Relationships Panel	Credit Card Interface	Accounting System Interface

TABLE 5-3   *Potential Control Classes for Remulak Productions*

Process Orders Controller	Maintain Orders Controller	Maintain Relationships Controller
Infrastructure Controller		

usually transient (not persisted to external storage). Their lifecycle is only as long as it takes the interaction to complete.

For example, where do we place the tasks necessary to orchestrate the messaging for the happy path *(Customer calls in and orders a guitar and supplies and pays with a credit card)* for the use case *Process Orders*? We'll place such "scripting" tasks in a control class. So, we create one control class for each use case. Table 5-3 shows the potential control classes for Remulak Productions's Increment One.

Relationships

Relationships between classes are necessary because object-oriented systems are based on objects collaborating together to accomplish some end goal (articulated in the use cases). Like a network, relationships define the pathways between classes and serve as the "messaging media" across which objects can communicate. Relationships also define a context between classes prior to instantiation and as objects after instantiation. They then define how the classes of the application function as an integrated whole.

The UML is quite rich in its ability to represent relationships between classes. It supports three types of relationships.

1. **Association**: The most common type of UML relationship, an association defines how objects of one class are connected to

objects of another class. Without this connection, or association, no direct messages can pass between objects of these classes in the runtime environment (note that dependencies, discussed later in the chapter, also indicate a messaging relationship). A simple association for Remulak Productions would be that defined between a *Customer* and its *Order*(s).

2. **Generalization**: A generalization defines a lattice of classes such that one class either refines, or specializes details, about a more general class. The generalized class is often called the *superclass*, and the specialized class the *subclass*. All structure (attributes) and behavior (operations) of the generalized class are available to (inherited by) the subclasses. (This applies only to those attributes and operations that have either public or protected visibility.) Generalizations are such that any subclass "is a" valid example of the superclass.

   An example of a generalization/specialization relationship for Remulak Productions is the `Product` (superclass) and the subclasses `Guitar`, `Sheet Music`, and `Supplies`. Structure (attributes) and behavior (operations) will be defined for `Product` and will apply to all of its subclasses. Structure (attributes) and behavior (operations) also will be defined for `Guitar`, `Sheet Music`, and `Supplies`. These are unique to the subclasses and further specialize the definition of a `Product`.

3. **Dependency**: A dependency is a situation in which a change to one class may impact the behavior or state of another class. Typically, dependencies are used in the context of classes to show that one class uses another class as an argument in the signature of an operation.

   Dependencies are more commonly found in package diagrams than in class diagrams. A dependency relationship exists between the three increments for Remulak Productions.

We use association and generalization relationships in the Remulak Productions class diagram.

Establishing Associations

Where do we find associations in the application domain? Explicit associations can be found in the use cases. Actually, however, an early indicator of associations can be found in the event table created during project scoping.

Recall that the use cases describe the intended uses of the system from the actor's perspective. For a event such as *Customer Places Order* that is encountered in the dialogue for the *Process Orders* use case, an explicit association exists between the two classes Customer and Order. When the use cases were initially created, we had no clear idea what the classes would be. Now that the class creation exercise is completed, we need to revisit the use cases in search of associations. Table 5-4 lists the associations for Remulak Productions.

Not all associations are explicitly stated in the use cases. For example, the association *Order is Paid By an Invoice* isn't stated directly in the use cases. However, it is an implicit association that is necessary to facilitate the messaging detailed in the pathways of the uses cases.

To construct the class diagram, we draw the classes as rectangles, connect the rectangles via a solid line, and place the verb describing the association on the line. In the UML, associations are read left to right, top to bottom. However, this isn't always possible, especially with complex diagrams. A small solid triangle can be placed next to the association name to indicate how to read the association. Finally, it isn't

TABLE 5-4   *The Remulak Productions Class Associations*

Class	Association	Class
Customer	Places	Order
Address	Locates	Customer
Order	Contains	OrderHeader
Order	Contains	OrderLine
Order	Contains	OrderSummary
Order	Paid By	Invoice
Order	Satisfied By	Shipment
Product	Specialized By	Guitar
Product	Specialized By	Sheet Music
Product	Specialized By	Supplies
Product	References	OrderLine

absolutely necessary to define association names, especially if the association is obvious from the classes involved. Figure 5-3 shows an example of a simple association for Remulak Productions.

Notice that the top of the rectangle contains the class name. A class has three compartments, which define the following.

Compartment 1: Class Name, displayed in proper case format

Compartment 2: Attributes (define the structure of the class)

Compartment 3: Operations (define the behavior supported by the class)

In many cases, depending on the stage the project and the reviewing audience is in, not all of the compartments will be displayed. Attributes and operations are explored in more depth later in this chapter.

Establishing Roles

A **role** is a UML construct that better qualifies how a particular object will play in its relationship to another class. Roles are optional but at times can clarify a class diagram, thereby preventing misinterpretation of what the authors meant (and misinterpretation often happens).

The role is placed next to the class on the association and is related to that class. In the case of Remulak Productions, *Order* could play the role of the purchase, while *Customer* could play the role of *Purchaser*. The next section shows how to diagram this, as well as how to correctly read the association.

Establishing Multiplicity

In the modeling of the application, it helps to define the number of possible objects involved in an association. This definition is expressed in the class diagram via the *multiplicity property*. Multiplicity can take

FIGURE 5-3   *A Remulak Productions association example.*

several forms, from very specific (1) to infinite (*). In addition, these can be combined to form unique multiplicity statements for the applications, for example 1..*, which means "1 or more." Figure 5-4 is an example of the `Customer` and `Order` association using all of the adornments discussed thus far.

The figure is read as follows.

`Customer` places zero or more `Order`(s) and the `Order` is acting in the role of `Purchase`.

`Order`(s) are placed by one and only one `Customer`, and the `Customer` is acting in the role of `Purchaser`.

Since the discussion of VB and the UML in Chapter 1, not much has been said about program code. However, some information about what the code generator (Rational Rose) will do might be helpful now.

If roles are present, then the class definition for, say `Customer`, will contain a variable that is defined as

```
Public purchase as Collection
```

Notice that the variable `purchase` is not declared as a type `Order`. This is because the multiplicity is 0..*, which means `Customer` can be related to many `Order`(s) and thus requires a `Collection` in VB. However, notice what the code generator does with the class definition of the class `Order`:

```
Public purchaser as Customer
```

Now notice that the variable `purchaser` is declared as type `Customer` and not as `Collection`. This is because the multiplicity is 1.

If no roles are defined on the diagram, then the code generator will supply default roles in the fashion `theClassName`, where `ClassName` is name of the target class. In the two previous examples, if role names

FIGURE 5-4   *A Remulak Productions fully adorned* `Customer`/`Order` *association.*

are not supplied, the following lines of code will be generated in the classes `Customer` and `Order`, respectively:

```
Public theOrder as Collection

Public theCustomer as Customer
```

Because Rational Rose is flexible in the automation it provides, we can modify this behavior if desired. We not only can turn off this automation feature but also change the naming pattern. Instead of "the" in `theCustomer`, perhaps "ref" or "my" would be more desirable; it is up to the modeler's discretion.

It really comes down to a matter of style. Role names can provide good customization for the code generation. On the other hand, roles often are extraneous information that might not add much value to the class diagram.

Advanced Associations

Many types of associations are possible, some are more complex than others. To better appreciate what the UML can offer regarding associations, we next explore more-advanced association types:

- Aggregation
- Composition
- Link (association class)
- Reflexive
- Qualification

Aggregation and Composition Associations

Aggregation and composition associations model "whole/part" contexts. In most application domains, a special relationship exists between a collection of classes where one class clearly exhibits either control or ownership of the others. Simple examples found in the everyday world are an investment portfolio or a book. An investment portfolio is made up of assets (stocks, bonds, and other securities), whereas a book is made up of lots of parts (cover, table of contents, chapters, index, and bibliography).

Distinguishing aggregation/composition associations from others is important because this will later impact how the application treats this from an implementation perspective (for example, messaging patterns and persistence). Aggregation can be viewed from two dimensions: aggregation and composition, with composition being a strong form of aggregation.

Aggregation means that any of the parts may also be related to other wholes. A good example of aggregation is the investment portfolio. For example, Remulak Productions's stock can be part of several individual portfolios. **Composition** means that any of the parts have one and only one whole. A book is a good example of composition. The table of contents for this book is associated with this book and this book alone.

For Remulak Productions, composition associations exist between Order and OrderHeader, OrderLine, and OrderSummary. Figure 5-5 shows an example of that composition association.

In the UML, composition is shown as a solid diamond and aggregation as a hollow diamond. Aggregation and composition might yield two different solutions, from a program code perspective, depending on the language being used. In VB, the effect will be the same. In C++, an aggregation relationship (the whole) will define its component vari-

FIGURE 5-5   *A Remulak Productions composition example.*

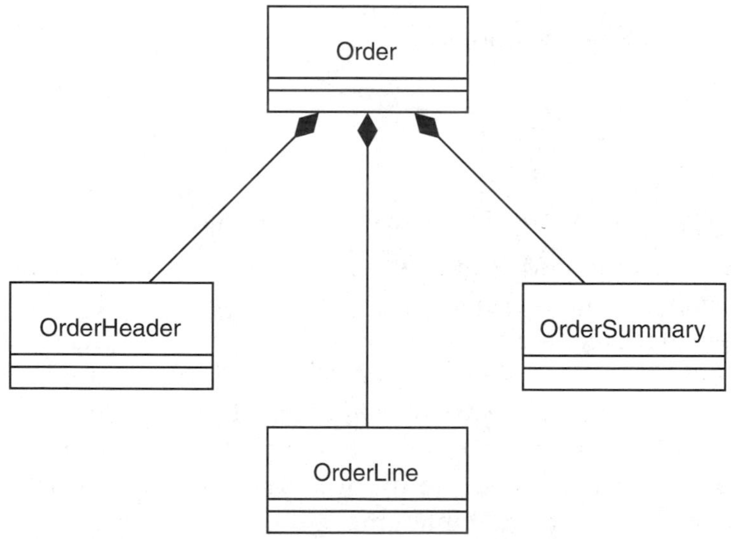

ables (the parts) by declaring them as "by reference" using a pointer. Composition, on the other hand, will be "by value" by declaring a variable of the class type. Put another way, with composition, when the whole is destroyed, the parts are destroyed with it. This is not the case with aggregation.

Remember that you do not always have to define an association name, especially when the name is obvious from the context. For example, placing the word "contain(s)" on each of the three composition associations would be redundant, so it is simply left off.

Link Associations (association class)

Often, there is no logical place to define certain information, usually attributes, about the association between two classes. You might need to define a class as a go-between for the actual link between two objects. A **link** is a runtime version of an association. *An important fact to note at this point: Links are to Objects as Associations are to Classes.*

From experience, I know that if an application has an `Address` class related to some other class (`Customer` in the Remulak case), then another type of class likely is needed to hold unique information about that association. This means that if a `Customer` can have different shipping and billing addresses, where should the attribute that defines the type of `Address` exist?

Be careful! An `Address` might be a physical shipping address for `Customer` Steve Jackson but might also be the billing address for `Customer` Mike Richardson. Thus the `Address` type attribute won't fit in either `Customer` or `Address`. This requires what the UML calls a **link association,** or **association class**, a class that is related to the association of other classes. Perhaps in this class (`Locale` for Remulak Productions), the attributes `addressType` and `dateAssigned` can be kept. Implicitly, the class also will contain the information necessary to distinguish exactly to which `Customer` and which `Address` these attributes relate. Figure 5-6 shows an example of an association class for Remulak Productions.

Reflexive Associations

Sometimes an association is needed between two objects of the same class. Called a **reflexive association**, this type of association is commonly used by many application domains. For Remulak Productions, we want

FIGURE 5-6   *A Remulak Productions association class.*

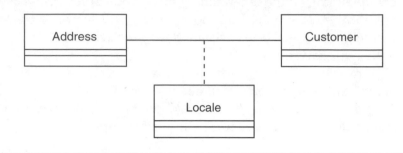

to relate products to other products. This could be beneficial, for example, when selling a guitar and then recommending some related supplies. To provide this feature, and to model it according to the UML, we need to set up a reflexive association on `Product`. Figure 5-7 shows an example of this association. Notice that the association leaves and returns to the same class.

Qualification Associations

When the class diagram is created, no distinction is made regarding how the association is traversed. Rather, one class is viewed as simply having access to all of the possible associations (links in runtime between objects) to their related classes. In some cases, it might be important enough in the domain to specify how the association will be traversed. Qualifiers provide this ability in the UML. A **qualifier** allows a set of related objects to be returned based on the qualification of some specific attribute(s).

For Remulak Productions, a qualifier could be placed, if needed, on the association between `Customer` and `Order`, as shown in Figure 5-8.

FIGURE 5-7   *A Remulak Productions reflexive association.*

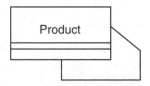

FIGURE 5-8   *A Remulak Productions qualified association.*

The source object (`Customer`), together with the qualifier's attributes (`orderId`), yield a target set of object(s) (`Order`). In the case of Remulak Productions, either nothing or one `Order` will be returned.

For the class diagram for Remulak Productions (outlined later in this chapter), we will diagram no qualified associations.

Generalization

Recall from earlier in the chapter that generalization is a way to depict a lattice of classes and to portray the fact that one class can be made to hold both structure (attributes) and behavior (operations) that apply to one or more specialized classes. These specialized classes can then add additional structure and behavior as necessary to portray their unique characteristics. Every instance of the specialized class also "is a" instance of the generalized class.

For Remulak Productions, a generalization/specialization relationship exists between Product, Guitar, Sheet   Music, and Supplies. Product is the generalized class and the other three are specializations on it. Common components will be defined in Product that will apply to all of the specialized classes. Figure 5-9 shows this generalization/specialization association.

Creating the Class Diagram

A word of caution, and perhaps comfort, is in order. The preliminary list of classes and associations are just that—preliminary. We will add more classes as we progress through the Elaboration stage of the project.

Some classes might be added to provide more detail about the project as it progresses. Some will be added to help resolve context-related

FIGURE 5-9 *A Remulak Productions generalization/specialization class diagram.*

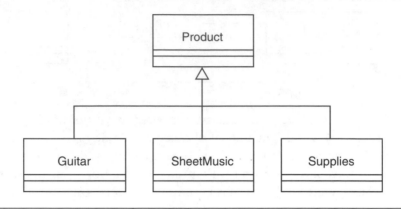

issues about other, already-defined associations. Figure 5-10 is a first cut at the class diagram for Remulak Productions.

The class diagram in the figure is rendered in the visual modeling tool (Rational Rose in this case). We do this to begin integrating

FIGURE 5-10 *The Remulak Productions class diagram.*

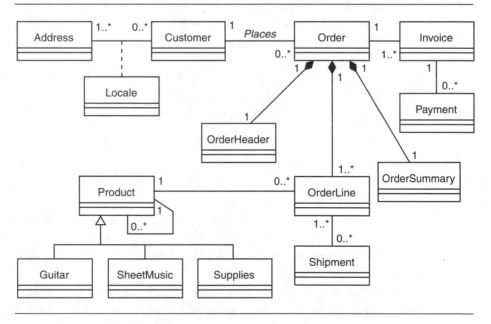

our requirements and analysis work within a tool that is going to extend, and make easier, our other deliverables. Figure 5-11 shows the user interface for Rational Rose and the class diagram for Remulak Productions. Notice the tree view pane on the left side of the window, which currently displays the logical view of Increment One entity classes.

Identifying Attributes and Operations

Until now, we haven't paid much attention to attributes or operations. In this section, we see how to identify both.

FIGURE 5-11   *The Remulak Productions class diagram in Rational Rose.*

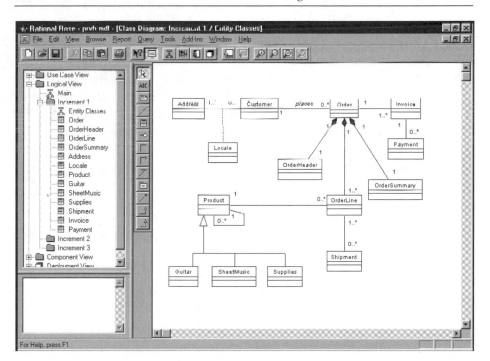

Attributes

We have already encountered several attributes, particularly during the class identification exercise . Recall that we identified many nouns that were actually attributes (rather than classes) because they didn't have structure and behavior in their own right but merely served as structural components of something else.

In the case of Remulak Productions, nouns such as "first name" and "last name" are part of the Customer class. Attributes such as address line 1, address line 2, address line 3, city, state, postal code, and country are part of the Address class, whereas attributes such as quantity, extended price, and line discount are part of the OrderLine class. Soon, the attributes that form the structural backbone of the Remulak Productions classes begin to take shape.

Recall that the previous UML class diagram showed three compartments for a class, containing the class name, attributes, and operations. The attributes go in the second compartment and have a defined structure; an example is shown in Figure 5-12.

The attribute name is entered in "camelback" notation, that is, the first letter is lowercase and the remaining full word components have their first letter capitalized. A colon separates the name from the attribute type. The type may be a primitive attribute defined for the particular language environment or a complex type such as other classes and structures. Any default initial value for a particular attribute may also be specified as shown. Other facets of the attribute specification, called *access visibility*, were explored in Chapter 2. They are Public (+), Private (−), and Protected (#) and preface the attribute name.

We don't want to get hung up on completing the entire attribute definition. We might not know the type or default initial values, if

FIGURE 5-12   *UML attribute definition.*

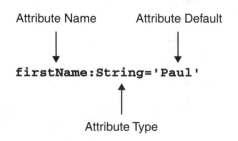

any, at this time. Eventually, however, we will need all of this information before we can generate any program code and use it meaningfully.

Operations

Operations define the behavior supported by a given class. At this point, we might not have a clear idea of the exact operations that each class will support; that will be driven by the work to be done as specified in the use cases. The operations will take more shape as the project moves into the dynamic modeling stage, which is explored in Chapter 7. However, answering some basic questions will help us begin to identify them, as well as provide a good brainstorming exercise to get at the operations of the classes.

1. What does the class know how to do?
2. What is the class expected to do for others?
3. What are the class's responsibilities?

For example, the `Order` class should know how to calculate some type of total due, as well as know if anything is backordered.

The operation goes in the class's third compartment and has a defined structure, as illustrated in Figure 5-13.

Like the attribute name, the operation name is entered in camelback notation. After the operation name, the parameters, or arguments, that make up the input to the operation are defined (within parentheses). The argument specification conveniently takes the same form as the attribute specification outlined in the attribute section.

FIGURE 5-13 *UML operation specification.*

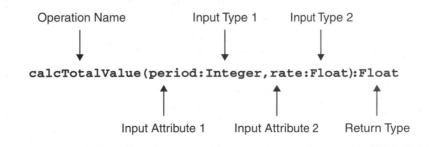

Multiple input arguments are allowed and are separated by commas. Finally, the type of the output, if any, returned by the operation may be specified.

The entire set of arguments and return types is called the **operation signature**. Operation signatures are important to polymorphism, as you will see when the nuances of polymorphism are explored during the Elaboration and Construction phases of the project.

Similar to attributes, we don't get hung up on completing the entire signature for each operation, as we might not know them at this point. We will need to complete all of this information before we can generate any program code and use it meaningfully.

All entity classes defined for an application support certain, basic services:

1. **getInfo**: Retrieves the contents of an object from persistent storage.

2. **create**: Creates an object.

3. **update**: Updates an object.

4. **delete**: Deletes an object.

These are some early standards that will begin to take shape for the project. These operations will allow us to implement some common services across all objects in the application.

Object Diagram

A UML **object diagram** is an improvisation of a class diagram, a snapshot of the lifecycle of a collection of objects. Like the balance sheet for a company, it is current only as of the time it is printed or rendered. However, depending on the audience, an object diagram can help to depict classes from a live perspective. It is most often used to depict the system to management and to members of the organization who are not as familiar with the project as the project team is.

Figure 5-14 shows an example of an object diagram for Customer Mike Richardson and his two Orders with Remulak Productions.

FIGURE 5-14   *A Remulak Productions object diagram for* Customer *and* Order.

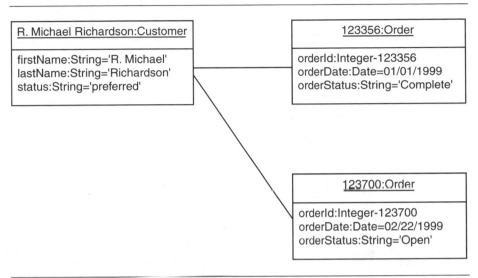

The object diagram is read as *the R. Michael Richardson object of class* Customer *is* linked *to both* *the 123356 object of class* Order *and* the *123700 object of class* Order. Notice that the attribute compartment shows the live object data for these instances. In addition, the operation compartment is dropped for object diagrams because operations are related to the class. Being a member of the class automatically gets the object access to the operations.

In later UML diagrams (sequence and collaboration), the object view is used. Otherwise, the project team will seldom use object diagrams.

Figure 5-15 is a class diagram of the relationships of several concepts discussed so far. The figure indicates that the use case is the embryo of all that we know about the project. Also shown are the primary, alternate, and exception pathways that we will model with an interaction diagram in Chapter 7. Classes initially show up in the use case and are used, as objects, in interaction diagrams.

FIGURE 5-15   *Class diagram of project concepts and UML deliverables.*

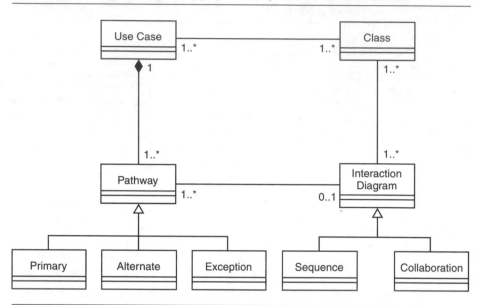

Finishing Up: The Analysis Model

With the completion of the use cases, classes (entity, control, and interface), class diagram, and related associations, we have completed the **analysis model**. The analysis model consists of everything completed so far. Recall that the requirements model consisted of the use cases delivered at the completion of the Inception phase. The use cases for Remulak Productions have been detailed extensively and from them we have derived additional diagrams and supporting artifacts (multiplicity, roles, and association names).

In the remaining chapters that deal with the Elaboration phase, we further flesh out the classes, adding more attributes and operations. In addition, the control and interface classes, in their own contexts with the entity classes, begin to meld. The eventual result will be the design model for Remulak Productions

Checkpoint

Where We Have Been

1. The first step in the Elaboration phase is to detail the alternate and exception pathways through all of the use cases in Increment One.

2. Categorization of business rules, although not UML artifacts, is key to the success and traceability of the project. Business rules are assigned to the use cases that enforce them.

3. We can develop a preliminary list of candidate classes by simply extracting nouns from the use cases and applying various class filters.

4. Classes are subdivided into three categories called stereotypes: entity, control, and interface. Entity classes are of most interest to the project sponsors, but all are vital to ensuring the application's flexibility as the business evolves. Sometimes Entity classes are called Domain classes.

5. Associations come in six forms: simple, aggregation, composition, link, reflexive, and qualification. They are instantiated to provide links over which messages flow to carry out the functionality of the use cases.

6. A class has three compartments containing the class's name, attributes, and operations. Not all of the detail for attributes and operations needs to be completely specified at this point in the project, but this needs to be done before generating program code.

7. The analysis model for Remulak Productions is complete and includes the details of all use case pathways, the results of the class identification process and assigning associations, and the detailing of multiplicity.

Where We Are Going Next

In the next chapter, we:

1. Begin a high-level prototype effort for some of the use case pathways.

2. Create screen flow structure charts (storyboards) before actually creating the prototype.

3. Identify ways to use the use cases and actors to match navigational requirements with the prototype.

4. Create screen dialogs to get the users' perspectives on the anticipated goals of the user interface and what they expect it to do.

5. Modify UML artifacts to reflect what is learned in the prototyping process.

6. Examine the need for change control and the ability to maintain traceability throughout the project deliverables.

CHAPTER 6

Building an Early Prototype

*At this point in the project, we need to create a concrete visualization, called a **prototype**, of some of what we have learned so far. This visualization should focus on those areas of the project that need further validation. It can also be an excellent way to discover more about the application requirements, which might involve not only new functionality but also usability needs.*

A prototype's goal is not only to mock up the visual interface but also to actually exercise many of the pathways through the use cases. In the case of Remulak Productions, the prototype focuses on the happy path through the Process Orders use case. It also sets the stage for establishing some future standards for the project team, particularly as those standards relate to the user interface.

GOALS

- Examine the use cases, focusing on gathering user interface requirements.
- Create a user interface artifacts section for each use case.
- Discuss the concept of use case coupling.
- Create screen structure charts as a preliminary storyboard of the user interface flow.

⮥ Construct the user interface prototype.

⮥ Create screen dialogs to outline perceived interactions and desired outcomes.

⮥ Evaluate the user interface prototype.

⮥ Outline the changes to the use case and class diagrams based on additional information found during the prototyping effort.

Building an Early Prototype

Before we begin reviewing the use cases, focusing on the user interface prototype, let's revisit the Synergy process model, as well as the project plan, this time emphasizing a new aspect of the Elaboration phase of the project. Figure 6-1 shows the process model with the focus of the project at this point highlighted.

In this chapter, we focus on the following:

• The "UI Prototype" block, which deals with the user interface prototype for Remulak Productions

FIGURE 6-1 *Synergy process model and the Elaboration phase.*

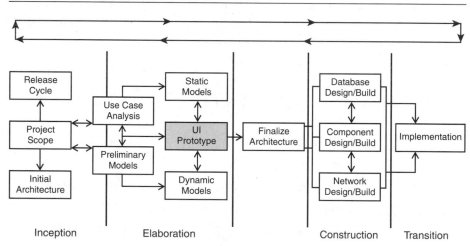

The Prototype

The user interface prototype serves many functions at this stage of the project:

- Further refines the actor and use case boundaries and clarifies any misconceptions or missing details that remain to be collected.

- Provides early feedback to the project sponsors of the many visual features that the application will provide.

- Further details the use cases by adding an additional section, *user interface artifacts*.

The prototype can also serve as an excellent eye-opener for many project participants. Many times in design sessions I have heard the statement, "I can't tell you what I want, but if I could show you a picture. . . ." The prototype is our first picture into the future.

Requirements Gathering

User Interface Prototype

In this chapter, we look at how we can use the UML deliverables created so far to leverage the prototyping effort. The prime input is the use cases. However, until now, we have purposely avoided adding to them any user interface specifications or usability requirements, instead keeping them technology-neutral. In fact, recall from Chapter 4 that the only mention of technology by Remulak was that the order inquiry component should support both a traditional VB front-end and an Internet or Web-based front-end. They also stipulated that the actual order entry component remain in a VB framework.

Before we begin the prototype discovery process, I want to offer a caution on using prototypes. Although the prototype succeeds in discovering and reconfirming existing requirements, it can foster unrealistic expectations by the project sponsors. Often I have heard from a project sponsor, "My, that took only two weeks, but you say the entire system will take a year and half . . . what gives?" It is very important that we educate the entire project team on the prototype's goal and do this early and with the right focus. The best method of communicating this is via the business members of the project team because the project sponsors consider them one of "theirs."

The goals of the prototype are as follows:

- Assess specific user interface requirements for the key pathways of the application.

- Provide feedback to the project sponsors in the form of visual clues that the stated requirements found in the use cases are understood and can be realized.

- Begin the early development of user interface standards for the project.

- Begin constructing the working on-screen templates to be used during the Construction phase.

We must tell the project sponsors up front that what is behind the prototype is actually "smoke and mirrors"; most of the logic and data aspects of the prototype are hard-wired. The only thing representative of the production deliverable is the anticipated flow and look and feel. We need to communicate this message early and often. Again, have the business team members on the project communicate this.

Actor and Use Case Boundaries

To reinforce the notion that the UML, combined with a sound process model such as Synergy, provides traceability, prototyping is driven by the use cases created at the project's beginning. To be more precise, the user interface prototype's initial focus is the actual point at which the actor crosses the boundary of the use case.

Every point in the use case at which the actor is involved warrants some type of user interface. The user interface doesn't have to be graphical. Recall from Chapter 3 that an actor can also be a hardware device, a timer, or a system. Thus it is also possible to prototype something that isn't visual. (This is certainly true for systems that have a very strong hardware element, which Remulak Productions does not.) However, for Remulak Productions, at least two system actors are needed: the *credit card switch* and the *accounting system*.

As in earlier chapters, we focus on the Remulak Productions *Process Orders* use case. Of the Remulak Productions use cases, *Process Orders* is probably the most challenging and probably the one with the highest risk. This is primarily because it is the most heavily visited use case (since it involves the taking of orders). In addition, it needs some serious consideration regarding component layout and user interaction.

The key pathways that we will prototype deal with order entry. This will actually exercise quite a bit of the flow of the application. Although the pathway details in the use cases so far have been technology-neutral, we still must provide a mapping between those "essential" steps and the realization of those steps into a physical user interface flow.

Figure 6-2 is a cutaway of the use case diagram created in Chapter 4, showing *Process Orders* and its specific actor interface, the order clerk.

A good way to begin the prototyping process is to investigate the actor's interface expectations with the use case by asking certain questions. Table 6-1 offers a set of questions geared toward human actors. The answers might lead the prototype into different directions based on the findings. In the table, the answers pertain to the order clerk actor.

Recall from Appendix A that the order clerk was given a rating of "complex" because it will deal with a *graphical* user interface (GUI). Responses to the questionnaire indicate that the order clerk has intimate knowledge about the business but can benefit from a sophisticated and somewhat complex user interface.

User Interface Artifacts

Each use case (or use case pathway, depending on the level of separation in the individual use case) will have a user interface artifacts section that will list key items geared toward the user interface for a

FIGURE 6-2   Process Orders *use case.*

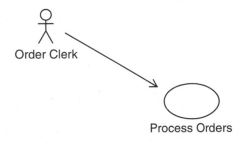

TABLE 6.1   *Sample Questions to Ask about a Human Actor at Remulak Productions*

Question	Answer
What level of skill does this actor need to have in order to perform its tasks irrespective of any computer knowledge?	The order clerk must be very knowledgeable about the order process. Often, the order clerk will be required to answer somewhat technical questions about musical instruments and supplies.
Does the actor have experience in a windowing environment?	Yes, all order clerks at Remulak Productions have extensive experience in using Microsoft Windows.
Does the actor have experience with an automated business application?	Yes, all order clerks are currently using Remulak Productions's older systems.
Will the actor be required to leave the application and consult manual information such as catalogs during the work processes?	Yes, order entry specifically will require external catalog resources. This is the only area of Remulak Productions that will require this.
Will the actor require that the application have a save and resume capability?	Yes, all pathways through the *Process Orders* use case will be dealing with an order that is new. An order is not saved until the order process is complete. If an order is partially completed but lacking something such as payment information, the order will be saved as an incomplete order.

particular actor/use case pair. In the case of *Process Orders*, there is only one primary actor.

What if a use case has more than one actor/use case pair? And what if the individual pairs require access to the same pathways but they differ vastly in their abilities to deal with a user interface, for example one is a novice and the other an expert? Many designs face this common dilemma. The only viable alternatives are to create either two different interfaces or one interface that has an option that provides for both novice and expert modes. Another possibility is that the user interface could be designed to support the common denominator, which is the easier of the two interfaces. However, I have found that this quickly alienates the expert user. (I also believe that humans improve over time and that those who start as novices will eventually become experts.)

Because there will probably always be new users, we have to deal with the dilemma. Often, novices can interface with a script manager in the user interface that guides them through the steps of the use case pathway. Scripts are much like the popular wizards in many Windows-based products. However, we won't have novice users.

Table 6.2 reviews the user interface artifacts section for each use case in Increment One. All of these artifacts are used as input to the user interface storyboarding and subsequent physical screen creation steps. They are very "soft" in that they often describe concepts and generalizations and seldom specifics such as "use a spinner control."

Use Case Coupling

Often we want to know if a given use case, from a workflow perspective, has a close association with other use cases. This provides some degree of coupling information that can be quite beneficial for the user interface flow. Using a matrix of use cases and describing their relationship can assess how closely use cases are related. Table 6-3 provides a first cut at the matrix based on what we know about Remulak Productions.

Here is an example of how to read the matrix. Consider the *Maintain Orders* use case from the *y*-axis and the *Maintain Relationships* use case from the *x*-axis. From this you can see that 60% of the time, a person who is in the *Maintain Orders* use case will subsequently navigate to the *Maintain Relationships* use case. Notice that this is not the same when taken in reverse. The person, while in the *Maintain Relationships* use case, has a 0% chance of going to the *Maintain Orders* use case.

You might want to use some other type of grading system instead of percentages (such as 0 for never, 1 for sometimes, and 2 for very often). Keep in mind that these occurrences are random and reflect the nature of the business at a given point in time. Note, too, that the relationships between use cases are not "includes" or "extends" relationships but merely related to workflow and navigation.

The matrix in Table 6-3 can help us determine how the user interface might be traversed, as well as demonstrate how easy it is to access other use cases from an associated use case pathway.

TABLE 6-2   *Use Case User Interface Artifacts Sections*

Use Case	User Interface Artifacts
Maintain Orders	Requires as few screens as possible because the user will be on the phone with the client and needs minimum "window open" sequences.
	Users want an easy way to tell who last changed an order and on what date.
Process Orders	Requires as few screens as possible because the user will be on the phone with the client and needs minimum "window open" sequences.
	Users want to have the payment methods displayed in a tabbed control. Many have used this in other Windows software, and they like its features.
	Product search should be maximized for performance and involve minimum keystrokes for access.
Maintain Relationships (*Customer* pathway only)	The customer search must be integrated onto the screen; the users want to avoid a separate screen if possible.
	Associating customers with addresses and specifying their associated roles should be very easy to do.
	Since many users work only certain states, default fields on the screens should be based on user preferences.
Application Infrastructure	This is a shadow use case and will have user interface components that are geared toward the information technology group.
Use Cases (general user interface comments)	All backgrounds will be white with black labels.
	All controls will come from the VB development environment supplied by Microsoft. No third-party ActiveX controls will be purchased for this project.
	The screens should be as lean as possible with no useless UI clutter.
	As much faultless entry of information as possible should occur in the user interface. Date processing is important; manually entering dates in a particular format should be avoided.

TABLE 6-3.   *Use Case Coupling Matrix*

	Maintain Orders	Maintain Inventory	Process Orders	Shipping	Invoicing	Maintain Relationships	Decision Support
Maintain Orders	X	0%	10%	40%	10%	60%	0%
Maintain Inventory	0%	X	0%	50%	0%	0%	0%
Process Orders	40%	0%	X	0%	0%	50%	0%
Shipping	30%	60%	0%	X	25%	5%	0%
Invoicing	20%	0%	0%	0%	X	0%	0%
Maintain Relationships	0%	0%	0%	0%	0%	X	0%
Decision Support	0%	0%	0%	0%	0%	0%	X

Iteration One

Screen Structure Charts

In my early days as a developer of client/server applications, I immediately created physical screen layouts during prototyping. All too often, I then found myself in discussions with my business sponsor along the lines of "move the OK button over 4 pixels" and "wouldn't a gray background be more appealing." Discussions like these shouldn't dominate the prototype. Instead, the prototype should initially identify *major* window groups and the *overall* look and feel strategy to be used while addressing more aesthetic issues last.

Researchers have found that 60% of an application's usability can be traced to how well the user interface maps to the mental model or the metaphor model of the user. Interaction accounted for 30%, while presentation accounted for 10%. Surprisingly, developers usually first approach the task that has the lowest impact on usability.

In an effort to streamline the prototyping process, we will create screen structure charts before creating any actual screens. A structure chart is a low-technology way to storyboard the application flow, specifically the flow of the pathways through the use cases. The chart consists of various easy-to-use symbols. Figure 6-3 shows an example.

The symbols that follow describe the major types of windowing activities in a graphical application.

- **Amodal (or modeless) window**: Does not require a response from the user. For example, the window might be invoked and then minimized or bypassed in favor of another window within the application or another application entirely. Any Microsoft Office application is a good example of an amodal window.

- **Modal window**: Requires a response from the user. For example, the window might be invoked but will require that the user complete the dialog box or cancel out of it. (This actually is misleading because Microsoft Windows allows the Alt+Tab key combination to invoke application toggle functionality on any other open

FIGURE 6-3   *Screen structure chart symbols.*

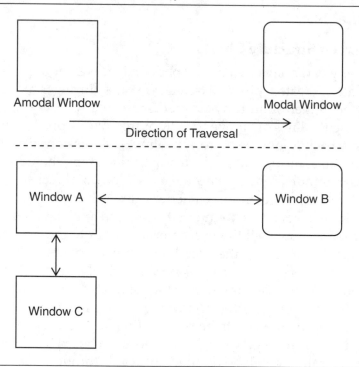

applications.) The Save As dialog box in most applications is a good example of a model window.

- **Direction of traversal**: Shows the pathway of window navigation. For example, suppose you are in a Multi-Document Interface (MDI) frame and a toolbar or menu item allows a transaction-based window to be opened with the option to return when that window is closed. Then the arrow will display as two-headed from the MDI frame to the transaction window.

This low-technology approach can yield high rewards. We also can model some of the more often-used controls, such as Tabbed controls, as we will do for Remulak Productions. A Tabbed control represents a form of logical paging and can be expressed with a focus block for a specific window, as shown in Figure 6-4.

The Tabbed controls, shown as windows in the figure, are embedded on the actual physical window, but they actually represent separate navigational elements of the user interface. They also are often mutually exclusive. Sometimes just showing window navigation alone isn't sufficient. In the case of windows, which use tabbed dialogs or in some cases master detail grids, distinguishing them as separate logical entities is important. Although these logical entities generally are layered onto one physical window, in some cases they are really user-driven navigational choices.

We create two structure charts for Remulak Productions in this chapter. Figure 6-5 depicts the overall screen structure chart for the order

FIGURE 6-4   *Logical paging using focus blocks.*

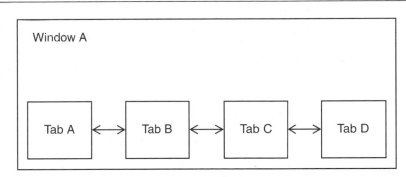

FIGURE 6-5   *The Remulak Productions overall screen structure chart.*

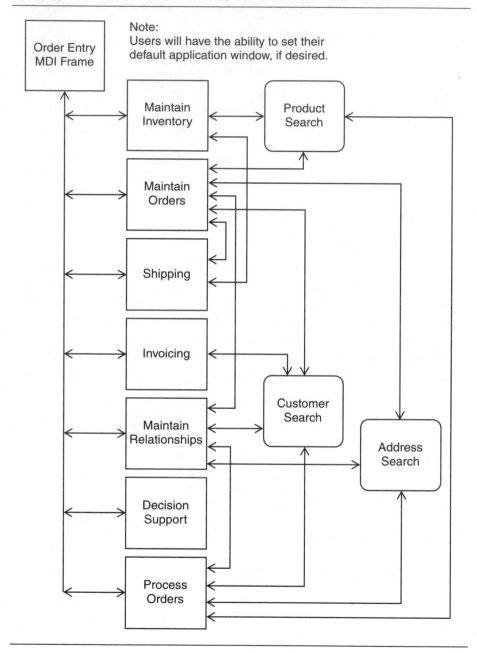

entry application. Figure 6-6 depicts the screen structure chart to support the *Process Orders* use case.

Notice that in Figure 6-6, the logical windows represent the payment processing tabs on the Process Order window. This example is more detailed about the window's look and feel. It also brings out some of the issues of the perceived mental model that will be employed in the design.

Creating the Prototype

VB is one of the best visualization tools ever built. Even companies that choose to build in C++ and Java often use VB to prototype their applications. This stems from VB's easy-to-use screen layout features. VB also makes it relatively easy for developers to build a flow that appears to work. Compare this with other development language environments in which pulling together a flow can take considerable effort.

We base our prototype on the MDI standard. In this way, we can provide a container in which all other forms are opened. Although not

FIGURE 6-6   *The Remulak Productions* Process Orders *screen structure chart.*

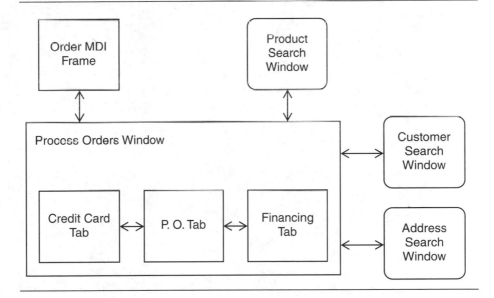

all applications today use the MDI approach, it remains a popular choice.

To start the Remulak Productions prototype, we create a project in VB.

1. Open Visual Basic. The New Project dialog box is displayed (Figure 6-7).

2. Double-click the Standard EXE option (which is highlighted by default). We select Standard EXE because the prototype will be form-intensive and forms are by nature always Standard EXEs (although forms may consist of several ActiveX DLLs).

FIGURE 6-7   *VB New Project dialog box.*

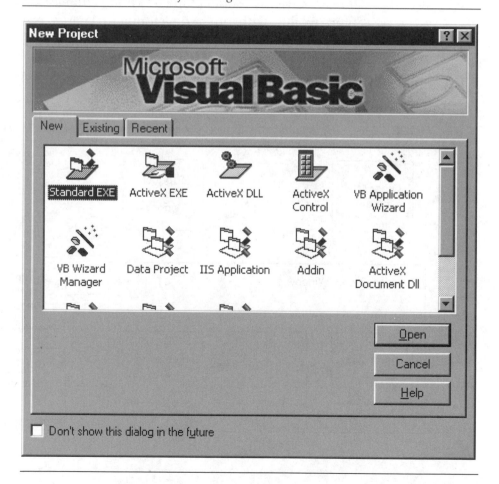

The project creation dialog box displays with a default name of Project1. We want to rename the project to "Remulak."

3. Right-click the Project1 attribute in the right-hand pane of the IDE.

4. Click Project1 Properties.

5. In the Project Name field in the Properties dialog box, change the name to "Remulak." Figure 6-8 shows the project form with the project renamed to "Remulak."

Next, we need to specify the controls that we will use to create some of the forms for the prototype. The prototype will need, at a minimum, the following controls:

- DateTimePicker
- Tabbed Dialog
- Grid

FIGURE 6-8   *The Remulak Productions project window.*

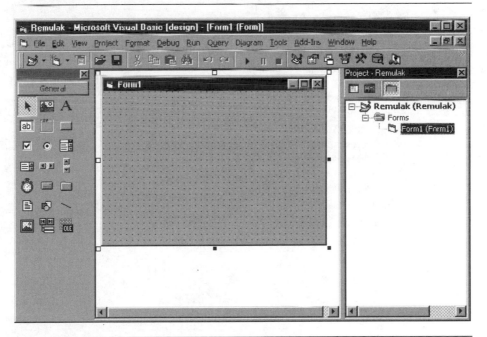

The Grid control, although a very low-technology grid, fits our purposes nicely because the prototype is somewhat static. Later, we might change the control, depending on whether we choose to go with disconnected recordsets that are bound to a grid or a control that works in an unbound mode. Actually, in the transition to VB v6.0, the old DBGrid control's replacement, the DataGrid, lost its ability to function in an unbound mode. DBGrid is still available in the Tools directory on the installation source but appears to be on the "soon to not be supported" list because it is not installed during VB v6.0 setup. Some excellent third-party products are available but Remulak Productions' President, Jeffery Homes, has asked that we limit our use of non-Microsoft controls. Time will tell if that aim is feasible.

We want to add the controls that we will use to the toolbar in the IDE. To do this, we need to add components as follows (Figure 6-9).

FIGURE 6-9   *Components dialog box.*

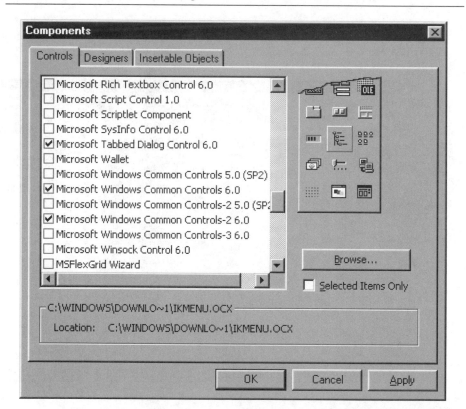

1. Click Project on the menu, and click Components from the drop-down menu to open the Components dialog window.

2. Scroll down the list as needed and click Microsoft Grid Control, Microsoft Tabbed Dialog Control 6.0, Microsoft Windows Common Controls 6.0, and Microsoft Windows Common Controls-2 6.0.

3. Click OK.

Next, we need to add the MDI form to the project and begin adding the menu items and basic task launch functionality.

1. Click Project on the menu.

2. Click the Add MDI Form menu item.

3. Double-click the MDI Form icon (Figure 6-10).

We want to change the default name of the MDI form to something more meaningful, as well as change some of the properties. Table 6-4

FIGURE 6-10   *MDI Form icon for inserting a new form.*

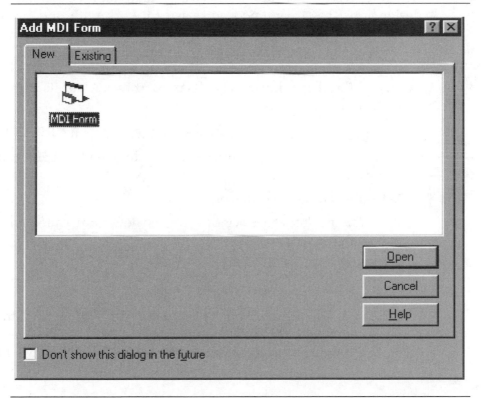

TABLE 6-4   *MDI Form Properties to Change*

Item	Value
Name	frmRemulakMDI
BackColor	Palette (White - &H00FFFFFF&)
Caption	Remulak Productions
WindowState	Maximized

lists the properties that we need to change for the MDI form. We do this using the Properties dialog box.

The MDI form always needs a way to launch the underlying application components. This can be done with toolbar or menu items. We use menu items for Remulak, listed in Table 6.5, by using the Menu Editor. The completed Menu Editor is shown in Figure 6-11.

We leave much of the functionality behind the MDI menu items empty because our goal is to prototype the *Process Orders* use case, which represents the hub of activity at Remulak Productions. The UI design must be streamlined and easy to work with and present as much information on one screen as possible, without the user having to go through many panels to get an order into the system.

To begin adding forms to the prototype, namely the Process Order form, and then changing some of its properties, such as its name, complete the following steps:

1. Right-click in the Project Explorer pane, and then click Add.
2. From the cascading menu, click Form to open the Add Form dialog box.
3. Double-click the Form icon.
4. Locate the Properties window for the new form, called Form1 by default.
5. Change "Name" to "frmProcessOrder."
6. Save the form as "Process Order."

Table 6-6 lists all of the Process Order form properties that we need to change. These changes will provide VB with the necessary input to allow the form to be opened as a child within the MDI frame `frmRemulakMDI`.

TABLE 6-5 *MDI Menu Items to Add to the MDI Form*

Menu Name	Submenu Name	Name
File		mnuFile
	New	mnuFileNew
	Open	mnuFileOpen
	Close	mnuFileClose
	-	line1
	Save	mnuFileSave
	Save As	mnuFileSaveAs
	-	line1
	Print	mnuFilePrint
Tasks		mnuTasks
	Process Order	mnuTaskProcessOrder
	Maintain Order	mnuTaskMaintainOrder
	Maintain Relationship	mnuTaskMaintainRel
	Inventory	mnuTaskInventory
	Shipping	mnuTaskShipping
	Invoicing	mnuTaskInvoicing
	Decision Support	mnuTaskDecisionSupport
Window		mnuWindow
	Tile Horizontally	mnuWindowHoriz
	Tile Vertically	mnuWindowVert
	Cascade	mnuWindowCascade
	Arrange Icons	mnuWindowArrange
Help		mnuHelp
	Order Help	mnuHelpHelp
	-	line1
	Contents and Index	mnuHelpIndex
	-	line1
	About Remulak Productions's Order Entry	mnuHelpAbout

FIGURE 6-11 *Completed MDI Menu Editor dialog box.*

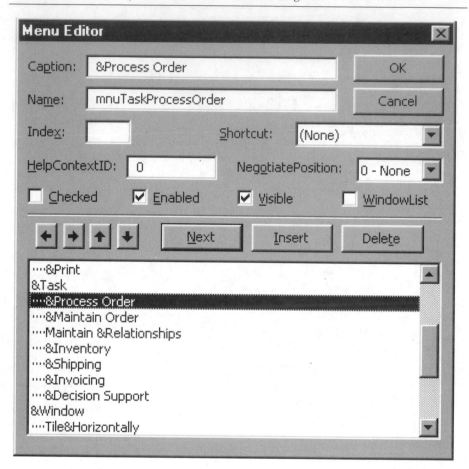

TABLE 6-6 *Properties of the Process Order Form to Change*

Item	Value
Name	frmProcessOrder
BackColor	Palette (White - &H00FFFFFF&)
BorderStyle	Fixed Single
Caption	Process Order
MDIChild	True

Without controls, the form is useless. Table 6-7 lists the controls that we want to add to the form (labels are not covered in the table).

TABLE 6-7   *Controls for the Process Order Form*

Control	Caption	Name
TextBox		txtCustomer
CommandButton	BMP showing Search Icon	cmdCustomer
TextBox		txtShipAddr
CommandButton	BMP showing Search Icon	cmdShipAddr
TextBox		txtBillAddr
CommandButton	BMP showing Search Icon	cmdBillAddr
ComboBox		lstTerms
DateTimePicker		lstDate
Grid		grdOrderLine
CommandButton	BMP showing Search Icon	cmdProduct
Tabbed Dialog Control		TabPayment
	Credit Card Tab	
RadioButton		rbVisa
RadioButton		rbMC
RadioButton		rbAmex
RadioButton		rbDiner
TextBox		txtCreditCard
TextBox		txtExpireDate
	Purchase Order Tab	
TextBox		txtPO
TextBox		txtAuth
DateTimePicker Control		LstThru
	Financing Tab	
TextBox		txtLoan
TextBox		txtScore
TextBox		txtLimit
TextBox		txtOfficer

To provide the grid formatting, we must add code to the `Form_Load()` event for the form `frmProcessOrder`, creating an event that looks like the following.

```
Private Sub Form_Load()
    grdOrderLine.Col = 1
    grdOrderLine.Row = 0
    grdOrderLine.Text = "Product"
    grdOrderLine.ColWidth(1) = 1000
    grdOrderLine.Col = 2
    grdOrderLine.Row = 0
    grdOrderLine.Text = "Description"
    grdOrderLine.ColWidth(2) = 1400
    grdOrderLine.Col = 3
    grdOrderLine.Row = 0
    grdOrderLine.Text = "Quantity"
    grdOrderLine.ColWidth(3) = 1000
    grdOrderLine.Col = 4
    grdOrderLine.Row = 0
    grdOrderLine.Text = "Price"
    grdOrderLine.ColWidth(4) = 1000
    grdOrderLine.Col = 5
    grdOrderLine.Row = 0
    grdOrderLine.Text = "Extended Price"
    grdOrderLine.ColWidth(5) = 1600
End Sub
```

So far we have laid out the menus on the `frmRemulakMDI` form as well as the controls on the `frmProcessOrder` form. We also need to write code to launch the `frmProcessOrder` form from the menu of the MDI frame, `frmRemulakMDI`, as follows.

1. Open the `frmRemulakMDI` form.

2. Right-click the form and click View Code.

3. Select `mnuTaskProcessOrder` from the object drop-down in the code pane. The default event for the menu object (and the only one) is the `click()` event.

Next, we add the following code to the event `click()`.

```
Private Sub mnuTaskProcessOrder_Click()
    Load frmProcessOrder
End Sub
```

We can run the application by clicking Run | Start from the menu; the RemulakMDI form will display as a blank frame. Or we can run it by selecting Task | Process Order from the menu; Figure 6-12 shows the resulting Process Order form. Notice along the bottom of the form the tabs representing the three forms of payment. By clicking a tab, we can uncover the tab to produce results that resemble Figures 6-13 and 6-14.

The DateTimePicker control makes date selection efficient for the application. To see how it works, click the Date field in the Process

FIGURE 6-12 *Process Order form.*

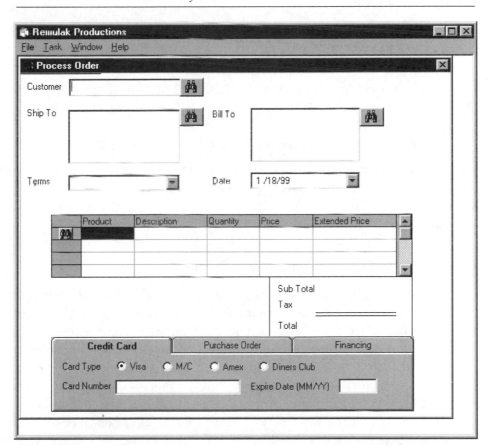

FIGURE 6-13 *Purchase Order tab uncovered.*

FIGURE 6-14 *Financing tab uncovered.*

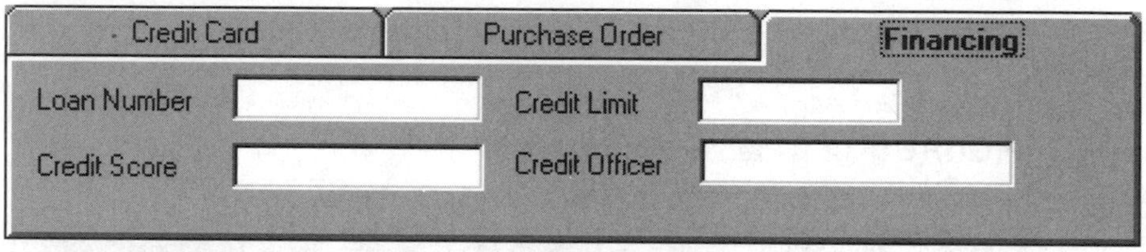

Order window and then the Good Thru Date field on the Purchase Order tab. Figure 6-15 shows the DateTimePicker control in action.

Collecting User Feedback by Using Screen Dialogs

User feedback about the screens benefits the prototype. This feedback should cover the following at a minimum:

- Logical function that is to be performed
- How is it done
- What happens as a result of the action

These might sound like the events identified in the earlier project scoping efforts; however, they concern the screens themselves. To gather this feedback, we follow a low-technology approach, by creating a screen dialog form. All of these prior tasks have been performed prior to any any "how" code being added to any windows.

To create a screen dialog, we take a screenshot of the screen and place a table below it that captures the key feedback points listed previously. It is a good idea also to capture any special edit notes, as well as any special processing information. Table 6-8 shows such a screen dialog for the

FIGURE 6-15   *DateTimePicker control.*

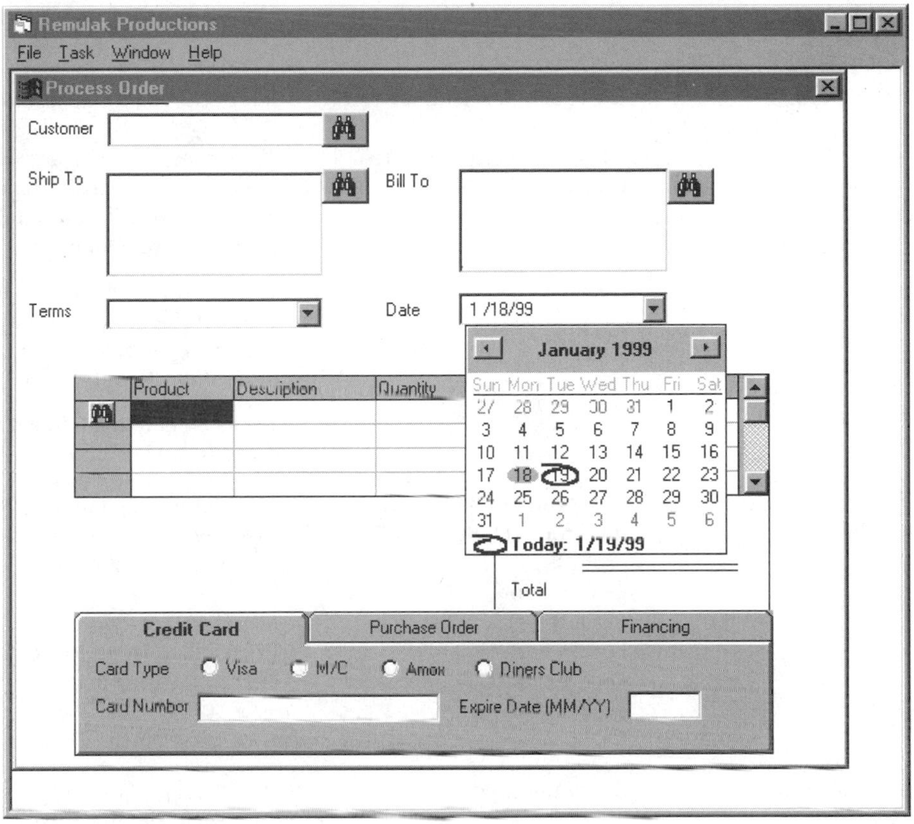

Process Order window, and Figure 6-16 shows the Special Edits/Notes section. Figures 6-12, 6-13, and 6-14 are used as the screenshots.

The project team members typically perform the screen dialog exercise. It is approached from the user's perspective. Like the use cases, the screen dialog focuses on the goals to be satisfied.

Learning from the Prototype

The final step is to review the static prototype with Remulak Productions's project sponsors and user team members. Suggestions for improving the user interface, as well as its functionality, always result from this step. If they don't, then either we are very good or we are dealing with very timid users.

TABLE 6-8   *Screen Dialog for the Process Order Form*

Action to Perform	How It Is Done	What Happens
Select a customer for order entry.	Enter customer id in the Customer field. -or- Click the customer search button and locate the customer.	Customer name appears to the left of the customer search button. Customer's Ship To and Bill To addresses are set. Customer's Terms are set. Date is defaulted to current system date. The payment tab is set to focus on the customer's default payment type and payment information is defaulted (if applicable). Focus is set to the first row of the order line grid.
Select the product to purchase.	Enter the product id into the Product field of the first order line. -or- Click the product search button to the left of the Product field and locate the product.	Product search dialog is displayed to allow product selection (if product search button is selected). Product's Description and (unit) Price is displayed in the grid next to the product id. Focus is set to the Quantity column.
Select a payment method of Credit Card.	Select the Credit Card payment tab. Select the appropriate Card Type. Enter the Card Number. Enter the Expire Date (MM/YY).	When the payment type is selected, the initial/default values in the other payment tabs are reset. Credit card number is validated against the current switch interface.
Select a payment method of Purchase Order.	Select the Purchase Order payment tab. Enter the P. O. Number. Enter authorization information. Override the Good Thru Date if necessary.	When the payment type selection is made, the initial/default values in the other payment tabs are reset. The Good Thru Date defaults to the current system date.
Select a payment method of Financing.	Select the Financing payment tab.	When the payment type selection is made, the initial/default values in the other payment tabs are reset.

(continued)

TABLE 6-8   *(continued)*

Action to Perform	How It Is Done	What Happens
Select a different Bill To address.	Click the Bill To search button.	Address search dialog is presented, thereby allowing the selection of another address for the customer.
		Revised address is returned and displayed.
Select a different Ship To address.	Click the Ship To search button.	To Address search dialog is presented, thereby allowing the selection of another address for the customer.
		Revised address is returned and displayed.
Save the order as entered.	Click File menu item. Click Save menu item.	Order is saved and order number is displayed.
Inquire on more-detailed product information.	Double-click the Product field. -or- Double-click the Description field.	Detailed product information window is displayed.
Get out of this window.	Click File menu item. Click Exit menu item. -or- Click System Exit icon on Process Order window. -or- Click System Exit icon on the MDI frame.	Window(s) are closed.

It is important that we incorporate suggested changes, within reason, into the prototype as quickly as possible. This is called **proto-cycling**. We also must separate user interface items from functional scope creep requirements and ensure that they go through some form of change control procedure. Many of the suggested changes are minor screen changes (for example, to icons or tab ordering) that are easy to change and can be dealt with effectively without change control.

FIGURE 6-16 *Special Edits/Notes section of Screen dialog for Process Order form.*

Edits

- Customer field id contains a Mod10 check digit that allows an initial verification of correct syntax.

- During product entry, if the customer's default payment type is Financing, then the order clerk should be notified if any one order line, plus outstanding accounts receivable balance, exceeds the customer's credit limit.

- American Express and Diner's Club credit card numbers should be edited to their respective valid mask. Due to variances in bank cards, this is not possible with Visa and Master Card numbers.

- The order clerk cannot modify the financing information.

Special Features/Notes

- Default payment type is kept at the customer level. Financing is the only option that retains state information. Credit card numbers are not kept from session to session or associated with a customer; only their order(s) are kept and associated.

- If the order clerk attempts to close the window without saving, a prompt for a save option appears. This applies to the Process Order window as well as the MDI frame that contains it.

Remulak Productions's user team members have reviewed the screens and completed the screen dialogs, and they raised some more-involved issues, including the following.

- No on-screen controls are available to save, add, exit, or print an order. Although the functionality is offered through menus, users felt that using them slowed down the process.

  Solution: Add Save, New, Exit, and Print command buttons to the window.

- No detailed product information on a given product is readily accessible to the order clerk. Although this was not considered a show stopper, users thought that it would be nice to have this information in case the customer asks for it. Also, products have associations with other products (that is, certain guitars are associated with certain brands of strings and other supplies). Users wanted to have this retrievable, if needed, from the Process Order screen.

Solution: Allow for product pop-ups that pop up by double-clicking on either the Product or Description field of the order line grid.

- The Credit Card Expiration Date field requires manual entry, which is more prone to error.

Solution: The Credit Card MM/YY field should also use the DateTimePicker control. Although credit card companies need just the month and year, the user interface could extract what is needed, thereby saving entry time and reducing errors.

- There is no predefined template order for special orders. Remulak Productions often has special offers that are handled by order clerks that only take those types of orders. Since calls go through a telephone response menu first, these special offer sales can be routed accordingly. The users want predefined template orders that are retrievable and set as the default based on order clerk and the clerk's immediate logon session.

Solution: Allow for a template order dialog box and the ability to associate the template with a user session so that subsequent new orders invoke the previously associated template.

The first three items are pretty straightforward, although the second item might require a little additional work. The last item might not be a difficult change, but it is a potentially broad one because it actually expands the functionality so as to add additional pathways through three use cases. Those use cases and their impact on other UML artifacts are listed in Table 6-9.

The result of the change control process confirms that we should go ahead with the necessary changes in scope and functionality. The resulting changes to the user interface from the user-supplied review are shown in Figure 6-17.

This exhaustive example is included because it reflects real life. The changes discussed here represent the expected types of changes we might encounter, and we need to show how the impact analysis might

TABLE 6-9 *Impact Analysis and Report to Change Control Management*

Use Case	Description of Change to Be Made
Process Orders	Allow for the creation of template orders. Instead of accomplishing this with a separate `ModelOrder` class, do so with an attribute within the existing entity class of `Order`. A more elegant solution is to employ some type of "factory" pattern that allows for the creation of template order objects, but that solution would be a bit of overkill for this change.
	Template orders will never have an association with a `Customer` object. This changes the multiplicity of the association between `Customer` and `Order`. An `Order` may now be associated with 0..1 `Customer` objects.
	Entry of a template `Order` should be transparent, with only a confirmation at saving to verify that the user intends to create a template order.
	Provide user interface input of a template order and associate this with the duration of a user's logon session. This template order will be invoked from the Process Order window and its context automatically carried forward from order to order for the duration of the user's logon session. The source of the template/user association will be made within the security subsystem with the addition of a `Session` object (long term).
Maintain Orders	Allow for the ability to change an order that is in the template status and any associated business rules that might be violated for in-process orders.
Security	This use case is not scheduled until Increment Three of the project. However, to support the session continuation feature for template orders, a `Session` class will be added in Increment One. This class will be void of any authorization knowledge, as is envisioned for Increment Three.

be performed and provide the traceability to the UML artifacts that require change. Figure 6-18 is a screenshot of the Maintain Relationships prototype.

The beauty of a process model such as Synergy or RUP, which support iterative and incremental development with the UML as the artifact trail, is that all of the pieces hang together. The crucial point is that everything is tied back to the use cases. If something isn't in the use case, then it won't be in the final deliverable. Changes to use cases should always go through change control.

FIGURE 6-17   *Remulak Productions's Process Order User Interface.*

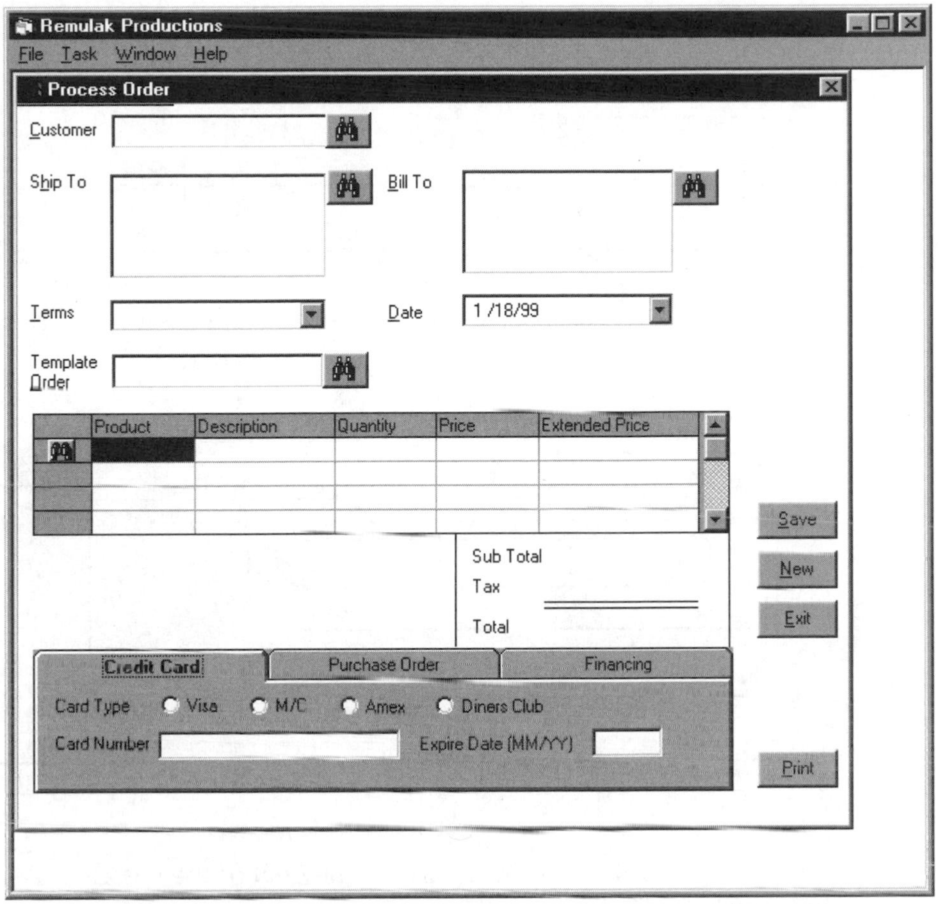

We can learn a lot from the prototype. The screen structure chart out-lines logical flow (at a high level). The prototype itself gives the unique look and feel perspective of the application. And the screen dialog enables the user to offer feedback regarding logical actions, how to perform them, and the results they are expected to produce.

Next, let's relate things to the UML deliverables produced thus far. The interaction begins with the actor's interface with the use case in the form of some initial event that the actor wants to perform, for example *Customer Places Order,* which is satisfied by a use case (from the user's perspective). This ultimately must be realized in some human/machine

FIGURE 6-18 *Remulak Productions's Maintain Relationships user interface.*

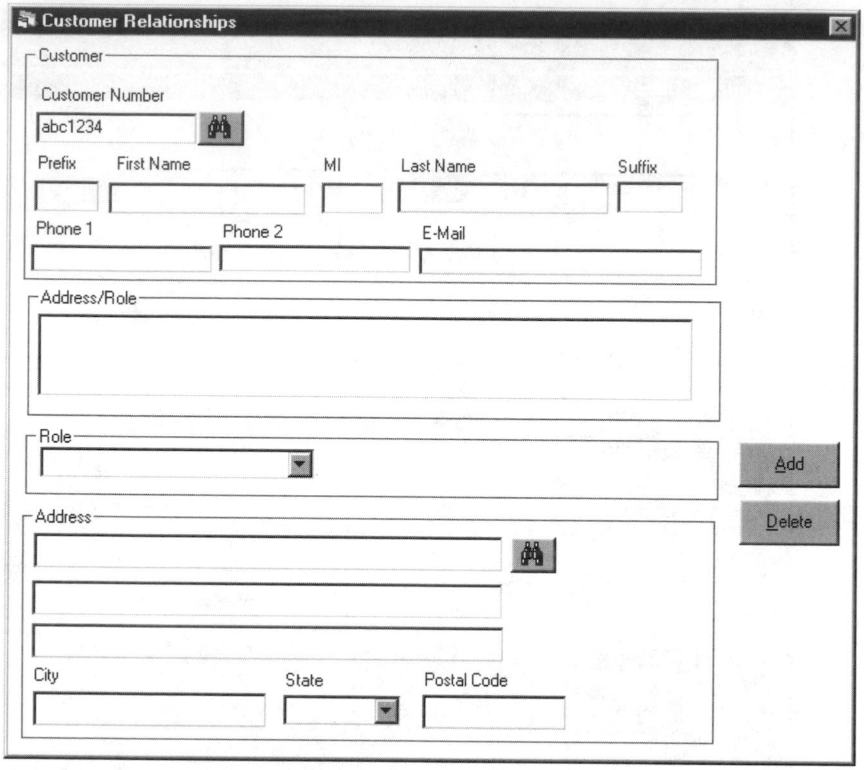

interface that will assist in satisfying the goal of the use case. As part of iteratively and incrementally developing applications, this type of feedback mechanism strengthens the final deliverable as well as builds confidence in the project team's ability to move forward.

Checkpoint

Where We Have Been

1. The primary goals of the prototype are to confirm actor and use case boundary relationships and to explore both functional and usability requirements.

2. Creating a user interface artifact section for the use cases enables the better definition of the detail about the interaction required between the actors and use cases.

3. Too often, project teams waste precious time creating a visual deliverable as the first step in the prototype. The screen structure chart is a low-technology approach to describing screen flow for the application.

4. The screen dialog is another low-technology effort. It captures the user's perceived expectations about interaction between the user interface and anticipated results.

5. Changes should be cycled back quickly into the prototype to give the user immediate feedback on suggested changes.

6. Any changes to the use cases that result from the prototype require a visit to the project's change control procedures.

7. By iteratively and incrementally developing the application, we can incorporate changes while still effectively managing scope creep. Changes are iteratively incorporated back into the use cases to ensure that the project, and any subsequent changes to its scope, leave traceability intact.

Where We Are Going Next

In the next chapter, we:

1. Begin to explore the project's dynamic aspects.

2. Synthesize the use case pathway detail into the two UML interaction diagrams: sequence and collaboration.

3. Review the state diagram and its usefulness in exploring classes that exhibit interesting dynamic behavior and explore the types of classes that might warrant the use of a state diagram to further our knowledge base.

4. Discuss the activity diagram and how we might use it both for complex operations and to detail the activities within use cases.

5. Create usage matrices to explore distributed loading characteristics of the Remulak Productions project.

6. Conduct dynamic modeling and use what is learned from this to enhance the class diagram.

CHAPTER 7

The Dynamic Elements
of the Application

In this chapter, we become more specific regarding how the project will realize its ultimate goal: constructing an order entry application for Remulak Productions. For it to do this, we need to add to the dynamic aspects of the project. More specifically, we add a dynamic model view of the project that depicts the collaboration of objects, with the sole goal of satisfying the pathways through the use cases. We have already explored some of the dynamic aspects when the detailed pathway task steps were captured in Chapters 4 and 5.

GOALS

- ⇨ Explore the mission of dynamic modeling and the perspective it brings to the project.

- ⇨ Review the components of the sequence diagram and how to effectively create them from the use case templates.

- ⇨ Create sequence diagrams for Remulak Productions's happy paths and alternate pathways.

- ⇨ Discover how knowledge learned from the creation of sequence diagrams is transferred to the class diagram.

↪ Review the components of the collaboration, state, and activity diagrams.

↪ Learn the circumstance under which to use a specify type of diagram.

↪ Explore the need for usage matrices and the perspective that they provide that isn't directly conveyed in any of the base UML diagrams.

Next Step of the Elaboration Phase

Before we explore the dynamic aspects of the project, let's revisit the Synergy process model and the project plan for this phase of the project. Figure 7-1 shows the process model, with the focus of the project at this point highlighted.

In this chapter, we focus on the following part of the model:

- The "Dynamic Models" block, which deals with the interaction of objects whose purpose is to satisfy the goals outlined in the use cases

FIGURE 7-1 *Synergy process model and the Elaboration phase.*

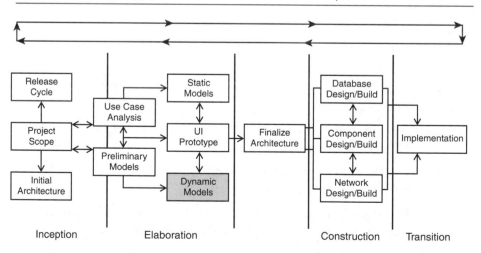

Dynamic Modeling

The dynamic models focus on the interactions between objects— instances of the classes identified in prior chapters that work together to implement the detailed pathways through the use cases. They add considerable value to the project, as follows.

- For the first time, we bring together the classes and use case pathways and demonstrate the ability to model the messaging necessary to implement them.
- Transfer knowledge learned from the dynamic model to the class diagrams in the form of operations, attributes, and associations.
- Incorporate knowledge learned from the use case and class diagrams to model the volumetric and loading characteristics of the application through the creation of usage matrices.

In our earlier work on the project, we explored the dynamic aspects of the Remulak Productions application. Many of the artifacts already captured add to the dynamic knowledge required to make the Remulak Productions system a reality, for example the following.

- The events identified during project scoping provide a clear picture of the external and internal stimuli to which the system must be prepared to respond.
- The pathways identified in the use case templates are dynamic in that they explain the logical steps necessary to satisfy the goal of the use case.
- The business rules capture the parameters and semantics that certain elements of the application must implement.

The dynamic models reviewed in this chapter provide a more formal approach to what has already been captured in various parts of the project's evolution. Chiefly, they reinforce the object-oriented concepts and principles to be used on the project.

Types of Dynamic Models

The UML offers four dynamic models in the form of diagrams that offer different views of the dynamic perspectives of the application. Each diagram's view provides its own unique focus and can be used in different instances depending on an application's needs.

- **Sequence diagram**: The sequence diagram, often called one of the *interaction diagrams* (the other being the collaboration diagram), is from my experience, the most often used dynamic model. Applications will always produce sequence diagrams. A sequence diagram is time-centered. Its focus is the linear flow of messages between objects. Time flows from the start of the diagram sequentially downward (see Figure 7-3).

- **Collaboration diagram**: A collaboration diagram is also called one of the interaction diagrams. It conveys the same meaning as the sequence diagram, except that it focuses on the individual objects and the messages that they send and receive. Collaboration diagrams are instance-centered. Some of the visual modeling tools available (for example, Rational's Rose and Computer Associates's Paradigm Plus) will generate collaboration diagrams from sequence diagrams.

    Note: The two interaction diagrams are the key link between the use case pathways and the code that will be constructed to actually implement the pathways.

- **State diagram**: A state diagram models the lifecycle of one class. More specifically, it models the various states that an object can be in and the events and associated actions and activities that are performed when an object transitions to a new state or while it is in a particular state. State diagrams add value only when the class exhibits interesting and complex dynamic behavior.

    Many classes in the application are, well, uninteresting concerning state (for example, `Customer` and `Address`), whereas others can be quite interesting (`Order`), divulging additional requirements knowledge about the application. Most applications will have a low ratio of state diagrams to classes. Applications of a more real-time embedded nature (for example, machine control, automotive, and telecommunications) typically have a higher ratio of state diagrams to classes.

- **Activity diagram**: An activity diagram models the steps in a complex operation. It can also be used to model the steps of a use case pathway. Activity diagrams are as close to a traditional flow chart as one can get.

Figure 7-2 provides a view of the application artifacts as they change focus toward the dynamic elements of the project; the sequence diagram is shown at the bottom of the figure. The roots of this sequence diagram can be traced to both the use case pathways and the class diagram.

The outlined steps or tasks necessary to implement a pathway through a use case eventually must be transformed into messages between objects. The dynamic models, particularly the sequence and collaboration diagrams, always view the live instances of the classes, that is, the objects. The objects are doing the interacting in the dynamic models (*Tammy Timmons Places an Order*). The classes define the rules regarding how each of their instances will undergo state changes, but each individual object then takes on a lifecycle of its own.

The following sections discuss the four diagrams in detail.

FIGURE 7-2   *Artifact flow to get at the sequence diagram.*

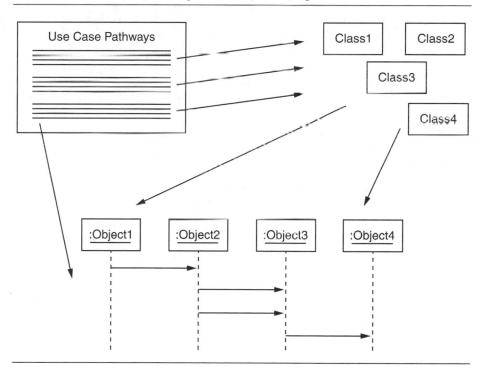

The Sequence Diagram

The sequence diagram is the most used of the dynamic models. It has a long and rich history tracing back to, among others, Rumbaugh's OMT (Object Modeling Technique) methodology. The diagram begins with instances of classes—objects—organized in "swimlanes" across the top of the diagram. Below each is a "lifeline." (See Figure 7-3.) Objects are drawn as boxes, with the class name preceded by a colon and then the entire name underlined. This can be verbalized as, for example, "any old `Customer` object." If a specifically named object is desired, then you precede the colon with the name of the object, for example <u>Rene Becnel:Customer</u>, which verbalized means "the `Rene Becnel` object of class `Customer`." Figure 7-3 shows an example of objects interacting in a sequence diagram.

The sequence diagram often uses the *focus of control rectangle*. It appears as a rectangular box imposed on top of the swimlane. This

FIGURE 7-3   *Enterprise-level use of the sequence diagram.*

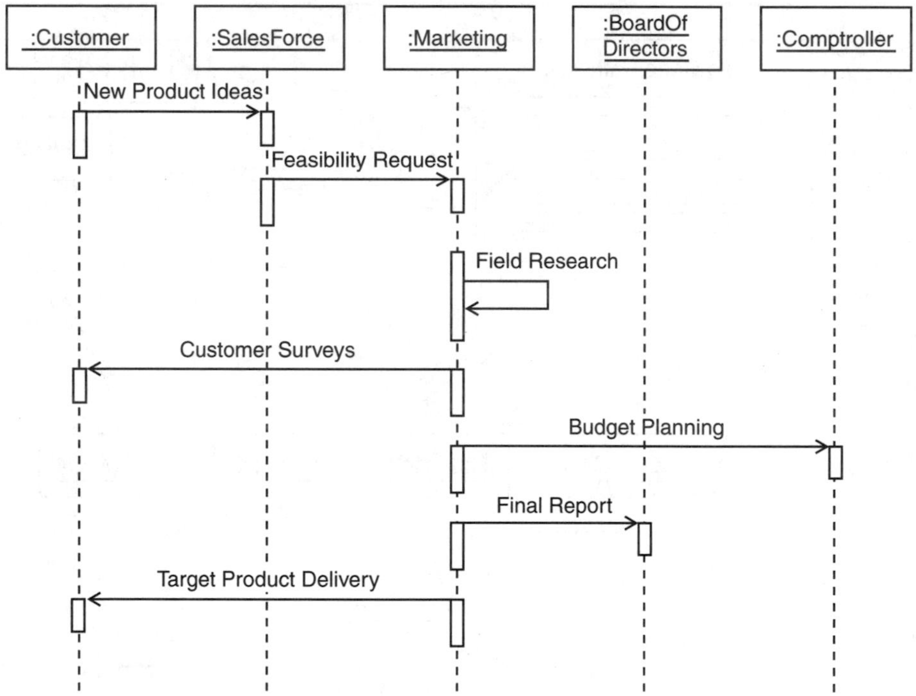

optional adornment indicates that this object is orchestrating the messaging activity and has control of that particular messaging sequence. Indicating this on the diagram, especially in multi-threaded applications, can be helpful.

In this book, we use the sequence diagram for a very specific purpose in the project's Elaboration phase. However, it also may be used for enterprise-level modeling, for example in business process reengineering efforts or even during a project's scoping phase. Figure 7-3 is an example of a sequence diagram depicting the overall enterprise-level interactions of departments within Remulak Productions. Note that this is a much higher-level use of the sequence diagram than we require here and doesn't specifically model a concrete use case pathway, at least not to the level at which we have defined our use cases.

Additional adornments can be added to the sequence diagram, key of which are the following.

- **Script**: A comment aligned to the left of each message flow. Many times a script details a task taken directly from the use case's pathway detail.

- **Latency and timing**: Allow us to designate time constraints on message send and receive semantics.

- **Guard condition**: A means to show condition checking. Allows us to introduce branching considerations.

- **Iteration**: Allows us to note repetitive message sequences until a given guard condition is met.

- **Synchronization semantics**: Allows us to identify messages that are nonblocking and that follow the "fire-and-forget" paradigm (asynchronous message—probably the most used). Others that fall into this category are simple (the default), synchronous, time-out, and balking.

Sequence Diagram of the Happy Path

We begin our modeling by creating a sequence diagram of the use case happy path. Recall that the happy path is the most commonly occurring pathway through the use case (*Customer calls in and orders a guitar and supplies and pays with a credit card*). By our modeling this pathway first, the other sequence diagrams should simply be variations of that pathway's diagram. In this way, we reduce the amount of work required, while adding the most artifacts (e.g., operations, attributes) to the class diagram in the shortest amount of time.

The class diagram benefits a lot from the dynamic modeling process. This is because every message sent to an object results in an operation being assigned to the target class. Figure 7-4 is the use case diagram we defined during project scoping. In particular, we deal in this chapter with dynamic models for the use cases that are part of Increment One of Remulak Productions's deliverable, as specified in Figure 7-5.

FIGURE 7-4   *The Remulak Productions use case diagram.*

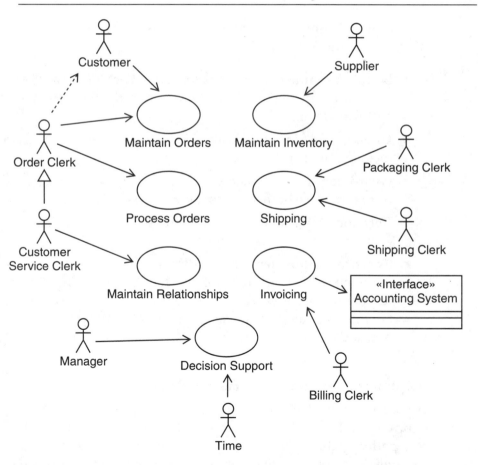

FIGURE 7-5   *Increment One package.*

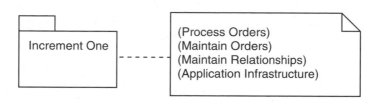

Recall from Chapter 4, Figure 4-9, the shadow technical use case—application infrastructure. The first increment outlined with the package diagram is shown in Figure 7-5. This shadow use case is not shown on the business view of the Remulak Productions use case diagram in Figure 7-4 because the use case focuses on the infrastructure needed for communication to occur among the user interface, the Business Rule Services layer, and Database Services layer of the application.

Following is the completed Use Case Template (without pathway detail) for the *Process Orders* use case. This is the same template introduced in Chapter 4.

Use Case Template

Use Case Name:	Process Orders
Use Case Description:	This use case starts when an order is either initiated or inquired about. It handles all aspects of the initial definition and authorization of an order. It ends when the order clerk completes a session with a customer.
Use Case Authors:	Rene Becnel
Actors:	Order clerk
Locations:	New Port Hills, Washington
Status:	Pathways defined
Priority:	1
Assumptions:	Orders are taken by the order clerk until the customer base is comfortable with the specialized services being provided now.
Preconditions:	Order clerk has logged onto the system.
Postconditions:	- Order is placed. - Inventory is reduced.

Primary Pathway:	Customer calls in and orders a guitar and supplies and pays with a credit card.
Alternate Pathway(s):	- Customer calls in and orders a guitar and uses a P. O.
	- Customer calls in and orders a guitar and uses the Remulak easy finance plan.
	- Customer calls in and orders an organ and pays with a credit card.
	- Customer calls in and orders an organ and uses a P. O.
Exception Pathway(s):	- Customer calls in to place an order using a credit card and the card is invalid.
	- Customer calls in with a P.O. but has not been approved to use the P. O. method.
	- Customer calls in to place an order, and the items desired are not in stock.

Following is the detail for the *Process Orders* happy path (*Customer calls in and orders a guitar and supplies and pays with a credit card*).

1. Customer supplies customer number.

2. Customer is acknowledged as current.

3. For each product that the customer desires:

    3.1 Request product ID or description.

    3.2 Resolve description to ID if necessary.

    3.3 Request quantity.

    3.4 Calculate item price.

4. Calculate extended order total.

5. Apply tax.

6. Apply shipping charges.

7. Supply extended price to the customer.

8. Customer supplies credit card number.

9. Validate customer credit card.

10. Reduce inventory.

11. Finalize and complete the sale.

We need to determine the objects needed to build the first draft of the sequence diagram. We choose from the class diagram in Figure 7-6. Following are the objects selected:

- `Customer`
- `Invoice`
- `Order`
- `OrderHeader`
- `OrderLine`
- `OrderSummary`
- `Payment`
- `Product`

Figure 7-7 shows a first attempt of the sequence diagram for Remulak Productions and the happy path of the *Process Orders* use case. In this view of the sequence diagram, sequence numbers are used to allow easier reference to various messages later. However, sequence numbers

FIGURE 7-6   *First draft of the Remuluk Productions class diagram.*

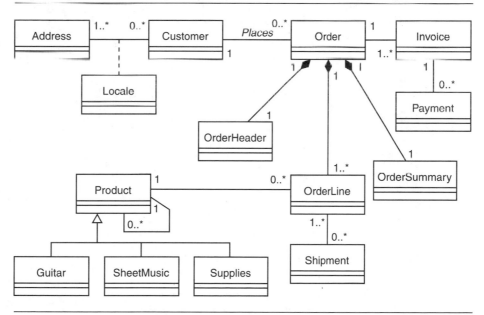

FIGURE 7-7 *First attempt at the Remulak Productions sequence diagram.*

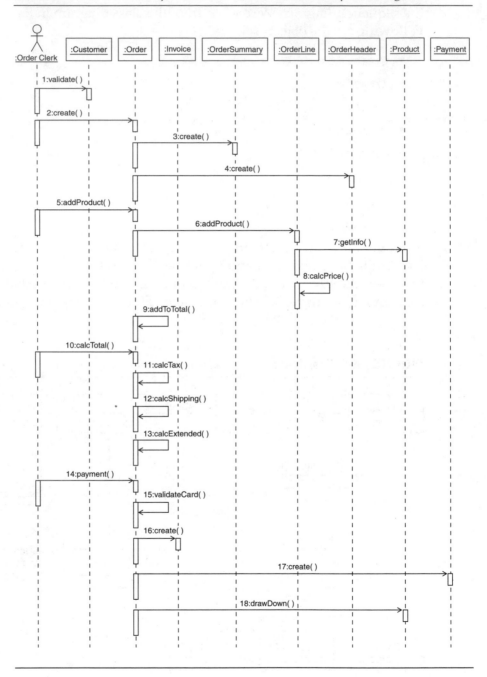

on a sequence diagram are optional, since time flows from top to bottom in such diagrams.

The sequence diagram forces us to ask some serious questions about the other UML artifacts, especially the classes and associations between classes. A message cannot be sent between two objects unless an association is defined between the classes that represent the objects. If a use case pathway requires communication between two objects whose classes have no such association, then the class diagram is incorrect. In addition, early iterations of creating a sequence diagram might require that additional classes be created to satisfy the requirements specified in the pathways. These new classes may be any of the three types discussed in Chapter 5: entity, interface, and control.

The sequence diagram also forces us to focus on good object-oriented design concepts. As messaging patterns begin to emerge, we will need to address some sound object-oriented design practices. One of these is the notion that classes in the solution set should be *loosely coupled* and *highly cohesive.*

Classes are considered loosely coupled if generally the associations between them are minimal. This doesn't mean that we should skimp on associations. If an association is needed, then by all means we should add it to the model. However, if a new class, usually a control or interface class, can be introduced to funnel messages and thus reduce the overall number of associations, then going this route will make the design more resilient in the long run. This is because every class association has eventual code ramifications in the form of references to other classes; these references are needed to allow messages to pass between the classes. Imagine the impact of a change to the domain and the resulting potential rippling to all of the associations. The amount of code that must be changed might be minimal, but if that code is in the class interface, massive amounts of regression testing might be necessary.

A good place to reduce class coupling is aggregation/composition associations. These, by nature, insulate their components from future changes. As an example, consider in the case of Remulak Productions the composition association between `Order`, `OrderHeader`, `OrderSummary`, and `OrderLine`. `Order` is the "boss"; all messages should flow through the boss if at all possible. Nothing prevents our adding several associations to all of `Order`'s components. However, if the structure of an `Order` later changes, the impact of the change could be substantial.

In the sequence diagram in Figure 7-7, notice that any messages dealing with a component of Order are initially sent to the Order object. Message 3:create() could have originated from the actor Order Clerk, but it actually originates from Order. The same is true for message 6:addProduct(). Although Order will have several "pass-through" shell operations that delegate work to its component parts, the solution is much more flexible.

You also can place classes that reduce coupling in the interfaces between packages (this will be required for Remulak Productions's security, audit, and archiving subsystems). These packages also happen to be use cases. Recall from Chapter 5 that there was a control class created for every use case in Increment One.

A class is considered highly cohesive if it sticks to the adage that "a class should do only one thing and do it well." Consider a class that does too many things. In our case, what if Order directly handles all of the responsibilities of all of its composites? Instead of four classes, we'd have but one. But Order will have taken on responsibilities that far exceed its original charter. The same issues that surfaced regarding coupling also show up with classes that are not highly cohesive. That is, a change to OrderLine processing might impact some of the functionality of OrderHeader and OrderSummary. The design is improved by having each of the four classes continue to do one thing well. We can enable this only by defining them as separate classes.

We learn as we go. In the case of Remulak Productions, some of the messaging didn't work, thereby requiring some changes. The issue here concerns tax calculation and shipping charges. The sequence diagram shows the messages 11:calcTax and 12:calcShipping being sent, privately, to the Order class. However, this raises the question about where to maintain the specific tax and shipping information. Order isn't a good solution. So we need to create a new class that manages not only the rates to charge but also the necessary algorithms to calculate the extended charges. For now, let's call this new class Charge. After further design of the class, we might find that Charge is an ancestor class to more specialized classes in the form of Shipping and Tax.

We also need to modify the message 15:validateCard(). The Order class isn't very smart regarding credit card validation—and it shouldn't be (remember: do one thing and one thing well). Thus the Order object should not receive the 15:validateCard() message. Recall from Chapter 5 that we identified the interface class

CreditCardInterface. This is the object that should receive the 15:validateCard() message.

One last observation about the sequence diagram: It doesn't reflect the iterative nature of buying multiple products. At present, the diagram applies to just one product. To make it more flexible, we add the ability to note iteration. We do this by simply adding a note and then referencing the exact sequences that can repeat. See Figure 7-8.

Sequence Diagram for an Alternate Pathway

Now that we've modeled the happy path with a sequence diagram, doing an alternate pathway is easy. Let's look at one of the alternate pathways for the *Process Orders* use case *(Customer calls in and orders a guitar and supplies and pays with a P. O.)*. The sequence diagram for the happy and alternate pathways differ only in the message 15:validateCard, as shown in Figure 7-9. We need a message sent back to the order clerk that validates the *authorization* and *good-thru-date* components of the Payment class. Figure 7-9 shows the sequence diagram for this alternate pathway of the *Process Orders* use case.

Although our biggest job generally will be diagramming the happy path, this could change depending on the complexity of the alternate pathways. Also, depending on the granularity of the project's use cases, the alternate pathways might be very distinct.

Transferring Knowledge to the Class Diagram

The power and benefits that result from using a visual modeling tool really become evident during the creation of sequence diagrams. (Note: VB's visual modeler does not support this.) Leading modeling products allow operations to be added dynamically to the classes represented by the objects on the diagram. This is fine, but its impact enforces two key elements of good project management and software design.

1. As operations are added to the classes, subsequent messages to the same class instance will display that newly added operation, thereby allowing it to be selected from the list. This forces us to focus on reusing existing operations instead of working in a vacuum and duplicating work.

2. Most class operations will be defined just by diagramming the happy path for each use case. The speed with which we diagram can increase a lot as the first few sequence diagrams take shape.

FIGURE 7-8 *The Remulak Productions sequence diagram with iteration.*

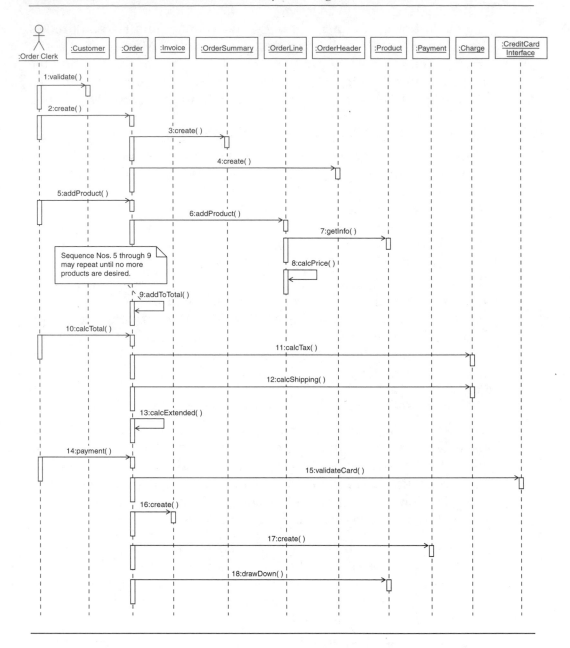

FIGURE 7-9   *The Remulak Productions sequence diagram for the alternate pathway.*

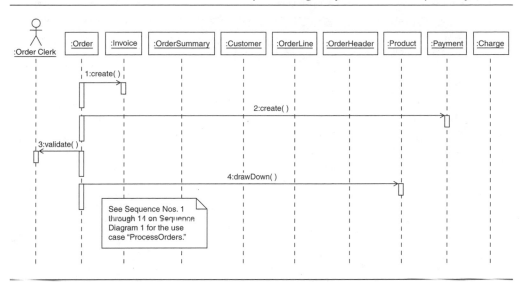

Figure 7-10 shows the use of Rational Rose to add or select operations during the sequence diagramming process. A new operation can be added by clicking the <new operation> option, which opens the operation creation dialog box. Also under the <new operation> option is a list of operations already present in the `Order` class (`calcExtended()` and `calcTax()`) from which we can select.

Also notice the diagram's tree view pane in the upper-left corner of the window. The *Process Orders* use case shows in the tree view; beneath it is a list of its sequence diagrams. The organization of the tree reinforces the steps taken in the Synergy process. What initially start out as events become pathways through a use case. Those pathways eventually are rendered as sequence diagrams that show the dynamic interaction of objects necessary to realize the goal of the use case.

Walking the Sequence Diagram

We still need to create a sequence diagram that shows how the user interface will communicate with the essential use case pathway of

FIGURE 7-10   *Rational's Rose visual modeling tool.*

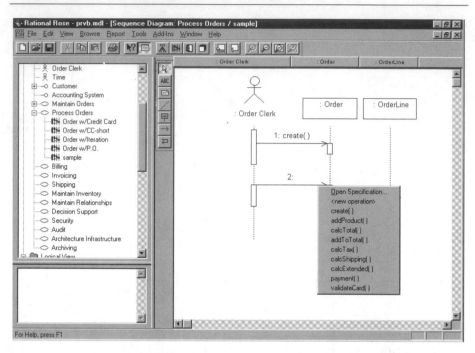

placing an order. We will do this in Chapter 10 . We turn our attention now to using the sequence diagram to walk-through the application to ensure its integrity. The sequence diagram is the primary vehicle for walk-throughs. Code walk-throughs become less of an issue when using the UML.

Although sound coding standards are still necessary (how will variables be defined?, how are classes defined?), the integrity of the system is depicted through the perspective of the sequence diagram. Once the project team gets used to the idea, it will become an invaluable task on the project plan.

The Collaboration Diagram

The collaboration diagram is the direct cousin of the sequence diagram. They differ only in their perspectives. The collaboration diagram has an "on top, looking down" view of the interaction. It focuses more on the actual objects and their roles in the interaction versus the linear flow of time expressed in the sequence diagram. Figure 7-11 shows a collaboration diagram of the *order with credit card* pathway.

Here is where sequence numbers become important. Whereas the sequence diagram works just fine without them, the collaboration diagram is useless without them because the order of the messages gets lost. The collaboration diagram offers a perspective of just how busy

FIGURE 7-11   *Collaboration diagram for the* order with credit card *pathway.*

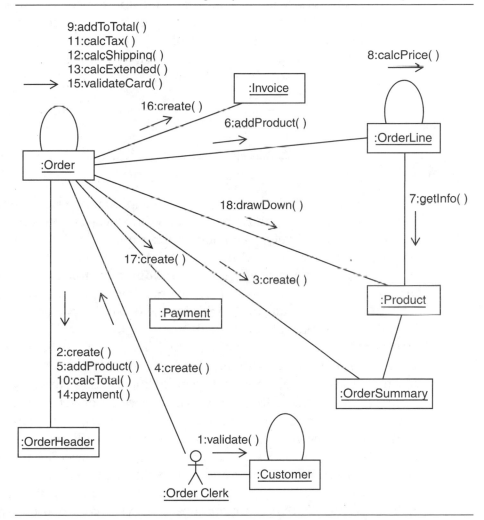

certain objects can be: sending messages, receiving messages, or both. An object being busy can mean that its lifecycle might be interesting and thus the project might benefit from a state diagram of it. State diagrams are discussed in the next section.

Some visual modeling tools will create a collaboration diagram directly from a sequence diagram. When using Rational Rose, you need only to have a sequence diagram open in a window and then click from the menu Browse | Create Collaboration Diagram. Rose also makes it easy to toggle back and forth between both types of diagrams.

Collaboration diagrams make it a bit easier to model complex branching conditions and the concept of multiple concurrent threads of activity. A thread identifier can be added to the sequence number, as well as merging and splitting of control.

I usually use a sequence diagram rather than a collaboration diagram, perhaps because I have used it much longer. Also, I think that it's clearer to the casual observer.

The State Diagram

Of the UML diagrams, the state diagram has probably been around the longest. Its initial uses had nothing to do with object-oriented concepts. In the design and development of complex integrated circuits, a model was needed that minimized the complexity of the various states that the system could be in at any specified moment in time. More important, the model needed to show the events that the system responded to when in a given state, and the type of work to be performed when the system changed states.

The state diagram can be a valuable tool. Today, we use them to model the lifecycle of one class (although the UML also supports the notion of sending events to other classes while modeling a class as to state). Think of the state diagram as the model that follows an object from birth to death (its final conclusion). As mentioned previously, many classes are uninteresting concerning state. For example, most of Remulak Productions's classes are rather mundane regarding their various states. Consider Customer. What states could it be in? Maybe Prospect, Active, and Inactive? Could we learn very much about the domain of Customer by modeling it in a state diagram and observing the work that the system needs to carry out as an object transitions from state to state? Probably not. The Order class is a little different. An Order object will go through many different states in its lifetime and will be influenced by many different events in the system. In addition, quite a bit of work needs to be done as an Order arrives at a given state, stays in a given state, and finally moves on to another state. In this section, we create a state diagram for the Order class, modeled for Remulak Productions.

In its simplest form, a state diagram consists of a set of states connected by transition lines (the subtleties of nested states and concurrent models are outside the scope of this book). On each transition line are captured (usually) events that stimulate an object to transition from one state to another. In addition, work also occurs during a transition—when the object enters or exits a state—and while the object stays in a given state. This takes the form of actions (uninterruptible tasks) and activities (interruptible tasks). Last, a state diagram can capture state variables that are needed for implementing the diagram (we don't do this for our example).

The process of modeling the state of a class is quite straightforward.

1. Identify states.
2. Select the happy path of any use case that utilizes the class.
3. Impose the context of the pathway on the state diagram.
4. Select another pathway from the same use case or a different use case until little additional knowledge remains to be learned.

Not all classes warrant a state diagram, for example those in most business-oriented applications. (Although this conclusion is a very broad generalization, I have found this case to be fairly consistent.) Following are some of the types of classes that usually warrant further exploration with a state diagram.

1. A class that takes on the role of "controller" (it might be quite dynamic in nature)
2. A class that appears to generate and/or receive high volumes of messages (as identified by the sequence or collaboration diagram)
3. A class that takes on the role of "interface" (such as an interface that represents a facade to a complex subsystem)
4. A class that has many different states that the domain is interested in capturing and that are relevant to the context of the application

Modeling the State Diagram of the Remulak Productions Order Class

Figure 7-12 shows the state diagram for the Remulak Productions Order class.

We can learn much from this state diagram. The event *Initiate Order* gets the ball started. It then transitions the Order to the Empty Order state. Upon entry, the system must perform an action, which is to "initialize order." Table 7-1 depicts the different types of work that can be performed and the different ways to model them.

As soon as the first line item is added (Add Item(1)), the Order transitions to the Adding Body state. Notice that there is a self-transition back

FIGURE 7-12   *State diagram for the Remulak Productions Order class.*

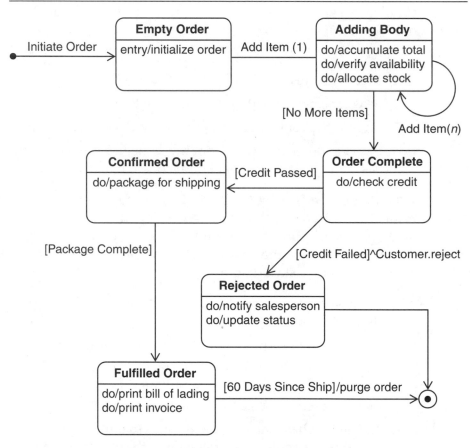

TABLE 7-1   *State Diagram Notation Elements*

Kind Of Action/Activity	Purpose	Syntax
External transition	Action to be performed during the transition from one state to another	Event/Action
Internal transition	Action to be performed in response to an event but while in the current state with no resulting transition	Event/Action
Entry	Action to be performed upon entry to a state	Entry/Action
Exit	Action to be performed upon leaving a state	Exit/Action
Idle	Activity to be performed while in a given state	Do/Activity

to the same state as additional items are added (Add item(n)). Next, note that we use a guard condition (no more items). Recall from the earlier discussion about the sequence diagram that a guard condition is a means to show condition checking and branching. The authors of the UML kindly used similar syntax constructs across many of the models.

Next, if the credit check fails ((credit failed)), then a special format is used to communicate with another object: ^Customer. reject. This is actually an event directed to the given Order's Customer object. This is the UML mechanism for signaling other objects while modeling the state of another class.

Note, too, how the Order eventually falls off the "radar screen"; that is, it reaches the final state, as noted by the bull's-eye in the figure. Assuming all goes well, then once the guard condition is met (60 days have transpired since shipment), the Order reaches its final state and will be purged. (The object also can reach its final state by being rejected because of bad credit.)

Modeling a class with a state diagram reveals the following.

1. Many of the events will result in the modeling of operations in the class.

2. All work (actions and activities) will result in the modeling of operations in the class. Many of the operations will be private to the class.

3. All messages to other objects (`^class.event`) will result in an operation being defined on the target class.

4. Any state variables identified will end up as member variables in the class that is being modeled. However, many of the variables will not be persisted during a single use of the system. Their purpose might be only to sustain a given state.

Alternative Way to View State Diagrams

A state diagram can be viewed in an alternative way, as a table. Although not an official UML view, it represents the same information. Some practitioners prefer it to a state diagram, especially when the state diagram is very complex and therefore becomes difficult to read. Table 7-2 is a table form of the state diagram in Figure 7-12.

TABLE 7-2   *State Information in Table Format*

Starting State	Event/Action	Ending State	Action/Activity
Null state	Initiate Order/Null	Empty Order	Enter/initialize order.
Empty Order	Add items(1)/Null	Adding Body	Do/accumulate total. Do/verify availability. Do/allocate stock.
Adding Body	No more items/Null	Order Complete	Do/check credit.
Adding Body	Add Item(n)/Null	Adding Body	Do/accumulate total. Do/verify availability. Do/allocate stock.
Order Complete	Credit Passed/Null	Confirmed Order	Do/package for shipping.
Order Complete	Credit Failed/ ^Customer.reject	Rejected Order	Do/notify salesperson. Do/update status.
Confirmed Order	Package Complete/ Null	Fulfilled Order	Do/print bill of lading. Do/print invoice.
Rejected Order	"automatic"	Final State	Null.
Fulfilled Order	60 days since ship /purge order	Final State	Null.

The table form also is a great way to document the dynamic nature of the VB Forms that will implement the user interface. The big difference is that the events are very user interface-oriented (button-clicked) and the actions are geared to the user interface (for example, load list box or disable text field).

The Activity Diagram

The activity diagram is the "new kid on the block," a special form of state diagram. Each state is considered an *activity state* that executes and then progresses to the next activity state. An activity diagram models workflows, computations, and complex operation steps.

Activity diagrams also are beneficial during the use case definition process. Pathways within the use cases can be easily modeled with an activity diagram (rather than an alternative outline format). Figure 7-13

FIGURE 7-13   *Activity diagram for* checkCredit *operation in the* Order *class.*

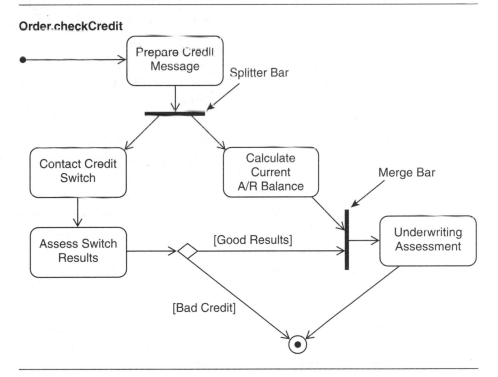

Order.checkCredit

shows an activity diagram for the `checkCredit` operation in the Remulak Productions `Order` class.

The activity diagram resembles a flowchart; notice that it includes a decision diamond. The presence of "merge" and "split" bars makes it very convenient to model concurrent activities and synchronization points.

Activity diagrams focus on the *what* of the flow, and not the *how*. For example, the activity state of *Prepare Credit Message* tells us what to do, but not how to do it.

Selecting the Right Diagram

As stated previously, the dynamic nature of the application domain can be viewed via four diagrams: the two interaction diagrams (sequence and collaboration), the state diagram, and the activity diagram. When should you use which one?

1. **Sequence diagram**: Use for the majority of your dynamic modeling as it pertains to the use case pathways. The big payback here is the creation of the operational signatures for the classes in the application.

2. **Collaboration diagram**: Use when the application includes complex branching dialogs that don't render well in the sequence diagram. (I rarely produce collaboration diagrams, instead opting for the more familiar and more orderly sequence diagram.)

3. **State diagram**: Useful only for a class that exhibits interesting and complex dynamic behavior. For real-time applications (for example, embedded systems), the ratio of state diagrams to classes will be higher than in non-real-time applications. However, the exact number will depend on the nature of the application. Most applications do not need state diagrams. (The entity classes are usually uninteresting regarding state. Usually, if I produce state diagrams, they are for controller and interface classes.)

4. **Activity diagram**: Can clearly depict a complex workflow. Activity diagrams are easy to read and very understandable to the business community. (I use them a lot during use case definitions. They sometimes produce a clearer picture than a verbal outline format in a use case template.)

The sequence diagram is the most commonly used, with the other three used only as needed. The project plan for Remulak Productions in Appendix E shows all four as tasks on the project plan. However, there they serve only as reminders that their use should be considered at this point.

Non-UML Extensions in the Design: Usage Matrices

The UML provides great artifacts that aid traceability from start to finish; however, they don't directly clarify the distributed or throughput requirements of the application. Although component and deployment diagrams can model the notion of "location," applications need a set of views that deal specifically with network and database loadings and distribution. The good news is that the input to this effort comes directly from the use cases, class diagram, and sequence diagrams; thus the project still weaves in traceability. These non-UML diagrams I call usage matrices. There are three types of matrices:

- Event/frequency
- Object/location
- Object/volume

Event/Frequency Matrix

The **event/frequency matrix** applies volumetric analysis to the events the system will automate. It begins to establish a basis for what will become important decisions about the location of both program code and data. The matrix applies to any application, regardless of whether the requirements call for distributed elements. Even if only one location will be served, this form of matrix will still present a network loading picture to the operations staff.

This form of matrix has as its input the event table created during the initial project scoping effort. Recall from Chapter 3, when we did project scoping for Remulak Productions, that we added more columns to the event table that attempted to capture the frequency information, albeit informally. This matrix also adds the element of location to the picture. The goal is to ask questions concerning throughput and growth spread over the dynamic spectrum of current and potential geographical locations. Table 7-3 is an event/frequency matrix (abbreviated) for Remulak Productions. This is an incomplete list of events and the growth percentage is specified as "per year."

Some of this information surfaced early during the project charter effort and by now has been refined and made more accurate. For example, early in the project, the number of changed orders was much lower. Further research has caused that number to increase tremendously.

Notice the column that represents a proposed East Coast location for Remulak Productions. Although this location isn't operational yet, we can take it into account when devising the final architecture solution and thereby improve the solution.

In a networked environment, an application's throughput is a function of not so much the media being used (fiber) or the data link layer being deployed (frame relay) but rather of the abuse that the application will inflict on the network technology. Granted, if the application will require subsecond response times to countries that have no communications infrastructure, then the network technology itself has a large impact. However, the very act of trying to collect these types of statistics might prove very difficult at best, and wrong information can be disastrous.

The operations element of the project might not care about 1,000 orders per day, but if 90% of those happen between 8:00 A.M. and 9:00 A.M., then that will raise their curiosity as a potential problem to be addressed. So, the application can be more effective by capturing potential peak hour frequency, input that will be much more meaningful to the operations staff.

TABLE 7-3   *Event/Frequency Matrix for Remulak Productions*

Event/Location	Newport Hills, Wash.	Raleigh, N. C. (proposed)
	Frequency ‖ Growth (% per year)	**Frequency ‖ Growth (% per year)**
Customer Places Order	1,000/day ‖ 20%	200/day ‖ 40%
Shipping Clerk Sends Order	700/day ‖ 20%	130/day ‖ 40%
Customer Buys Warranty	60/day ‖ 5%	10/day ‖ 10%
Customer Changes Order	200/day ‖ 20%	80/day ‖ 20%
Supplier Sends Inventory	10/day ‖ 10%	3/day ‖ 10%

Based on the numbers and the anticipated growth rates, decisions will be made that affect the following:

1. Where the processes (objects) that actually satisfy the events will reside

2. The communications infrastructure that might need to be in place to satisfy the desired throughput levels

3. Component granularity (the number of EXEs and DLLs and how the classes are packaged)

Eventually, we will be able to approximate just what the *Customer Places Order* event is in terms of the amount of information moving across the "pipe." This is ultimately what the network staff will require. However, it can simulate different loadings so as to anticipate potential bottlenecks much earlier than most project teams realize.

Object/Location Matrix

The **object/location matrix** focuses on the potential location in which various objects may need to reside to meet performance criteria. The matrix is really useful when multiple locations will require access to the application. For this matrix to be effective, we need information about not only the locations but also the kind of access that the objects will require.

The object/location matrix captures two dimensions of the application concerning objects and locations:

- Breadth of object access, where

  A = All object occurrences

  S = Subset of object occurrences (specify subset)

- Pattern of object access, where

  R = Read-only (no operations require update activity)

  U = Update (implies all possible types of operations, including read)

In the current case, Remulak Productions wants the Newport Hills facility to have update access (U) to all objects in the system (A), including the proposed new location at Raleigh. The Raleigh location will need read-only access (R) to all objects in the system (A), but it will be able to update (U) only those objects that are serviced at Raleigh (S). An 800 number will enable customers to reach a dynamic call routing system that is based on the calling area code and that will shuttle calls to the appropriate call center. Table 7-4 is an object/location matrix for Remulak Productions.

This matrix quickly paints a picture of eventual object distribution in the system and the ultimate determination of how any database replication strategies might be laid out. Specifically, the object/location matrix influences decisions that will affect the following.

- Where physical objects will reside in the application. Unless the application is going to use an object-oriented database, which

TABLE 7-4   *Object/Location Matrix for Remulak Productions*

Object/Location	Newport Hills, Wash.	Raleigh, N. C. (proposed)
Customer	AU	AR,SU
Order	AU	AR,SU
OrderHeader	AU	AR,SU
OrderLine	AU	AR,SU
OrderSummary	AU	AR,SU
Shipment	AU	AR,SU
Address	AU	AR,SU
Locale	AU	AR,SU
Invoice	AU	AR,SU
Payment	AU	AR,SU
Product	AU	AR,SU
Guitar	AU	AR,SU
SheetMusic	AU	AR,SU
Supplies	AU	AR,SU

AU: update access to all object occurrences allowed

AR: read access to all object occurrences allowed

SU: update access to a subset of object occurrences

Remulak will not, this decision will affect the design of the underlying relational database.

- Data segmentation and distribution strategies, such as replication and extraction policies.

Common patterns found in the matrix will lead to specific solutions (or at least consideration of them). A classic pattern, which does not show up in the Remulak Productions object/location matrix, is one location that has update access to all object occurrences (AU), with the remaining sites having read access to all object occurrences (AR). This pattern might be common when code tables and, in some cases, inventory are housed and managed centrally. It usually leads to some type of database snapshot extraction approach by which locations get refreshed copies of a master database.

Another similar pattern involves one location that has update access to all object occurrences (AU), with the remaining sites having read access to their own unique subset (SR). Depending on the database technology being chosen, such as Oracle or Microsoft SQL Server, many of these issues can be dealt with by using out-of-the-box solutions.

Object/Volume Matrix

The **object/volume matrix** is intended primarily to look at the number of objects used at specific locations and their anticipated growth rate over time. It is beneficial for single- or multi-location application requirements. Like the object/location matrix, it uses the same x- and y axis (object and location). Table 7-5 is the object/volume matrix for Remulak Productions.

The object/volume matrix will affect several areas of the design, including the following.

- Server sizing, as it pertains to both the database server and the application server that might house the application's business rule services layer. The sizing pertains not only to disk storage but also to memory and CPU throughput and quantity of CPUs per server.

- Database table size allocations, free space, and index sizing. Also affected will be the logging activities and how often logs are cycled, as well as backup and recovery strategies, given the volumes expected at a given location.

TABLE 7-5   *Object/Volume Matrix for Remulak Productions*

Object/Location	Newport Hills, Wash.	Raleigh, N. C. (proposed)
	Volume (100s) ‖ Growth (% per year)	Volume (100s) ‖ Growth (% per year)
Customer	750 ‖ 20%	150 ‖ 60%
Order	1,400 ‖ 25%	275 ‖ 30%
OrderHeader	1,400 ‖ 25%	275 ‖ 25%
OrderLine	3,400 ‖ 35%	700 ‖ 35%
OrderSummary	1,400 ‖ 25%	275 ‖ 25%
Shipment	2,200 ‖ 10%	500 ‖ 10%
Address	2,000 ‖ 10%	450 ‖ 20%
Locale	2,600 ‖ 10%	600 ‖ 10%
Invoice	1,700 ‖ 25%	500 ‖ 25%
Payment	1,900 ‖ 25%	400 ‖ 25%
Product	300 ‖ 15%	300 ‖ 15%
Guitar	200 ‖ 5%	200 ‖ 5%
SheetMusic	50 ‖ 5%	50 ‖ 5%
Supplies	50 ‖ 5%	50 ‖ 5%

Obviously, for any application, many of these numbers will not be so exact that no changes will be made. They are approximations that allow for planning and implementation tactics for the application.

The usage matrices introduced in this section add additional perspective to the four dynamic UML diagrams. They enforce traceability, as they get their input directly from the artifacts produced earlier in the chapter.

Checkpoint

Where We Have Been

1. The UML offers four diagrams to model the dynamic view of the application domain.

2. The interaction diagrams—sequence and collaboration—are used primarily to model the objects as they interact to satisfy the pathway of a given use case.

3. Sequence diagrams have a longer history than collaboration diagrams and are typically preferred over collaboration diagrams. Both relay the same message, but in different formats. Of all of the UML dynamic diagrams, the sequence diagram is the most heavily used.

4. The state diagram models the lifecycle of one class. These diagrams appear most often in applications that have a real-time element (for example, an embedded system). Often, controller and interface classes might contain interesting state information that can be further detailed through the use of state diagrams.

5. An activity diagram models complex workflows, operations, or algorithms. These diagrams closely follow flowchart notation and can be used to model the pathways through a use case.

6. Usage matrices allow a dynamic view of the application as it deals with loadings from both a network and database perspective.

Where We Are Going Next

In the next chapter, we:

1. Explore the technology landscape as it pertains to projects being implemented today with VB as the solution set.

2. Review the differences between logical and physical tiers and how an application can plan ahead to eventually take advantage of an N-tier solution.

3. Discuss Microsoft's strategy for implementing N-tier solutions, incorporating Distributed Component Object Model (DCOM) concepts.

4. Review the different mechanisms by which tiers can communicate.

5. Explore issues concerning the management of transaction scope with and without using Microsoft Transaction Server (MTS).

6. Examine how to leverage the Internet to migrate portions of the Remulak Productions application to the Web.

CHAPTER 8

The Technology Landscape

Keeping up with technology has always been a concern of Remulak Productions. Chapter 1 presented the preliminary execution architecture of the company's order-processing application, based on what was known at that point in the project. Much of that preliminary architecture still holds true. However, the architectural components set out then dealt more with the technical architecture, that is, the tools and product sets for building and implementing the solution. We have not yet determined the approaches to take for the application architecture and data access architecture. This chapter reconfirms the technology architecture selected earlier and explores options for the other two types of architectures.

GOALS

⟳ Review the need for a sound technical architecture.

⟳ Discuss the application architecture and why separation of services is so critical to the application's resiliency.

⟳ Explore the issues concerning the selection of a data access architecture.

⟳ Review the Microsoft solution options for implementing the different architectures.

- Discuss the mechanisms available for communication to occur among the application's logical layers.

- Explore the Microsoft DCOM (Distributed Component Object Model) and how it enables communication outside of the realm of a single desktop.

- Cover how to manage transactions within the application either internally or via the MTS (Microsoft Transaction Server) solution.

- Discuss how to Internet-enable an application while preserving the layered architecture and the separation of services.

Next Phase of the Elaboration Phase

Prior to exploring the technology landscape of the project, let's revisit the Synergy process model and the project plan for this phase of the project. Figure 8-1 shows the process model, with the focus of the project at this point highlighted.

In this chapter, we focus on the "Finalize Architecture" block, which actually consists of three distinct architectures:

FIGURE 8-1   *Synergy process model and the Elaboration phase.*

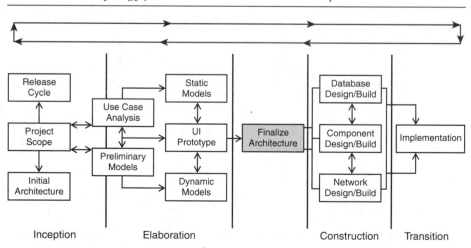

- **Technology**: Deals with the many tools required to construct the application. These include the database technology, construction tools, source control, configuration management, transaction monitor software, and software distribution. Although we might know going into the project which tools to use, focusing on the technology architecture now will serve to confirm that our choices are correct based on what is currently known about the application.

- **Data Access Technology**: Deals with how the data will be accessed in the application, including the database replication technology and the data access infrastructure (native database APIs versus ODBC).

- **Application Technology**: Deals with how to segment the application, including the layering strategy that will separate the various layers of the application and how the layers will be managed.

These three architectures are assessed collectively as to known requirements, and the appropriate mix for the application is selected. This unique set of technology, product, and architecture choices is called the application's **execution architecture**.

Separating Services

Long before client/server and the Internet came into the forefront of technology, the layers of an application were thought best kept distinct and separate. Commingling of, for example, the data access and business logic led to "spaghetti" code that was difficult to maintain and to understand. However, very few applications followed this approach, that is, until the technology horizon changed and client/server and distributed computing became possible.

The term *legacy application* traditionally has characterized mainframe-centric applications. However, many applications built in the past 7 or 8 years that wear the client/server label are also legacy applications because the logical layers of the applications were not separated in their design or implementation. Further exacerbating this situation is the nature of the unique graphical front-end used to build many of these applications, which makes maintaining them more difficult.

Although the concepts of layering functionality are easy to comprehend, we absolutely must make the application architecture extensible and isolate the logical layers of the application. Figure 8-2 depicts those logical layers, and Table 8-1 lists the scope and objective of each.

The Presentation Services layer traditionally is graphical in nature (for the typical reader of this book) but also may take the form of a report or even an external feed to some interface. The GUI (graphical user interface) layer evolves with time. For example, as recently as 1997, few would have thought that the user interface to the Internet would be not a VB form but a browser interacting with the application. If the Presentation Services layer that a given application supported had been separate from the Business Services layer when originally designed, snapping on a new front-end would have involved minimal pain. Unfortunately, for most applications a better solution was to scrap what was there and start over, and that is what many organizations did.

The Business Services layer, and to some degree the Presentation Services layer, will likely be the most dynamic of all of the layers. Years of experience with software development have taught us that an application's rules and functionality change the most. Thus if the Business Services layer is isolated from the other two layers, then changes will impact the application less. When possible, the Business Services layer needs to be void of all user interface and data access logic.

The Data Services layer often will be the most static aspect of the application. The data structures and their relationships are usually less effected by changes compared to the Business Services layer. However, significant change does occur regarding data access. The data might

FIGURE 8-2 *Logical layers of the application architecture.*

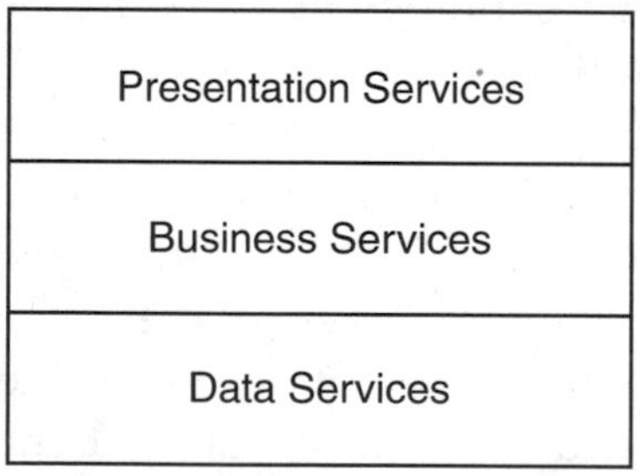

TABLE 8-1   *Scope and Objective of Each of the Logical Layers*

Layer	Scope	Objectives
Presentation Services	Data presentation	Ease of use
	Data acceptance	Natural, intuitive user interactions
	GUI	Fast response times
Business Services	Core business rules	Rigid enforcement of business rules
	Application/dialogue flow control	Preservation of investment in code
	Data integrity enforcement	Reduced maintenance costs
Data Services	Durable data storage and retrieval	Consistent, reliable, secure database
	DBMS accessed via APIs	Information sharing
	Concurrency control	Fast response times

still be in the same repository that it has always been in, for example Microsoft SQL Server or Oracle, but the number of access models varies one or more times a year. The technology options range from native drivers specific to a given database vendor to Microsoft's latest OLE/DB technology using ActiveX Data Objects (ADO). Later in this chapter, we explore the data access services layer closely and segment it further, separating the logical request for data, such as a Structured Query Language (SQL) request, from the physical access technology, such as a Data Access Object (DAO), Remote Data Object (RDO), or ADO. Constructing an application using good object-oriented design concepts can further insulate the layers. Note that the partitioning design presented in this chapter for the different layers relates to the shadow use case called application infrastructure, which is discussed in Chapter 4.

Logical versus Physical Tiering

These three layers are often called *tiers*, or in this case, *three logical tiers*. They might be separated by well-defined interfaces, thereby allowing for less troublesome changes in the future, but they are considered logical because they may be implemented on only *two physical* tiers. Figure 8-3 depicts the notion of logical versus physical tiers.

This very common implementation scheme represents a logical three-tiered solution that is actually implemented on two physical tiers: the client and server. This solution initially served the push into distributed client/server computing quite well, but it soon began to show signs of wear and tear, as follows.

- Increased burden on an organization's infrastructure to distribute software to more and more clients when any part of the application changed and to configure software on more and more clients when new distributions were made. The latter applies especially to the database access component and the troublesome nature of installing and configuring ODBC drivers on multiple machines.

- Nonoptimal transaction throughput as a result of poor resource pooling in the form of database connections. Depending on the physical database technology, the resulting increase in cost could

FIGURE 8-3   *Logical versus physical tiers.*

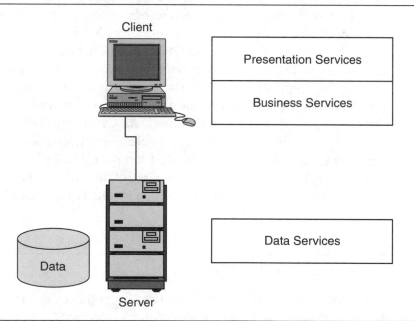

be substantial, as each client workstation required an access license to the database.

- Inappropriate resource utilization because some business service activities (for example, complex mathematical calculations) might not be appropriate for the platform that is serving as the client; if placed there, they could result is poor performance.

Figure 8-4 depicts the same model presented in Figure 8-3, except that it implements the logical layers individually, as three separate physical tiers rather than two.

The figure illustrates where the term *three-tier* derives. One needs to understand the context of the term when used because the individual might be referring to logical rather than physical tiers. Actually, a better name is *N-tier* because multiple physical tiers could be implementing

FIGURE 8-4   *Mapping logical to appropriate physical tiers.*

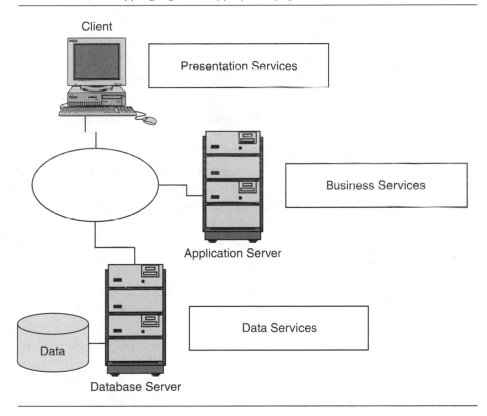

the three logical tiers (multiple Business Service layer servers and multiple Data Services layer servers).

Microsoft's Tiering Strategy

Many options are available to a project team that wants the best and most flexible design strategy. At a minimum, any application built today that wants to be around longer than a year or two without experiencing a major reworking must implement a minimum of three logical tiers. This minimum is specified because the traditional three-tier model needs further categorizing, for the following reasons.

- The Business Services layer actually consists of two types of services: Business Context and Business Rule. The first deals with the user interface as it pertains to filtering and cleansing information as it enters the system, for example a value entered in one field limits the allowable values entered in another field. The other service deals with the more traditional business rules, for example a Remulak Productions customer that places over $10,000 in orders in a given year receives 10% off of its next purchase.

- The Data Services layer actually consists of three types of services: Data Translation, Data Access, and Database. The first deals with translating a logical request for information services (for example, Select, Update, or Delete) into a language that is compatible for the data repository, such as SQL. The second service deals with the execution of the request by some API , such as a native database interface, ADO using OLE/DB, or an ODBC driver. The third service is the actual database technology (Oracle or Microsoft SQL Server).

Figure 8-5 depicts the logical layers that could be used on any application—the *six logical tier model*—along with a description of the services provided at each layer.

The Presentation Services and Database Services layers require the least amount of attention (we have to build forms and design tables, of course). The remaining four layers must be very sound and well built to hold up over time. Actually, if we do our job right, we should easily

FIGURE 8-5   *Six logical tier model.*

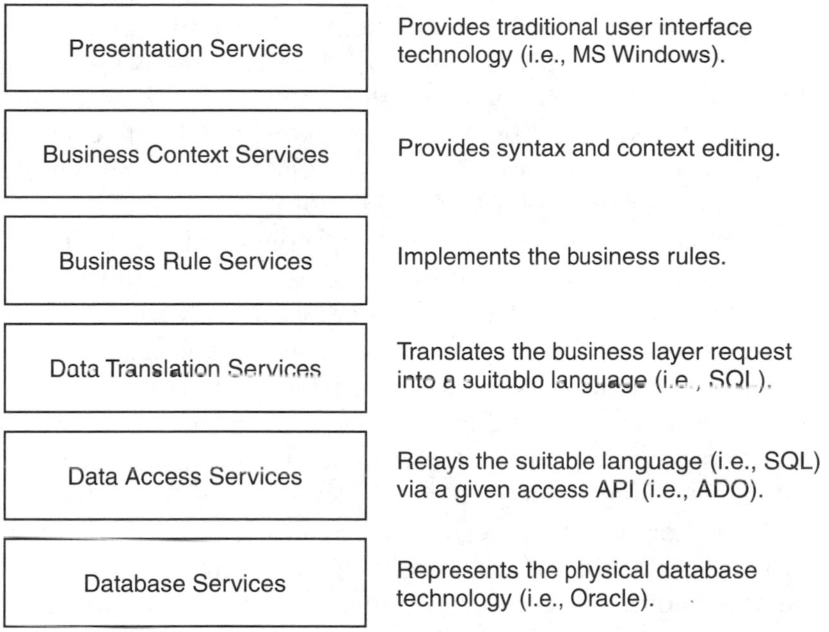

Presentation Services	Provides traditional user interface technology (i.e., MS Windows).
Business Context Services	Provides syntax and context editing.
Business Rule Services	Implements the business rules.
Data Translation Services	Translates the business layer request into a suitable language (i.e., SQL).
Data Access Services	Relays the suitable language (i.e., SQL) via a given access API (i.e., ADO).
Database Services	Represents the physical database technology (i.e., Oracle).

be able to later replace the Presentation Services and Database Services layers with different presentation services such as the Internet and different database technology such as Oracle (to replace Microsoft SQL Server).

Communication among the Six Layers

We need to determine the most appropriate mechanism to enable communication among the six layers. To do so, we first should ask the following questions.

1. What inter-process communication (IPC) technology should be used among the layers?

2. What mechanism should be utilized to communicate among the layers when the IPC is used?

These two questions are addressed in the next two subsections.

Inter-Process Communication Architecture

The IPC mechanism can be handled by any of many different technology options, including native Remote Procedure Calls (RPC) and Common Object Request Broker Architecture (CORBA) technology. However, our technology platform is being built with Microsoft products, so we use Microsoft's Component Object Model (COM) and DCOM (to the builder, DCOM is COM with a "long wire"). Appendix D offers a primer on COM and DCOM.

Microsoft makes building COM-enabled applications very easy. When a component that implements COM is built in VB, the project type is selected up front as either an ActiveX DLL or ActiveX EXE. In this way, VB does a lot of the work automatically. This also allows the project to talk with other COM-enabled applications.

For Remulak Productions, each layer that we implement will be packaged as an ActiveX DLL, with the exception of the Presentation Services layer, which will be implemented as both a Standard EXE (VB forms) or, in some cases, as a Web front-end. Later, some of the components, when distributed, *might* be recompiled as ActiveX EXEs. (When MTS is used, the components might still be distributed, but they are left as ActiveX DLLs. We'll discuss more about MTS later in this chapter.)

Layer Communication Architecture

The second question deals with methods for communicating, from the application's perspective, among the layers. This communication method will use the IPC services (COM/DCOM). Several choices are available.

- Pass individual attributes and objects, as needed, between each layer.

- Pass VB collections, containing attributes and objects, between each layer.

- Pass Variant arrays, containing attributes and objects, between each layer.

- Pass disconnected recordsets (ADO), containing all information needed, between each layer.

- Pass String arrays and attributes between each layer.

Before discussing the pros and cons of each alternative, let's take a look at the "under the covers" story of what goes on when COM components communicate, either locally or remotely (via DCOM).

Inside COM Communication

A COM communication is *in-process* when a VB executable, say the VB forms for Remulak Productions, needs to send a message to an object that resides in an ActiveX DLL, which resides on the client. In-process COM communication is good because it is as fast as communication gets, while still using a solid, logically separated services architecture. Since fast is good, we want as much in-process COM communication as possible.

Every program that executes gets a **call stack**—a place to keep variables as well as registers that keep track of where the next line of code is to execute. Without getting too gory here, any component that is an ActiveX DLL, running in-process, gets to share the same virtual memory space—play in the same backyard, so to speak—that the caller (VB forms EXE) already has allocated. The good news is that we, as VB developers, don't have to worry about how this happens; VB shields us from this. But as soon as an ActiveX component is created as an *out-of-process* component (an ActiveX EXE in most cases), then the whole situation changes; but again, VB shields us from all of this.

Suppose the same Remulak VB forms project invokes an ActiveX component that is now out-of-process. Then the caller must deal with the component inside its own backyard. This event is called a **context switch** and is common in many operating systems. The caller must completely change the context with which it is dealing—its own—and now deal with some other virtual address space. This causes additional overhead to the caller and will, in most cases, extract a bit of performance from the application. The increased complexity results because *marshalling* must take place to ensure that the data that gets passed to the out-of-process component gets translated properly—not only on the way out, but also on the way back in. Figure 8-6 shows an example of what COM must do when dealing with an out-of-process component.

In the figure, the proxy acts as a stand-in for the real object A that has been instantiated as an out-of-process component. The VB program doesn't have a clue, from the developer's view, that the object isn't in its own process space.

FIGURE 8-6 *Out-of-process COM in action.*

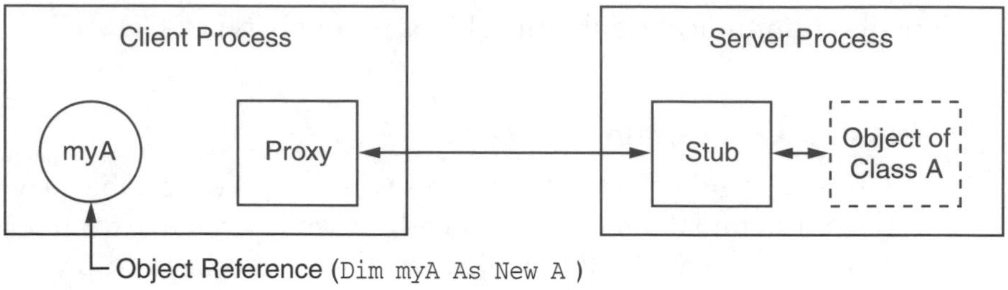

Performance can suffer if the out-of-process component is executed remotely (on another machine). This is where DCOM comes into play. The same scenario in Figure 8-6 also happens when DCOM steps in, except that the Stub and the instantiated object A reside on another machine. When distributed components are used, performance is at the mercy of both the in-place network infrastructure (for example, bandwidth and existing congestion) and how poorly the application uses the network.

We can't control who else uses the network, but we can be careful how we plan to use the network. Following are some practices to absolutely avoid when communicating out-of-process.

- **Do not pass any parameters by reference (ByRef).**

  Common practice is to declare parameters in VB procedures ByRef if they will be used to pass large strings and Variant arrays, even if the procedure doesn't make any changes to the parameter. It's much faster to pass a 4-byte pointer to the data than to copy the entire string or array and pass a pointer to the copy.

  Passing ByRef works within the address space of the invoker's own process space. This is because the method to which you pass the parameter can use the pointer to access the data directly.

  Out-of-process marshalling reverses this practice. Data for a ByRef method argument is copied into the component's address space, and the method is passed a pointer to the local copy of the data.

  The method uses the pointer to modify the copy. When the method completes, the data for any ByRef parameters is copied back into the client's address space. Thus a parameter declared ByRef will be passed out-of-process *twice* per method call.

Declaring a parameter of a method ByRef in an out-of-process component prevents developers who are using the component from avoiding the effects of marshalling (for example, by putting parentheses around the parameter or by using the ByVal (by value) keyword when they call the method). In this case, VB will create a copy of the data, but COM and Automation will have no way of knowing that the data is just a copy. Thus VB will marshal the copy back and forth between processes, and the data ends up being copied a total of three times. Ugly stuff.

- **Do not pass an object or a VB collection**.

   Objects and VB collections that are passed out-of-process are actually passed ByRef and therefore require quite a bit of marshalling.

- **Avoid passing Variant arrays**.

   A Variant array can be sent ByVal, as opposed to ByRef. This aids marshalling, but it also consumes a lot of stack space and therefore carries high overhead. A Variant takes 16 bytes, compared to 2 bytes for an Integer and 8 bytes for a Double. Variable-length String variables use 4 bytes plus 1 byte per character in the string, but a Variant that contains a String takes 16 bytes plus 1 byte per character in the string.

- **Avoid setting object properties individually.**

   When a program sets the properties of an out-of-process object individually, each property set or get will involve a round-trip. Instead of the program's doing this, have one operation that will pass either an array or individual parameters and have the target object set the properties.

Deciding whether to code in-process or out-of-process needs to be considered from the "long view." What you run in-process today might tomorrow be run out-of-process. The in-process versus out-of-process issue is transparent to the code that is invoking the component; with the exception of a few recompiles, no code changes need to be made for the switch to occur. So, code all of your components as if one day they will be out-of-process.

Five Options on Which to Base an Infrastructure Architecture

Five options are available regarding what to pass between each layer in an infrastructure architecture. The following subsections discuss these.

- **Pass Individual Attributes and Objects.**

    Passing individual *attributes* between each layer is partially acceptable. However, passing *objects* is not a good idea, for the reasons discussed previously (all objects get passed ByRef regardless of what you do to avoid this). In addition, if parameters will be passed, it is better to package them as a User-Defined Data Type (UDT) or as a String array of parameters.

- **Pass VB Collections That Contain Attributes and Objects.**

    As indicated earlier in the section, passing VB collections that contain attributes potentially will require quite a bit of marshalling because the VB collection is passed ByRef. Passing objects, too, is not a good idea, for the same reason.

- **Pass Variant Arrays That Contain Attributes and Objects.**

    As mentioned earlier in the section, passing Variant arrays that contain attributes and objects can result in a larger amount of information being sent across the network. However, this method of passing is flexible in that any type of attribute, regardless of data type, can be placed in the Variant array and passed ByVal. (The exception is if the Variant array contains an object, in which case we suffer the same as with pass ByRef.)

    A related approach is use of the PropertyBag object. Using the PropertyBag, objects can be converted to variants or byte arrays and passed.

- **Pass Disconnected Recordsets That Contain All of the Information Needed.**

    Passing disconnected recordsets (ADO) that contain all of the information needed is new with VB v6.0. It allows the database services layer to sever its database connection, after recordset instantiation and retrieval, and pass an ADO recordset back to the client. The information can be manipulated at the client, as if the client is connected, and then passed back to the data layer for application to the database. This approach allows the recordset to be passed ByVal. But it suffers from a long-term downside: If the disconnected recordset technology is later replaced (as is rumored with the Extensible Markup Language (XML) being Microsoft's future format of choice), the technical infrastructure will have to be changed and retested. Also, if the client will be dealing with an ADO recordset and the VB forms are replaced later with a Web-based front-end, then the browser option would be limited to only Microsoft Internet Explorer (although Netscape's Navigator can deal with ActiveX and ADO via a plug-in.) Lastly, I have found the performance of disconnected recordsets very spotty at best. This anomaly seems to be supported by other dialog found on various newsgroups and VB forums.

- **Pass String Arrays and Attributes.**

  As indicated previously, passing String arrays and attributes adds additional sizing overhead because the array will be of a variable length and therefore require a length indicator. However, it has great appeal because all traffic sent between components will use a common denominator to resolve many of the potential problems referred to previously. For example, a multiple-row result set from a query will be packaged in a variable-length, dynamically adjusted String array before being returned from the Data Access Services layer. This approach offers the flexibility that the components need in order to communicate. This architecture is the primary one that we will implement for Remulak Productions to facilitate layer communication.

Managing Transaction Scope within the Application and Microsoft Transaction Server

An application that will interact with any type of data repository can face the somewhat daunting task of managing the **transaction scope**. Transaction scope is the entire process of establishing a database connection, communicating with the resource at the end of the connection, eventually committing any changes made, and then closing the connection.

Managing transaction scope is more difficult if the scope crosses physical database boundaries. For example, suppose that a transaction must update both an Oracle database and a Microsoft SQL Server database within the scope of one transaction and ensure that both servers get updated at the end of the transaction. This is difficult to do because talking to each database product (Oracle and SQL Server) requires a connection to each that must be managed individually. Figure 8-7 depicts a transaction scenario between two database products.

One solution to this problem is to use a **transaction monitor**. A transaction monitor acts as a watchdog over any utilized resources and is delegated the task of monitoring transaction scope. This is where MTS enters the application architecture. However, this is just a small portion of what MTS can do for the application. MTS is reviewed in detail in Chapter 13. Meanwhile, following are some of the many other problems that it addresses.

- **Database connection pooling**: MTS can pool database connections. Sadly, many developers write poor code and in the scope of just one transaction end up with several database connections

FIGURE 8-7   *Transaction scope with two databases.*

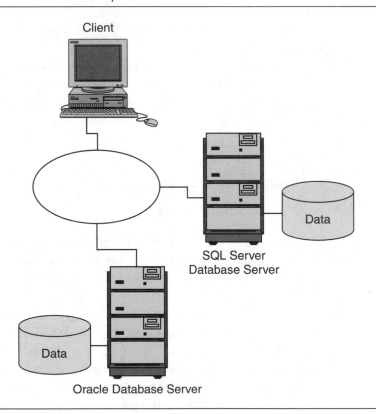

open to a database. Not only does this waste precious memory resources on the client and server; it also can increase the project's cost if the database vendor is charging per connection.

- **Thread pooling**: Each component can be written as if it is single-threaded; MTS will take care of the rest. MTS also leaves threads open, preallocated, to allow for quicker response to clients that request thread activation.

- **Reduction of transaction management logic**: Each transaction must explicitly issue a "begin" transaction and an "end" transaction. In addition, the application must deal with a myriad of return code checks and error handling pertaining to the database with which it is interfacing. MTS takes care of this by virtually connecting transaction components together via a common transaction context.

- MTS offers a **flexible security model** for the application's implementation. Users can be assigned to roles, and then those roles can be assigned to components and interfaces within the components.

MTS can obviously assist the application in reducing the amount of overhead logic and transaction management requirements. On the surface, it appears to be the answer for all transaction management needs. However, sometimes it can be an overkill solution or, worse, not even viable for some applications. Following are some of its characteristics that drive home this point.

- **MTS v2.0 operates only with databases that support OLE transactions.**

    Further, if Oracle also is used, a Microsoft ODBC v3.0 driver also must be used. And if the application requires access to any other database technology, then MTS can't manage the transaction scope.

- **MTS runs primarily on Windows NT platforms (it has only limited running ability on Windows 95/98).**

    If the application doesn't utilize Windows NT as a server platform, then MTS is not a viable solution. Even when running under Windows NT, the application must manage the components remotely under MTS on a Windows NT machine. This means, for example, that if the application is using Microsoft SQL Server on a Windows NT platform and the Business Services

layer is still running on the client, then using MTS doesn't buy
you anything. For smaller applications, and especially those with
only one back-end technology to deal with, MTS might be a
Cadillac solution when a Volkswagen would do.

- **MTS strongly favors stateless objects.**

  By "stateless," it is meant an object that does not keep state
  information (for example, references to variables, other objects,
  and database connections) for longer than absolutely necessary.
  This notion flies in the face of object-oriented programming concepts, which usually espouses stateful objects.

- **MTS does not yet support object pooling.**

  The ability to support object pooling would allow for objects,
  such as `Order` or `Customer`, to be left instantiated and thereby
  readily available for clients. This would be extremely beneficial to
  many larger-scale applications because the overhead for object
  instantiation could be reduced and in some cases removed. Several
  program solutions to this issue in the form of code to preinstantiate
  objects, but these objects must be customized by each application.

  It is rumored that this ability will be part of a future release of
  MTS that is coupled with the release of Windows 2000 and the
  introduction of COM+. (See Appendix D for a review of COM.)

- **MTS does not support load balancing.**

  The ability to support load balancing would allow objects, for
  example `Order` and `Customer`, to be instantiated on multiple
  applications servers, based on how busy the existing component
  hosts were. It also would dynamically direct clients to servers that
  are available for hosting object instances based on current system
  loadings.

  It is rumored that this ability, too, will be part of a future release
  of MTS that is coupled with the release of Windows 2000 and the
  introduction of COM+. (See Appendix D for a review of COM.)

Despite the pros and cons regarding MTS-enabled applications, the
direction and emphasis that Microsoft places on the technology attests
that MTS will continue to be integrated into core product architectures.
However, for smaller applications, MTS is clearly overkill. To deal with
this, we will implement both types of transaction management solutions
for Remulak Productions. This will allow you to use whatever mecha-

nism best suits their needs. We also will leverage some areas with well-defined interfaces to ease future transition into an MTS environment by applications that did not choose to initially utilize the technology.

Incorporating the Internet into the Solution

Chapters 6 and 7 both commented on Remulak Productions's need for Internet access by some of its use case pathways. The goal was to Web-enable the order inquiry functionality of the application. This would enable customers to check on the status of their orders without human intervention, while still allowing Remulak the control it feels it needs to actually place the orders.

The Internet plays a large role in the solution strategies from Microsoft and will continue to do so well into the future. In fact, the Internet is so key to these strategies that Microsoft has given it its own unique name: DNA, or Distributed Internet Application Architecture. DNA's technology goal is to serve as a relationship between the three logical layers addressed earlier in this chapter.

Figure 8-8 reviews the architecture for enabling DNA, matching technology features with the layers. Some of the technologies are not in their final form (for example, COM+). However, to implement applications based on the concept of DNA capabilities is very much a reality.

FIGURE 8-8   *DNA architecture strategy.*

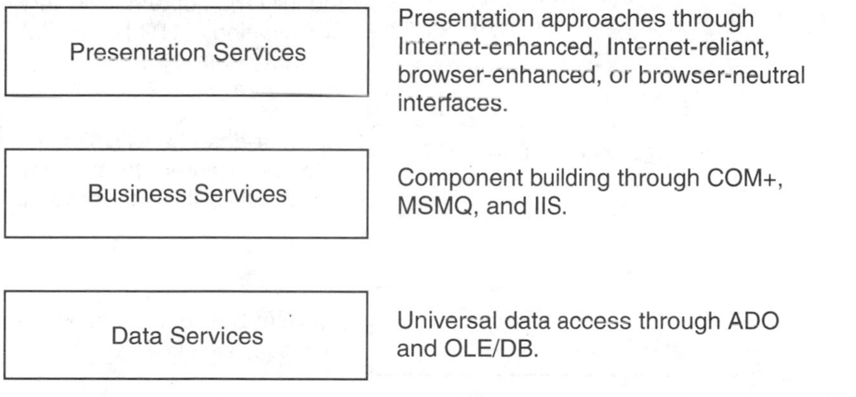

Presentation Services	Presentation approaches through Internet-enhanced, Internet-reliant, browser-enhanced, or browser-neutral interfaces.
Business Services	Component building through COM+, MSMQ, and IIS.
Data Services	Universal data access through ADO and OLE/DB.

We need to decide on the DNA presentation approach to use for the order entry application for Remulak Productions. DNA options range from EXE-based to Page-based. We will need solutions from both ends of this spectrum. This is addressed in more detail shortly.

- The Presentation Services layer suggested by DNA consists of four scenarios, illustrated in Figure 8-9. We will use a variation of two of these to deliver the Remulak Productions user interface.

- The Business Services layer will use both COM and MTS. COM+ will eventually incorporate MTS under its umbrella. Actually, all of our components will talk COM. Remember that COM is our IPC protocol for the application.

- The Data Services layer will utilize ADO and OLE/DB to implement the navigational and connectivity infrastructure. This is the easiest of all of the decisions to make. ADO provides a rich interface to the application, and OLE/DB provides the ability to connect later to nonrelational data stores, if needed.

FIGURE 8-9   *DNA Presentation Services layer strategy.*

Internet-Enhanced "a connectable application"	Non-browser-based application that utilizes the Win32 API, while still Internet-enabling the application via hosting a Web browser and/or hosting hyperlinks within the application.
Internet-Reliant "a connected application"	Non-browser-based application that utilizes the full range of Windows services. Uses a combination of HTML, DHTML, Scripting, and ActiveX controls.
Browser-Enhanced "a dynamic Web application"	Browser-based application that utilizes Internet Explorer. Uses a combination of HTML, DHTML, and Scripting.
Browser-Neutral "a basic Web application"	Browser-based application that utilizes any browser. Uses HTML.

Initially, all of the presentation services will be implemented as standard executables, with the addition of a hyperlink to Remulak Productions in the About dialog box and a hyperlink to the trouble-ticket system of Remulak Productions on the Internet (in a future version). This layer is considered Internet-enhanced.

The order inquiry function, represented by the *Process Order* use case, will be available via the Internet, in addition to being supported via standard VB forms. Remulak Productions, however, cannot dictate which Web browser a client will use, so we will test the application's functionality using the two most common browsers: Microsoft's Internet Explorer and Netscape's Navigator. The *Process Order* use case pathway will support the browser-enhanced model because JavaScript can be used to add more dynamic abilities to the page.

This browser-enhanced functionality for order inquiry will require an interface of some type between the Web page and the Business Services layer. This interface will consist of Active Server Pages (ASP) that will run on an Internet Information Server (IIS). The ASP will actually act as both the interface and controller of the process. They will have to broker the request from the browser and then instantiate and message to the appropriate object to return information suitable for building a return HTML reply. Figure 8-10 is an overview of the Internet architecture.

FIGURE 8-10   *The Remulak Productions Internet strategy.*

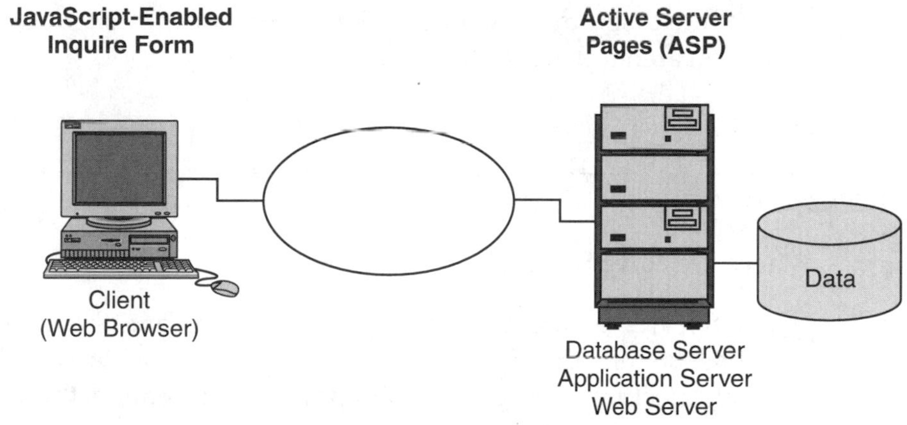

JavaScript-Enabled
Inquire Form

Active Server
Pages (ASP)

Client
(Web Browser)

Data

Database Server
Application Server
Web Server

FIGURE 8-11   *Summary of the execution architecture.*

Presentation Services	• Visual Basic Standard EXE • HTML and Scripted Forms
Business Context Services	• Visual Basic Standard EXE • Active Server Pages (Internet)
Business Rule Services	• Visual Basic ActiveX DLL or EXE • Managed Traditionally or by MTS
Data Translation Services	• Visual Basic ActiveX DLL or EXE • Managed Traditionally or by MTS • SQL
Data Access Services	• Visual Basic ActiveX DLL or EXE • Managed Traditionally or by MTS • ADO and OLE/DB (native and ODBC)
Database Services	• Microsoft SQL Server (production) • Oracle (investigate)

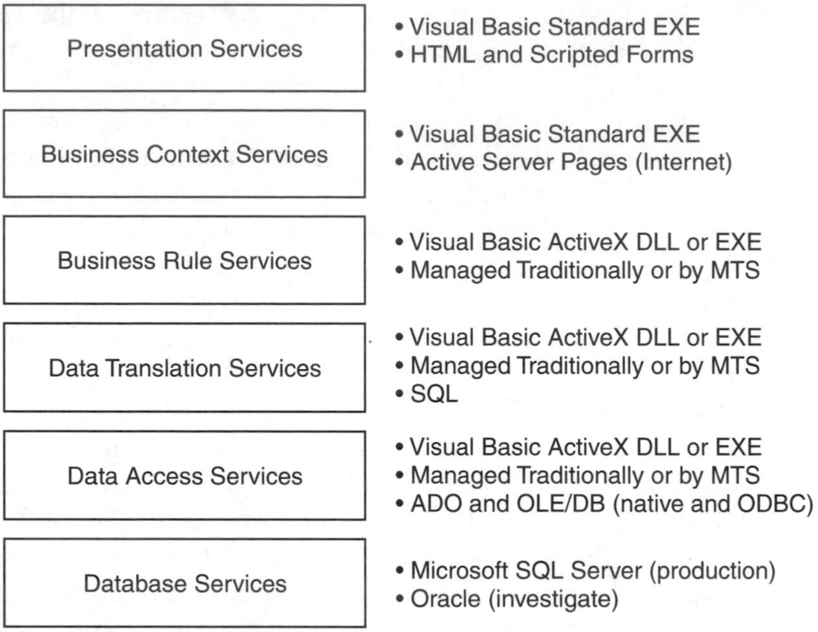

Remulak Productions Execution Architecture

We have had quite a technology discussion in this chapter. We could use a summary of what is on the table for us to implement. Figure 8-11 is the same diagram presented in Figure 8-5, except that it outlines the execution architecture for Remulak Productions.

Checkpoint

Where We Have Been

1. After the requirements have been solidified and the design work has begun, three architectures must be considered. The final architecture selected for the application is called the execution architecture.

2. The IPC mechanism can be handled by any of many different technology options. This project will use COM as its standard.

3. Many mechanisms are available for communicating between the layers of the application. All have strengths and weaknesses. The one with the most appeal for Remulak Productions passes String arrays and attributes.

4. Transaction management is the ability of the application to ensure that changes are either committed to the database, if all goes as planned, or rolled back and discarded otherwise. MTS provides this ability. Remulak Productions will utilize MTS as well as traditional transaction management techniques.

5. The Internet offers an audience unlike any the technology industry has ever known. Remulak Productions's use of the Internet will consist primarily of enabling customers to link to its Web site and to inquire about their outstanding orders.

Where We Are Going Next

In the next chapter, we:

1. Explore the issues regarding transitioning from the logical perspective offered by the design view of the class diagram to the physical persistence layer (this assumes the existence of a relational database).

2. Review the issues concerning the use of a visual modeling tool such as Rational's Rose to generate a DDL from the class diagram.

3. Discuss how to translate inheritance modeled on the class diagram to a table structure and how to translate aggregation/composition on the class diagram to a table structure.

4. Explore how to keep the class diagram and tables in sync.

5. Review the benefits and weaknesses of implementing the query access as stored procedures and triggers.

CHAPTER 9

Data Persistence: Storing the Objects

We have now reached a significant point in the Remulak Productions's project lifecycle. In the next several chapters, we will consider many traditional design issues. Iterative development fosters the notion of learning a little, designing a little, and then constructing a little. In this chapter, we construct the necessary database components to implement the physical tables for the Remulak Productions solution.

GOALS

- ⮕ Review the issues encountered when mapping the class diagram to a relational database management system (RDBMS).
- ⮕ Discuss the mapping of simple associations to table structures.
- ⮕ Explore the options when mapping generalization/specialization hierarchies to the table structures.
- ⮕ Discuss the mapping of aggregation and composition to table structures.
- ⮕ Explore how to select the proper key structure for tables and for normalization issues.
- ⮕ Review how visual modeling tools generate data definition language (DDL) statements for the database.

↬ Discuss how to improve the output from visual modeling tools to better approximate the final generated DDL.

↬ Review the pros and cons of using stored procedures and triggers to implement aspects of the data layers.

↬ Explore the pros and cons of using VB's data-aware classes for the data layers.

↬ Examine the Data Translation and Data Access Services layers.

Construction Phase

Before venturing into the Construction phase as it pertains to the database, let's revisit the Synergy process model and the project plan for this phase of the project. Figure 9-1 shows the process model, with the focus of the project at this point highlighted.

Although the Construction phase considers several different areas of focus, in this chapter we focus on the following:

• The "Database Design/Build" block, which deals with transitioning from the class diagram created for Remulak Productions to a

FIGURE 9-1 *Synergy process model and the Construction phase.*

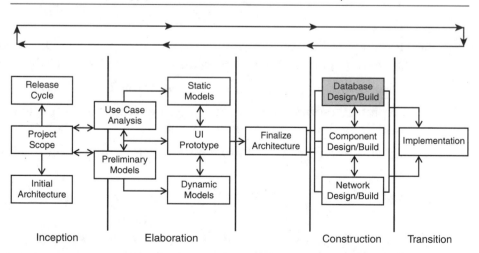

design that can support a relational database. Microsoft SQL Server is our initial target, but we will also test the database against an Oracle implementation.

The database design, and its transformation from the class diagram, is critical not only to the other layers that will request the services of the database, but also to the performance of the database in a production environment.

Object-Oriented Concepts and Translating to the Physical Design

Until now, we haven't needed to translate what we modeled with the UML into something that isn't object-oriented in order to implement the application. To some degree, we addressed this when reviewing VB's lack of implementation inheritance and how we might physically implement it (which we do in Chapter 11). However, the implementation inheritance issue didn't require that much handling. The same is not always true for the transition necessary from the class diagram to an entity relationship diagram (ERD).

The next several sections deal with many aspects of this transition. We assume that the repository being used as the persistence layer is some type of RDBMS. Most issues addressed here don't come up if the persistence layer is going to be an object-oriented database management system (OODBMS). OODBMSs are still by far the minority (although I encounter them more and more often in my consulting practice). Most applications that utilize an OODBMS are also using C++, Java, or Smalltalk as their language implementation. This is primarily because OODBMS vendors usually directly support bindings between their products and those languages; this doesn't mean that you can't use VB paired with an OODBMS. However, the mainstream VB development being done today is against an RDBMS.

Before progressing down the translation path, we need to visit each class and ensure that we completely identify all of the attributes for each, specifying their unique data types. We've already identified many along the way, but now we need to apply more rigor to the process because we soon will be generating relational tables to support them.

FIGURE 9-2   *Class Diagram for Remulak Productions.*

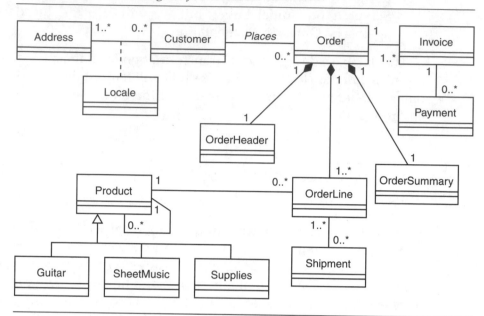

Mapping Classes to Tables

The easiest and simplest way to translate classes to tables is to make a one-to-one mapping from the classes to the tables (see the classes in Figure 9-2). I strongly recommend against this. Yet it is done more often than you might realize. One-to-one mapping can lead to the following problems.

- **Too many tables**

    In most object-to-relational translations done using this approach, more tables result than are actually necessary.

- **Too many joins**

    If there are too many tables, then logically there will be too many SQL join operations. It's likely that several one-to-one table relationships (such as `Order` to `OrderSummary` and `Order-Header` for Remulak Productions) would be better implemented as one table (in this case, `Order`).

- **Missed tables**

  Any many-to-many association (for example, Customer and Address) will require a third relational table to physically associate a given Customer with a given Address. At a minimum, the columns found in that table will be the primary identifier (primary key) from both Customer and Address.

  In the Remulak Productions class diagram, outlined again in Figure 9-2, an association class, Locale, is defined between Customer and Address. This was defined because we want to capture important information about the association, namely the role that Address was serving (mailing, shipping, and billing) for a given Customer/Address pair. This also conveniently handles the relational issue of navigating in either direction.

  However, in the association between OrderLine and Shipment, no association class is defined. This is completely normal and common from the object viewpoint (this association has no interesting information that we care to capture), but from the relational perspective, an intersection table is necessary to implement the relationship.

- **Inappropriate handling of generalization/specialization (inheritance) associations**

  Most often, the knee-jerk reaction is to have a table for each class in the generalization/specialization association. This can lead to nonoptimal solutions that impair performance. Later in this chapter, we review specific implementation alternatives.

- **Denormalization of data**

  Many applications are report-intensive, and the table design might be directed to address their unique needs. For such applications, more denormalization of data might occur (that is, the same data is duplicated in multiple tables).

Rather than one-to-one mapping of classes to tables, a better approach is to revisit the pathways through the use cases, especially how they manifest themselves as sequence diagrams. The class diagram, too, should be addressed. Other useful artifacts are the usage matrices created in Chapter 7.

Rumbaugh once used the term *object horizon* when referring to the available messaging pathways that objects have in a given domain. For example, if the sequence diagrams suggest a number of occurrences of `Customer` messaging to `Order` objects and then to `OrderHeader` and `OrderSummary` objects, then the physical DBMS must be structured so as to support this navigation very efficiently.

The action/frequency matrix we created in Chapter 7 also is invaluable during this phase. Any action (event) will trigger a given sequence diagram into action. The frequency of these actions forces us to focus more closely on their performance. The biggest bottleneck in most applications is usually disk input/output (I/O). Too many tables will lead to excessive joins, which leads to additional I/O. This is not to say that poor key selection (addressed later in the chapter) cannot also impact performance. But too many tables in the first place will lead to additional I/O. And whereas CPU speeds are doubling in speed every 18 months (Moore's Law), raw disk I/O speeds have less than doubled in the last 5 years.

Mapping Simple Associations

Before we can begin transforming classes to relational entities, we must ask a question of each class: Does it even need to be persisted? Some classes will never be persisted to a physical repository, for example most interface and control classes. Classes that are not persisted are called *transient* because they are instantiated, typically used for the life-cycle of either a transaction or the actor's session (in which many transactions might be executed), and then destroyed. Visual modeling tools use this property of classes to determine whether to consider them when generating the SQL DDL for the RDBMS table structures. Figure 9-3 shows the Class Specification for the Order dialog box in Rational's Rose, with the Detail tab showing the specification of the persistence property of the class `Order`.

We have not yet addressed navigation. When creating the initial class diagram, we usually consider every association as **bidirectional**, which means that it can be traversed in either direction of the association (however, in my experience most associations are unidirectional). Treating every association as bidirectional is a good policy because we momentarily cease to consider whether we actually need to be able

FIGURE 9-3   *Class Specification for Order dialog box for Rational's Rose.*

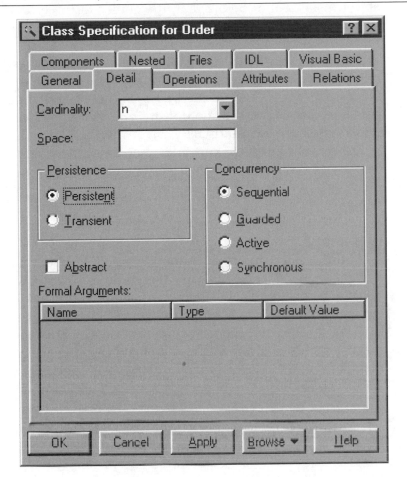

to navigate from, say, Customer to Order as well as from Order to Customer. This decision will impact the language implementation as well as the translation to the relational design.

Semantically, navigation in the UML pertains to objects of a given class being able to message to other objects with which they might have an association. Nothing is said about the implications that navigation might impose on the supporting RDBMS table design. However, this is a very important consideration. On the surface, we are referencing an object instance, but below that, the ability to traverse an association will ultimately depend on the database technology (at least for classes that are persisted).

The UML represents navigability as a stick arrowhead pointing in the direction of the navigation. Figure 9-4 illustrates a scenario involving the Customer and Order classes and the fact that Customer will navigate only in the direction of Order (each Customer has a list of Orders because the multiplicity can be infinite).

From this figure, we can infer that an Order does not know its Customer. However, this isn't very practical for our use and as such won't meet our navigational requirements (Remulak Productions system requirements state we must be able to navigate in both directions). Figure 9-5 shows Customer and Order taken from the class diagram for Remulak given in Figure 9-2.

At this point, you might be thinking that based on our definition of navigation, we can't navigate in either direction. In the UML, the navigational adornments may be omitted as a convenience and to manage clutter. A problem could result, however, if in fact we did have an association that didn't have navigational requirements in either direction. As this is in practice highly unusual, the navigational indicators are typically left off. In the case of the class diagram for Remulak Productions, every relationship will be bidirectional and implied in the model (arrowheads omitted).

FIGURE 9-4   Customer *and* Order *classes with explicit navigation.*

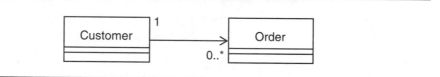

FIGURE 9-5   Customer *and* Order *classes with implied navigation.*

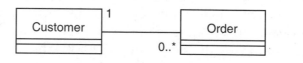

Suppose that we want to translate the two classes, with their multiplicity and dual navigability, into relational tables for the Oracle RDBMS. This would require the following DDL.

```
CREATE TABLE T_Customer(
    customerId INTEGER NOT NULL UNIQUE,
    customerNumber CHAR(14) NOT NULL,
    firstName CHAR(20) NOT NULL,
    lastName CHAR(20) NOT NULL,
    middleInitial CHAR(10) NOT NULL,
    prefix CHAR(4) NOT NULL,
    suffix CHAR(4) NOT NULL,
    PRIMARY KEY(customerId));

CREATE TABLE T_Order(
    orderId INTEGER NOT NULL UNIQUE,
    customerId INTEGER NOT NULL UNIQUE,
    FOREIGN KEY (customerId) REFERENCES
    T_Customer,
    PRIMARY KEY(orderId));
```

Note: Class names in tables are prefaced by a T_. This is in accordance with the default naming convention used by Rational's Rose when generating a DDL from the class diagram.

Notice in the DDL fragment the other artifacts that are strictly relational in nature and that are not part of the class diagramming specifications (although they can all be handled as tagged values in the UML). These artifacts include such items as data types for the relational database (for example, Char and Decimal) and precision (for example, Decimal(9,2)).

Notice also the absence of a reference in the table T_Customer to the T_Order table. This is because a Customer can have many Orders but the RDMBS cannot handle multiple Orders in the T_Customer table.

Note: Many RDBMSs today, including Oracle 8, support the concept of nesting relationships. RDBMSs are slowly crafting themselves as object-relational in their ability to model more-complex relationships.

A Customer can find all of its Orders simply by requesting all Orders from the T_Order table, in which the customerId is equal to a supplied number.

Table 9-1 sets out the translation regarding multiplicity and the resulting RDBMS action. Keep in mind, this is after deciding whether a table is to be persisted or not.

Next, we review the classes that have simple associations (including association classes such as `Locale`) for Remulak Productions and apply the rules for translation. The result is shown in Table 9-2.

TABLE 9-1 *Class/Multiplicity to Relational Mapping*

Multiplicity between Classes	RDBMS Action
One to one	Creates a table for each class (Table A, B).
	The primary key of each table (Table A, B) is also a foreign key in the related table.
	If the relationship is actually 1 to optionally 1, then a benefit might result from implementing the association in the RDBMS as two separate tables. However, if there are a high number of cases in which an association between the two exists or if the multiplicity is truly 1:1, then the best solution is to implement the association in the RDBMS as only one table.
One to many	Creates a table for each class (Table A, B).
	The primary key of the table on the One side of the association (Table A) is a foreign key in the table on the Many side of the association (Table B).
Many to many	Creates a table for each class (Table A, B).
	Creates an additional intersection table (Table C).
	The primary keys of each table (Table A, B) are defined as foreign keys in the intersection table (Table C).
	The primary key of the intersection table may be a separate, unique column (surrogate primary key, which is generated). Or it may be the composite of the two foreign keys from the other tables (Table A, B) or the composite of the two foreign keys from the other tables (Table A, B) along with some meaningful identifier (role, type).

TABLE 9-2   *Class to Table Translation: Simple Association*

Class	Table
Address	T_Address
Locale	T_Locale
Customer	T_Customer
Invoice	T_Invoice
Payment	T_Payment
Shipment	T_Shipment
	T_OrderLineShipment (intersection table for OrderLine and Shipment)

The other classes and related tables are addressed in the next several sections.

Mapping Inheritance to the Relational Database

Creating generalization/specialization associations (inheritance) is one of the more interesting translation exercises when implementing an object design in an RDBMS. Similar constructs that might have appeared in relational modeling are the subtype/supertype relationships.

Figure 9-6 shows the Remulak Productions class diagram, with its generalization/specialization association detailed.

We can follow any of three alternatives when translating a generalization/specialization association to a relational design, as outlined in Table 9-3.

These choices might seem a bit overwhelming, but which one to choose is usually clear. Following are some example scenarios to help you decide which to choose.

- If the number of rows is somewhat limited (in Remulak Productions's case, if the product database is small), then the preference might be to insulate the application from future change and provide a more robust RDBMS design. Thus option 1 in Table 9-3 might be more flexible. However, if performance is a concern,

FIGURE 9-6   *Generalization/specialization and relational design.*

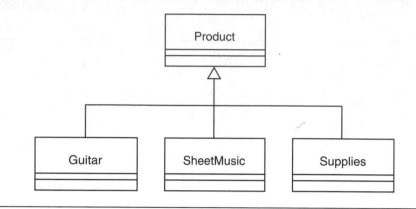

TABLE 9-3   *Three Options for Mapping Inheritance to a Relational Design*

Option	Benefits/Drawbacks
1. Create a table for each class and an SQL view for each superclass/ subclass pair.	This option results in a more flexible design, thereby allowing future subclasses to be added with no impact on other classes and views.
	It results in the most RDBMS objects (in the case of Remulak Productions, seven separate objects: four tables and three views).
	It might hinder performance, since each access will always require an SQL join through the view.
2. Create one table (of the superclass), and denormalize all column information from the subclasses into the one superclass table.	This option results in the least number of of SQL objects (and in the case of Remulak Productions, only one table, `T_Product`).
	It typically results in the best overall performance because there is only one table.
	It requires table modifications and, if future subclassing is needed, possibly data conversion routines.

(continued)

TABLE 9-3   *(continued)*

Option	Benefits/Drawbacks
	It requires "dead space" in the superclass table, T_Product, for those columns not applicable to the subclass in question. This ultimately increases row length and could impact performance because fewer rows are returned in each physical database page access.
3. Create a table for each subclass and denormalize all superclass column information into each subclass table.	When a change is required, this option results in somewhat less impact than option 2. If further subclassing is required, the other subclasses and the superclass will require no modifications.
	If the superclass later must be changed, then each subclass table also must be changed and potentially undergo conversion.
	This option results in adequate performance because in many cases, fewer tables are needed (in the case of Remulak Productions, only three tables would be needed: T_Guitar, T_SheetMusic, and T_Supplies).

then this option yields the least optimum performance (it involves lots of joins).

- If the number of attributes in the superclass is small compared to the number of its subclasses, then option 3 in Table 9-3 might be a more prudent choice. Better performance than that provided by option 1 would result, and extending the model by later adding more classes would be easier.

- If the amount of data in the subclasses is sparse, then option 2 might be best. This option enables the best performance, although it has the worst potential for future flexibility.

In the case of Remulak Productions, we use option 1 because the company later might want to expand its product line and would want the least amount of disruption when that happened.

TABLE 9-4   *Classes and Tables for Inheritance Association*

Class	Table
Product	T_Product
Guitar	T_Guitar
	V_Product_Guitar (view of joined Product and Guitar)
SheetMusic	T_SheetMusic
	V_Product_SheetMusic (view of joined Product and SheetMusic)
Supplies	T_Supplies
	V_Product_Supplies (view of joined Product and Supplies)

Remember, this decision in no way changes the programmatic view of the business (except for the SQL statements). To the VB developer, the view of the business remains based on the class diagram.

Table 9-4 outlines classes and their associated tables.

Mapping Aggregation and Composition to the Relational Database

In a relational database, aggregation and composition are modeled as standard relations. The same rules that apply to the entries in Table 9-4 also apply to aggregation and composition. Often, aggregation and composition relationships involve many one-to-one relationships. Composition relationships almost always are implemented as just one relational table (that being the aggregation or composition owner, such as T_Order for Remulak Productions). If the composition is implemented as separate tables, then the cascading of deletes must be addressed and implemented in the physical DBMS. Aggregation relationships, however, might end up as separate tables because the leaf classes (those being aggregated) can stand on their own.

FIGURE 9-7   *Aggregation and composition and the relational design.*

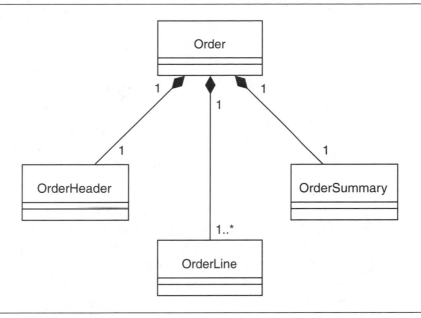

For Remulak Productions, we create three composition associations as shown in Figure 9-7. We also create two relational tables: T_Order and T_OrderLine. The attributes defined in the classes OrderHeader and OrderSummary will be collapsed into T_Order, since they are one-to-one associations and serve no purpose as their separate tables. Table 9-5 recaps the class-to-table translations for the Remulak Productions composition association.

TABLE 9-5   *Aggregation and composition and the relational design*

Class	Table
Order	T_Order
OrderLine	T_OrderLine
OrderHeader	Attributes migrate into T_Order
OrderSummary	Attributes migrate into T_Order

FIGURE 9-8 *The Remulak Productions reflexive association.*

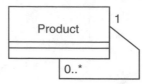

Mapping Reflexive Associations to the Relational Database

Remulak Productions's order entry application has one reflexive association, the Product class, as shown in Figure 9-8.

Recall that this association is necessary to support the requirement that products be related together for cross-selling opportunities. A reflexive association, called a *recursive relationship* in relational modeling, results in a column being added that is itself a primary key to another product. So, each row in the T_Product table will have not only a productId column as its primary key but also another productId column as a foreign key. This would allow, for example, a specific set of strings (Supplies) to be related to a particular guitar (Guitar).

Key Structures and Normalization

You might have seen some column names such as customerId and productId in previous tables. They relate to keys and normalization. Every persistent object in the system must be uniquely identified; the nature of object design and implementation frees us, somewhat, from having to worry about object uniqueness. When an object of a given class is created, it is assigned a unique ID for its lifetime; this is done internally in the language subsystem. However, this doesn't apply when the object is persisted to, for example, Microsoft SQL Server or Oracle. When making the transition from the object view to the relational view, we need to consider the primary identifiers, or keys, that will make every row in a table unique.

We can take either of two approaches to identify keys in a relational database. The first is to select natural keys. A **natural key** is a meaning-ful column, or columns, that have a context and semantic relationship to the application. A good example is in the DDL presented earlier in the chapter. The `T_Customer` table has a 14-character column called `customerNumber` (although this column contains both numbers and characters, it is still called a number). This column is an ideal, natural primary key for the `T_Customer` table because it is unique and has meaning to the application domain.

The second approach to identify keys in a relational database is to pick keys that have absolutely no meaning to the application domain. This type of key is called a **surrogate**, or **programming**, **key**. Most often this type of key is a random integer or a composite creation of a modi-fied timestamp. At first glance, this approach might seem absurd. However, it can have some very positive ramifications on the design and performance of the system, as follows. (I have used surrogate keys exclusively for years.)

- The primary key of every table in the system is of the same data type. This promotes consistency, as well as speed in joins. Most RDBMS optimizers are much more efficient when joining on columns that are an integer. This is because the cardinality, or the distribution of possible values, is much smaller (a 14-byte charac-ter field versus a 4-byte Integer).

- Joins will be limited to single columns across tables. Often, if the primary key selection results in a compound composite key (more than one column is needed to uniquely identify the rows in the table), the ability to join on that key results in poorer performance and much more difficult SQL code.

- Storage needs are reduced. If the natural key of `customerNumber` is chosen as the primary key of `T_Customer`, then the `T_Order` table will contain a `customerNumber` column as a foreign key in order to facilitate the join. This key will require 14 bytes in `T_Order`. However, if the primary key of `T_Customer` is a 4-byte Integer, then the foreign key in `T_Order` will be only 4 bytes. This might not seem like much saved space, but for thousands or tens of thousands of orders, the amount quickly adds up.

- More rows are returned in a physical page I/O. All RDBMSs fetch rows at the page level (at a minimum). They access pages ranging from 2K to 8K. Actually, in some cases, if a database vendor "senses" you are reading sequentially, it might access pages in 32K and 64K increments. Thus many rows reside inside of one page of accessible storage. This results in more data being in memory when the next row is requested. Memory access is always faster than disk access, so if smaller primary keys exist, then those same efficient keys will also be defined as foreign keys elsewhere. Overall, a physical page typically has more rows, thereby resulting in a few more rows being made available to the application at a much higher potential access rate.

The Remulak Productions's relational design will use a surrogate key as the primary key of every relational table. The column names will be similar across tables, each using the mask of *tablenameId*, where *tablename* is the respective table in the system. This surrogate key

FIGURE 9-9 *ERD for Remulak Productions.*

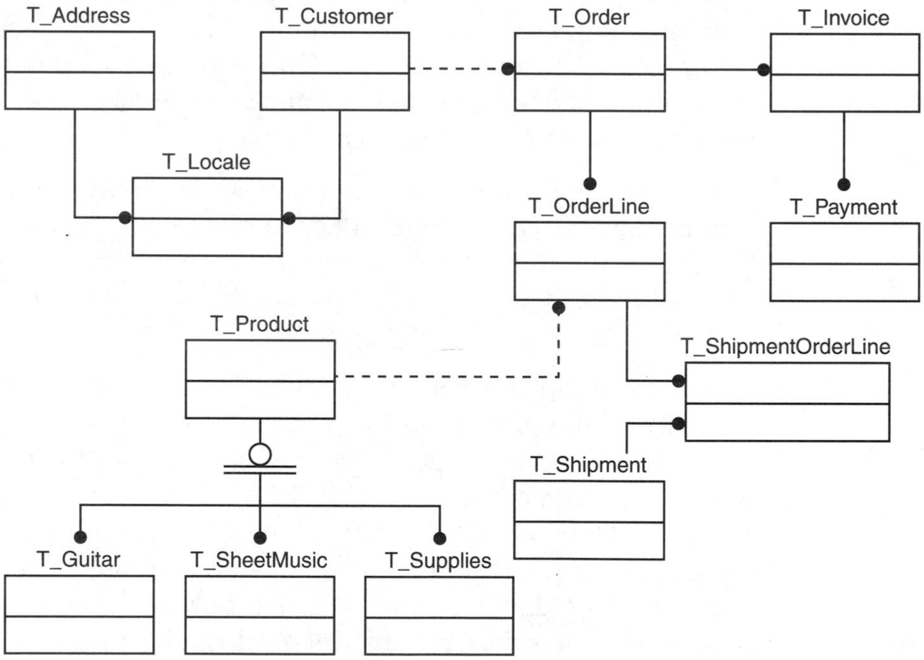

will be stored as an Integer in the database and programmed as a Long in VB. The next chapter introduces code that generates this surrogate key prior to the row being inserted into the table.

Figure 9-9 is an ERD (entity relationship diagram) that shows the tables necessary to implement the Remulak Productions class diagram. The notation is in the industry standard entity definition schema, the IDEF1X format.

Using a Visual Modeling Tool to Generate the Data Definition Language

Visual modeling tools are a must have for integrating UML with an implementation language. Chapter 10 shows that the interative and incremental approach to building software relies on quick and accurate forward and reverse engineering. This modeling/code generation approach is called **roundtrip engineering**.

When we are using the SQL DDL to generate the table structures, it becomes just as critical as the implementation language (VB) is to the project. Some visual modeling tools do a better job than others at generating table structures. As before, we use Rational's Rose. It does an adequate job, provided that the mapping from classes to tables is one-to-one. It also generates inheritance implementations quite nicely, although it uses only one approach (the one we conveniently chose for Remulak Productions).

When using Rose, we need to manually intervene in a few areas, as follows.

- If class attributes will be collapsed into another table, then the table definitions will have to be modified manually after the tool does its job.

- Rose will not generate the intersection table if the table involves a many-to-many association. By default, if an association class is defined, then the association class becomes the intersection table.

- If two classes, such as classA and classB, have a one-to-many relationship and the association is bidirectional, Rose will erroneously place a foreign key in classA that points to classB.

- Rose does not support transient attributes, only transient classes. During DDL generation, each class attribute is given a corresponding column in the target relational table. There might be attributes that are needed at runtime only (`isDirty`, `isNew`) that we won't want persisted.

None of these problems are showstoppers because Rose is very flexible. With it, DDL generation is done with a scripting language (similar to VB) that interprets the model and then writes out the DDL. This script is completely modifiable. In the next section, we will make Rose a better citizen by adding our own custom scripting that will resolve, at a minimum, the last two issues in the previous list.

Figure 9-10 shows Rational's Rose and the current class diagram for Remulak Productions.

DDL generation in Rose is very easy. Following is an example that generates DDL for the `Customer` class.

1. Select the `Customer` Class, and select Tools from the menu.

FIGURE 9-10   *Rational's Rose and the current class diagram for Remulak Productions.*

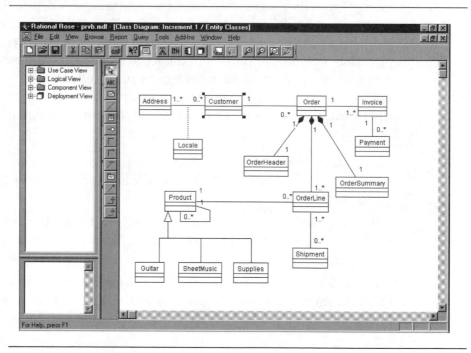

2. Select DDL from the Tools menu, and then select DDL | Generate DDL. The DDL Setup dialog box opens (Figure 9-11).

We need to select a target database platform and output file. We can take the default or can change the selections.

3. Select Oracle, and then click the OK button. A confirmation message box appears, indicating that the DDL generation is complete.

Next, we can browse our new DDL.

4. Select the Customer Class.

5. Click Tools from the menu, and then click DDL from the Tools menu.

6. Click DDL | Browse DDL. The Rose DDL script for Oracle appears in Notepad (Figure 9-12).

FIGURE 9-11 *Rose DDL Setup dialog box.*

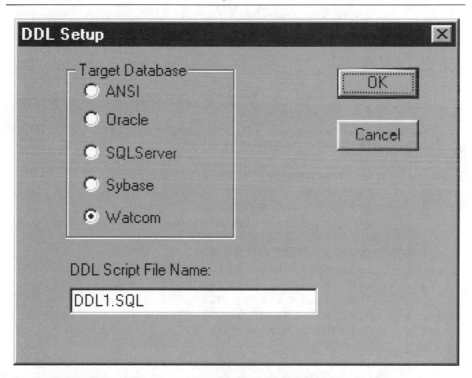

By going through the same process but selecting SQL Server as the target database, we can get the DDL output shown in Figure 9-13.

If you are familiar with DDL, you'll likely notice a few problems with this script.

- Columns declared as `Integer`, such as `customerID`, are followed by parentheses, ( ). If we try to process this through our database, these characters will cause an error.

- The `T_Customer` table has foreign keys for both the `T_Address` and `T_Order` tables. This is incorrect because `T_Customer` can have many `T_Address` and `T_Order` rows to which it is related.

We correct these problems in the next section when we look at enhancing Rose to better generate the DDL.

Enhancing the Visual Modeling Tool

Next, we want to enhance Rational's Rose to provide more flexibility in DDL generation. Rose uses a scripting language called Summit Basic-

FIGURE 9-12 *Rose DDL script for Oracle.*

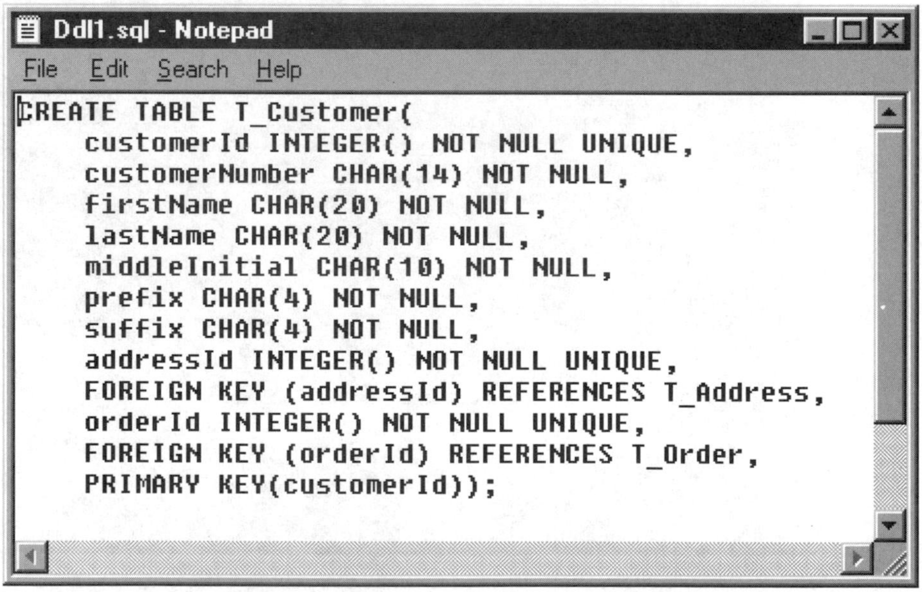

```
Ddl1.sql - Notepad
File  Edit  Search  Help
CREATE TABLE T_Customer(
    customerId INTEGER() NOT NULL UNIQUE,
    customerNumber CHAR(14) NOT NULL,
    firstName CHAR(20) NOT NULL,
    lastName CHAR(20) NOT NULL,
    middleInitial CHAR(10) NOT NULL,
    prefix CHAR(4) NOT NULL,
    suffix CHAR(4) NOT NULL,
    addressId INTEGER() NOT NULL UNIQUE,
    FOREIGN KEY (addressId) REFERENCES T_Address,
    orderId INTEGER() NOT NULL UNIQUE,
    FOREIGN KEY (orderId) REFERENCES T_Order,
    PRIMARY KEY(customerId));
```

FIGURE 9-13   *Rose DDL script for SQL Server.*

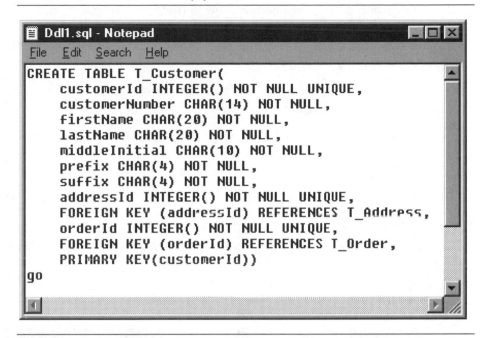

```
CREATE TABLE T_Customer(
    customerId INTEGER() NOT NULL UNIQUE,
    customerNumber CHAR(14) NOT NULL,
    firstName CHAR(20) NOT NULL,
    lastName CHAR(20) NOT NULL,
    middleInitial CHAR(10) NOT NULL,
    prefix CHAR(4) NOT NULL,
    suffix CHAR(4) NOT NULL,
    addressId INTEGER() NOT NULL UNIQUE,
    FOREIGN KEY (addressId) REFERENCES T_Address,
    orderId INTEGER() NOT NULL UNIQUE,
    FOREIGN KEY (orderId) REFERENCES T_Order,
    PRIMARY KEY(customerId))
go
```

Script to drive all of its generation processes. The models within Rose are all addressable from this language platform because they are all stored as objects—an object model of the model, so to speak. This powerful extensibility feature is called the **Rose Extensibility Interface** (REI).

Using Rose, we can edit the script, ddlgen.ebs, that generates the DDL and thus fix the problems mentioned earlier in the chapter. Before beginning, we need to make a copy of the file—located in the Scripts subdirectory of either Rose or Microsoft's Visual Modeler—and place the copy in that same subdirectory.

1. Open the Rose model for Remulak Productions.

2. Select the Customer Class, and click Tools on the menu.

4. Click Open Script on the Tools menu to open the File Open dialog box.

5. Double-click the Scripts subdirectory, and click the file DDLGEN.EBS.

We are now in Edit mode in the script that generates DDL. Recall the first problem that we encountered in the previous subsection: the stray parentheses, ( ), after columns marked Integer. To fix that problem, we need to find and correct the subroutine that is at issue (in this case, PutAttr).

6. Click Edit | Find to search for the subroutine PUTATTR. The subroutine is shown highlighted in Figure 9-14 and on the screen.

The problem is that the script is checking the attribute's Length property for a null value. We need to change it to test for a value of zero. If the value is zero, then there is no length and the pair of parentheses should not be generated. Using the highlighted code in Figure 9-15, we make the change in the script.

This small fix also will clean up several other similar problems related to such data types as Date, DateTime, Number, and TimeStamp,

FIGURE 9-14 *Rose DDL generation script with error highlighted.*

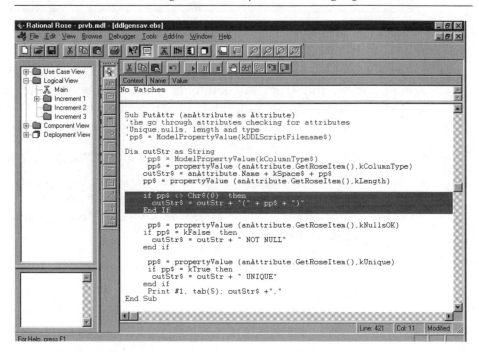

which require no specific length. Each could have similar stray ( ) characters generated after the data type.

The second problem mentioned previously concerns the incorrect generation of foreign keys on the one-to-many associations (we don't want a foreign key of `orderId` in the `T_Customer` table). To fix this, we need to make another change to the generation script.

We return to Edit mode on the DDL generation script to find the affected subroutine, dotable, shown highlighted in Figure 9-16.

In this case, the problem is that the script is not checking whether the role multiplicity is 1, 0..1, or blank. If it is either of these, then a foreign key should be generated; otherwise, no foreign key should be generated. We need to change this code to test the Role.Cardinality property. This additional `If` test can be added to the other two `If` tests already in the code. Using the highlighted code in Figure 9-17, we make the change in the script window.

FIGURE 9-15 *Rose DDL generation script with correction.*

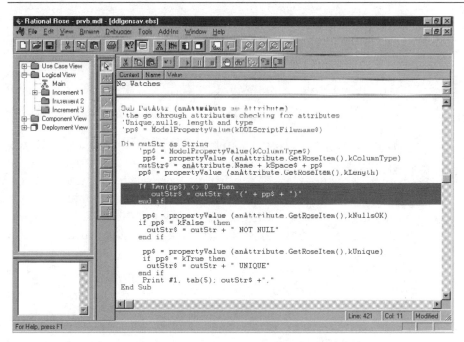

FIGURE 9-16   *Rose DDL generation script with another error.*

Finally, we save our changes to ddlgen.ebs and run our DDL generation process again for T_Customer as outlined previously. The results should resemble Figure 9-18.

This is much better. Fixing these problems demonstrates one of Rose's strengths: its flexible and extensible environment, which, as shown here, allows us to modify, or fix, Rose to do what we want.

We can take further advantage of Rose's extensibility to build an extension that will enable Rose to mark an attribute as transient. Then, at DDL generation time, we can bypass those attributes in the class that shouldn't have a corresponding table column, although they will be needed at runtime in the programming environment. This change is more involved but still very easy and understandable, so it is covered in Appendix B. However, the result is shown in Figure 9-19. Notice the extra property, Persistent, on the DDL tab. This indicates that the isNew attribute in the Customer class is not persistent. The DDL generation script can now check this value and act accordingly.

FIGURE 9-17   *Rose DDL generation script with second error corrected.*

FIGURE 9-18   *Corrected DDL script.*

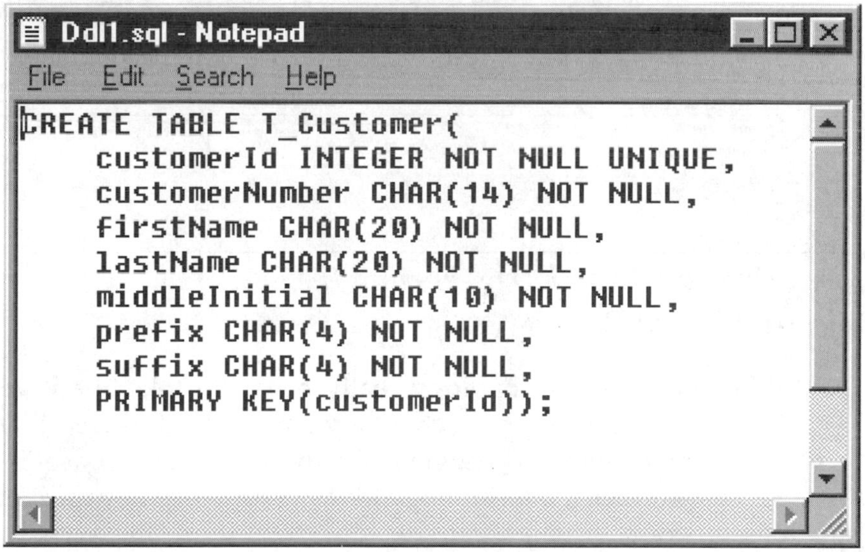

```
CREATE TABLE T_Customer(
    customerId INTEGER NOT NULL UNIQUE,
    customerNumber CHAR(14) NOT NULL,
    firstName CHAR(20) NOT NULL,
    lastName CHAR(20) NOT NULL,
    middleInitial CHAR(10) NOT NULL,
    prefix CHAR(4) NOT NULL,
    suffix CHAR(4) NOT NULL,
    PRIMARY KEY(customerId));
```

FIGURE 9-19   *Rose DDL attribute modification.*

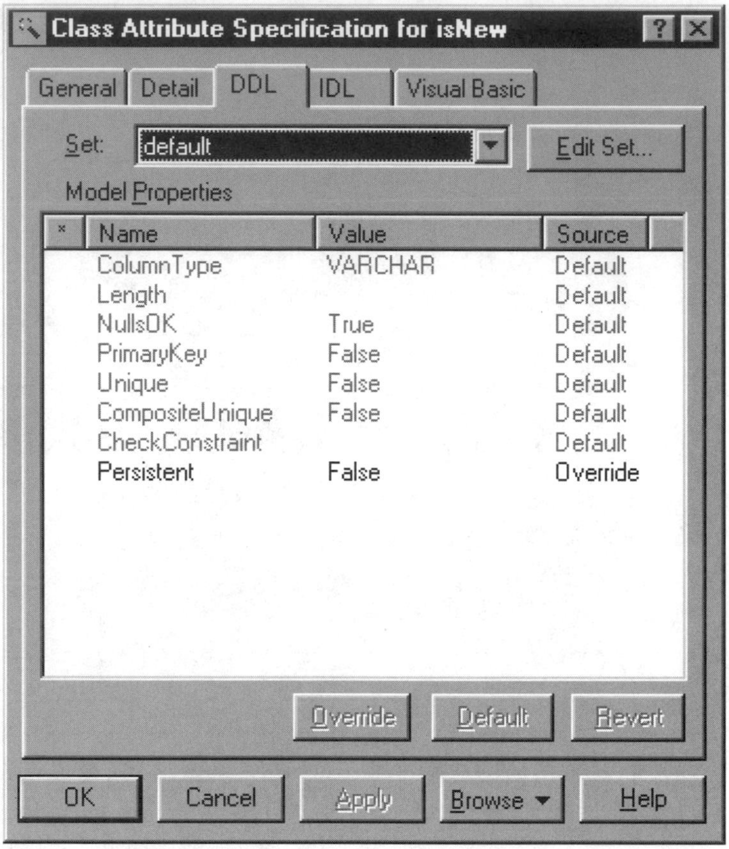

Stored Procedures and Triggers and the Object-Oriented Project

As client/server technology really began to take shape in the later 1980s and early 90s, one technology that boosted its credibility was the stored procedure and trigger. Initially offered by Sybase in their SQL Server product, the technology today is supported by most major database vendors.

Stored procedures and triggers gained wide acceptance for several reasons.

1. They provide for the precompilation of SQL and procedural programming logic (if..then..else) into a tightly bound database object that can be invoked from a client or other server.

2. They provide performance advantages over dynamic SQL (that is, SQL that originates at the client and is then passed across the network). Dynamic SQL must be parsed, validated, and optimized before execution, whereas stored procedures and triggers wait to be invoked in an executable state.

3. They provide a common, central repository for data access, thereby reducing redundant SQL code that might spread across multiple client sources.

Despite the promise of stored procedures and triggers, they fly in the face of object-oriented principals and concepts, for example, as follows.

1. They are written in a DBMS-dependent language, such as SQL Server's Transact-SQL or Oracle's PL/SQL. These are not transportable across database platforms (Note: This is destined to change as most database vendors are announcing support of Java as their stored procedure language).

2. They contain business rules specific to a given application and tie the rules not only to a specific DBMS language but also to the data access language (SQL).

This technology has both opponents and proponents. Those who want an extensible design that is portable across database platforms support never using it. Proponents argue that if a stored procedure or trigger can make a poor-performing transaction really fast, then who cares what is used to meet the service-level agreement with one's clients.

I use stored procedures and triggers as the ultimate screwdriver to fine-tune the application. I initially approach my design without them. Then if I experience problems with performance, I use a stored procedure to perform the typical Create, Read, Update, Delete (CRUD) activities in SQL (Insert, Select, Update, and Delete). As a last resort, if a complicated business rule that requires access to many rows of information is simply not performing, I will use a stored procedure or trigger. However, keep in mind that this migration from a program code solution to a database code solution is not trivial and will take some time.

The key point is that the option exists. The bottom line in the decision process is meeting the performance goals of the application. Show me the last systems designer who was able to get away with 10-minute response times by saying, "We did it for object purity." Don't laugh—I actually heard that line used once.

Visual Basic Support of Data-Aware Classes

New in VB v6.0 is the concept of a **data-aware class**. A data-aware class can be classified as either a *data consumer* or a *data provider*. Data consumers can be bound to data providers, and one data provider can service many data consumers.

For example, suppose the `Customer` class is a data consumer and a new `CustomerDP` class is a data provider (note the DP in the class name, which stands for data provider). The new class has the logic to be able to populate single or multiple ADO recordsets (for example, `Customer` by `customerNumber`, `Customer` by `customerId`, and `Customer` by `lastName`) and expose them to any consumer that wants the populated recordset. Then any time that a consumer wants information, a special method in the data provider, called `GetDataMember`, is fired. This method has a case statement for each recordset that it exposes. The requested recordset then is opened and returned to the data consumer.

Data-aware classes are very efficient, but they are not a flexible solution for a component-building strategy like the one we are basing our design on for Remulak Productions. This is because our data acquisition logic will be compiled as a separate ActiveX DLL, and this won't work if we use data-aware classes defined as data sources, which must be declared private. (Note: This applies only if the consumer is an ActiveX EXE.) You cannot bind to a data-aware class that is in another component outside of the consumer. For the previous example to work, `Customer` and `CustomerDP` would have to be in the same ActiveX DLL. However, this is not good design because the former implements the business rules of the application, whereas the latter deals with data access.

The Data Translation Services and Data Access Services Layers

Recall that Chapter 8 discussed the six layers of an application, shown again in Figure 9-20.

Recall also from Chapter 8 that for Remulak Productions, the Data Translation Services layer will be implemented as an ActiveX DLL. We established that we will use COM or DCOM as our IPC (inter-process communication) protocol and use the method of passing String arrays back and forth across the layers. At that time, however, little was said about how this layer functions.

FIGURE 9-20   *Six logical tier model.*

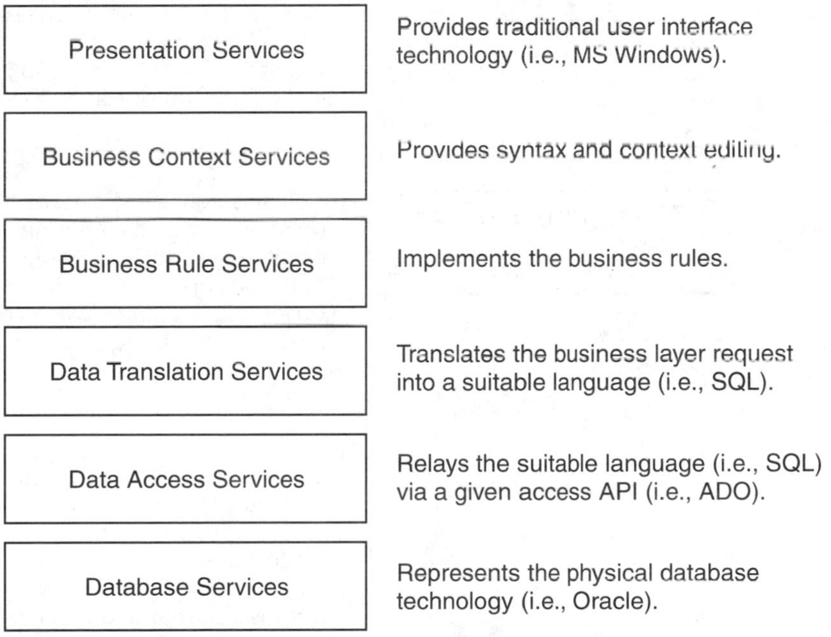

Presentation Services	Provides traditional user interface technology (i.e., MS Windows).
Business Context Services	Provides syntax and context editing.
Business Rule Services	Implements the business rules.
Data Translation Services	Translates the business layer request into a suitable language (i.e., SQL).
Data Access Services	Relays the suitable language (i.e., SQL) via a given access API (i.e., ADO).
Database Services	Represents the physical database technology (i.e., Oracle).

We can take either of two approaches in packaging the Data Translation Services layer. One is to have one class that has a public operation for each logical request for service (for example, retrieve all orders greater than a specific date). Another is to have a data translation class, for example `CustomerDT` (DT stands for Data Translation), for each business class, for example `Customer`.

The first approach has the benefit of fewer classes in the system. However, its downside is a potentially very heavy class that doesn't follow the class motto of doing only one thing and doing that one thing well.

The second approach has the benefit of being a more object-oriented solution, providing for smaller classes that are highly cohesive. However, its downside is more classes in the system.

For flexibility and future extensibility, we elect the second approach: one ActiveX DLL with several business classes in it to serve as the Data

FIGURE 9-21   *Data Translation Services layer.*

Business Rule Services BRSVC.DLL	• Contains business classes such as `Customer`, `Order`, and `OrderLine`. • Handles much of the workflow and provides the U/I with an easy-to-use object interface. • Communicates with its sibling classes in the Data Translation Services layer.
Data Translation Services DTSVC.DLL	• Contains translation classes that match, one-to-one, with their business counterparts, such as `CustomerDT`, `OrderDT`, and `OrderLineDT`. • Builds SQL statements and communicates those to the Data Access Services layer.
Data Access Services DASVC.DLL	• Contains generic SQL access operations such as `DARetrieve` (Select) and `DAQuery` (Update, Delete, Insert) that utilize ADO. • For requests to `DARetrieve`, a String array will be returned with the query results.

Translation Services component. Each of the business classes can also leverage from a common interface. Actually, each data translation class will expose a CRUD interface. This interface will be the same for all Data Translation Services layer classes because all will have to Select, Update, Delete, and Insert data. (Maybe we should call it SUDI . However, I won't burden our industry with yet another acronym.) Figure 9-21 reviews the components and their logical services.

The Data Translation Services layer, housed in the ActiveX component DTSVC.DLL, will host several classes, all ending with the letters DT. Each class will have a one-to-one mapping to its business counterparts. In addition, each, such as CustomerDT, will expose a common interface called ICrud. Figure 9-22 shows a UML diagram with the interface rendered as a "lollipop" icon attached to the class CustomerDT.

This means that CustomerDT implements the ICrud interface. In VB, ICrud will be defined as a class as well and CustomerDT will contain an Implements ICrud reference. The dashed line with the arrow pointing from Customer to the interface icon (the "lollipop") means that Customer depends on the ICrud interface that is implemented by CustomerDT.

The ICrud interface exposes four operations. Each class will implement these differently, although their signatures are the same (polymorphism). This will provide some flexibility later when we begin fleshing out the code within the Business Rule Services layer.

FIGURE 9-22   ICrud *interface in a UML diagram.*

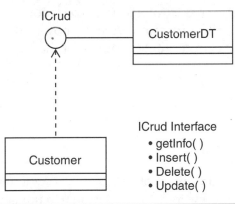

The data translation classes will support other operations in addition to those in the ICrud interface, for example a browseByName operation in CustomerDT. All of these operations for CustomerDT, as well as those for the other classes for the Remulak Productions's project, are detailed in Chapter 10.

The Data Access Services layer is the smallest layer that we will build. Although it does just a few things, it is very powerful and really drives home the benefits of service separation and component building. The ActiveX component, DASVC.DLL, will host two main operations, DARetrieve and DAQuery.

- DARetrieve takes in a connection string, an SQL query (Select only), and an empty String array. A generic ADO recordset is created and "walked" until no more rows remain to be retrieved. Each row is packed into the String array. The result, if successful, is a populated String array that will find its way back through the layers.

- DAQuery handles all other types of SQL queries (Delete, Update, and Insert). It takes in a connection string and an SQL query. A generic ADO Execute against the connection is issued.

This design approach is resilient because only one class in the entire system issues database API calls. If the technology changes later—which we know it will (who ever thought using the native ODBC API would ever be in its way out)—then the API access logic found in these two operations will need to be rewritten. But this involves only a simple recompile of the DASVC.DLL component, and no one will be the wiser. (This assumes that the interface doesn't change and that binary compatibility is selected in the project options. More on this in Appendix D.)

We have met our goal of service separation while keeping performance and flexibility in mind. Armed now with a good design, we begin in the next chapter to flesh out all of the code.

Checkpoint

Where We Have Been

1. Several issues must be considered when mapping an object view of the system to a relational database design. The early

inclination is to create one-to-one mappings, but this usually results in too many tables.

2. Generally, most one-to-one class associations can be collapsed into one relational table. This might not be the case if the association is optional (0..1).

3. Three common approaches to mapping inheritance to the relational model are available. One is to create a table for each class involved and a view for each subclass. Another is to collapse all of the attributes from the subclasses into a table matched to the superclass. The last is to take the attributes found in the superclass and duplicate them in each table for each of the subclasses.

4. Aggregation and composition associations are mapped in the same way as simple associations.

5. We have many options for identifying primary keys. A common approach that offers significant flexibility is to use surrogate, or programming, keys.

6. A visual modeling tool is a must for any project team that is serious about building object-oriented systems. Such tools can generate code, as well as SQL DDLs.

7. Rational's Rose modeling tool can be customized to add additional flexibility to the DDL generation process.

8. Stored procedures and triggers should be viewed as the ultimate screwdriver for fine-tuning the application. If they are commingled with the business logic, then the application becomes more dependent on the product architecture choices.

9. Data-aware classes do not facilitate a component-building strategy unless the provider class is packaged in the same component (ActiveX DLL or EXE) as the consumer class.

10. The Data Translation Services layer hosts a translation class for every business class in the Business Rule Services layer.

11. The Data Access Services layer is the only area in the application that database API calls will be made. It also is generic enough to execute all of the SQL that will be passed in from the Data Translation Services layer.

Where We Are Going Next

In the next chapter, we:

1. Explore the needs of the infrastructure layers as a whole, and establish our layer communication mechanisms and error handling process.

2. Review the identified classes, and assess all attributes that have been defined to ensure completeness.

3. Build a template for applying the layered code.

4. Begin to generate code components from the class diagram.

CHAPTER 10 · *Applying the Infrastructure*

The previous chapter introduced some of the elements of the infrastructure necessary to support our design. This primarily dealt with the back-end and the database technology. That chapter stressed the need to separate physical access technologies, such as ADO (ActiveX Data Objects), and the logical request for information, such as "give me a list of orders that are backordered."

The same message will be emphasized in this chapter, but the focus will be on separating the user interface, such as a Visual Basic (VB) form, from the relaying of the form's intent to the business layer. Too often, applications will meet the initial goal of delivering a system but begin to self-destruct as soon as enhancements are requested. At other times, they will also self-destruct if the technology changes, such as new data access services or different presentation services. These systems soon wear the "legacy" hat. The goal of this chapter is to ensure that we have a robust implementation, while providing an extensible architecture that will evolve as the business does.

GOALS

⮑ Review the infrastructure issues in communicating from the user interface all the way to the persistence layer at the back-end.

⮑ Explore the other layers not defined in the previous chapter (presentation and business context) and assign them to components.

⮑ Review the importance of keeping the user interface as light as possible.

⮑ Bring back the three types of classes (interface, control, and entity) and apply them to the layered architecture for Remulak.

⮑ Review the final component infrastructure to support all the use cases and related pathways.

⮑ Revisit the UML class diagram and further refine the operation signatures necessary to support automatic code generation.

Construction Phase

Synergy Process

Before exploring the Construction phase as it pertains to the technical infrastructure, let's visit again the Synergy process model and the project plan for this phase of the project. Figure 10-1 is the process model, highlighting the focus of the project at this point.

Although the Construction phase considers several different areas as outlined in Figure 10-1, the focus of this chapter will be on the following:

FIGURE 10-1   *Synergy process model and the Construction phase.*

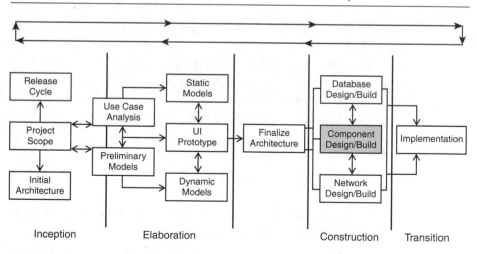

- The "Component Design/Build" block, which will deal with transitioning from the many artifacts we have produced so far to a component design strategy and construction process to realize the product

The component design will be realized using VB. There will also be UML component and deployment diagrams produced to show the packaging strategy of the software, as well as how it will be physically deployed. There will be more options presented because of the two environments that we may have (MTS versus no MTS).

Component—Infrastructure Issues and Communicating with All the Layers

Remember from the database chapter that we successfully laid out an architecture that separated the physical DBMS, Microsoft SQL Server, from the access services, ADO. The data access services were further separated from the data translation services, used to build SQL statements. In this chapter, our goal will be to do the same but this time from the front-end, working inwards until the two ends meet in the middle.

Figure 10-2 is our layered architecture introduced previously and then reintroduced in the database chapter. Again, these layers are both logical and, in some cases, physical as well.

Remember, just because they are individual layers, many may still run together on the same machine. At least three of them, Presentation Services, Business Context Services, and perhaps some of the Business Rule Services, will probably be on the client. I say probably because, depending on the Presentation Services technology (VB forms versus a Web browser), the Business Context Services may be on a Web server in the form of ASP (Active Server Pages) and JavaScript. Then again, the Business Context Services could be implemented in the browser as well in the form of VBScript or JavaScript.

Figure 10-3 focuses on those layers to be reviewed in this chapter and a more in-depth review of the roles that they will be serving.

In Figure 10-3, the Business Rule Services layer is repeated from the previous chapter to provide some continuity. All the layers will be presented, in their entirety, in the form of a component diagram at the end of this chapter.

FIGURE 10-2 *Services layers.*

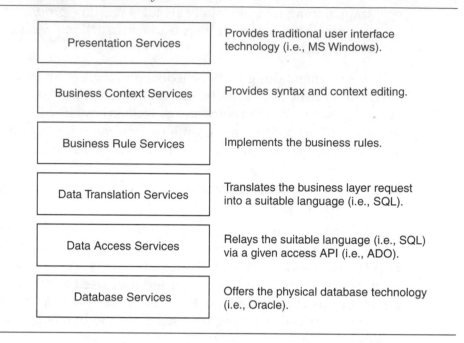

Presentation Services	Provides traditional user interface technology (i.e., MS Windows).
Business Context Services	Provides syntax and context editing.
Business Rule Services	Implements the business rules.
Data Translation Services	Translates the business layer request into a suitable language (i.e., SQL).
Data Access Services	Relays the suitable language (i.e., SQL) via a given access API (i.e., ADO).
Database Services	Offers the physical database technology (i.e., Oracle).

Component—Exploring the Presentation Services Layer

The Presentation Services layer will be the most volatile layer in the entire application. New technologies will present themselves of which the project must be able to take advantage. In addition, as time passes, the project sponsors will want to see information in different ways that the project must be able to quickly and easily provide.

One way to facilitate the ever-changing presentation requirements, and to provide a better design for extensibility, is to implement a *model, view, and controller* (MVC) framework. MVC got its start in the Smalltalk world and has been used extensively in many commercial frameworks. Before we lay out the Remulak architecture, some terminology discussion is in order.

- **Model** in the MVC framework is the Entity class (for example, Customer, Order). The goal of the model is to keep the framework pure, void of any user interface knowledge. The model is represented in our application via VB class modules packaged in the BRSVC.DLL ActiveX component.

FIGURE 10-3   *Presentation, Business Context, and Business Rule Services layers.*

Presentation Services
EXE (VB Forms), Browser w/JScript
Business Context Services
EXE (VB Forms), Browser w/JScript

- Contains the visual components of the application.
- Layer is technology-dependent. Most common will be either VB forms or Internet-based. However, it could be any presentation technology that can talk COM (Excel).
- Contains syntax and context edits that will filter and cleanse input before it is passed through the other layers.
- Implements user interface-related business rules.

Business Rule Services
BRSVC.DLL

- Contains business classes such as Customer, Order, and OrderLine.
- Handles much of the workflow and provides the user interface with an easy-to-us object interface.
- Communicates with its sibling classes in the Data Translation Services layer.

- **View** in the MVC framework is the rendered interface that will be delivered to the client. The view can know about both the controller and the model. The view is represented in our application via VB forms packaged in the UISVC.EXE standard executable.

- **Controller** in the MVC framework is the service that most often acts as the go-between for the model and the view. There is a one-to-one relationship between a view and a controller. So, in the Remulak Productions system, there will be a VB class module stereotyped as a controller for every VB form that we create.

One benefit of letting the controller broker requests between the view (form) and the model (entity class) is that it keeps the user interface light. Although there is nothing to prevent the user interface from calling into the entity classes to retrieve information, by keeping the VB forms relatively clueless, we end up with services layers that are highly cohesive and less coupled to the other services layers. Figure 10-4 is a representation of the MVC pattern and how it is used in Remulak Productions.

FIGURE 10-4   *Model, view, controller framework.*

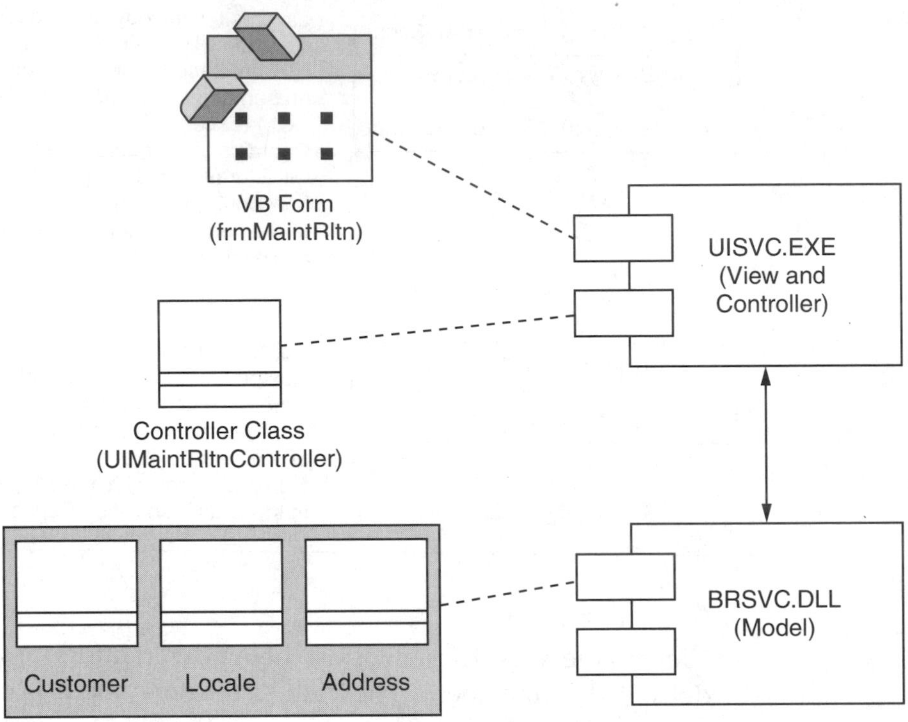

Figure 10-4 outlines the framework to support the Maintain Relationships use case. There is one form, called frmMaintRltn, in the Remulak Productions project that carries out the user interface aspects. This form resides in the Standard EXE, UISVC.EXE, and implements the view aspects of the MVC framework. A class module, called UIMaintRltnController, also resides in the Standard EXE and implements the controller aspects of the MVC framework. The entity classes that are the source of all the business information are implemented as class modules (Customer, Address, Locale) and reside in the ActiveX component, BRSVC.DLL.

Component—Exploring the Business Context Services Layer

The Business Context Services layer of the application works very closely with the specific presentation technology. It is responsible for much of the editing that transpires during the user interface interaction. Some of these logical services are split between the actual form-level code, packaged in the `UISVC.EXE` component, and the Business Rule component, `BRSVC.DLL`.

This logical layer focuses on what is happening during a given interaction between the system and the application and in particular on syntax and context edits. These various edits perform as follows for the application.

- **Syntax edits** focus on formatting and cleansing information before it ever leaves the user interface. These edits can range from numeric range checks to valid date formatting.

- **Context edits** focus more on the business aspect of the information. For instance, if someone selects a payment type of finance and they have a credit score below 50, then a finance officer approval is required for a sale. This is a classic type of business rule, but it is better implemented somewhere on the client, as that is where this information originally becomes available. This type of rule would probably end up as an operation defined on the `Payment` class that will reside in the Business Rule component `BRSVC.DLL`.

Someone could make the point that we should not have any type of syntax or context editing going on in the form-level code. The reason is that these types of edits would apply whether the user interface was a VB form or a Web-based front-end. I have seen some designs that actually package the edits as a single method inside of the user interface controller class and pass all the screen information to the edit operation to perform the edit. This would allow some level of reusability should the front-end change to a Web-based solution. However, depending on the technology selected for a Web-based front-end, something as simple as preventing the entry of a field based on the value entered in another field (context edit) may require a trip all the way back to the Web server to be edited. This is clearly a case where purity and performance will butt heads.

Component—Exploring the Business Rule Services Layer

Although the industry overutilizes the term "Business Rule," it is important to place it in a context of how we will use it. What really resides in this layer? We have been using the term *entity class* quite a bit in this book, and this is where those classes will live. Initially, the implementation constructs of each will mirror the attributes defined in the class diagram. There will also be Get and Let operations for each attribute because all attributes will be declared as private. Then, there will be services that each entity class will provide, such as a way to request the retrieval of information about itself for eventual use by some aspect of the system. The classes will also have to be able to respond to update requests, thereby resulting in some form of persistence management that will be implemented by another layer in our application. Table 10-1 is a table of the operations that will be required of every entity class implemented in the Remulak Productions system.

The logical layer of Business Rules actually has a dual spirit. The Business Rules physically implemented in the ActiveX component BRSVC.DLL are very workflow-oriented. There are other Business Rule services that deal with the business aspect of data management. This will actually be implemented in what we have referred to in the previous chapter as the Data Translation Services layer.

The BRSVC.DLL component that contains all the entity class will most probably be distributed to the server, especially if the implementation involves the Web. However, there is nothing from preventing its distribution to the client. The other prime candidates for server-side implementation are both the Data Translation and the Data Access Services layers. The Business Rule Services layer maintains state about itself (firstName, lastName), while the two Data layers are somewhat

TABLE 10-1 *Common Entity Class Operations*

Operation Name	Purpose
getInfo	Used to retrieve information about an instance of a class.
update	Used to update information about one instance of a class.
delete	Used to delete information about one instance of a class.
Insert	Used to insert information about one instance of a class.
unPack	Used to populate object member variables using the results retrieved from a select call to the Data Translation Services layer.

stateless (they do their work and then they are done). This will be a key consideration when we explore the impact of MTS on our application in a later chapter.

Component—Cooperating Classes: Interface, Control, and Entity

Let's now take a simple interaction, the retrieving of customer information via the Maintain Relationships use case, and map into the layers of the application. This exchange of messages will be initially mapped out at a high level and then will get much more concrete (as to full operation signatures) as we move through the example. Figure 10-5 outlines the UML sequence diagram depicting the interaction.

In this depiction of the messaging between the objects, we see a pattern. The controller class, `UIMaintRltnController`, does much of the go-between work of the form and the other layers of the application. It also allows the controller to act as a traffic cop based on the context of the interaction.

Let's take a walk through the messaging. I have asked Rose to put sequence numbers on the diagram for readability; however, they are unnecessary for sequence diagrams, as order flows top to bottom. Figure 10-6 is a snapshot of the Customer Relationships screen taken from the Remulak Productions Project Deliverables to provide you with a frame of reference.

1. The clerk interacts with the form, thus causing the form to load and execute the `form_load` event.

2. The form asks itself to `initialize`.

3. During the initialization function, a new `UIMaintRltnController` is instantiated.

4. The clerk enters a customer number and clicks the Search command button.

5. The form sends a message to its controller instance that it wants to `getInfo`, passing it the `customerNumber`.

6. During the `getInfo` operation, a new `Customer` is instantiated.

7. The `Customer` instance is then asked to `getInfo` using the `customerNumber`.

FIGURE 10-5 *Customer inquiry sequence diagram.*

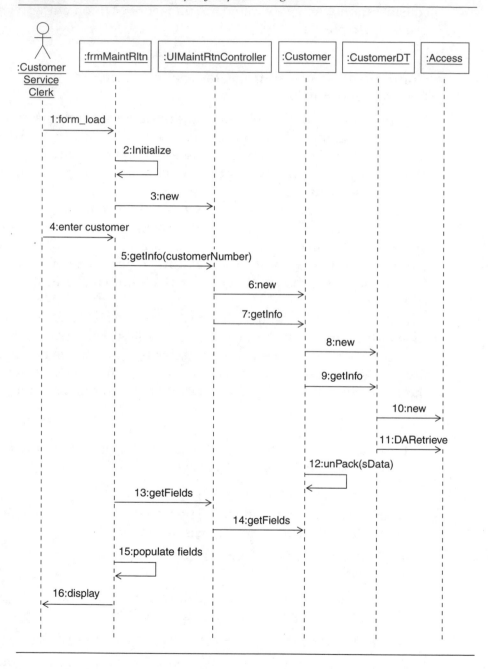

FIGURE 10-6   *Customer Relationships screen.*

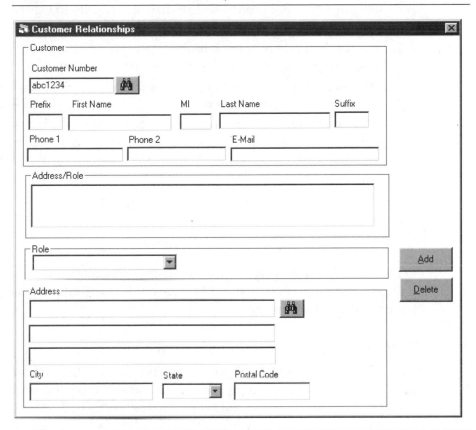

8. During the `getInfo` operation, a new `CustomerDT` is instantiated. Remember from the previous chapter that DT classes perform the business function of translating the logical request for information into an SQL statement.

9. The `CustomerDT` instance is then asked to `getInfo` using the `customerNumber`.

10. During the `getInfo` operation, a new `Access` instance is instantiated. Remember from the previous chapter that the `Access` class applies the data access API of choice, in our case ADO, using the SQL statement built in the DT module.

11. The `Access` instance is asked to `DARetrieve`, which actually executes the SQL query and returns the results to `CustomerDT` inside of a string array `sData`.

12. `sData` finds its way back to the Customer instance, which asks itself to `unPack` the array into its member variables.

13. All the messages eventually cascade back to the form, which begins to assign its text boxes (`txtFirstName`, `txtLastName`) with information from the controller's instance of `Customer`. The diagram shows `getFields`. There is no actual operation by this name. This is used instead of showing an individual message for each attribute.

14. Same as 13.

15. Fields are populated.

16. The form is displayed with the results.

This interaction is very typical of all the interactions on which the Remulak Productions system will be based. It is actually a framework that can be applied time and time again.

Component—Layer Communication

Remember from the technology landscape chapter that we looked at many ways to facilitate layer communication. We settled on a String array because string arrays are relatively low overhead, especially the way that we want to use them. Although all arrays are passed `ByRef`, in our case we need to pull information from a target layer. The good news is that on the call to the target layer, the `ByRef` String array, `sData`, will be empty. The valid argument against `ByRef` is that the data has to marshaled out to the target and then back again. In our case, nothing has to get marshaled out, only back. VB handles all this for us. Figure 10-7 is a diagram depicting how this communication will look once we get really serious about building code in the next chapter.

Figure 10-7 shows how database rows get retrieved and find their way back through the layers all the way to the user interface. The secret of the success of this approach is that all rows returned from the result set of a query will be packed into a two-dimensional array. This array is a dynamic String array that is resized with the `ReDim` statement as the number of rows increases. So, whether you are returning one row or

FIGURE 10-7   *Layer communication.*

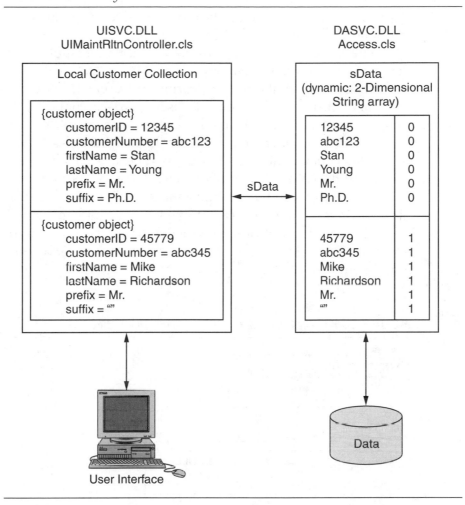

UISVC.DLL
UIMaintRltnController.cls

DASVC.DLL
Access.cls

Local Customer Collection

{customer object}
   customerID = 12345
   customerNumber = abc123
   firstName = Stan
   lastName = Young
   prefix = Mr.
   suffix = Ph.D.

{customer object}
   customerID = 45779
   customerNumber = abc345
   firstName = Mike
   lastName = Richardson
   prefix = Mr.
   suffix = " "

sData
(dynamic: 2-Dimensional
String array)

12345	0
abc123	0
Stan	0
Young	0
Mr.	0
Ph.D.	0
45779	1
abc345	1
Mike	1
Richardson	1
Mr.	1
" "	1

sData

User Interface

Data

five hundred, the services that `DARetrieve` provides within the `Access` class are the same.

Since `sData` is passed `ByRef`, when it first arrives at the `Access` object, along with the SQL statement that `CustomerDT` built, it is empty because it will have been `Erased` prior to the invocation. After the array is packed, control eventually returns to the initial caller. At this point, the class instance `Customer` is instantiated and then its member variables set. (These instances will be UDTs.)

Component—Implementation of the Infrastructure

The infrastructure for the application can now be rendered as a UML component diagram, shown in Figure 10-8.

The initial component maps to the logical Presentation and Business Context Services layers. This component, UISVC.EXE, will be a standard VB EXE and will contain all the forms and user interface controllers. Remember that there will be one user interface controller for every screen. UISVC.EXE depends on the next component, BRSVC.DLL.

The next component maps to the logical Business Rule Services layer. This component, BRSVC.DLL, will be an ActiveX DLL and will contain all the entity classes. This ActiveX component will stay a DLL under either of these two circumstances: (1) It runs in-process on the client or (2) it runs under MTS. It will be made into an ActiveX EXE if we wish to run it out-of-process, whether or not we remote it to another server, or if it resides on the client. BRSVC.DLL depends on the next component, DTSVC.DLL.

FIGURE 10-8 *The Remulak Productions component diagram.*

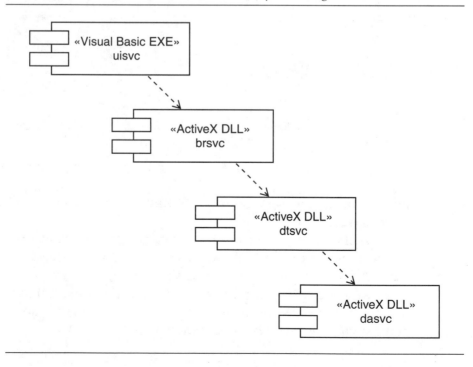

The next component maps to some elements of the logical Business Rule Services layer as well as the logical Data Translation Services layer. This component, DTSVC.DLL, will be an ActiveX DLL and will contain a translation class for each entity class. Their primary goal is to build SQL statements. This ActiveX component will stay a DLL under either of these three circumstances: (1) It runs in-process on the client, (2) it runs under MTS, or (3) it runs in-process on the server using the remoted BRSVC.EXE as its client. It will be made into an ActiveX EXE if we wish to run it out-of-process, whether or not we remote it to another server, or if it resides on the client. DTSVC.DLL depends on the next component, DASVC.DLL.

The next component maps to the logical Data Access Services. This component, DASVC.DLL, will be an ActiveX DLL and will contain database API logic, in our case ADO. This ActiveX component will stay a DLL under either of these three circumstances: (1) It runs in-process on the client, (2) it runs under MTS, or (3) it runs in-process on the server using the remoted DTSVC.EXE as its client. It will be made into an ActiveX EXE if we wish to run it out-of-process, whether or not we remote it to another server, or if it resides on the client. DTSVC.DLL depends on the next component, DASVC.DLL.

There are quite a few options for distributing our application. In the case of Remulak Productions, the probable deployment strategy will be to run UISVC.EXE on each client. The BRSVC.DLL, DTSVC.DLL, and DASVC.DLL components will run on the server. Figures 10-9 and 10-10 depict the likely deployment strategies using UML component and deployment diagrams. Note that Figure 10-9 depicts a traditional DCOM strategy without MTS and Figure 10-10 depicts MTS.

In both cases, the Database Server is shown as an Active Object, as it runs in its own process and has its own thread of control. In a later chapter, when we look at alternative interfaces, we will offer yet another view depicting the packaging with the Web. Figure 10-10 will also be explored further in a later chapter when an MTS solution is reviewed.

Component—Revisiting the UML Class Diagram to Refine Operation Signatures

We are now getting close to the point of generating code from the class diagram as constructed in Rational Rose. First, we have to make sure that we have all the classes we need, along with operations and the

FIGURE 10-9   *Remulak Productions's deployment strategy using traditional DCOM without MTS.*

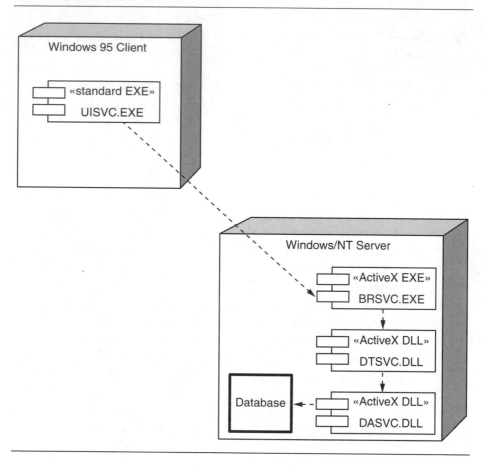

attributes as well as the signatures (names, input parameters, and return parameters) for all the operations. It isn't absolutely necessary that we get everything exactly right because we will also be reverse-engineering. Remember that reverse-engineering is letting Rational Rose use our VB project as its source, and based on what it finds in our code, it will update the class diagram accordingly. We need to add the classes that were reviewed in this chapter, as outlined in Table 10-2.

Also, in Table 10-1, there were operations that were identified that must be added to the entity classes. Again, don't think that this will be the last time that you see your class diagram. Your project team will

FIGURE 10-10 *Remulak Productions's deployment strategy using traditional DCOM with MTS.*

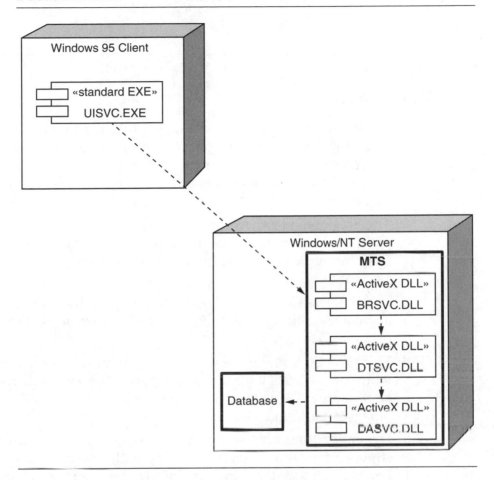

TABLE 10-2 *New Classes for the User Interface Interaction*

Class	Description
UIMaintRltnController	User interface controller for the Maintain Relationships form.
UIProcessOrderController	User interface controller for the Process Order form.
UIMaintainOrderController	User interface controller for the Maintain Order form.
UISearchController	User interface controller for the generic search form.

make the act of reverse engineering and forward engineering a weekly, if not daily (in the beginning), event.

Checkpoint

Where We Have Been

1. A well-designed application requires that the logical layers be treated with care when the physical implementation occurs. This is because, as the business evolves, a shift in either the business model or the technology framework won't leave the application in the legacy bin.

2. The Presentation Services layer will change often in the life span of an application. It is paramount to separate the user interface from the implementation. Today, VB forms may be used; tomorrow, the Internet.

3. The Business Context Services layer is responsible for the syntax and context editing. This logical layer will be implemented in the user interface component.

4. The Business Rule Services layer is responsible for the many workflow issues that the application faces. This layer will contain all the entity classes and they can be deployed on either the client or server platform.

5. Dynamic String arrays provide for a powerful mechanism to shuttle information from the back-end to the client requestor. The key is to insulate the unpacking of the array from the client and isolate it in its own class, that of the entity.

6. The deployment options are varied, but the two key ones that will be pursued for Remulak Productions are the Presentation Services executing on the client and the Business Rule Services, Data Translation Services, and Data Access Services executing on the server. This will also apply to an MTS scenario. The only difference is that the Business Rule Services layer will be an ActiveX DLL instead of an ActiveX EXE.

Where We Are Going Next

In the next chapter, we:

1. Explore the remaining setup issues that are required of Rational Rose before we generate our code skeletons.

2. Uncover what must be added after the generation process is complete.

3. Explore the subtleties of reverse engineering and getting the work done on the project that isn't reflected in the model.

4. Explore the subtleties of forward engineering after a reverse engineering has been completed.

5. Review what is necessary to attach the user interface to the layers of the application.

CHAPTER 11

Generating Code from the UML Class Diagram (Part 1)

Now that we have the infrastructure chapters behind us, it is time to generate lots of VB code. This is where our hard work of laying out the architecture will pay off. Decisions have been made about what the layers will be, how they will communicate, and how we will actually deliver our software. There shouldn't be a lot of architecture-related decisions to be made from this point forward.

Our focus in this chapter will be to take the class diagram that we built in Rational Rose and generate the initial code skeletons. From there, we have to begin filling in code to make the skeletons actually do something for us. We will also get into the nuances of reverse engineering from code back into our class diagram to pick up additional attributes, operations, and maybe even classes that we will add while coding.

We will salvage as much from the prototype as possible. I have found that with practice, a prototype can be evolved into something useable. Most of the code in the prototype was to make the screens flow and work when buttons were pressed. There was no code in the way of class modules created during the prototype.

My focus on the coding aspect of the project is to lay the foundation to support a use case transaction from start to finish. All the code for Remulak Productions's order entry application will be available to the reader in its entirety in a format described at the end of this book. However, I will not be devoting precious page real estate to describe, for instance, how to add items

*to a listbox control, as it is beyond the scope of this book. I am making the
assumption that you can figure that out by examining the code provided
with this book or spend time with some of the excellent introductory books
available in the technical book marketplace today.*

GOALS

⇨   Review the mission of the visual modeling tool as it pertains to
program code generation.

⇨   Review the mission of the visual modeling tool as it pertains to
reverse engineering program code into the visual modeling
tool.

⇨   Review the setup issues in preparing to generate program code.

⇨   Review items to watch out for after generation is complete.

⇨   Review the notion of interface versus implementation inheritance.

⇨   Review how the visual modeling tool implements generalization/specialization for VB.

⇨   Explore how to simulate implementation inheritance through
containment and delegation.

⇨   Explore how to reengineer program code back into the visual
modeling diagram.

⇨   Explore the necessary code that must be added to support a
simple inquiry transaction from start to finish.

Construction Phase

Synergy Process

This chapter continues our exploration of the Construction phase as it
pertains to the implementation of the technical infrastructure as well as
the business aspects of Remulak Productions's order entry application.
Let's visit again the Synergy process for this phase of the project. Figure

11-1 shows the process model, highlighting the focus of the project at this point.

Although the Construction phase considers several different areas, as outlined in Figure 11-1, the focus of this chapter will be on the following.

- The "Component Design/Build" block, in this chapter, will deal with creating much of the code that drives the application.

In the next chapter, we will add more complex transaction support, such as update, insert, and delete processing. In chapters following that, we will take this solution and modify it to support MTS as well as the Internet.

Visual Modeling—The Mission of the Visual Modeling Tool as It Pertains to the Project

To again stand on my soapbox: Too many VB projects fail because their desire to produce code far outweighs the importance of sound project planning and a precise understanding of the application's requirements. There is no reason why VB applications can't sit at the shoulder of well-built C++, Java, and COBOL applications as being resilient and production-worthy, while at the same time perform with admirable abilities.

FIGURE 11-1   *Synergy process model and the Construction phase.*

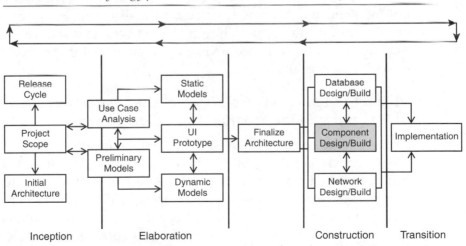

To reemphasize from a previous chapter, if you have come this far in the book and not seen the benefit of using a visual modeling tool, then this chapter is either going to finally convince you or merely cement your already positive conclusion. Besides the obvious benefits of having a repository of artifacts and a consistent approach to creating them, the visual modeling tool really excels in getting the programming effort started. It also gets high marks for the ongoing evolution of the application by bringing code artifacts back into the model.

In this book, we have used Rational Rose as the visual modeling tool. Like its many competitors in the marketplace, this generation of Computer Aided Software Engineering (CASE) tools is a skeleton-generation product. Modeling tools are either analysis-focused, design-focused, or a combination of the two. Unfortunately, I have been the victim, in a previous life, of being "welded" to my modeling tool, always forced to take the code output it produced and forced again to get it to run in a production environment. These integrated CASE tools demanded that the user learn a new language that would eventually translate into code (for example, COBOL, C, or C++); usually, not a pretty picture.

The current generation of skeleton-generation tools provides both the analysis and design transition support, but only the code structure and framework is generated from the model. I really like this approach. It still allows the project to apply the rigor of keeping true to the structure of the application design, while not dictating the solution for the *how*. It will, for instance, put in place the class structures, operation signatures, and available message paths to calculate an order discount but not force me to tell it how to calculate the discount. My once negative opinion of integrated modeling tools has been swayed into the positive. In summary, you need a visual modeling tool that generates code in your language of choice.

Visual Modeling—The Mission of the Visual Modeling Tool as It Pertains to the Program Code Generation

Rational Rose generates code strictly from the information found in the class diagram, along with some physical attributes that we give the UML component that has been assigned to realize, or implement, the classes. Components in Rational Rose end up being EXEs or DLLs in VB.

There is a completed Rational Rose model that you can use if you have either Microsoft's Visual Modeler or a copy of Rational Rose. You can enter each class by hand, along with all of its support material (attributes, operations) or use my model as a start to generate your code. I highly recommend the latter.

Review the Setup Issues in Preparing to Generate Program Code

We need to revisit our class diagram for Remulak Productions and see how some of the components have been arranged. This will facilitate how we work with the diagram, as well as help us to better manage all the aspects of the code generation. Figure 11-2 shows the Remulak Productions model `prvb.mdl`.

On the right-hand side of Figure 11-2 is the overall package diagram that is broken out by the increments, with a note attached describing the use cases that are being realized. In the browser tree view on the left-hand side, there are now packages under each increment that weren't there before. These packages reflect the physical layering decided on in the prior two infrastructure chapters.

Figure 11-3 shows the Data Access Services package expanded along with the `Access` class and its operations. If you desire, you can

FIGURE 11-2   *Rose model organization.*

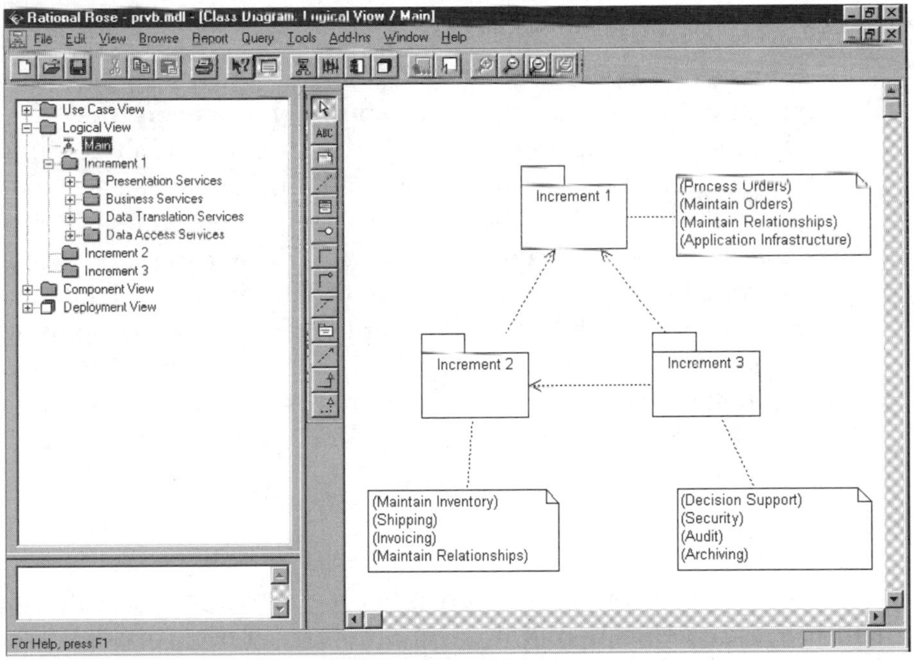

FIGURE 11-3 *Data Access Services package, expanded.*

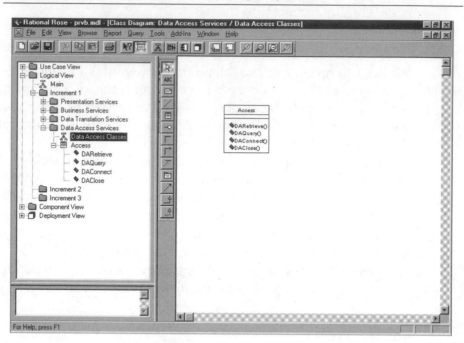

double-click the `Access` class and inspect the full signatures of all the operations (input parameters and output parameters).

I reemphasize here that, in practice, you shouldn't get hung up on being totally accurate with your signature layouts. The model delivered with the book is complete. Just remember, in reality this knowledge will grow with the code. Better still, when we reverse engineer our code back into the model, a lot of information will be updated for us. For instance, when adding input parameters for operations, you can specify `Optional`, `ByRef`, and `ByVal`. However, don't bother to add them to the class diagram because when we reverse engineer the code, Rational Rose will fill in that information for us. We want to get to the code as soon as we can.

Modifying the Code Generation Parameters

Before we tell our tool to generate code, we need to tweak some of the VB code generation options that Rational Rose provides. Figure 11-4 shows the Options dialog for the Remulak Productions model.

FIGURE 11-4   *Changing the code generation properties.*

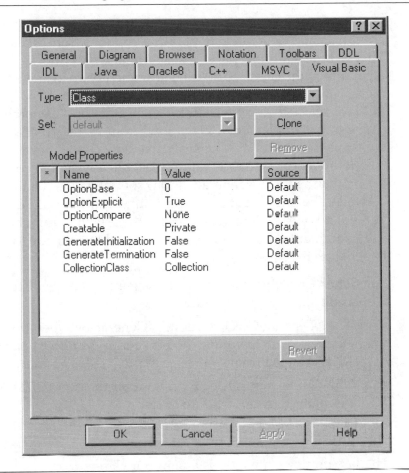

To get to this screen, do the following.

1. Select the "Tools" from the menu, and then select Options from the drop-down menu.

2. Select the "VB" tab.

Notice that the drop-down for "Type" indicates "class." These are all the default options defined at the class level for code generation. We want to change the "Creatable" option from "Private" to "Mult-Use." If we don't, all of our classes will be generated as private. You can subsequently go in and set these parameters uniquely for each class if you so desire.

3. Select the Type drop-down and select Attribute.

We want to change the "GenerateGetOperation," "GenerateSetOperation," and "GenerateLetOperation" options from "False" to "True." This will generate property `get`, `set`, and `let` blocks for all of our attributes in the classes. You can subsequently go in and set these parameters uniquely for each attribute if you so desire.

Now select the "Type" drop-down and the "Generalize" option. Change the "ImplementsDelegation" from "True" to "False." Because we have several of the Data Translation classes implementing the `ICrud` interface, we don't want to generate delegation code. However, we do want it for the generalization/specialization relationship found between `Product`, `Guitar`, `SheetMusic`, and `Supplies`. I will show you what Rational Rose generates for those later in this chapter.

In summary, the following changes need to be made to get the code to generate the way we want.

- The "Creatable" option for class generation needs to be changed from "private" to "multiuse."

- The "GenerateGetOperation," "GenerateSetOperation," and "GenerateLetOperation" options for the attribute generation need to be changed from "False" to "True."

- The "ImplementsDelegation" option for generalization needs to be changed from "True" to "False."

Assigning Classes to Components

The last thing we must do is assign our classes to components. Create four components that look like the ones shown in Figure 11-5.

We saw these in the last chapter. The only addition is the lollipop icon extending off of the `dtsvc` component. This is indicating that the component implements the `ICrud` interface and automatically shows up if the component implements a class stereotyped as an "Interface." To make our first code generation process small and easy, let's start at the back-end, with the Data Access Services layer, and work our way up to the Presentation Services layer.

To assign classes to components do the following.

1. Double-click the component labeled "dasvc."

2. Select the "Realizes" tab (See Figure 11-6).

FIGURE 11-5   *The Remulak Productions components.*

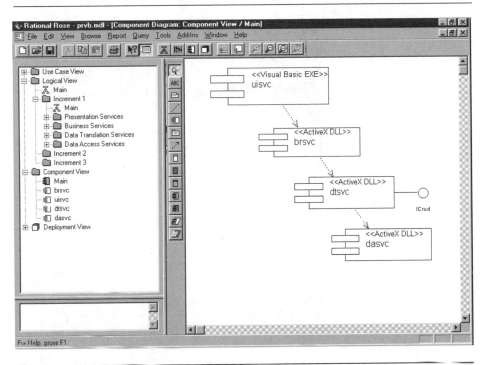

3. Select the "VB" tab.

4. Scroll down until you find the class called Access.

5. Right-click the class and select "Assign."

Notice that there is a check mark on this class, shown in Figure 11-6. Now it is time to generate code.

Generating Our First Code from the Visual Modeling Tool

While still on the component diagram, do the following.

1. Right-click the "dasvc" component.

2. Select Generate Code.

You are now looking at the Code Generation Wizard. Just keep hitting "Next" until you get to the screen for selecting options shown in Figure 11-7.

FIGURE 11-6 *Component assignment.*

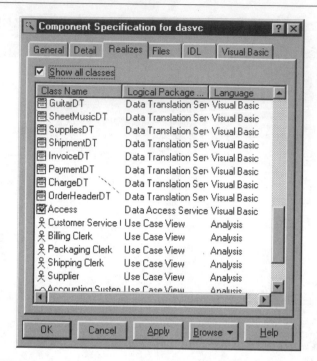

Uncheck the two options that deal with Debugging and Error handling. Continue through the screens until you get to the last one and select "Finish." Now the VB Integrated Development Environment (IDE) will be launched, and you can sit back and watch a project be built on-the-fly. You should end up with something that looks like Figure 11-8.

Save this project in its own directory called "dasvc." Our first project skeleton is complete. Let's move on to the next layer.

Generating the Remaining Code from the Visual Modeling Tool—Data Translation Services

If the previous exercise went smoothly, then the remaining generation tasks should be just as straightforward—just a lot more code will be generated. Let's keep working our way up the chain from where we started with the Data Access Services component, `dasvc.dll`.

The next component is the Data Translation Services component, `dtsvc.dll`. Refer to Figure 11-5, where you created it previously.

FIGURE 11-7 *Code Generation Wizard.*

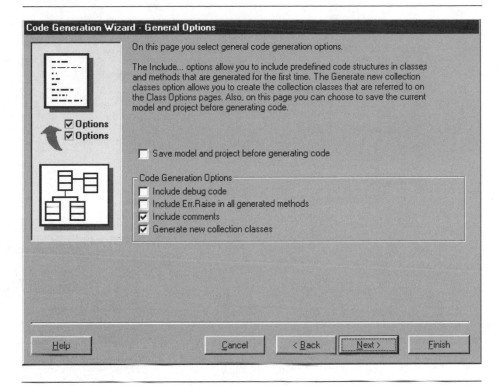

You want to perform the same steps as before in assigning classes to a component. With this component, all the DT classes need to be assigned.

You need to make a small change to your generation process from here forward. Once the change is made, you can forget about it, as the setting will be maintained for you. The second screen you arrive at allows you to select a class; make sure the "manually" option is chosen and not "automatically." If "automatically" is chosen, Rational Rose will try to generate all the code for everything that has changed since the last forward generation. By selecting the manual path, you get only the component that you requested.

Now, much as we did in the previous section, where we generated our first code, we perform the same exercise, only now for the dtsvc.dll component. You should end up with something that looks like Figure 11-9.

FIGURE 11-8   *VB after code generation.*

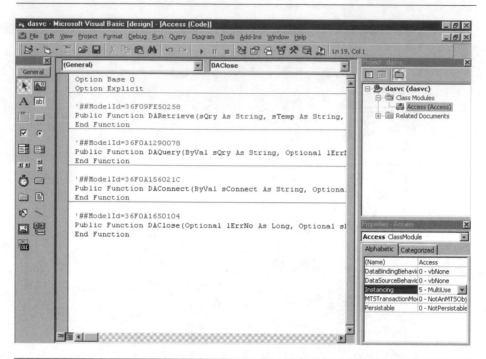

Save this project in its own directory called "dtsvc." Notice a few interesting things in Figure 11-9, such as the `Implements ICrud` interface statement in the `CustomerDT` class. Also, notice how the functions defined match the signature of the `ICrud` interface. We know that they belong to the `ICrud` interface because `ICrud_` is appended to the front of each operation. Also, don't be fooled by the fact that they are declared `Private`. We can still message to them from other classes, but they must be declared `Private` or otherwise the `CustomerDT` class base interface, which are its other operations, would be commingled with the `ICrud` interface. Lastly, note the declaration:

```
Public theAccess As Access
```

This declaration came from the class diagram and the fact that there was an association between `CustomerDT` and `Access` that was a navigable. Our second project skeleton is complete. Let's move on to the next layer.

FIGURE 11-9   *VB after code generation of the Data Translation Services compo-*

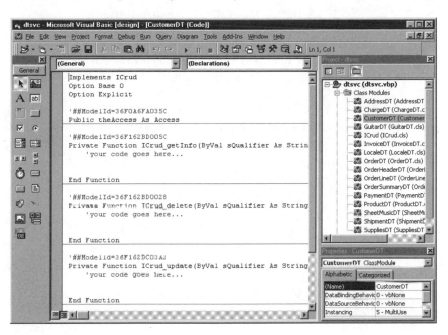

Generating the Remaining Code from the Visual Modeling Tool—Business Rule Services

The next component is the Business Rule Services component, `brsvc.dll`. Refer to Figure 11-5, where you created it previously. You want to perform the same steps as before in assigning classes to a component. With this component, all the entity classes need to be assigned, along with the use case controller classes, `UCMaintRltnController` and `UCProcessOrderController`. Remember, these latter classes will orchestrate the actual interaction with the entity classes to implement the pathways, or transactions, defined in the use cases (for example, Relationship Inquiry, Place Order, Maintain Order, and Change Order).

I want to live up to my promise on detailing how we can let the visual modeling tool handle the containment/delegation strategy for simulating implementation inheritance in VB. Remember that we want to do that for the generalization/specialization relationship found between `Product`, `Guitar`, `SheetMusic`, and `Supplies`. To get at this feature, do the following.

1. Select "Tools" from the menu.

2. Select "Options" from the drop-down menu.

3. Select the "VB" tab.

4. Now select the "Type" drop-down and the "Generalize" option. Change "ImplementsDelegation" from "False" to "True."

Let's now perform the same code generation exercise, only now for the `brsvc.dll` component. You should end up with something that looks like Figure 11-10.

A few things to note about what got generated. Because we told Rose that `ImplementsDelegation` was `True` this time around, we got the following line of code:

```
Private mProductObject as New Product
```

FIGURE 11-10   *VB after the code generation of Business Rule Services component.*

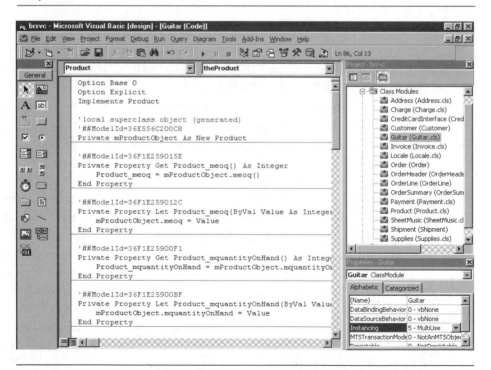

This is containment in action. Contained within the `Guitar` class is the declaration of its parent, or superclass: an object of type `Product`. Now find the operation that looks like this:

```
Private Property Let Product_quantityOnHand(ByVal _
   Value As Integer)
     mProductObject.quantityOnHand = Value
End Property
```

This is delegation in action. If another object tries to assign a value to the attribute `quantityOnHand` found in `Guitar`, which is an attribute of the superclass `Product`, the `Guitar` class delegates that task to the contained instance of its superclass, `mProductObject`. You would find the same exact containment and delegation code in both the `SheetMusic` and `Supplies` classes as well.

This is how we resolve the implementation inheritance issue in VB. So, in my opinion, with a visual modeling tool, if you can select how you want the code generated as it pertains to containment and delegation, then the often over-hyped issue of no implementation inheritance is less of an issue with which to deal. That said, I still want implementation inheritance natively supported in VB.

Generating the Remaining Code from the Visual Modeling Tool—Presentation Services

The last component is the Presentation Services component, `uisvc.exe`. Refer to Figure 11-5, where you created it previously. You want to perform the same steps as before in assigning classes to a component. With this component, the only two classes we have right now are the user interface controllers, `UIMaintRltnController` and `UIProcessOrderController`.

Now, just like we did for the `brsvc` component, we perform the same code generation exercise, only now for the `uisvc.exe` component. You should end up with something that looks like Figure 11-11.

This layer doesn't have much in it yet, but it won't be long before we have forms to add, as well as operations that allow the forms to talk to the other layers through the user interface controller classes.

Review Items to Watch Out for after Generation Is Complete

Don't be surprised if your class diagram looks a bit different after this code generation exercise. For instance, each class will be stereotyped as

FIGURE 11-11 *VB after the code generation of the Presentation Services component.*

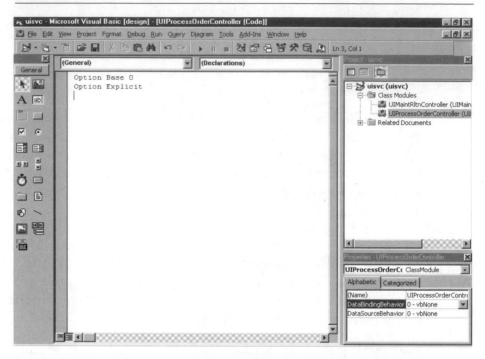

a "Class Module." Also, if you didn't have roles assigned to your relationships, which we didn't have, Rational Rose generates roles for you and adds them to the diagram.

From this point forward, it is paramount to the success of the project and the perpetuation of traceability that a cycle of reverse engineering and forward engineering (round-trip reengineering) be a common and consistent practice within the project team.

Explore How to Reengineer Program Code Back into the Visual Modeling Diagram

Before we move on to building a real transaction and adding a lot of "how to" code to go along with our empty skeletons, a quick tour through the Reverse Engineering Wizard is in order.

There are a few things that we can do to the uisvc project we have loaded.

1. Add three of the forms that we identified during the course of the book. They are `frmMaintRltn`, `frmProcessOrder`, and `frmRemulakMDI`.

2. Add an operation to the `UIMaintRltnController` that would allow the user interface to request information about a customer through the `UCMaintRltnController` found in the `brsvc` component. For starters, we will need a `customerNumber`, something to package the result in, an error number, and an error description.

We should end up with something like this for the operation skeleton:

```
Public Function getInfo(ByVal sCustomerNumber As _
    String, sData() As String, Optional lErrNo As _
    Long, Optional sErrDescr As String) As Boolean

End Function
```

Figure 11-12 is what our `uisvc` project should look like after completing the previous steps.

To start the reverse engineering process, do the following while in the `uisvc` project in VB.

1. Select "Add-Ins" from the menu.

2. Select "Rational Rose 98" from the drop-down menu.

3. Select "Reverse Engineering Wizard" from the drop-down menu.

4. Select the Rose model to which to apply the reverse engineering task. This will default to the one from which you originally generated the code.

After the wizard starts, take all the defaults until you get to the screen shown in Figure 11-13.

The Assignment of Project Items window gives us the chance to assign the components that we are reverse engineering to specific parts of our model. The `UIMaintRltnController`, to which we added the declarations and attributes, already has a home, as a result of our forward engineering effort, in the Presentation Services layer. However, the three forms we added don't have a home. Simply drag and drop them into the Increment 1, Presentation Services package. Keep stepping through the screens until the process is complete. What you should have now is shown in Figure 11-14.

FIGURE 11-12 *UISVC project with changes made for the reengineering exercise.*

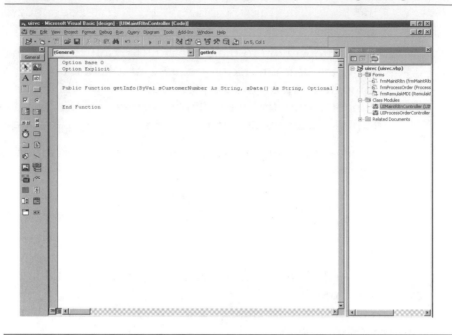

FIGURE 11-13 *Reverse Engineering Wizard for assignment of items.*

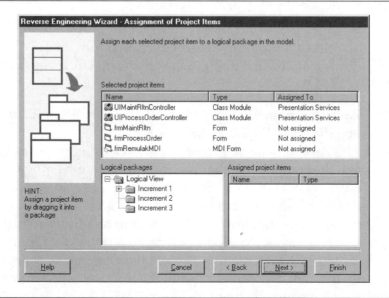

FIGURE 11-14   *Reverse-engineered UISVC project.*

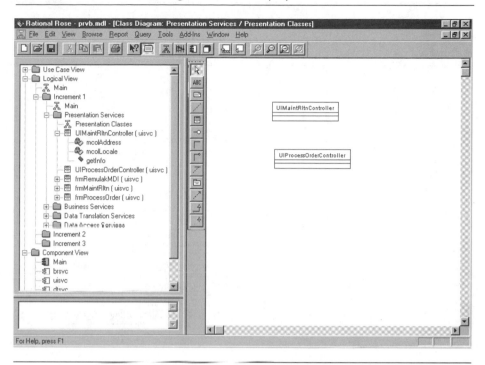

Notice that the forms and attributes are showing up in the left-hand tree view. Forms look just like classes in Rational Rose. In fact, they are classes as far as the visual modeling tool is concerned. They are stereotyped as "Form."

So, from here we could add more classes, new operations, new attributes, take both items away and then forward engineer to VB. This entire process is round-trip reengineering in action.

Adding Code to Realize a Use Case Pathway

Explore the Necessary Code That Must Be Added to Support a Simple Transaction from Start to Finish

It's time to fill in the gaps. We will add the code necessary to execute a use case transaction from start to finish. We will start with something easy, such as inquiring through the Relationship Maintenance form

FIGURE 11-15   *Sequence diagram of the Relationship Inquiry pathway.*

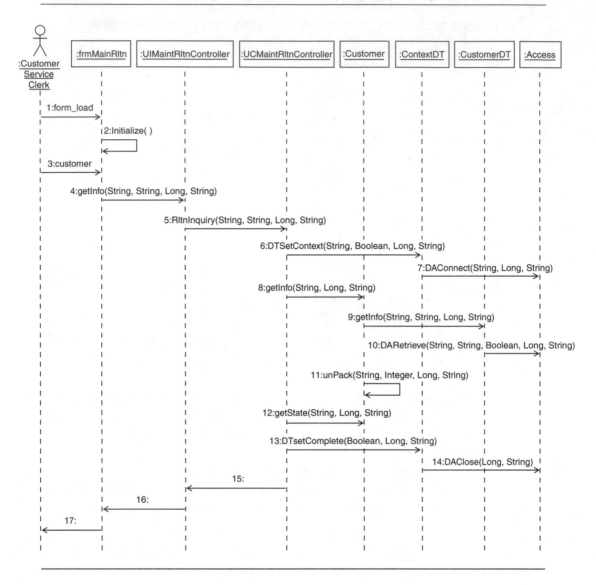

using a valid customer number. This is a pathway through the Maintain Relationships use case. Although the story will unfold as we go through all four layers of the application, a sequence diagram of this interaction is outlined in Figure 11-15.

Data Access Service Layer: DASVC Component

As with the previous code generation exercise, let's begin at the back-end with the dasvc project and work toward the user interface, a great start given how components will reference other components in our project. Beginning with the four operations already defined, but still quite empty, let's flesh out DARetrieve, DAQuery, DAConnect, and DAClose. We will also find that other operations will be required as well, and we will add them as we go. Then when we are comfortable with things, we'll reverse engineer the code back into Rational Rose.

Connecting to the Data Source and Executing a Select Query

This project will use ADO to retrieve information from some repository. I have used the framework presented next against Oracle (v7.*x* and v8.*x*) and Microsoft SQL Server (v6.5 and v7.0), as well as Jet (Microsoft Access). Remember that the layer that communicates with the Data Access Services layer, the Data Translation Services layer, doesn't know what database we are using, let alone access API (ADO, RDO, DAO).

First of all, the class will require ADO Connection and Recordset objects. So let's define two private ones at the top of the Access class, right under the two Option statements.

```
Private moConn As ADO.Connection
Private mrsTemp As ADO.Recordset
```

Next, we need to create a Connection object somewhere, and a good place to do that is in the Class_Initialize operation.

```
Private Sub Class_Initialize()
    Set moConn = New ADODB.Connection
End Sub
```

DAConnect is an operation whose task is to establish the connection to an ADO resource. It sends the ADO Open message, along with the connection string passed in, sConnect, and establishes a connection.

```
Public Function DAConnect(ByVal sConnect As _
    String, Optional lErrNo As Long, Optional _
    sErrDescr As String) As Boolean
    On Error GoTo DAConnectErr
    DAConnect = False
```

```
    'Call open method to open the DSN
    moConn.Open sConnect
    DAConnect = True        'Return TRUE for function
    Exit Function
DAConnectErr:
    lErrNo = Err.Number
    sErrDescr = Err.Description
End Function
```

Let's turn our attention to the DARetrieve operation. This operation is going to be a real workhorse for the application. It is surprisingly simple in its approach to taking an SQL statement, passed from dtsvc, executing it, and then walking the recordset, packing each row/column combination into a two-dimensional string array sTemp. It can deal with one row or hundreds of rows. Let's look at the code in chunks for this operation. Remember from the chapter that dealt with the architecture for Remulak Productions, we chose to use String arrays between the layers as our communication mechanism because that is one approach that will remain stable going forward. Although disconnected recordsets have somewhat less overhead from a programming perspective, the overall performance is better with the String arrays.

The first part of the function sets up some working variables and executes the SQL query passed in from dtsvc in the sQry parameter.

```
Public Function DARetrieve(ByVal sQry As String, _
    sTemp() As String, bAddColumnName As Boolean, _
    Optional lErrNo As Long, Optional _
    sErrDescr As String) As Boolean
    On Error GoTo DARetrieveErr
    Dim sRet        As String
    Dim lCurRow     As Long
    Dim iCols       As Integer
    Dim iCurCol     As Integer
    DARetrieve = False
    Set mrsTemp = moConn.Execute(sQry)
```

The next part of the operation checks to see if any rows were found for the query and if the requestor wants the column names back as part of the String array based on the request parameter bAddColumnName. Think of the column names as a metadata feature of the operation. If they are being requested, then the ADO recordset `names` property is cycled for each column until they are all assigned.

```
'Check the existence of records before filling
'up array
If Not (mrsTemp.BOF And mrsTemp.EOF) Then
    iCols = mrsTemp.Fields.Count - 1
    'If meta data desired, go get it
    If bAddColumnName Then
        lCurRow = 0
        ReDim sTemp(iCols, lCurRow + 1)
        For iCurCol = 0 To iCols
            sTemp(iCurCol, lCurRow) = _
            mrsTemp(iCurCol).Name
        Next iCurCol
        lCurRow = 1
    Else
        lCurRow = 0
    End If
```

The next block of code actually does the populating of the data rows returned from the query into `sTemp`. Notice the use of the `ReDim Preserve` statement to dynamically adjust the size of the array without destroying the information already contained. Each column returned in the query is converted into a string with `CStr` before being placed in the array. The `CheckType` function, shown later in the chapter, will default a value for null columns based on the data type of the column.

```
Do Until mrsTemp.EOF
    ReDim Preserve sTemp(iCols, lCurRow)
    For iCurCol = 0 To iCols
        If IsNull(mrsTemp(iCurCol)) Then
            'For nulls, get default value
            CheckType mrsTemp(iCurCol).Type, _
              sRet
            sTemp(iCurCol, lCurRow) = sRet
        Else

            sTemp(iCurCol, lCurRow) = _
            Trim$(CStr(mrsTemp(iCurCol)))
```

```
                  End If
              Next iCurCol
              lCurRow = lCurRow + 1
              mrsTemp.MoveNext
          Loop
          DARetrieve = True
      End If
```

The upside of using the String array is that all data types can be treated the same and the amount of information pushed back and forth is much smaller, per our previous discussion on the overhead imposed by the Variant data type. The downside is that the process that must unravel the String array is going to have to know the data type of each element (that is, Long, Integer, Date) and convert it back from a String into its intended type. If you were using a Variant array, that wouldn't be necessary. This routine and the subsequent architecture could easily be changed to use Variants if desired. I personally am always focused on reducing network loads if possible; less overhead is always better.

The last part of the function closes the recordset and then sets the Recordset object reference to Nothing.

```
          mrsTemp.Close          'Close the recordset
          Set mrsTemp = Nothing  'Clear the recordset
                                 'object
          Exit Function          'Exit the function
  DARetrieveErr:
      lErrNo = Err.Number
      sErrDescr = Err.Description
  End Function
```

The last piece of code for DARetrieve is the CheckType subroutine, which assigns a default value for those columns that may be null.

```
Private Sub CheckType(ByVal lType As Long, sRet As _
   String)
      'Assign the default value
      Select Case lType
          Case adDate, adDBDate, adDBTime, _
          adDBTimeStamp
```

```
            sRet = 0
        Case adBigInt, adCurrency, adDecimal, _
            adDouble, adInteger, adNumeric, adSingle, _
            adSmallInt, adTinyInt, adUnsignedBigInt, _
              adUnsignedInt, adUnsignedSmallInt, _
            adUnsignedTinyInt
            sRet = 0
      End Select
End Sub
```

That's all there is to our universal SQL select processor. This could be used on any project going forward. Actually, when it is used for a new project, this layer and the accompanying `dasvc.dll` is ready to work the minute you install them.

Closing the Connection to the Data Source

Our Data Access Services will also have to close connections as well as open them. The function `DAClose` will do that for us, and it is called after the recordset has been completely traversed.

```
Public Function DAClose(Optional lErrNo As Long, _
    Optional sErrDescr As String) As Boolean
    On Error GoTo DACloseErr
    DAClose = False
    'Close the connection
    moConn.Close
    DAClose = True      'Return TRUE for function
    Exit Function
DACloseErr:
    lErrNo = Err.Number
    sErrDescr = Err.Description
End Function
```

This function simply issues the `Close` message to the `moConn` `Connection` object. The last piece we need in place after the eventual destruction of our `Access` object is to set our `moConn` object to `Nothing`. This can be done in the `Class_Terminate` operation.

```
Private Sub Class_Terminate()
    Set moConn = Nothing
End Sub
```

So, the previous collection of operations, defined in the Data Access Services component, can be used to get an SQL select query executed. This request will be driven by one of the DT classes residing in the Data Translation Services layer.

Connecting to the Data Source and Executing an Insert, Update, or Delete Query

Although we won't need it for our first use case pathway which was to inquire through the Relationship Maintenance form using a valid customer number, let's introduce the process necessary to execute Insert, Update, and Delete SQL statements. This primary function is called DAQuery, and it does surprisingly little. Since there is no data to return or manipulate after the execution of a query, it merely executes the query against the connection.

```
Public Function DAQuery(ByVal sQry As String, _
    Optional lErrNo As Long, Optional sErrDescr As _
    String) As Boolean

    On Error GoTo DAQueryErr
    DAQuery = False
    'Execute the query
    moConn.Execute sQry
    DAQuery = True        'Return TRUE for function
    Exit Function
DAQueryErr:
    lErrNo = Err.Number
    sErrDescr = Err.Description
End Function
```

Regardless of whether the update-oriented query is successful or unsuccessful, the caller will be notified via the error number and message.

In the bigger scheme of things, there is going to be more required to execute update-oriented transactions. We have the whole unit of work issue to deal with, such as beginning, committing, and rolling back a transaction. Toward that end, we need three additional functions that must be supported by our Data Access Services layer. These functions, DABeginTrans, DACommitTrans, and DARollBack, will be made public and, when combined, will expose the functionality to support update-oriented transactions.

The DABeginTrans function messages to the ADO Connection object moConn that we wish to start a transaction. This transaction may be a series of SQL statements, the effect of which should be an "all or nothing" outcome. If we update Order and try to update Customer and it fails, we want to be able to issue a rollback and have the Order update undone for us by the DBMS.

```
Public Function DABeginTrans(Optional lErrNo As _
   Long, Optional sErrDescr As String) As Boolean
      On Error GoTo DABeginTransErr
      DABeginTrans = False
      'begin transaction
      moConn.beginTrans
      DABeginTrans = True
      Exit Function
DABeginTransErr:
      lErrNo = Err.Number
      sErrDescr = Err.Description
End Function
```

The DACommitTrans function messages to the ADO Connection object moConn that we wish to commit a transaction. Any and all update-oriented SQL statements since the start of the message to DABeginTrans will be committed to the DBMS.

```
Public Function DACommitTrans(Optional lErrNo As _
   Long, Optional sErrDescr As String) As Boolean
      On Error GoTo DACommitTransErr
      DACommitTrans = False
      'commit the transaction
      moConn.commitTrans
      DACommitTrans = True
```

```
        Exit Function
DACommitTransErr:
    lErrNo = Err.Number
    sErrDescr = Err.Description
End Function
```

The DARollBackTrans function messages to the ADO Connection object moConn that we wish to rollback a transaction. Any and all update-oriented SQL statements since the start of the message to DABeginTrans will be rolled back out of the DBMS.

```
Public Function DARollBack(Optional lErrNo As _
  Long, Optional sErrDescr As String) As Boolean
    On Error GoTo DARollBackErr
    DARollBack = False
    'rollback the transaction
    moConn.RollbackTrans
    If Not DAClose(lErrNo, sErrDescr) Then
       Exit Function
    End If
    DARollBack = True
    Exit Function
DARollBackErr:
    lErrNo = Err.Number
    sErrDescr = Err.Description
End Function
```

This pretty much wraps up the entire functionality of the dasvc component. We shouldn't have to do much to it for the completion of this chapter. We will, though, have to address this architecture once we take into account an application that wants to operate within the MTS environment. This component maintains quite a bit of stateful information in between calls from the dtsvc component. In addition, all the begintrans, committrans, and rollback logic is completely unnecessary when running within MTS. Keep in mind that we want a design that can work in or out of MTS, using the same code. We will face that challenge when we look at implementing the Remulak Productions system within the MTS environment.

Before we compile the component, and since we are sure that there will be no compile errors, we need to reference the ADO type library. To do that we need to do the following.

1. Select the Project menu item.

2. Select "Components" from the drop-down menu list.

This will present the Components dialog window.

3. Scroll down the list and select the "Microsoft ActiveX Data Objects 2.0 Library."

4. Select "OK."

Figure 11-16 is what the References dialog window should look like when the ADO type library is selected.

FIGURE 11-16   *References dialog box for the ADO type library.*

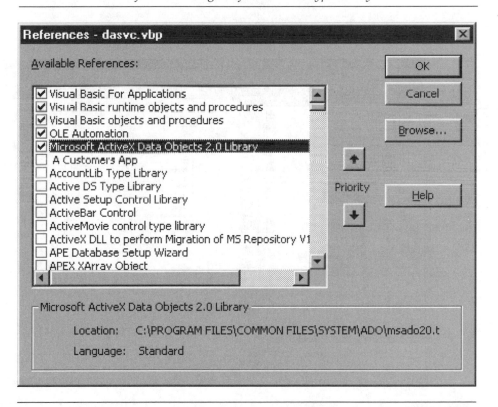

The last thing we might want to do is reverse engineer all the work we did back into the Rational Rose model. Some might think of this as a waste of time, but they couldn't be further from the truth. First, it allows other developers and designers to see the inner workings of the application from the class diagram perspective. Second, as more sequence diagrams are created, these new operations will now appear and can be used to quicken the dynamic modeling iterations. Third, it enforces traceability and we don't have to rely on "code experts" to understand the system. The design view of the class diagram is invaluable for the evolution of the application.

We have already done a reengineering exercise previously, so I won't go through the steps in detail again. If you have the `dasvc` project open, refer back to Figure 11-13; all should work as before. What you end up with should look like Figure 11-17.

FIGURE 11-17 *Rose model after reengineering the DASVC project.*

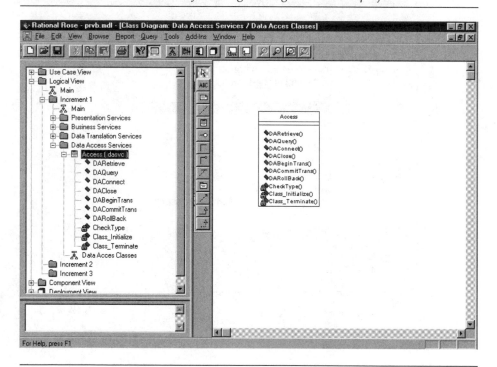

Data Translation Services Layer: DTSVC Component

Building the SQL to Be Executed by the Data Access Services Layer

The `dtsvc` project implements this layer, and it contains a one-to-one mapping between the entity classes found in the Business Rule Services layer. We generated these classes in a previous step in this chapter.

This layer also does some additional work for us. Since the Business Rule Services layer will be driving all of our transactions via the use case controller classes mentioned previously, they need a way to request services through this layer to establish a connection as well as a unit of work for multistep, update-oriented SQL statements. Before we build our first entity-related translation class, let's add a new class to our `dtsvc` project called `ContextDT` and five operations to perform the services of this class (`DTSetContext`, `DTSetConnect`, `DTSetComplete`, `DTSetAbort`, and `DTSetClose`). These support-oriented classes will work hand-in-hand with all the other classes in this project, as well as the `Access` class in the `dasvc` component. To add the class, do the following.

1. Right-click the `dtsvc` project in the project explorer window.
2. Select "Add" from the drop-down menu list.
3. Select "Class Module."
4. Double-click the "class module" icon.

We need to now add code to support the five operations mentioned previously. You can do this in two ways. You could set up the class using the Class Wizard, add the operations through that route, and then add the code that we are about to present. The other approach is to just enter the information as is outlined below.

For the `DTSetContext` operation, we need to add support for not only setting a connection, via a call to `DTSetConnect`, but also the ability begin a transaction if asked to do so by the `bAction` setting passed in.

```
Public theAccess As Access
Public Function DTSetContext(ByVal sConnect As _
   String, Optional ByVal bAction As Boolean,
Optional lErrNo As Long, Optional sErrDescr As _
   String) As Boolean
```

```
            On Error GoTo DTSetContextErr
            Set theAccess = New dasvc.Access
            Set goAccess = theAccess
            DTSetContext = False
            If DTSetConnect(sConnect, lErrNo, sErrDescr) _
              Then
                If bAction Then
                    If Not theAccess.DABeginTrans(lErrNo, _
                      sErrDescr) Then
                        DTSetContext = True
                        Exit Function
                    End If
                Else
                    DTSetContext = True
                    Exit Function
                End If
                DTSetContext = True
            End If
    DTSetContextErr:
        lErrNo = Err.Number
        sErrDescr = Err.Description
    End Function
```

To support this new class, we need the ability for all the classes in the project to communicate with the same instance of the Access object. To do this, we need to create a standard BAS module. Call it dtBAS. Follow the same procedure as for adding a class, with the exception of selecting "module" instead of "class module." Add one line of code to this module:

```
Dim goAccess as dasvc.Access
```

The previous DTSetContext function calls DTSetConnect. Let's define it next.

```
Public Function DTSetConnect(ByVal sConnect As _
    String, Optional lErrNo As Long, Optional _
    sErrDescr As String) As Boolean
    On Error GoTo DTSetConnect
    DTSetConnect = False
```

```
      If theAccess.DAConnect(sConnect, lErrNo, _
         sErrDescr) Then
           DTSetConnect = True
           Exit Function
      End If
DTSetConnectErr:
      lErrNo = Err.Number
      sErrDescr = Err.Description
End Function
```

This function simply calls the `Access` function `DAConnect` to get a connection to the database.

The next operation to define is `DTSetComplete`.

```
Public Function DTsetComplete(Optional ByVal _
   bAction As Boolean, Optional lErrNo As Long, _
   Optional sErrDescr As String) As Boolean
      On Error GoTo DTSetCompleteErr
      DTsetComplete = False
      If bAction Then
         If Not theAccess.DACommitTrans(lErrNo, _
            sErrDescr) Then
                   Exit Function
         End If
      End If
      'Close the connection
      If DTsetClose Then
          DTsetComplete = True
      End If
DTSetCompleteErr:
      lErrNo = Err.Number
      sErrDescr = Err.Description
End Function
```

If the prior activity had been part of a unit of work (`bAction = True`), then `DACommitTrans` would have been called. The next operation is `DTSetAbort`.

```
Public Function DTsetAbort(Optional lErrNo As _
   Long, Optional sErrDescr As String) As Boolean
```

```
      On Error GoTo DTsetAbort
      DTsetAbort = False
      If theAccess.DARollBack(lErrNo, sErrDescr) _
        Then
           DTsetAbort = True
           Exit Function
      End If
DTSetAbortErr:
      lErrNo = Err.Number
      sErrDescr = Err.Description
End Function
```

The last operation for this new class is `DTSetClose`.

```
Private Function DTSetClose(Optional lErrNo As _
  Long, Optional sErrDescr As String) As Boolean
      On Error GoTo DTSetClose
      DTSetClose = False
      'Close the connection
      If Not theAccess.DAClose(lErrNo, sErrDescr) _
        Then
           Exit Function
      End If
      DTSetClose = True
DTSetCloseErr:
      lErrNo = Err.Number
      sErrDescr = Err.Description
End Function
```

Let's now add some code to the `CustomerDT` class that will retrieve information from the database. I am assuming that you have run the setup DDL scripts for your database of choice. Microsoft SQL Server v7.0 scripts accompany the code for this book. This code can be found as per the directions in the appendix. There isn't too much setup required because for our first pass, we will retrieve only customer information. To facilitate the construction of SQL, we will want to add quite a few global String constants, such as quotes and spaces, to make the construction much simpler. These can be added to the `dtBAS` module created previously. In the code that follows, reference to the "gs" variables can be found in the dtBAS module.

```
Private Function ICrud_getInfo(ByVal sQualifier As _
   String, sData() As String, Optional lErrNo As _
   Long, Optional sErrDescr As String) As Boolean
   Dim sQry As String
   ICrud_getInfo = False
   'Build query string
   sQry = gsSELECT
   sQry = sQry & "mcustomerID" & gsCOMMASPACE
   sQry = sQry & "mcustomerNumber" & gsCOMMASPACE
   sQry = sQry & "mfirstName" & gsCOMMASPACE
   sQry = sQry & "mlastName" & gsCOMMASPACE
   sQry = sQry & "mmiddleInitial" & gsCOMMASPACE
   sQry = sQry & "mprefix" & gsCOMMASPACE
   sQry = sQry & "msuffix" & gsCOMMASPACE
   sQry = sQry & "mphone1" & gsCOMMASPACE
   sQry = sQry & "mphone2" & gsCOMMASPACE
   sQry = sQry & "meMail"
   sQry = sQry & gsFROM
   sQry = sQry & msCustomer
   sQry = sQry & gsWHERE
   sQry = sQry & "mcustomerNumber" & gsEQUALS
   sQry = sQry & gsSQ
   sQry = sQry & sQualifier
   sQry = sQry & gsSQ
   'Call the operation on the Access class
   If goAccess.DARetrieve(sQry, sData, False, _
   lErrNo, sErrDescr) Then
       ICrud_getInfo = True
   End If
End Function
```

Remember that the DT classes, with the exception of the newly created ContextDT class, all implement the ICrud interface. The SQL statement executes a query on the T_Customer table, matching on the customerNumber passed in from the Business Rule Services layer. That is all that we are going to build into the dtsvc project for now.

Our goal initially is to get a use case pathway completed from start to finish.

Business Rule Services Layer: BRSVC Component

Building the Rules That Govern Processing

The brsvc project implements the Business Rule Services layer, and it contains our entity classes for Remulak Productions. As said previously, there are really two kinds of business rules—those that deal with the user interface and how we enforce certain syntax/context edits and those that govern the business and how it operates. Also said was that the DT classes defined in the previous section are a kind of business rule in that they deal with how we translate a logical request for service into an SQL call. As you can conclude, the definition of a business rule is a bit subjective.

There are two additional classes we added that are called controllers: UCProcessOrderController and UCMaintRltnController. These classes represent the use case. Each operation within the controller class maps to a pathway through the use case. It will be the responsibility of these "pathway operations" to orchestrate the messaging necessary to satisfy the use case pathway.

There will be other operations found in these classes that deal with preparing, for instance, the user interface so that a use case pathway can be performed, such as loading list boxes and so on. The previous chapter introduced four different use case controllers. In this chapter, we will acknowledge two of them and flesh out one of them. Eventually, the completed code for the first increment will have all four in use.

The goal of the use case controller classes is to orchestrate the messaging for a use case pathway. These classes can range from something simple, such as the one we will initially put together, to quite complex, such as the one for entering a new order. The controller also acts as an excellent surrogate to the Business Rule Services layer and the entity classes. All messaging from the Presentation Services layer will go through the use case controllers. The use case controllers will also become vital to the implementation of units of work that require an all or nothing series of transactions for our database updates.

In the following code review for the `brsvc` layer, there will be several global variable references, such as `giFirstName`. We know they are global because we have prefaced them with a "g." These are not found in a BAS module but in a new class called `Dictionary`. `Dictionary` is nothing more than a series of ENUM blocks defining our array offsets for each class. This allows the Business Rule Services and Presentation Services layers to refer to logical names instead of ugly array offsets (that is, `sData(3,5)`). There will be an ENUM block for each and every entity class that we define. This class is duplicated in both the `brsvc` and `uisvc` projects. In the `brsvc` project, it must be marked as "globalmulti-use" so that we can refer to them just like global variables.

```
'these represent enums for public consumption
Public Enum enumCustomer
    giCustomerId = 0
    giCustomerNumber = 1
    giFirstName = 2
    giLastName = 3
    giMiddleInitial = 4
    giPrefix = 5
    giSuffix = 6
    giPhone1 = 7
    giPhone2 = 8
    giEMail = 9
End Enum

Public Enum enumArrayOffsets
    giZERODIM = 0
    giONEDIM = 1
    giTWODIM = 2
    giTHREEDIM = 3
    giFOURDIM = 4
    giFIVEDIM = 5
End Enum
```

When we initially generated our code skeletons into our VB projects, we added the previous two controllers. Now we need to add some code to them. Let's start out by adding an operation that deals with the use case pathway that we are implementing first, a Relationship

Inquiry by customer number. Let's call the operation `RltnInquiry` and assign it to the `UCMaintRltnController` class.

```
Public Function RltnInquiry(ByVal sCustomerNumber _
   As String, sData() As String, Optional lErrno As _
   Long, Optional sErrDescr As String) As Boolean
   On Error GoTo RltnInquiryErr
   Dim oCustomer As New Customer
   RltnInquiry = False
   Set oContextDT = New dtsvc.ContextDT
   If oContextDT.DTSetContext(msDSN, False, _
     lErrno, sErrDescr) Then
   If oCustomer.getInfo(sCustomerNumber, lErrno, _
     sErrDescr) Then
         If oCustomer.getState(sData, lErrno, _
           sErrDescr) Then
           RltnInquiry = True
           Set oCustomer = Nothing
         End If
      End If
   End If
   If RltnInquiry Then
      If oContextDT.DTSetComplete(False, lErrno, _
        sErrDescr) Then
         Set oContextDT = Nothing
         Exit Function
      End If
   End If
 RltnInquiryErr:
   lErrno = Err.Number
   sErrDescr = Err.description
End Function
```

From where is this operation called? This operation is called from the user interface controller `UIMaintRltnController`. Notice that the signature of this operation is passing in a customer number, `sCustomerNumber`, from the screen, as well as a dynamic array, `sData()`, that must be populated and returned.

The operation then gets a handle to both a `Customer` object, `oCustomer`, as well as a `ContextDT` object, `oContextDT`. We get a connection to the database by calling the `DTSetContext` operation. Notice that we are passing in the connect string. In our example, this is defined as a constant string value with the DSN specified. This string value is defined in the `UCMaintRltnController` class. A better solution would be to keep this value in a Registry key or an INI file and get it dynamically during application load.

The operation `getInfo` is called on the `Customer` object, passing in again the `sCustomerNumber` that came from the user interface request. The result of this call to `Customer` is that it populates its member variables.

Before we can move on with what our use case controller is doing, let's look at the details of what is happening in the `Customer` class and, in particular, the `getInfo` and `getState` operations.

```
Public Function getInfo(ByVal sCustomerNumber _
  As String, Optional lErrno As Long, Optional _
  sErrDescr As String) As Boolean
    On Error GoTo getInfoErr
    Dim sData() As String
    Dim oICrud As ICrud
    getInfo = False
    Set theCustomerDT = New dtsvc.CustomerDT
    'Talk to the DT interface
    Set oICrud = theCustomerDT
    If oICrud.getInfo(sCustomerNumber, sData, _
      lErrno, sErrDescr) Then
      If unPack(sData, giZERODIM) Then
        getInfo = True
        Exit Function
      End If
    End If

getInfoErr:
    lErrno = Err.Number
    sErrDescr = Err.description
End Function
```

The `getInfo` operation for `Customer` gets a reference to a `CustomerDT` object and then assigns it to an object of type `ICrud`. Remember, `ICrud` is our interface class. All DT classes support the

ICrud interface. The CustomerDT object, oICrud, is sent the get-Info message. We reviewed what CustomerDT's getInfo does in the previous section when we covered the Data Translation Services layer and the dtsvc project.

After the information is returned in sData(), we need to populate the Customer object's member variables, such as mfirstName and mlastName. We do this with the Customer's unPack operation.

```
Private Function unPack(sData() As String, iIndex _
   As Integer, Optional lErrno As Long, Optional _
   sErrDescr As String) As Boolean
   On Error GoTo unPackErr
   unPack = False
   customerId = CLng(sData(giCustomerId, iIndex))
   customerNumber = CStr(sData(giCustomerNumber, _
      iIndex))
   firstName = CStr(sData(giFirstName, iIndex))
   lastName = CStr(sData(giLastName, iIndex))
   middleInitial = CStr(sData(giMiddleInitial, _
      iIndex))
   prefix = CStr(sData(giPrefix, iIndex))
   suffix = CStr(sData(giSuffix, iIndex))
   phone1 = CStr(sData(giPhone1, iIndex))
   phone2 = CStr(sData(giPhone2, iIndex))
   eMail = CStr(sData(giEMail, iIndex))
   unPack = True
   Exit Function

unPackErr:
   lErrno = Err.Number
   sErrDescr = Err.description
End Function
```

The unPack operation takes the results of the call to the Data Translation Services layer that was returned by getInfo and converts the data types back to their native format for storage in the Customer class's member variables. This is a nice example of encapsulation, in that only Customer has to know about how values from a database call eventually got assigned to member variables.

The next operation called in the `RltnInquiry` operation is the `getState` operation. This operation is also directed at the `oCustomer` object. This operation just grabs all the local member variables in one operation.

```
Public Function getState(sData() As String, _
    Optional lErrno As Long, Optional sErrDescr As _
    String) As Boolean

    On Error GoTo getStateErr

    getState = False

    ReDim sData(9)

    sData(giCustomerId) = customerId
    sData(giCustomerNumber) = customerNumber
    sData(giFirstName) = firstName
    sData(giLastName) = lastName
    sData(giMiddleInitial) = middleInitial
    sData(giPrefix) = prefix
    sData(giSuffix) = suffix
    sData(giPhone1) = phone1
    sData(giPhone2) = phone2
    sData(giEMail) = eMail

    getState = True
    Exit Function

getStateErr:
    lErrno = Err.Number
    sErrDescr = Err.description
End Function
```

Back to the `RltnInquiry` operation in the `UCMaintRltnController` class, the `getState` operation returned all the customer attribute values in the `sData` dynamic string array.

If everything went as planned, then the `DTSetComplete` message is sent to the `oContextDT` object. This will result in the connection to the database being closed. Control is now returned back to the

UIMaintRltnController class found in the uisvc project, which we will cover in our next section.

Presentation Service Layer: UISVC Component

What the User Sees: Attaching the User Interface to the Business Rule Services Layer

The uisvc project implements the Presentation Services layer, and it contains the forms along with a controller class for each form. The form that we will focus on in this chapter is Customer Relationships.

The primary interface between the user interface and the other layers is through the user interface controller. The previous chapter, in the discussion about the MVC (model view controller) framework, said that there was one user interface controller for each form. We added the UIMaintRltnController class in this chapter when we generated the code out of Rational Rose. However, there wasn't much in it. Let's explore what we need to do to hook the Presentation Services layer and the Business Rule Services layer together, along with setting up the communications necessary to talk to the Business Rule Services layer. Figure 11-18 is the Maintain Relationships form.

The first thing that we need to do is initialize the form and get an instance of our UIMaintRltnController class so that the form can talk to the other layers. These few lines of code in frmMaintRltn will do that for us.

```
Private moMyController As UIMaintRltnController
Private Sub Form_Load()
    If Not Initialize Then
    End If
End Sub

Function Initialize() As Boolean
    Set moMyController = New UIMaintRltnController
End Function
```

The form, during load, will create an instance of the user interface controller with which we will interact. Once the form is displayed, we will need to inform the controller of our intentions. By entering a "Cus-

FIGURE 11-18 *Maintain Relationships form.*

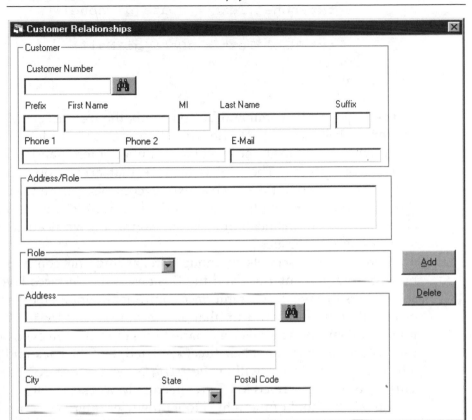

tomer Number" and clicking the "Find" command button located to
the right of the field, we will request the information for that customer
number to be returned.

```
Private Sub cmdCustomer_Click()
    Dim sData() As String
    If moMyController.getInfo(txtCustomerNumber.Text, _
      sData) Then
        txtFirstName.Text = sData(giFirstName)
        txtLastName.Text = sData(giLastName)
        txtMInitial.Text = sData(giMiddleInitial)
        txtPrefix.Text = sData(giPrefix)
```

```
                txtSuffix.Text = sData(giSuffix)
                txtPhone1.Text = sData(giPhone1)
                txtPhone2.Text = sData(giPhone2)
                txtEMail.Text = sData(giEMail)
        End If
    End Sub
```

The logic in this command button sends the `getInfo` message to the form's instance of the `UIMaintRltnController` class. It passes along with that request the customer number entered and a dynamic string array, `sData`. The goal is to have that array populated with attributes to place in the screen's textbox controls. Before we examine the `getInfo` operation that exists in the `UIMaintRltnController` class that the command button is messaging to, we need to review some architecture issues.

There are two schools of thought regarding the communication between the user interface and the Business Rule Services layer. One school says to have the user interface controller maintain local arrays of objects that are messaged to (that is, `Customer` and `Order`). This is fine, and I have done it this way many times myself. However, now the user interface component has direct knowledge of the back-end layers, albeit they are hidden within the `UIMaintRltnController` class. This is how we described MVC architecture to work as well.

The other school of thought is to let the user interface controller on the front-end communicate with the use case controller in the `brsvc` layer. Let the use case controller class, `UCMaintRltnController` in our case, work directly with our user interface controller, `UIMaintRltnController` (revisit Figure 11-15). Any object references that must be kept will be in the use case controller class. This will make the user interface very light, but then with the user interface in a constant state of flux, maybe that will pay off in the long-run (remember that we have an Internet requirement to deal with later). Let me say, this is where the use of disconnected recordsets handled at the client would make the interaction a bit easier. Then, of course, we would still have to contend with passing VB-specific recordsets all over the place.

To communicate with our use case controller, `UCMaintRltn Controller`, we need a local reference to it in our user interface controller:

```
Private moUCMaintRltnController _
As brsvc.UCMaintRltnController
```

Then, to send our request along the way through the layers previously described, we need to request that the use case controller execute our use case pathway for us.

```
Public Function getInfo(ByVal sCustomerNumber As _
   String, sData() As String, Optional lErrNo As _
   Long, Optional sErrDescr As String) As Boolean
   On Error GoTo getInfoErr
   getInfo = False
   Set moUCMaintRltnController = New _
     brsvc.UCMaintRltnController
   If moUCMaintRltnController.RltnInquiry _
     (sCustomerNumber, sData, lErrNo, sErrDescr) _
      Then
     getInfo = True
     Set moUCMaintRltnController = Nothing
     Exit Function
   End If

getInfoErr:
   lErrNo = Err.Number
   sErrDescr = Err.Description
End Function
```

This request is made against the local instance of the use case controller `moUCMaintRltnController`. It is sent the `RltnInquiry` message passing `sCustomerNumber` and the dynamic string array `sData`.

Referring back to the code within the previous `cmdCustomer` command button, if the use case pathway is successful, then the individual textbox fields are populated with the results. You should get something back as shown in Figure 11-19. This results from using the sample data that comes with the database accompanying this book.

Now that we have made it all the way through a use case pathway, it is now time to reverse engineer what we have done back into Rational Rose. Go ahead and do that as we did previously in this chapter.

FIGURE 11-19 *Maintain Relationships form after execution.*

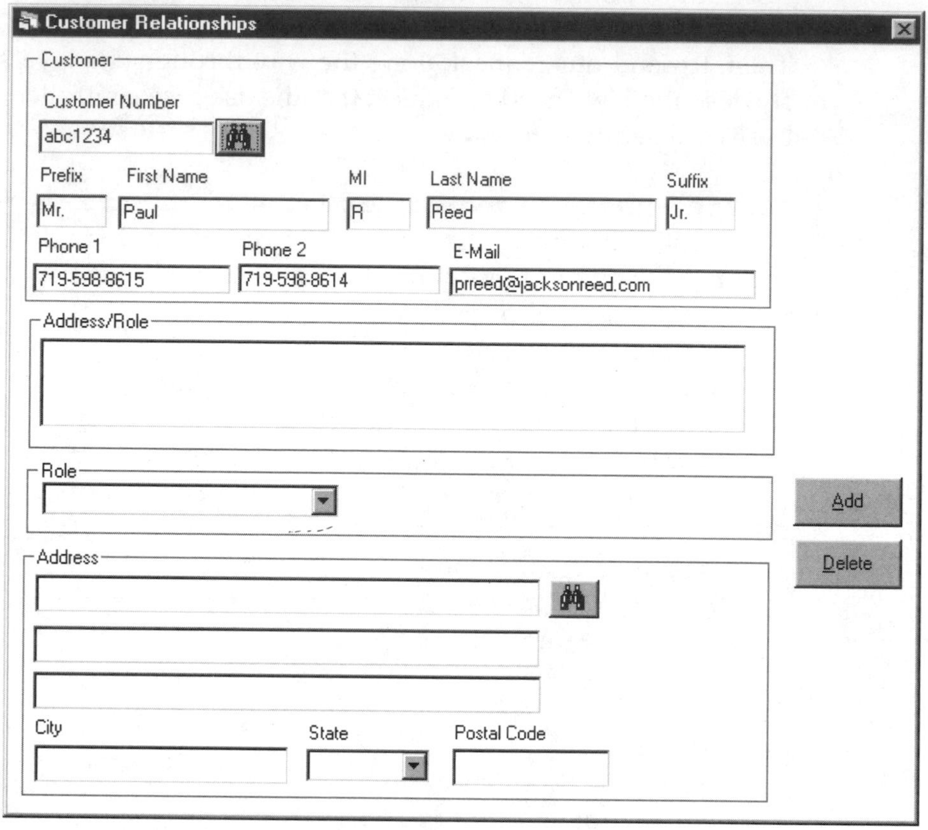

Building Blocks for the Future

There was a lot of code presented in this chapter. We started out by generating all of our code from the nucleus of our class diagram. Because we are iteratively developing the system, we then coded a little, reverse engineered, and then coded some more. It is important to revisit Figure 11-15. It will be much clearer to you now that you have walked through the code that implemented that particular sequence diagram.

The goal of this chapter was to get us through a relatively simple use case pathway from start to finish. The good news is that with much of the infrastructure code now built, we won't have to do as much the next time around. It also helped to solidify our architecture by going through the construction process. Our next challenge will be to do some more-complicated pathways, such as adding addresses and assigning them to customers along with roles. The order entry portion of the application will show up when we do the Internet front-end for the order inquiry.

Checkpoint

Where We Have Been

1. A visual modeling tool is necessary to expedite the process of program code development. The primary source for the code is both the class and component diagrams.

2. Just as forward engineering is beneficial, it is important to reverse engineer the application code back into the visual model. This iterative process—forward engineering, coding in VB, and then reverse engineering—is ongoing.

3. The Data Access Services layer implemented our physical access API, in our case ADO. This API could be replaced with something else, and the other layers in the application wouldn't have to change at all.

4. The Data Translation Services layer built the physical SQL statements to implement the request for information. The SQL is passed to the Data Access Services layer.

5. The physical layers of the application must stay contained. We enforce that with the use of controller classes in both the Presentation and Business Rule Services layers.

Where We Are Going Next

In the next chapter, we:

1. Explore the changes and additions needed to support the more robust functionality, such as inserting, updating, and deleting information from the Remulak Productions system.

2. Review what is necessary to implement the functionality to fully support the customer relationship portion of the application.

3. Explore the use of the Remulak Productions coding framework to support transactions that can be committed or rolled back based on the conditions met in the application.

CHAPTER 12

Generating Code From the UML Class Diagram (Part 2)

In the last chapter, we accomplished quite a lot. Code was generated from the Rose diagram. We then fleshed out the four layers of the application with enough detail to support a use case pathway, Customer Inquiry, from start to finish. In that process, we added new classes and then reverse engineered those back into the Rose model. This round-trip engineering will be continual throughout the project. In fact, it was stated strongly that if this type of back and forth synchronization wasn't performed between code and the model, then the hope of traceability for the application would be lost.

This chapter will focus on adding more code to the Remulak Productions system. While it is fresh in our minds from the last chapter, we will continue with the Customer Relationship effort and enhance the inquiry, as well as add update capabilities.

GOALS

⇨ Review the Customer Inquiry pathway through the Maintain Relationships use case and add additional inquiry functionality. Primarily, expand the notion of what a `Customer` contains by retrieving not only its properties but also the objects that it contains, such as `Locale` and `Address`.

↪ Review a growing trend to split the "business object" between client and server, thus losing much of the benefit of keeping a class's implementation cohesive. An alternative will be proposed that keeps the notion of complete classes intact, while still preparing the design for an eventual distributed implementation.

↪ Explore an alternative to dealing with String arrays at the client: UDTs (User-Defined Types) and the unique capabilities added to them in VB v6.0.

↪ Explore how the architecture will support insert, update, and delete functionality as it pertains to the Customer Relationship pathway.

Construction Phase

This chapter adds to the Construction phase as we implement more of the Remulak Productions system. Our efforts will focus on expanding the functionality already presented with additional capabilities and features.

FIGURE 12-1 *Synergy process model and the Construction phase.*

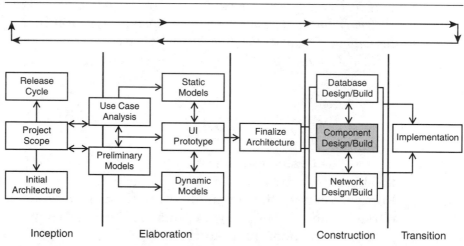

Although the Construction phase considers several different areas, as outlined in Figure 12-1, the focus of this chapter will be on the following.

- The "Component Design/Build" block, in this chapter, will deal with creating much of the code that drives the application.

In following chapters, we will take this solution and modify it to support DCOM and MTS, as well as the Internet.

Enhancing the Customer Inquiry and Introducing the Notion of Shallow and Expanded Objects

Our Customer Relationship Inquiry efforts from the last chapter accomplished the goal of getting a transaction to work from start to finish. They exercised our architecture ideas and forced us to make some alternative decision about how the design was actually realized. However, there were some aspects of our work that you may have noticed were incomplete. Specifically, it didn't address the following:

- The ability to retrieve not only `Customer` information but also other information about a customer, such as its `Addresses` and the `Locale` information. Remember that `Locale` defines the role that a given `Customer` plays with an `Address`.
- A mechanism to support the inserting, updating, and deleting of `Customer` and `Customer`-related objects such as `Address` and `Locale`.

To address the first item, a brief discussion is necessary about a troublesome issue regarding object attributes and their status during instantiation. Take the `Customer` class that we dealt with in the last chapter. Besides the obvious `Customer` attributes, such as `firstName` and `lastName`, there were also the following attributes:

```
Public theLocale As Collection
Public theOrder As Collection
```

The question arises, if we just want to retrieve what are called *base Customer attributes* but not their contained attributes (relationships) that are in and of themselves objects, what do we do? This is a common problem that presents itself in most object designs. There are two ways, generally, to deal with this issue, and they each have pros and cons.

- Upon instantiation of an existing `Customer`, via `getInfo` as discussed in the last chapter, all contained objects are also retrieved and instantiated.

   Pros
   - The customer is completely expanded, with all contained objects, and allows the observer to always view an object as a cohesive whole at runtime.

   Cons
   - Performance can degrade severely and in many cases unnecessarily. Why instantiate, for instance, all of a `Customer`'s `Order` and `Locale` objects, which could escalate into the hundreds, if all that is desired are base class attributes?

- Part of the instantiation request will be a parameter request to expand the object or not. That is, if the expansion is not requested, it will be instantiated as a shallow instance, except with its base attributes intact.

   Pros
   - Performance is improved, especially for those objects that have many complex relationships. Given the business context, only those aspects of the object are retrieved that need to be.

   Cons
   - The object will be in an incomplete state, with all of its parts not fully expanded. This will require that the user of that object either understand its incomplete state or request that it be expanded should the need arise. A solution to this potential problem is to provide expansion on demand. That is, if a message is sent to a contained object, then it will need to expand itself as needed.

   In our design, the second strategy will be pursued. This will be the goal of our next major coding exercise, expanding the functionality of the Customer Relationship Inquiry to bring back all of an object's properties when requested.

Code Changes to the Customer Relationship Inquiry

Let's focus our attention on the changes necessary to the work done so far to support the notion of shallow and expanded objects. A good place to start is the `Customer` class itself and the operations already in place. To get the ball rolling, we must tweak our Rose model a bit, due to a deficiency in how Rose generates VB code for association classes, specifically that of the `Locale` class. Figure 12-2 shows the association class, `Locale`.

If we generate VB code from this model, Rose will generate the following attributes in the following classes.

```
'Address Class
Public theCustomer As Locale
'Customer Class
Public theAddress as Locale
'Locale Class
Public theCustomer As Collection
Public theAddress As Collection
```

What should be generated for the three classes is the following.

```
'Address Class
Public theLocale As Collection
'Customer Class
Public theLocale as Collection
'Locale Class
Public theCustomer As Customer
Public theAddress As Address
```

To do this, we are going to have to change the model to get the code to generate properly. I don't think of this as necessarily being a negative

FIGURE 12-2   *The Association class* `Locale`.

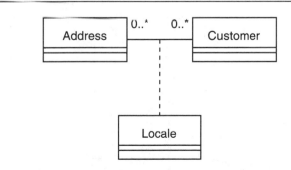

thing. Granted, I wish the tool generated it properly in the first place, but this is the design model, not the analysis model, and thus things do require changing to accommodate the implementation semantics. What we want the class diagram to look like is shown in Figure 12-3.

The changes suggested in Figure 12-3 will end up generating the correct relationships that we need.

Code Changes to Support Expanding Objects

It is a reality that performance should usually be the most primary concern when compared to all other factors. Perhaps one area that is even more important is an application that is easy to change and enhance. Regardless, there are compromises that we must make from time to time. This is the focus of this section and how we can deal with shallow and fully expandable objects.

It is important to note that almost any class in the project could benefit from optionally being expanded or not. It is possible, though, that an object may not have any contained references to other objects, especially if the navigability is in the direction of the object in question. I usually choose in my designs to make this feature at least published in the signature of the getInfo operation for every class, whether it supports it or not. This allows the designer some flexibility in the future should the underlying associations change.

Remember from the last chapter the elegant and rather simplified manner that each layer used when requesting services of the next. Specifically, the use case controller class UCMaintRltnController

FIGURE 12-3   *The modified class diagram to support code generation.*

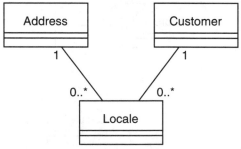

contained the `RltnInquiry` operation that implemented the Customer Relationship Inquiry use case pathway.

```
Public Function RltnInquiry(ByVal sCustomerNumber _
   As String, sData() As String, Optional lErrno _
     As Long, Optional sErrDescr As String) _
     As Boolean On Error GoTo RltnInquiryErr
     Dim oCustomer As New Customer
     RltnInquiry = False
     Set oContextDT = New dtsvc.ContextDT
     If oContextDT.DTSetContext(msDSN, False, _
       lErrno, sErrDescr) Then
         If oCustomer.getInfo(sCustomerNumber, _
           lErrno, sErrDescr) Then
             If oCustomer.getState(sData, lErrno, _
               sErrDescr) Then
                 RltnInquiry = True
                 Set oCustomer = Nothing
             End If
         End If
     End If
     If RltnInquiry Then
         If oContextDT.DTSetComplete(False, lErrno, _
           sErrDescr) Then
             Set oContextDT = Nothing
             Exit Function
         End If
     End If
RltnInquiryErr:
     lErrno = Err.Number
     sErrDescr = Err.description
End Function
```

The important line of the previous code is the `getInfo` message being sent to `oCustomer`. It is here that we need to decide what type of service we are requesting of this object. When printing mailing labels or producing a demographics report of customers, the only thing I really care about are the base `Customer` attributes. I don't care about contained `Orders` or `Locales`.

What is needed is a way to request of an object just base attributes (shallow) or the fully instantiated object (expanded). For this to be supported, the signature of getInfo, as it resides in the Customer class, needs to be changed.

```
Public Function getInfo(ByVal sCustomerNumber As  _
    String, Optional bExpand As Boolean, Optional  _
    lErrno As Long, Optional sErrDescr As String)  _
    As Boolean
```

The only change in the signature is this newly defined parameter:

```
Optional bExpand As Boolean
```

Now, we need to make some changes within the getInfo operation of Customer to support this. The driving portion of the getInfo operation within Customer needs to interrogate this parameter and, if a shallow object is being requested, proceed as before. However, if an expanded object is being requested, then we must dig down into our association horizon and realize those relationships.

```
If oICrud.getInfo(sCustomerNumber, sData, lErrno, _
    sErrDescr) Then
        If unPack(sData, giZERODIM, True) Then
            getInfo = True
            If bExpand Then
              Set oLocale = New Locale
              Set oLocale.theCustomer = Me
              If oLocale.getInfoByCustomerId(lErrno, _
                sErrDescr) Then
                  Set theLocale = oLocale.colLocale
              End If
            End If
        End If
    End If
```

Notice that this code creates a new Locale object and sets its contained reference of theCustomer to Me. This is simply saying, "Hey, I am creating you and here is your reference you need to me." The next thing we do is send the getInfoByCustomerId message to the oLocale object that we just created. The goal will be to get all the

`Locale` objects to which this `Customer` is related. Those related `Locales` are being assigned to the `Customer`'s `theLocale` collection by the next line of code:

```
Set theLocale = oLocale.colLocale
```

We will explore this in depth shortly. Before we proceed, what is actually taking place in this code is a fabrication of something that VB does not support—class operations and attributes.

Don't be confused—I mentioned this shortcoming at the beginning of the book. It is a minor one but important to point out. There is the notion that classes can have operations and attributes that aren't related to any given instance of a class. They represent structure and behavior that apply to all instances of a class. A good case in point is our operation `getInfoByCustomerId`. We are asking for a collection of `Locales`, not just one. This kind of operation in C++ or Java would be declared `static`—this distinguishes it from traditional instance-related operations.

VB has no distinction as such. There is a way to simulate this: by declaring a separate class for the sole purpose of holding class-level attributes and operations and assigning it a property of `Global Multi-Use`. This allows us to use an operation without creating a reference to the object prior to its use. I don't like this approach to class-level simulation, although I admit to having done it before, because now the designer has two classes that really are one and the same thing.

So, the `oLocale` object that we instantiated previously is going to act as our proxy to which to send the `getInfoByCustomerID` message. Let's now explore what is going on inside of `oLocale` when it gets this message.

```
Public Function getInfoByCustomerId(Optional _
  lErrno As Long, Optional sErrDescr As String) _
  As Boolean
    On Error GoTo getInfoErr
    Dim sData() As String
    Dim lCustomerId As Long
    Dim oICrud As ICrud
    Dim oLocale As Locale
    Dim iIndex As Integer
```

```
        getInfoByCustomerId = False
        Set theLocaleDT = New dtsvc.LocaleDT
        'Talk To The Interface
        Set oICrud = theLocaleDT
        lCustomerId = theCustomer.customerId
        If oICrud.getInfo(CStr(lCustomerId), sData, _
          lErrno, sErrDescr) Then
            If unPack(sData, True, lErrno, sErrDescr) Then
                getInfoByCustomerId = True
            End If
        End If
        Exit Function
getInfoErr:
        lErrno = Err.Number
        sErrDescr = Err.description
End Function
```

Like we did previously in our simple `Customer` inquiry, we set the operation to talk to its `ICrud` interface and send a `getInfo` message to its Data Translation counterpart, `LocaleDT`. Remember that the `ICrud` interface is the same for all DT classes. We basically pass in a String array, which gets returned to us. However, this time, unlike in the previous chapter's `getInfo`, we may get multiple rows back, as a `Customer` can have more than one `Address` and this is what `Locale` tells us. I won't show the code for `LocaleDT`'s `getInfo`; it is an SQL select statement, just as we reviewed in the last chapter for `Customer`. Again, all the code is available to you as described in the back of this book.

Since we are digging deeper and deeper into this request, let's explore what `oLocale`, our surrogate class to which we send the `getInfoByCustomerID` message, does when it returns with a populated String array from `LocaleDT`. There is an attribute defined in `Locale` that looks like this:

```
Public mcolLocale As Collection
```

The `unpack` operation is going to cycle through the returned result set, make `Locales` out of them, and load them into this collection.

```
Private Function unPack(sData() As String, _
  Optional ByVal bInquiry As Boolean, _
```

```
      Optional lErrno As Long, Optional sErrDescr _
         As String) As Boolean
On Error GoTo unPackErr
Dim iIndex As Integer
Dim oLocale As Locale
Dim bOk As Boolean
Set mcolLocale = New Collection
unPack = False
bOk = False
For iIndex = LBound(sData, giTWODIM) To UBound(sData, _
   giTWODIM)
    Set oLocale = New Locale
    Set oLocale.theCustomer = theCustomer
    Set oLocale.theAddress = New Address
    With oLocale
        .role = CInt(sData(giRole, iIndex))
        .localeId = CLng(sData(giLocaleId, iIndex))
        .theAddress.addressId = CLng(sData _
          (giLocaleAddressId, iIndex))
        If bInquiry Then
           .isDirty = False
           .isDeleted = False
           .isNew = False
        Else
           .isDirty = CBool(sData(giLocaleISDirty, _
              iIndex))
           .isDeleted = CBool(sData(giLocale _
              ISDeleted, iIndex))
           .isNew = CBool(sData(giLocaleISNew, _
              iIndex))
        End If
    End With
    If bInquiry Then
       If Not oLocale.theAddress.getInfo(oLocale. _
          theAddress.addressId,
           lErrno, sErrDescr) Then
           Exit Function
       Else
          bOk = True
```

```
            End If
          Else ' this is an update, delete, insert
            bOk = True
          End If
          If bOk Then
            mcolLocale.Add oLocale, CStr(sData _
              (giLocaleId, iIndex))
            unPack = True
          End If
      Next
      Exit Function
unPackErr:
      lErrno = Err.Number
      sErrDescr = Err.description
End Function
```

What is important to note about unpack is how the For loop uses the Upper and Lower bounds of the second dimension of our returned String array. If you remember from our discussion about the String array, the second dimension is the row indicator. Notice that for each of the rows found, another oLocale is created. This one is a real one, not a proxy used to get work done. It will actually contain information pertaining to what was found on the database.

Since this is an inquiry use of unpack—more on that later in the chapter—we default all the transient attributes such as isNew and such to False. Now the plot thickens. Notice this line of code:

```
oLocale.theAddress.getInfo(oLocale.theAddress. _
  addressId, lErrno, sErrDescr)
```

What is this doing? You guessed it—we are sending a message to the newly created, but as of yet empty, theAddress object, which is contained in oLocale, the getInfo message. Why? To get back an expanded Address object. Sometimes we need a picture to visualize what it is we are unraveling, as shown in Figure 12-4.

To complete the picture, following is Address's getInfo operation, although it is a bit redundant.

```
Public Function getInfo(ByVal lAddressId As Long, _
  Optional lErrno As Long,
```

FIGURE 12-4 *Visualization of the* Locale **class.**

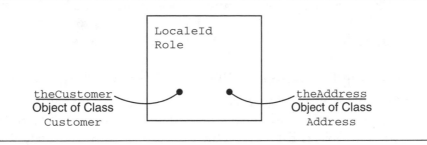

```
    Optional sErrDescr As String) As Boolean
On Error GoTo getInfoErr
Dim sData() As String
Dim oICrud As ICrud
getInfo = False
Set theAddressDT = New dtsvc.AddressDT
'Talk to the DT interface
Set oICrud = theAddressDT
If oICrud.getInfo(CStr(lAddressId), sData, _
  lErrno, sErrDescr) Then
    If unPack(sData, giZERODIM, True) Then
       getInfo = True
       Exit Function
    End If
  End If
getInfoErr:
  lErrno = Err.Number
  sErrDescr = Err.description
End Function
```

Back to the unpack of the Locale object. So, we now are loading our returned address into the theAddress reference. The last thing of importance is the addition of our newly completed Locale, complete with Address, to the collection contained in our proxy Locale.

```
mcolLocale.Add oLocale, CStr(sData(giLocaleId, _
  iIndex))
```

Again, remember, the unpack found in the Locale object is having to retrieve and unravel multiple occurrences of Locale objects. The goal is to get this collection, mcolLocale, back to Customer so that it can be assigned to its Locale collection, theLocale.

Making Life Easier for the User Interface: User-Defined Types

Our prior discussion revealed a much more flexible framework for retrieving information from our system. We added the ability to have smarter objects that, given the proper stimulus, can instantiate themselves in a shallow fashion, with base attributes only or fully expanded. As a result of adding the expansion logic, we are able to retrieve all of a customer's relationships as they deal with Addresses. We will address a Customer's Orders when we look at the Internet portion of the application.

Remember from the last chapter that we carried String arrays, as a result of the retrieval process, all the way back to the client. This worked quite well and met the requirements of the user interface, but could it be better still? Let's next explore a way to make what is presented to the user interface a bit more palatable. We will do that with User-Defined Types (UDT).

UDTs have been around for quite a while in VB. They also have a strong root in that they highly resemble structs for those C programmers out there and also resemble copybooks for those of us who have dabbled in COBOL in one lifetime or another. A UDT in VB looks something like this:

```
Public Type CustomerUDT
    customerId As Long
    customerNumber As String
    firstName As String
    lastName As String
    middleInitial As String
    prefix As String
    suffix As String
    phone1 As String
    phone2 As String
    eMail As String
    isDeleted As Boolean
    isNew As Boolean
```

```
    isDirty As Boolean
End Type
```

Then to use the UDT, we might have something in our code that looks like this:

```
Dim customerInfo as CustomerUDT
CustomerInfo = mcolCustomer.Item(CStr _
  (lcustomerId))
```

These last few lines assume that mcolCustomer is a collection with Customer objects in it. The Item operation is doing a key lookup based on a customerId, which happens to be the key to the collection. We can then do things like the following.

```
txtFirstName.Text = customerInfo.firstName
txtLastName.Text = customerInfo.lastName
txtMInitial.Text = customerInfo.middleInitial
```

This is a bit more appealing than doing the following.

```
txtFirstName.Text = msData(giFirstName, iIndex)
txtLastName.Text = msData(giLastName, iIndex)
txtMInitial.Text = msData(giMiddleInitialName, _
  iIndex)
```

In VB v6.0, UDTs got a bit of a boost in where they can be used and how they can be used. UDTs can now be the return parameter of a function. So, something like the following is possible:

```
Public Function getCustomer(sKey, lErrNo, _
  sErrDescr) As customerInfo
```

CustomerInfo could be populated within the getCustomer operation and returned. Be advised that the CustomerInfo UDT is coerced into a Variant to make this happen. This isn't necessarily bad, just worth noting based on our prior discussions on the extra overhead associated with the Variant data type.

UDTs can make life much easier for the developer if used wisely. In the Remulak Productions application, we will upgrade our approach presented in the previous chapter as it dealt with exposing String arrays back to the client. What we will implement are collections of

UDTs kept in the user interface controllers. The user interface forms will interact with and manipulate these, rather than have to parse String arrays.

It is worth noting at this point that a very similar construct to UDTs, but with more programmatical abilities, are the new, disconnected recordset features offered in VB v6.0. Disconnected recordsets provide for even more powerful client-side manipulation. The only drawback is that they represent a very database access-centric interface that is completely reliant on Microsoft's data access evolution. In addition, disconnected recordsets have been proven not to perform as well as some of the other options discussed.

For Remulak Productions, we are going to use UDTs strictly as a manipulation mechanism for the user interface. We will keep them in the `Dictionary` class that we introduced in the previous chapter. Don't think we got rid of the String arrays. They are still our primary means of communication all the way from the back-end `dasvc` layer to the `uisvc` layer on the front-end. It will be the `uisvc` layer that will work with them directly. The `uisvc` layer, and specifically the user interface controller classes, will load the UDTs into collections using the String arrays.

Each class will now have a pair of definitions: one `ENUM` as the means of manipulating the String array and a related `Type` structure for the user interface manipulation. Here is the definition for `Customer`.

```
Public Type CustomerUDT
    customerId As Long
    customerNumber As String
    firstName As String
    lastName As String
    middleInitial As String
    prefix As String
    suffix As String
    phone1 As String
    phone2 As String
    eMail As String
    isDeleted As Boolean
    isNew As Boolean
    isDirty As Boolean
End Type
```

```
    Public Enum enumCustomer
        giCustomerCount = 13
        giCustomerId = 0
        giCustomerNumber = 1
        giFirstName = 2
        giLastName = 3
        giMiddleInitial = 4
        giPrefix = 5
        giSuffix = 6
        giPhone1 = 7
        giPhone2 = 8
        giEMail = 9
        giCustomerISDeleted = 10
        giCustomerISNew = 11
        giCustomerISDirty = 12
    End Enum
```

Let's now look at how the user interface controller manipulates the String array returned and gets it into collections of UDTs. The following code is from the `UIMaintRltnController` class.

```
Public Function getInfo(ByVal sCustomerNumber _
  As String, Optional lErrNo As Long, Optional _
  sErrDescr As String) As Boolean
On Error GoTo getInfoErr
    Dim customerInfo As CustomerUDT
    Dim localeInfo As LocaleUDT
    Dim AddressInfo As AddressUDT
    Dim sDataLocale() As String
    Dim sDataAddress() As String
    Dim sData() As String
    Dim iIndex As Integer
    getInfo = False
    Set moUCMaintRltnController = New
    brsvc.UCMaintRltnController
    If moUCMaintRltnController.RltnInquiry _
      (sCustomerNumber, sData, sDataLocale, _
      sDataAddress, lErrNo, sErrDescr) Then
```

```
freeCollection mcolCustomer
For iIndex = LBound(sData, giTWODIM) To _
   UBound(sData, giTWODIM)
     With customerInfo
          .customerId = CLng(sData(giCustomerId, _
             iIndex))
          .customerNumber = CStr(sData _
             (giCustomerNumber, iIndex))
          .firstName = CStr(sData(giFirstName, _
             iIndex))
          .lastName = CStr(sData(giLastName, _
             iIndex))
          .middleInitial = CStr(sData _
             (giMiddleInitial, iIndex))
          .prefix = CStr(sData(giPrefix, iIndex))
          .suffix = CStr(sData(giSuffix, iIndex))
          .phone1 = CStr(sData(giPhone1, iIndex))
          .phone2 = CStr(sData(giPhone2, iIndex))
          .eMail = CStr(sData(giEMail, iIndex))
          .isDeleted = False
          .isNew = False
          .isDirty = False
     End With

     mcolCustomer.Add customerInfo, _
        CStr(customerInfo.customerId)
Next
freeCollection mcolLocale
If sDataLocale(0, 0) = "" Then
Else
For iIndex = LBound(sDataLocale, giTWODIM) To _
             UBound(sDataLocale, giTWODIM)
      With localeInfo
           .localeId = CLng(sDataLocale _
              (giLocaleId, iIndex))
           .addressId = CLng(sDataLocale _
              (giLocaleAddressId, iIndex))
           .customerId = CLng(sDataLocale _
              (giLocaleCustomerId, iIndex))
```

```
                .role = CInt(sDataLocale(giRole, _
                    iIndex))
                .isDirty = False
                .isDeleted = False
                .isNew = False
            End With
            mcolLocale.Add localeInfo, CStr _
                (localeInfo.localeId)
        Next
    End If
    freeCollection mcolAddress
    If sDataAddress(0, 0) = "" Then
    Else
        For iIndex = LBound(sDataAddress, _
            giTWODIM) To _
                    UBound(sDataAddress, giTWODIM)
            With AddressInfo
                .addressId = CLng(sDataAddress _
                    (giAddressId, iIndex))
                .addressLine1 = _
                CStr(sDataAddress(giAddressLine1, _
                    iIndex))
                .addressLine2 = _
                CStr(sDataAddress(giAddressLine2, _
                    iIndex))
                .addressLine3 = _
                CStr(sDataAddress(giAddressLine3, _
                    iIndex))
                .city = CStr(sDataAddress(giCity, _
                    iIndex))
                .state = CStr(sDataAddress(giState, _
                    iIndex))
                .zip = CStr(sDataAddress(giZip, _
                    iIndex))
                .isDirty = False
                .isDeleted = False
                .isNew = False
            End With
            mcolAddress.Add AddressInfo, _
```

```
            CStr(AddressInfo.addressId)
        Next
    End If
    getInfo = True
    Set moUCMaintRltnController = Nothing
    ReDim sData(0, 0)
    ReDim sDataAddress(0, 0)
    ReDim sDataLocale(0, 0)

    Exit Function
  End If
getInfoErr:
  lErrNo = Err.Number
  sErrDescr = Err.description
End Function
```

This code is a bit long, but notice that it is a result of all the attributes that require assigning into the UDTs; the logic itself is quite straightforward. The String arrays that came back from the `brsvc` layer (`msData`, `msDataAddress`, and `msDataLocale`) are cycled through, assigned to a respective UDT (`CustomerInfo`, `AddressInfo`, and `LocaleInfo`), and then added to an appropriate collection.

```
Public mcolCustomer As New Collection
Public mcolLocale As New Collection
Public mcolAddress As New Collection
```

The key to each collection is the primary key of the class as it resides in the database. In our case, remember that all of our primary keys are surrogate keys that are `Longs` in VB and `Integers` in the database.

Notice that the signature for this `getInfo` operation has changed from the last chapter. It is even simpler; no String array goes back to the VB form now. The user interface will totally interface with their user interface controller collections. Let's look at how that happens by examining some of the code in the `frmMaintRltn` form.

```
Public Sub RetrieveData()
  Dim sCustomerNumber As String
  sCustomerNumber = txtCustomerNumber.Text
  If moMyController.getInfo(sCustomerNumber, _
```

```
    mlErrNo, msErrDescr) Then
        'Populate Customer Fields
        SetCustomer
        mbNewCustomer = False
        mbExistingCustomer = True

        'No role address information for this customer
        If moMyController.mcolLocale.Count > 0 Then
            'Populate Role Fields
            SetLocale

            mbNewAddress = False
            mbExistingAddress = True
            mbNewLocale = False
            mbExistingLocale = True
        End If
    Else
        'No Customer Found
        If moMyController.mcolCustomer.Count > 0 Then
            MsgBox "Customer " + sCustomerNumber + _
                " Does Not Exist", , "Customer Inquiry"
        End If
    End If
End Sub
```

The `retrieveData` operation eventually gets called once a user requests a customer number and selects the Search command button. Its mission is to send `getInfo`, along with the customer number, off to its controller class `UIMaintRltnController`. This interaction was documented in the sequence diagram at the end of the last chapter. What has changed is how the form gets at the attributes.

```
Public Sub SetCustomer()

    Dim customerInfo As CustomerUDT

    'Talk to UI Controller Collections
    customerInfo = moMyController.mcolCustomer(1)
```

```
txtFirstName.Text = customerInfo.firstName
txtLastName.Text = customerInfo.lastName
txtMInitial.Text = customerInfo.middleInitial
txtPrefix.Text = customerInfo.prefix
txtSuffix.Text = customerInfo.suffix
txtPhone1.Text = customerInfo.phone1
txtPhone2.Text = customerInfo.phone1
txtEMail.Text = customerInfo.eMail
'this is property is invisible
txtCustomerId.Text = customerInfo.customerId
End Sub
```

The setCustomer operation gets called from retrieveData if a customer was found. You can see that the interaction at the client is made a bit simpler by referring to UDT members and assigning those to controls. The same thing happens for Locales and Address (if there are any). The code for Address follows.

```
Public Sub attachAddress()

    Dim sTemp As String
    Dim localeInfo As LocaleUDT
    Dim AddressInfo As AddressUDT

    mbScroll = True

    sTemp = lstRoleAddress.ItemData(lstRoleAddress. _
        ListIndex)

    'Talk to UI Controller Collection
    localeInfo = moMyController.mcolLocale. _
        Item(sTemp)

    AddressInfo = moMyController.mcolAddress. _
        Item(CStr(localeInfo.addressId))

    txtAddr1.Text = AddressInfo.addressLine1
    txtAddr2.Text = AddressInfo.addressLine2
    txtAddr3.Text = AddressInfo.addressLine2
    txtCity.Text = AddressInfo.city
    txtZip.Text = AddressInfo.zip
    'this field is invisible
```

```
    txtAddressId.Text = localeInfo.addressId
    'this field is invisible
    txtLocaleId.Text = localeInfo.localeId

    selectGivenItemDataOfComboBox cmbRole, _
      CStr(localeInfo.role)
    selectGivenItemOfComboBox cmbState, _
      AddressInfo.state

    mbScroll = False
End Sub
```

What we end up with after a query resembles Figure 12-5.

FIGURE 12-5 *Customer Relationship Inquiry with addresses.*

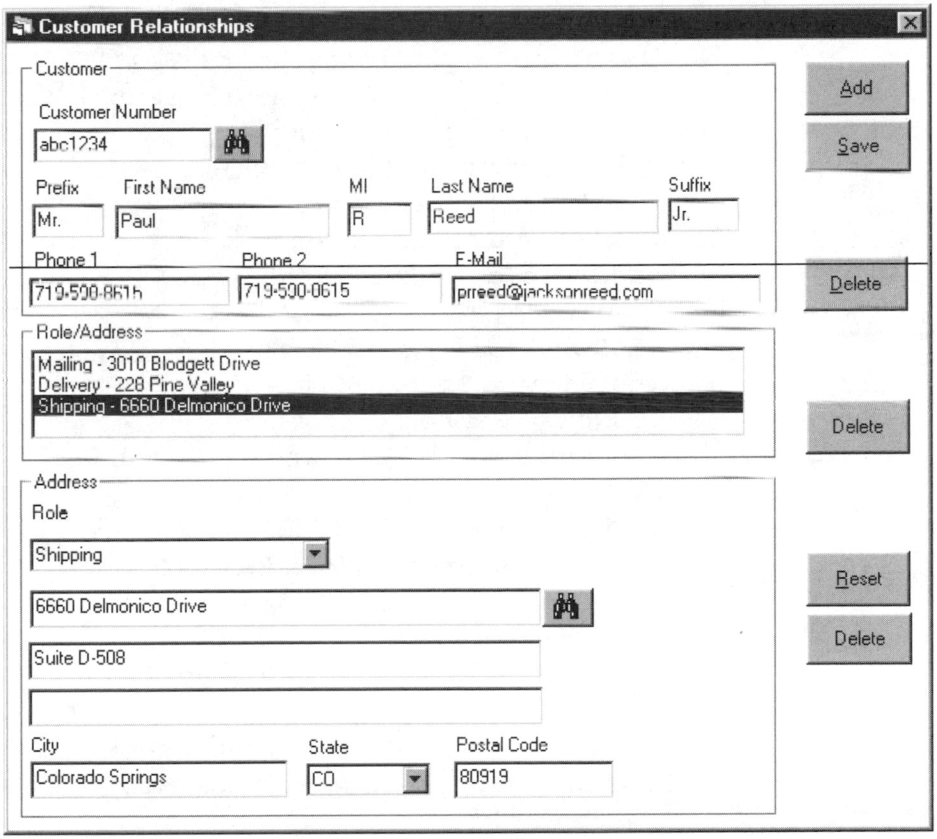

The user interface allows for easy navigation using the scroll window in the middle of the screen. It is clear that Paul R. Reed, Jr., has three different role/address combinations. The current role/address with focus causes the bottom portion of the address detail to be displayed.

Much like with disconnected recordsets, a user can enter additional addresses, one after the other, and click "Add" for each. What this does is add each as a UDT entry into the collection residing in the UIMaintRltnController class. All interaction stays at the client until a "Save" is requested. Following is the code executed when a new Address is added.

```
Public Sub AddAddress()
    Dim AddressInfo As AddressUDT
    If editAddress Then
      With AddressInfo
            .addressLine1 = (Trim(txtAddr1.Text))
            .addressLine2 = (Trim(txtAddr2.Text))
            .addressLine3 = (Trim(txtAddr3.Text))
            .city = (Trim(txtCity.Text))
            .state = (Trim(cmbState.Text))
            .zip = (Trim(txtZip.Text))
            If mbExistingAddress Then
                .addressId = CLng(txtAddressId. _
                  Text)
                .isDeleted = False
                .isDirty = True
                .isNew = False
                'remove the old one and add it back
                'updated
                moMyController.mcolAddress.Remove  _
                    CStr(AddressInfo.addressId)
                moMyController.mcolAddress.Add _
                  AddressInfo, _
                    CStr(AddressInfo.addressId)
            Else
                .addressId = moUtility.getRandom
                txtAddressId.Text = AddressInfo. _
                  addressId
```

```
            .isDeleted = False
            .isDirty = False
            .isNew = True
            'add it to collection in UI Controller
            moMyController.mcolAddress.Add _
                AddressInfo,
                CStr(AddressInfo.addressId)
        End If
    End With
    If mbNewAddress Or mbChangedAddress Then
        If Not mbSaveMode Then
            If lstRoleAddress.ListCount > 0 Then
                If Not mbNewLocale And Not
                    mbChangedLocale Then
                    removeAllItemsFromListBox _
                        lstRoleAddress
                    SetLocale
                End If
            Else
            'the list is empty, it will get refreshed
            'in Locale
                End If
            End If
        End If
    End If
End Sub
```

Notice that the addAddress subroutine simply goes through each field and assigns each to an element in a new, empty addressUDT. It then checks to see whether this is a change to an existing address or it is a new Address. If it is new, then isNew is set to True; otherwise, isDirty is set to True. This small fact will become important later when we talk about storing the changes in the other layers.

If the entry is a change, the old one is removed from the collection and added back with the updates. If it is a new Address, it is just added to the collection. There is similar logic for the Locale class. The collections again are in the UIMaintRltnController class that resides in the uisvc layer. Before we move on to show how updates make their way through the layers to the database, let's talk a bit about design philosophy.

Client-Side Objects or No Client-Side Objects

Many of you at this point may be wondering why you should go through all the trouble of using UDTs at the client? Why not just reference the business classes directly from the user interface and assign their properties directly? Perhaps my pitch about our modified MVC framework in the last chapter didn't convince you of the need for this separation. Many applications are written to talk directly to the business layer. Here is a common scenario.

```
txtFirstName.Text = oCustomer.firstName
txtLastName.Text = oCustomer.lastName
```

The same thing applies when modifications are requested of an object.

```
oCustomer.firstName = txtFirstName.Text
oCustomer.lastName = txtLastName.Text
```

This is very similar in format to the UDT solution, but with the UDT solution, I will admit that we had to write a little more support code. However, with the direct object reference shown previously, the object oCustomer may one day live on a server as part of a distributed implementation strategy and not on the client. Objects are just references. Objects don't get marshaled across the wire like base data types that are passed ByRef; they stay where they were created. Each one of the oCustomer requests is a trip across the network in a distributed implementation. Several developers state that out-of-process remote access is 1,000 times slower than in-process local access, although this figure is unofficial and very much dependent on network loadings. Now, 1,000 times slower may still be under a second, so don't throw in the towel just yet. But this is worth being aware of.

Some of the performance concerns can be made less troublesome by providing a getState operation on each entity class, like we showed in the last chapter, which gets everything about a Customer all at one time. We would also want a setState operation like the one we will cover in this chapter that does the same thing but for updates. This is better than the individual attribute references given previously, but we are still maintaining a reference to an object that may be on another machine one day. Furthermore, if we are going to use MTS, the last thing we want is a stateful entity object such as Customer hanging around instantiated on a server.

We shall see when we follow this solution to the back-end that our hold time to objects is kept to a minimum. In the previous example, once the data got to the `uisvc` layer, the other three layers were no longer referenced. These references are reborn once we need to request additional services either for inquiry or update. This is why I strongly encourage the VB community that is building applications that may need to scale in throughput either to follow an approach similar to the one being presented here or to utilize disconnected recordsets.

A Disturbing Trend with the Advent of Distributed Implementations

Let's expand a bit more this notion of keeping references to objects outside of their immediate use for long periods of time. This relates to a disturbing trend that I see in increasing numbers related to VB design architecture. It is particularly obvious with the introduction of MTS, which we will focus on in the next chapter.

The issue that prompts this discussion is the latest mantra of distributed development: the server-side stateless object, whose definition is quite simple. For any and all work done by an operation in a class, the operation should receive everything it needs to do its job via parameters passed in during its invocation. Upon completion of that work, it should leave nothing behind in the way of references to other objects. In a nutshell, this would mean that there would be little use for a class to have properties (for example, `Get`, `Let`, and `Set`). Our `Customer` class, given this definition, would need to be either a client-side-only class, with properties, or a server-side class, with nothing but operations. This completely flies in the object-oriented face of what a class is in the first place. There is a justification for this concept, although we shall take a middle-of-the-road approach that will soon be introduced.

The reasoning behind using stateless objects is that for us to take complete advantage of Microsoft's evolving distributed design strategies, instances of objects should be very short-lived, be built to do something very quickly, and then destroy themselves. The perceived motivation for this is to reduce the overhead on the server, which must keep the overhead intact in order to manage stateful objects. This is a misleading myth.

The real reason is that supporting a seamless transaction management system, such as MTS, requires that transactions begin and commit themselves with very little overhead. It does no good, for instance, to have a `Customer` object referenced in a VB form somewhere if a transaction was recently submitted that changed its state. This is really just age-old transaction management 101 in my opinion. So the reasoning for stateless objects is acknowledged. However, the extremes to which I see it being implemented is unacceptable. This is primarily because many of the benefits from an object design are lost and we end up with code that is no easier to maintain and, worse yet, a design that separates the notion of what a class is by splitting its structure and behavioral features. Figure 12-6 is a diagram detailing this emerging design pattern, which I call the *fragmented business object*.

What is most troubling about Figure 12-6 is that I see one monster operation-only class being implemented in some designs. It sits on the server and just executes client requests. It certainly does the job, but all identity of the class behavior is completely lost.

Our approach, after UDTs have just been introduced, will be to keep the entity classes intact, as is. They will have both properties and, more important, the business rules and interfaces implemented in the same class (just as classes in VB have always had). The difference in our design approach is that when a class is retrieved and instantiated, it is

FIGURE 12-6 *Fragmented* `Entity` *class.*

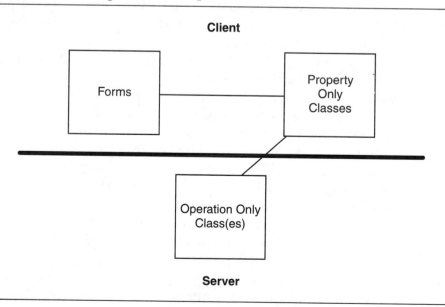

done so in time to package the class in a form that is presentable to a client, as a UDT kept in collections. After that transformation takes place, the object reference is destroyed.

For update activity, the reverse will happen. The future object will be passed in from the client as a UDT and the object that it represents will be instantiated in the `brsvc` component. Then any changes that must be applied will be done to those in-memory objects and persisted out to storage. The client will hold a reference to a server-side object only long enough to get something it has requested or to send something off to be persisted. So our objects will remain intact, but not for long periods of time. Figure 12-7 is the outline of this architecture that we have been working on so far.

Updating Information from the User Interface to the Back-End

Now that we have shown how information gets from the back-end, through our layers, and into the user interface, let's continue where we left off on the outbound trip from the form to perform an insert. Figure 12-8 is a sequence diagram depicting the messaging. It is important to

FIGURE 12-7   *Real-enough time objects.*

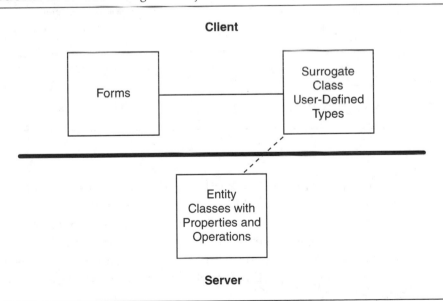

FIGURE 12-8 *Sequence diagram for Customer insert.*

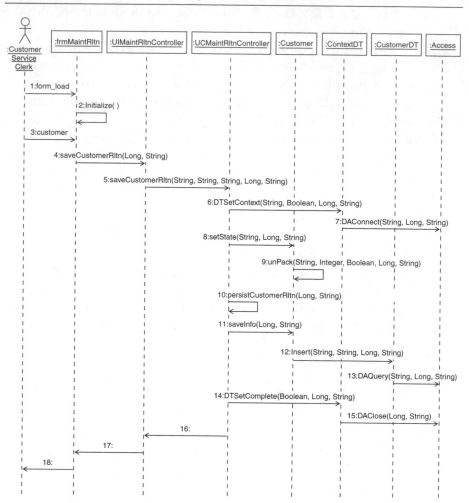

point out, for brevity's sake, that sequence numbers 8 and 9 would also be sent to `Address` and `Locale`, respectively.

Previously, we saw how the user interface creates new UDT structures, populates them with information from the screen, and adds them, or replaces them, in the collections stored in the user interface controller classes. Let's start out by seeing how the save process gets started.

```
Private Sub cmdSave_Click()
    mbSaveMode = True
    'see if anything changed and hasn't been added
    'yet
    ProcessScreen
    If mbScreenChanged Then
        Screen.MousePointer = vbHourglass
        If moMyController.saveCustomerRltn _
          (mlErrNo, msErrDescr) Then
            RefreshFields
        Else
            setMessage txtCustomerNumber, "Save _
              Failed", msTitle
        End If
        Screen.MousePointer = vbDefault
    End If
    mbSaveMode = False
End Sub
```

After we make sure that nothing is left behind, the saveCustomerRltn operation is sent to the form's reference to the UIMaintRltnController class, moMyController. It passes nothing but a receptacle for an error number and message. The saveCustomerRltn in UIMaintRltnController looks like this.

```
Public Function saveCustomerRltn(Optional lErrNo _
  As Long, Optional sErrDescr As String) As Boolean
    On Error GoTo saveCustomerRltnErr
    Dim customerInfo As CustomerUDT
    Dim localeInfo As LocaleUDT
    Dim AddressInfo As AddressUDT
    Dim iIndex As Integer
    saveCustomerRltn = False
    'Set dynamic String arrays in preparation for
    'trip out
    ReDim msCustomerData(giCustomerCount - 1, 0)
    ReDim msLocaleData(giLocaleCount - 1, 0)
    ReDim msAddressData(giAddressCount - 1, 0)
```

```
        'assign it to UDT
    customerInfo = mcolCustomer(giONEDIM) 'only
    'one customer
    loadCustomerData msCustomerData, customerInfo, _
      giONEDIM
    For iIndex = 1 To mcolLocale.Count
        'assign it to UDT
        localeInfo = mcolLocale(iIndex)
        If localeInfo.isDeleted = True Or _
            localeInfo.isDirty = True Or _
              localeInfo.isNew = True Then

            loadLocaleData msLocaleData, localeInfo, _
              iIndex
        End If
    Next
    For iIndex = 1 To mcolAddress.Count
        'assign it to UDT
        AddressInfo = mcolAddress(iIndex)
        If AddressInfo.isDeleted = True Or _
            AddressInfo.isDirty = True Or _
              AddressInfo.isNew = True Then
          loadAddressData msAddressData, _
            AddressInfo, iIndex
        End If
    Next
    Set moUCMaintRltnController = New brsvc. _
      UCMaintRltnController
    If moUCMaintRltnController.
    saveCustomerRltn(msCustomerData, _
            msLocaleData, msAddressData, lErrNo, _
              sErrDescr) Then
        saveCustomerRltn = True
    End If
    Exit Function
saveCustomerRltnErr:
    lErrNo = Err.Number
    sErrDescr = Err.description
End Function
```

After some preparation work, the `Customer` information is the first to get massaged for the trip to the `brsvc` layer by calling the private `loadCustomerData` operation. This operation expects a String array (`msCustomerData`) that will be the recipient of the UDT information (`customerInfo`), the UDT record from the collection, and an index offset for the position within the String array. The operation `loadCustomerData` doesn't do much other than populate the outbound String array.

```
Private Sub loadCustomerData(msCustomerData() As _
  String, udtTemp As Variant, iIndex As Integer)

  ReDim Preserve msCustomerData(giCustomerCount _
    - 1, iIndex - 1)

  msCustomerData(giCustomerId, iIndex - 1) = _
    udtTemp.customerId
  msCustomerData(giCustomerNumber, iIndex - 1) = _
    udtTemp.customerNumber
  msCustomerData(giFirstName, iIndex - 1) = _
    udtTemp.firstName
  msCustomerData(giLastName, iIndex - 1) = _
    udtTemp.lastName
  msCustomerData(giMiddleInitial, iIndex - 1) = _
    udtTemp.middleInitial
  msCustomerData(giPrefix, iIndex - 1) = _
    udtTemp.prefix
  msCustomerData(giSuffix, iIndex - 1) = _
    udtTemp.suffix
  msCustomerData(giPhone1, iIndex - 1) = _
    udtTemp.phone1
  msCustomerData(giPhone2, iIndex - 1) = _
    udtTemp.phone2
  msCustomerData(giEMail, iIndex - 1) = _
    udtTemp.eMail
  msCustomerData(giCustomerISNew, iIndex - 1) = _
    udtTemp.isNew
  msCustomerData(giCustomerISDirty, iIndex - 1) _
    = udtTemp.isDirty
```

```
  msCustomerData(giCustomerISDeleted, _
    iIndex - 1) = udtTemp.isDeleted
End Sub
```

Similar load routines are called for `Locale` as well as `Address`. It is also important to point out that only those UDT members within the collections that have changed in some way based on their state (`isNew`, `isDirty`, or `isDeleted`) are packed into the String arrays.

The next thing that must happen is to pass all this hard work off to the `brsvc` layer and specifically to the `UCMaintRltnController` class. The operation `saveCustomerRltn` takes with it the three String arrays `msCustomerData`, `msAddressData`, and `msLocaleData` that were extracted from the UDT records in the collections.

We are now back in the use case controller class. Use controller classes control the flow that must occur to implement a use case pathway.

```
Public Function saveCustomerRltn(sCustomerData() _
  As String, sLocaleData() As String, sAddressData() _
    As String, Optional lErrno As Long, Optional _
      sErrDescr As String) As Boolean

  On Error GoTo saveCustomerRltnErr

  Dim oCustomer As New Customer
  Dim oAddress As New Address
  Dim oLocale As New Locale
  Dim sCustomerNumber As String

  saveCustomerRltn = False

  sCustomerNumber = sCustomerData _
    (giCustomerNumber, 0)

  Set oContextDT = New dtsvc.ContextDT

  'Start transaction with bAction set to True
  'for Unit of work
  If oContextDT.DTSetContext(msDSN, True, _
    lErrno, sErrDescr) Then
      If sCustomerData(giCustomerISNew, 0) = True _
      Then 'new customer
```

```
If oCustomer.setState(sCustomerData, lErrno, _
  sErrDescr) Then
  mcolCustomer.Add oCustomer, CStr(oCustomer. _
    customerId)
  If oAddress.setState(sAddressData, lErrno, _
    sErrDescr) Then
    Set mcolAddress = oAddress.mcolAddress
    Set oLocale.theCustomer = oCustomer
    If oLocale.setState(sLocaleData, lErrno, _
      sErrDescr) Then
      Set oCustomer.theLocale = oLocale. _
        mcolLocale
      'now our objects are in memory and
      'reflect the work
      'done in the UI...but not persisted
      'yet. Any unique
      'business rules would be sent from here
      If persistCustomerRltn(lErrno, _
        sErrDescr) Then
          saveCustomerRltn = True
      End If
    End If
  End If
End If
Else 'Customer is not new
  If oCustomer.getInfo(sCustomerNumber, True, _
    lErrno, sErrDescr) Then
    If oCustomer.setState(sCustomerData, _
      lErrno, sErrDescr) Then
      mcolCustomer.Add oCustomer, CStr _
        (oCustomer.customerId)
      If oAddress.setState(sAddressData, _
        lErrno, sErrDescr) Then
        Set mcolAddress = oAddress. _
          mcolAddress
        If oLocale.setState(sLocaleData, _
          lErrno, sErrDescr) Then
          Set oCustomer.theLocale = _
            oLocale.mcolLocale
```

```
                            'now our objects are in memory
                            'and reflect the work
                            'done in the UI...but not
                            'persisted yet. Any unique
                            'business rules would be sent
                            'from here
                          If persistCustomerRltn(lErrno, _
                            sErrDescr) Then
                              saveCustomerRltn = True
                          End If
                      End If
                  End If
              End If
          End If
      End If
  End If
  If oContextDT.DTSetComplete(True, lErrno, _
    sErrDescr) Then

      Set oContextDT = Nothing
      Exit Function
  End If

saveCustomerRltnErr:
    lErrno = Err.Number
    sErrDescr = Err.description
End Function
```

There are two main branches to this use case pathway, one for when the customer is new and another for when it isn't. We will explore the pathway for when the customer is new. The first thing to note, as we saw in the `rltnInquiry` operation, is that a message, `DTSetContext`, is sent to the `ContextDT` class. Remember, this establishes a connection for us. More important to note about this invocation is that `True` is being passed as the `bAction` parameter. `bAction` is checked in the `DTSetContext` operation and if it is `True`, it will issue a `beginTrans` on the connection. This is so that we can make lots of database changes and subsequently issue a `rollback` if things don't go as planned or a `commitTrans` if everything turns out ok. All of this is determined by the value of bAction contained in both the DTSetContext and DTSetComplete operations.

Previously I mentioned that a setState operation would be nice to have so that we could pass along everything that we needed to update an object at one time. We now call setState on our oCustomer object, passing in the String array for Customer. setState just sets its internal member variable values as they come in as part of the array.

```
Public Function setState(sCustomerData() As String, _
  Optional lErrno As Long,
   Optional sErrDescr As String) As Boolean
    On Error GoTo setStateErr
    Dim i As Integer
    setState = False
    If sCustomerData(giCustomerISNew, 0) = True Or _
        sCustomerData(giCustomerISDeleted, 0) = True Or _
         sCustomerData(giCustomerISDirty, 0) = True Then

      If unPack(sCustomerData, giZERODIM, False) Then
        setState = True
      End If
      setState = True
    End If
    Exit Function
setStateErr:
    lErrno = Err.Number
    sErrDescr = Err.description
End Function
```

The message unPack is fired on Customer within setState. Notice, this is the same unPack operation that was used in getInfo to get data out of the database. The only difference is that we interrogate the bInquiry flag to determine whether this is a unPack request as a result of a getInfo or a setState request.

```
Private Function unPack(sData() As String, iIndex _
  As Integer, Optional bInquiry As Boolean, Optional _
    lErrno As Long, Optional sErrDescr As String) As _
    Boolean
```

```
    On Error GoTo unPackErr

    unPack = False

    customerId = CLng(sData(giCustomerId, iIndex))
    customerNumber = CStr(sData(giCustomerNumber, _
      iIndex))
    firstName = CStr(sData(giFirstName, iIndex))
    lastName = CStr(sData(giLastName, iIndex))
    middleInitial = CStr(sData(giMiddleInitial, _
      iIndex))
    prefix = CStr(sData(giPrefix, iIndex))
    suffix = CStr(sData(giSuffix, iIndex))
    phone1 = CStr(sData(giPhone1, iIndex))
    phone2 = CStr(sData(giPhone2, iIndex))
    eMail = CStr(sData(giEMail, iIndex))

    'If the unpack is the result of an inquiry then
    'default
    'the state flags to false, else...use what was
    'passed in
    'from the client
    If bInquiry Then
       isDeleted = False
       isNew = False
       isDirty = False
    Else
       isDeleted = sData(giCustomerISDeleted, _
         iIndex)
       isNew = sData(giCustomerISNew, iIndex)
       isDirty = sData(giCustomerISDirty, iIndex)
    End If

    unPack = True
    Exit Function

unPackErr:
    lErrno = Err.Number
    sErrDescr = Err.description
End Function
```

Back to the `saveCustomerRltn` operation in the use case controller class `UCMaintRltnController`, the `setState` operation is subsequently sent to the `Address` object, passing in its String array of addresses. The result of this is a collection of `Address` objects that are assigned to `UCMaintRltnController`'s collection, `mcolAddress`. The same thing occurs for `Locale`, with the result that a collection of `Locales` are assigned to `mcolLocale`. If everything goes as planned, the final private operation, `persistCustomerRltn`, will be invoked on itself, the `UCMaintRltnController.persistCustomerRltn` `(lErrno, sErrDescr)`.

This operation will be instigating the actual updates to the database. All that we have done to this point is to build objects and populate their instances with information from the user interface. They are sitting in memory, with their state attributes set accordingly (`isNew = True` in this example).

Persisting the Objects

By sending `persistCustomerRltn` to `UCMaintRltnController`, we start the process of getting all of our objects persisted to the database. The source for this effort is the object collections that we built as a result of our `setState` messages.

```
Private Function persistCustomerRltn(Optional _
  lErrno As Long, Optional sErrDescr As String) As _
    Boolean
    On Error GoTo persistCustomerRltnErr
    Dim iIndex As Integer
    persistCustomerRltn = False
    'persist address
    For iIndex = 1 To mcolAddress.Count
        If mcolAddress(iIndex).saveInfo(lErrno, _
          sErrDescr) Then
            persistCustomerRltn = True
        End If
    Next
    'persist customer....within customer, locale
    'will be persisted
    For iIndex = 1 To mcolCustomer.Count
```

```
        If mcolCustomer(iIndex).saveInfo(lErrno, _
          sErrDescr) Then
            persistCustomerRltn = True
        End If
    Next
    Exit Function
 persistCustomerRltnErr:
    lErrno = Err.Number
    sErrDescr = Err.description
End Function
```

The persistCustomerRltn operation starts out by looping through its local Address collection, mcolAddress, and sending each Address the saveInfo message. Let's see what saveInfo in the Address class does.

```
Public Function saveInfo(Optional lErrno As Long, _
  Optional sErrDescr As String) As Boolean

    On Error GoTo saveInfoErr
    Dim oICrud As ICrud
    Dim sAddressData() As String
    saveInfo = False
    Set theAddressDT = New dtsvc.AddressDT

    'Talk to the DT interface
    Set oICrud = theAddressDT

    'get address information into an array to send
    'onward
    getAddressBase sAddressData

     'Depending on internal state, the correct
     'message is invoked
    If isNew Then
      If oICrud.Insert("", sAddressData, lErrno, _
        sErrDescr) Then
          saveInfo = True
          Exit Function
      End If
    Else
```

```
      If isDirty Then
         If oICrud.Update("", sAddressData, _
            lErrno, sErrDescr) Then
            saveInfo = True
            Exit Function
         End If
      Else
         If isDeleted Then
            If oICrud.Delete("", sAddressData, _
               lErrno, sErrDescr) Then
               saveInfo = True
               Exit Function
            End If
         End If
      End If
   End If
   Exit Function
SaveInfoErr:
   lErrno = Err.Number
   sErrDescr = Err.description
End Function
```

The `saveInfo` interrogates itself as to its state by asking, "Am I new, dirty or deleted?" Depending on what it finds out, it sends the appropriate message to the `ICrud` interface for its DT class. So, if it is a new `Address`, which it will be in this leg of our investigation, It will send the `insert` message along with the column information, `sAddressData`, with which to do the inserting. Let's visit the `insert` operation in the `AddressDT` class.

```
Private Function ICrud_insert(ByVal sQualifier As _
   String, ByRef sData() As String, Optional lErrNo _
   As Long, Optional sErrDescr As String) As Boolean
   Dim sQry As String
   ICrud_insert = False
   'Build query string
   sQry = gsINSERT & gsINTO
   sQry = sQry & msAddress & gsSPACE
   sQry = sQry & gsOP & "maddressId" & _
```

```
        gsCOMMASPACE
    sQry = sQry & "maddressLine1" & gsCOMMASPACE
    sQry = sQry & "maddressLine2" & gsCOMMASPACE
    sQry = sQry & "maddressLine3" & gsCOMMASPACE
    sQry = sQry & "mcity" & gsCOMMASPACE
    sQry = sQry & "mstate" & gsCOMMASPACE
    sQry = sQry & "mzip"
    sQry = sQry & gsCP
    sQry = sQry & gsVALUES & gsOP
    sQry = sQry & sData(giAddressId, 0) & _
        gsCOMMASPACE
    sQry = sQry & gsSQ & sData(giAddressLine1, 0) & _
        gsSQ & gsCOMMASPACE
    sQry = sQry & gsSQ & sData(giAddressLine2, 0) & _
        gsSQ & gsCOMMASPACE
    sQry = sQry & gsSQ & sData(giAddressLine3, 0) & _
        gsSQ & gsCOMMASPACE
    sQry = sQry & gsSQ & sData(giCity, 0) & gsSQ & _
        gsCOMMASPACE
    sQry = sQry & gsSQ & sData(giState, 0) & gsSQ & _
        gsCOMMASPACE
    sQry = sQry & gsSQ & sData(giZip, 0) & gsSQ
    sQry = sQry & gsCP

    'Call the operation on the Access class
    If goAccess.DAQuery(sQry, lErrNo, sErrDescr) Then
        ICrud_insert = True
    End If
    'ReDim the dimension so the data doesn't get
    'passed back
    ReDim sData(0, 0)
End Function
```

Much like we saw with our investigation of the getInfo operation for the DT classes in the last chapter, the insert operation is very focused in its purpose. It inserts a row into the Address table in this case. However, for all SQL statements, with the exception of selects, we message to DAQuery. Note the last line of code, ReDim sData(0,0).

Remember that the sData array contains the information passed in from the brsvc layer with the information to be inserted. If the sData array isn't reset to contain nothing, then the array and all of its information will get dragged back to the Address class unnecessarily on return from the insert operation. This reduces the network load and makes for a much more efficient implementation.

Back to the persistCustomerRltn operation, the process continues by persisting the Customer object. Within the Customer object, the theLocale collection is iterated over and sent the saveInfo message. This is outlined at the bottom of Customer's saveInfo.

```
Public Function saveInfo(Optional lErrno As Long, _
  Optional sErrDescr As String) As Boolean

    On Error GoTo saveInfoErr

    Dim iIndex As Integer
    Dim oICrud As ICrud
    Dim sCustomerData() As String

    saveInfo = False

    Set theCustomerDT = New dtsvc.CustomerDT

    'Talk to the DT interface
    Set oICrud = theCustomerDT

    'get customer information into an array to
    'send onward
    getCustomerBase sCustomerData

    'Depending on internal state, the correct
    'message is invoked
    If isNew Then
        If oICrud.Insert("", sCustomerData, lErrno, _
          sErrDescr) Then
            saveInfo = True

        End If
    Else
        If isDirty Then
            If oICrud.Update("", sCustomerData, _
```

```
                     lErrno, sErrDescr) Then
                  saveInfo = True

              End If
          Else
            If isDeleted Then
              If oICrud.Delete("", sCustomerData, _
                 lErrno, sErrDescr) Then
                 saveInfo = True

              End If
            End If
          End If
      End If

      For iIndex = 1 To theLocale.Count
          If theLocale(iIndex).saveInfo(lErrno, _
            sErrDescr) Then
             saveInfo = True
          End If
      Next
      Exit Function
SaveInfoErr:
      lErrno = Err.Number
      sErrDescr = Err.description
End Function
```

This completes our upgrading of the Customer Relationships Inquiry pathway within the Maintain Relationships use case of the order entry application for Remulak Productions. Although this may seem like a small part of the application, it is a vital piece to the system. It is also a good example to use in demonstrating the architecture used in the system.

Hopefully, this chapter demonstrated the ability to keep the object concept of classes intact while not sacrificing performance and the need to keep stateful objects to a minimum. This will become very important in the next chapter when DCOM and MTS are introduced into the Remulak Productions application.

Checkpoint

Where We Have Been

1. Retrieving objects must incorporate all aspects of the object, including all contained relationships. However, sometimes the entire object may not be necessary; only its base attributes are needed. It is necessary for some classes in a design to have both shallow and expanded object instantiation abilities.

2. UDTs offer a worthy compromise solution to providing the user interface with an easy to work with programming model. At the same time, the entity classes remain intact and can be easily migrated to other physical platforms.

3. With the advent of MTS and the presumed assumption that all objects must be stateless, there is a growing trend to split object functionality in half, one portion dealing with properties and how the client manipulates them and the other being the workflow and business rules, which stay server focused. Unfortunately, the business rules and properties must stay as a cohesive whole or much of the benefit derived from a strong object design is lost. This can be accomplished without the sacrifice of performance.

4. The Data Translation Services layer is easily enhanced to support update functionality as well.

Where We Are Going Next

In the next chapter, we:

1. Explore the changes and additions needed to support a distributed implementation of the Remulak Productions application.

2. Review the requirements of utilizing native DCOM to distribute all but the Presentation Services layer to a Windows NT server.

3. Review the requirements of utilizing MTS to distribute all but the Presentation Services layer to a Windows NT server.

CHAPTER 13

Creating a Distributed Implementation: DCOM and MTS

In the last chapter, we added more code to the Remulak Productions project, thereby enabling it to perform updates as well as inquiries. With the basic structure of the application in place and working, it is time to address the issue of a distributed implementation.

In this chapter, we will cover two different forms of distribution: native DCOM and MTS. This may seem a bit like double-talk because MTS still relies heavily on DCOM as its IPC (inter-process communication) mechanism. However, as we will see, enabling access with native DCOM takes a bit more work to get the pieces in place and usually requires some handholding. MTS, on the other hand, makes the act of moving components from client to server as easy as drag-and-drop, regardless of whether you use any of MTS's transaction management services.

GOALS

- Review the reason why applications may benefit from a distributed implementation.

- Review the tools necessary to utilize DCOM as a distributed solution. Create an install-set to distribute a portion of the application and walk through the scenario from start to finish.

⮑ Explore the concepts behind MTS and the changes necessary to utilize MTS in the Remulak application. Create an MTS install set to distribute a portion of the application and walk through the scenario from start to finish.

Construction Phase

Synergy Process

This chapter adds additional features to the project as it pertains to distributing the solution to an application server.

Although the Construction phase considers several different areas, as outlined in Figure 13-1, the focus of this chapter will be on the following.

- The "Component Design/Build" block, in this chapter, will deal with creating much of the code that drives the application.

In the chapters that follow, we will take this solution and modify it to support the Internet.

FIGURE 13-1 *Synergy process model and the Construction phase.*

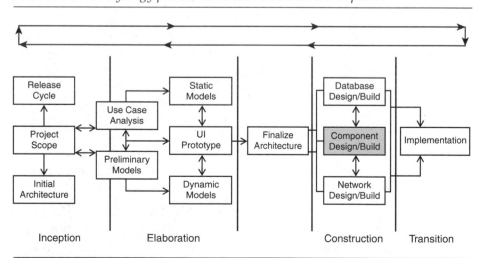

Construction—Distributed Applications: Nirvana or Overkill?

In an earlier chapter, where our architecture solution was reviewed, it was stated clearly that Remulak Productions may need the ability to distribute its application logic to improve management with server-side support. This is especially true if a portion of the order entry inquiry is going to be supported over the Internet.

Distributed applications, as a topic, have been quite popular with both the seminar-going and book reading crowd. Before we delve into the nuances of making Remulak Productions a candidate for distribution, there should be a business reason why the application should be distributed in the first place. Just because the tool can do it, doesn't mean it should be done. Of more importance is to ensure that the architecture framework that the application is built on affords distribution as a viable choice now and into the future.

One of the initial reasons for partitioning the application between different machines was to remove some of the burden that client-centric, or fat client, applications placed on the organizational infrastructure. Not only did the operational strains of distributing massive amounts of client code to perhaps hundreds of workstations add complexity, it also limited the ability of the business to tweak its operational rules easily without triggering an outward exodus of program code.

If the application could maintain its business rules on an application server, then changes would have to be made maybe at only one location in the organization without burdening the organization with yet another client-side software install. Another infrastructure savings feature of physical partitioning was the reduction of the complexity as it pertained to database connectivity. In the majority of client/server applications today, each client machine must maintain the necessary database drivers to afford server-side data access. If I have ever personally experienced frustration, it is in the fragile nature of the client as it pertains to keeping ODBC drivers and such up-to-date and protected from invasion by an uninformed client population. Moving the business rules to a server also means that the Data Access Services layer would move as well. Instead of hundreds of client-side ODBC drivers having to be set up and installed, a server solution could limit that to one install. In addition, depending on the DBMS platform, this could substantially reduce the overall cost of the application by requiring fewer driver and database connection licenses.

Given all of these positive aspects, why would someone not automatically assume a distributed solution? First of all, the sheer size of the application must be considered, as well as the audience being targeted. Surely, if the application is itself quite small, with only a few users, then physically partitioning the application may not make sense. Another aspect to consider is cost. To distribute the application will require additional server resources. I don't mean just hardware, but also the operational skills to set it up, back it up, and keep it up and running.

Businesses that maintain a large non-Windows platform for server operations may not yet be ready for the introduction of the Windows NT operating system into their environments. Both server-side DCOM and MTS require it. There have been ports of DCOM to non-Windows platforms such as Hewlett Packard's UNIX (HP/UX), but these environments still can't execute VB code, so they would give us no benefit.

However, without a doubt, if an application must scale to hundreds of users or if an application has a very dynamic business environment requiring frequent rule-oriented changes, then a well-conceived distribution strategy can pay off handsomely. This is true even with the extra overhead that the client experiences with executing some of the application remotely.

Construction—The Remulak Productions Partitioning Strategy—Payback Time

As was just pointed out, the most important element of the distribution strategy is the framework used to build the application in the first place. If that decision is correctly made, then whether the organization decides to distribute now rather than later becomes a nonissue.

Remember from prior chapters that the components utilized in the Remulak Productions design are well positioned to take advantage of a distributed solution. At the end of the chapter prior to our first big coding effort, we suggested several different potential distribution strategies. In this chapter, we will look at following the strategy outlined in Figure 13-2.

In this case, everything but the `uisvc` component will be distributed to a server. For the sake of simplicity, everything will reside on one Windows NT server. This includes all of the application logic as well as the physical database. In a production environment, to increase scalability and reduce the impact on the database machine, the application logic may well be installed on a server separate from the database. This

FIGURE 13-2 *The Remulak Productions distribution strategy.*

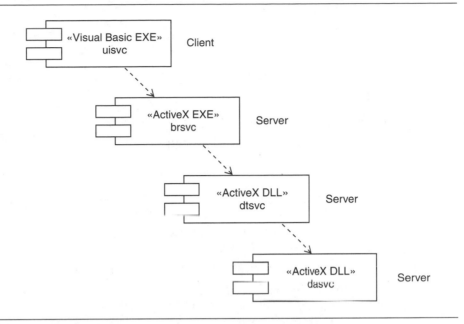

would especially be true if our DBMS was going to be running on a non-Windows platform. In addition, Microsoft highly recommends that MTS not be installed on a primary domain controller of a Windows NT machine. The primary reason is that both services are very CPU- and disk access-intensive, which will slow them both down.

This section's title is "payback time." This will become very evident when we see just how easily we can adjust our physical partitioning strategy because we followed, early on, a sound logical partitioning strategy. So, without any further delay, let's move into our first distribution strategy using native DCOM.

Remote Solutions—Distributed Component Object Model

As was stated in a prior chapter, DCOM is nothing more than COM with a long wire. I don't mean to trivialize the technology that implements DCOM, but it is really easy to get the grasp of things if one keeps that frame of reference. To take advantage of DCOM, we must do three things concerning the Remulak Productions application.

1. Decide what components—`uisvc`, `brsvc`, `dtsvc`, and `dasvc`—should run where.

2. Install the server-side software on the server and set up its permissions correctly.

3. Inform the client-side software of where to find the now remoted portions of the application.

We already made the first decision. The only thing that will remain on the client will be the `uisvc` component, which contains our forms and the UI controller classes.

To install the server-side software on the Windows NT platform, we must recompile a few things and create an install package to run on the server. To take advantage of the remoted Remulak Productions components, we must recompile just one component, `brsvc`. Remember that all of our components at present, with the exception of the `uisvc` layer, are ActiveX DLLs. The first component accessed from the client, at least in the Remulak Productions application, must be an ActiveX EXE if it is going to be out-of-process. This is true regardless of whether it is local or remote. Both the `dtsvc` and `dasvc` components may remain DLLs. The reason is that the `brsvc` layer will continue to use those as in-process ActiveX DLLs (remember, in-process is always faster than out-of-process). Now, if we wanted, for instance, to have the `brsvc` layer on one server and the other two components on their own server, maybe with the database itself, then both the `brsvc` and `dtsvc` components would have to be ActiveX EXEs.

Because we have followed a very structured application partitioning strategy, the number of decisions we will have to make about what should be an EXE and what can remain a DLL are straightforward. Each layer knows nothing more than how to talk to its closest component going outward toward the database. When we get to MTS, you will really like your options because everything we distribute will remain a DLL (actually they must be a DLL).

Construction—Preparing the Components for DCOM Distribution

The attractive thing about the DCOM approach is that we can get things ready in advance and test the revised component structure before we distribute the code. We must recompile the `brsvc` layer into an ActiveX

EXE as well as change a few of its project properties. Keep in mind that up to this point in the project, everything developed has been running as in-process servers to the `uisvc` component (actually, `brsvc` has been in-process to `uisvc`, `dtsvc` has been in-process to `brsvc`, and `dasvc` has been in-process to `dtsvc`). This is about to change. The `brsvc` component needs to run as an out-of-process component with respect to the `uisvc` component. Both the `dtsvc` and `dasvc` components will remain in-process servers to `brsvc`. Let's begin our changes.

Open the `brsvc` project by itself as shown in Figure 13-3.

Next, in the right-hand pane, right-click on the item which reads "brsvc(brsvc.vbp)" and select "brsvc properties." You will be presented with the Project Properties dialog box, as shown in Figure 13-4.

We want to make some changes to the "General" tab.

1. Change the "Project Type" from "ActiveX DLL" to "ActiveX EXE." This will make our project an out-of-process ActiveX server. In our case, `uisvc` will reference this new `brsvc.exe`.

FIGURE 13-3 *BRSVC project.*

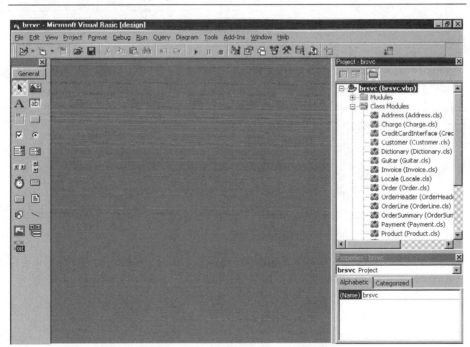

FIGURE 13-4   *BRSVC Project Properties dialog box.*

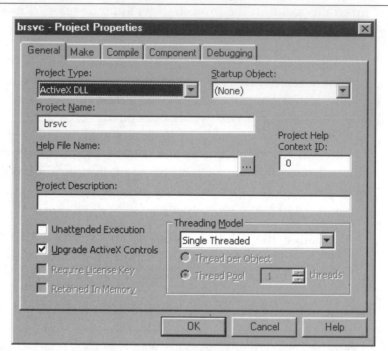

2. Select "Unattended Execution." This states that our component will utilize no user interface facilities. Any that are used would be written to an event log. This actually could have been set this way when the component was still a DLL.

3. Deselect "upgrade ActiveX controls." This feature allows only for the automatic update of controls, which we aren't using.

Now, let's make some changes that will prepare the `brsvc` component to be distributed in the future. Select the "Component" Tab. We need to make two changes.

1. Select the "Remote Server Files" checkbox. This will produce two very important files for the project when we recompile it to an EXE. It will create a `brsvc.tlb` file and `brsvc.vbr` file. The TLB file is a type library that basically acts like a calling card for the component, describing its interfaces. Remember that the native interface for any class in VB is the sum of all of its Public

operations and attributes. If it also implements another interface, like our DT classes do, then it would have two interfaces defined in the TLB file: its native one and, in the case of the DT classes, the `ICrud` interface. The TLB file will become very important once we remote the `brsvc` component. The VBR file assists VB in locating our remoted component.

2. Select the "Binary Compatibility" radio button. This option will act like a cut-off point for our component. Basically, any component that references a binary compatible component doesn't require a recompile when that component changes (see the COM appendix for exceptions to this). If not selected, then each and every time we recompile this component, it would generate new Globally Unique Identifiers (GUID) for the project and/or new GUIDs and Class Ids (CLSID) for the classes that it contains. Refer to the appendices for a discussion on COM architecture, GUIDs, and CLSIDs. All of the components in the Remulak Productions application, with the exception of `uisvc`, should be marked as "Binary Compatibility." In a nutshell, if we didn't do this, every time a business rule changed in the `brsvc` layer, we would have to recompile all of the clients that reference it.

We should have a dialog box that looks like Figure 13-5 after completing this last step.

Now we should recompile the component by doing the following.

1. Select "File."

2. Select "Make brsvc.exe."

If we test the application, all should work as planned. The `uisvc` component is accessing the out-of-process (but still local) `brsvc` component. Also remember, we didn't have to do anything to the other two layers; they are still happy DLLs that are accessed as they always have been.

Construction—Distributing the Server Components

The next step in our DCOM saga is to create a server-side installation package for all the components that we are going to run on the Windows NT server. To do that, we need to run the Package and Deployment Wizard (See Figure 13-6).

FIGURE 13-5 *BRSVC-completed Component tab.*

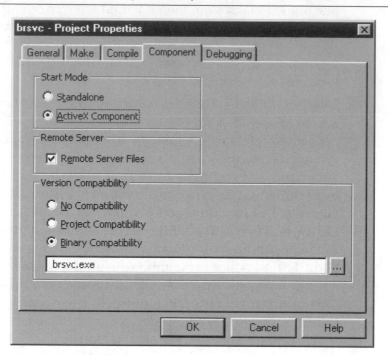

1. Select the "Start" button on the toolbar.

2. Select "Programs."

3. Select "Microsoft Visual Studio 6.0."

4. Select "Microsoft Visual Studio 6.0 Tools."

5. Select "Package and Deployment Wizard."

6. Browse until you find the `brsvc.vbp` project file that represents our project for the Business Services layer component. Then select the first button, "Package."

There will be several screens that appear. Take all the defaults until you get to a screen that prompts you for a question regarding remote automation, as shown in Figure 13-7.

This is a misleading question and your inclination is to say yes, as it is the default. Remote Automation is used very seldom since the introduction of DCOM. It is really only useful if you are still dealing with

FIGURE 13-6   *Package and Deployment Wizard.*

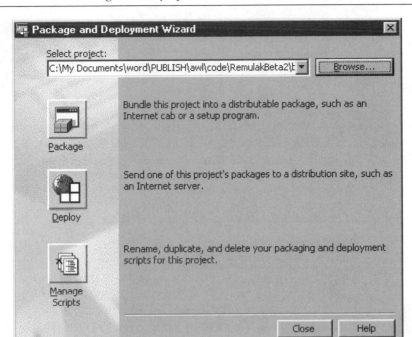

clients still running 16-bit Windows v3.1 or if you don't have available TCP/IP as a network protocol. So, in our case, we want to say "No "

Keep taking defaults from here forward until you reach a screen that gripes about a dependency missing, as shown in Figure 13-8.

This notice is just informing us that VB can't interrogate any dependencies for this component and would we like to mark it to permanently have no dependencies. Just leave it as it is and select "OK." There will eventually be a summary screen that will be presented, showing what is going to get built into the package (Figure 13-9).

We need to add one more component. It actually ties into the previous dialog. The component dtsvc depends on dasvc, so we need to manually add it by selecting "Add," to eventually end up with the dialog box shown in Figure 13-10. Notice that all of the three components being distributed show up in the "Include Files" dialog box.

Select "Next" and continue with the package creation. The next question that will require answering is shown in Figure 13-11.

FIGURE 13-7   *Remote Automation warning.*

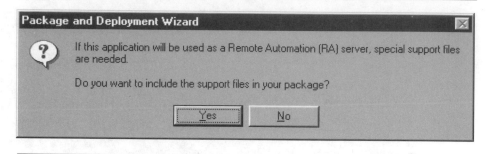

FIGURE 13-8   *Missing dependency notice.*

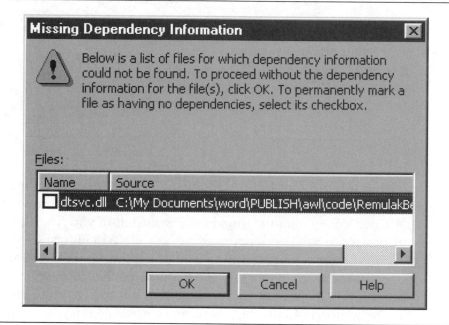

This question can be answered either way. If you feel that there will be several applications that may be accessing this component on your server, select the checkbox; otherwise, just take the default. Finally, there will be a prompt that displays what has happened and gives us the option to save the packaging report. Just select "Close" (Figure 13-12).

FIGURE 13-9 *Completed Included Files dialog box.*

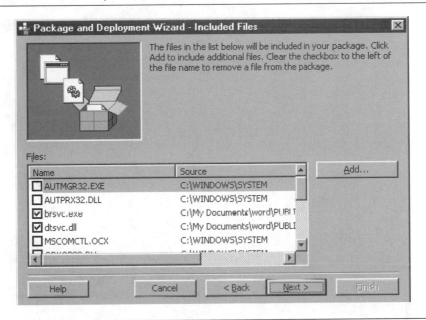

FIGURE 13-10 *Adding the DASVC component.*

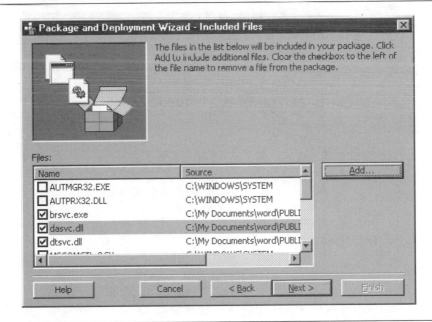

FIGURE 13-11   *Shared Files request dialog box.*

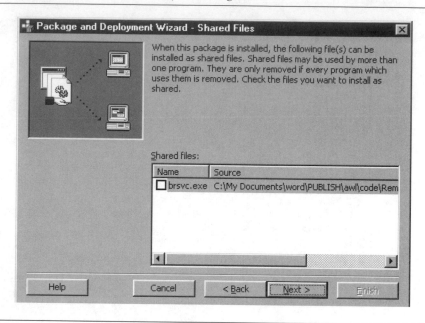

FIGURE 13-12   *Packaging Report dialog box.*

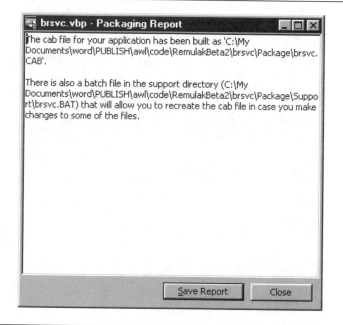

There will now be a "Package" folder in the directory that contains the `brsvc` component, as shown in Figure 13-13.

If you double-click this folder, you will notice a `setup.exe` file that will allow the application to be installed on the server.

Construction—Installing the Components on the Server

At this point, you would want to logon to your Windows NT server and navigate to the directory on the development machine where the install package resides. I am assuming that you are using two machines, developing on one and then deploying the `brsvc`, `dtsvc`, and `dasvc` components to another, a Windows NT server machine. Figure 13-14 shows the initial setup prompt once the `setup.exe` file is executed.

The next important thing that must be done is to establish the security for the remotely installed components. This requires that we run a program, on the Windows NT machine, to set these parameters. This program is called `dcomcnfg.exe`.

Figure 13-15 shows the dialog box that `dcomcnfg` will initiate. Select the `brsvc` server and double-click "Properties." You may be wondering what the "brsvc.SysCodes" means. `SysCodes` is just one class within the `brsvc` component. We are actually working with the entire EXE, not just this one class. The display is vague, but don't let it fool you.

FIGURE 13-13 *Package components.*

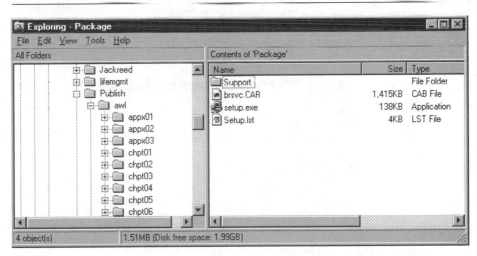

FIGURE 13-14 *Installing the server-side components.*

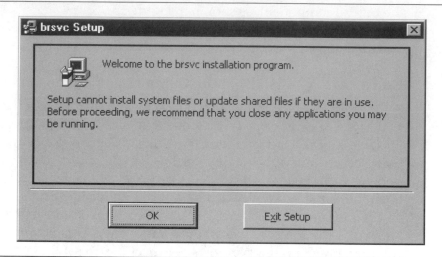

FIGURE 13-15 *Running* `dcomcnfg` *to set security.*

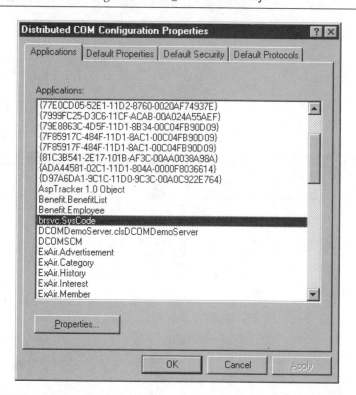

The next few screens will show how we establish the permissions for not only accessing the component but also who can launch the application. After the application is initially installed on the server, the component will still be in a "lock-down" status, so to speak.

Figure 13-16 shows the "Security" tab for the `brsvc` component. When the tab is first displayed, the "use default" radio buttons will be selected for the top two options.

We need to change these to use custom security. Select "Edit" for the first one, and you should see what Figure 13-17 presents.

Although in a production environment you would want to give careful consideration to the security access rules, for starters, I usually

FIGURE 13-16   *Security tab of the SysCode Properties dialog box.*

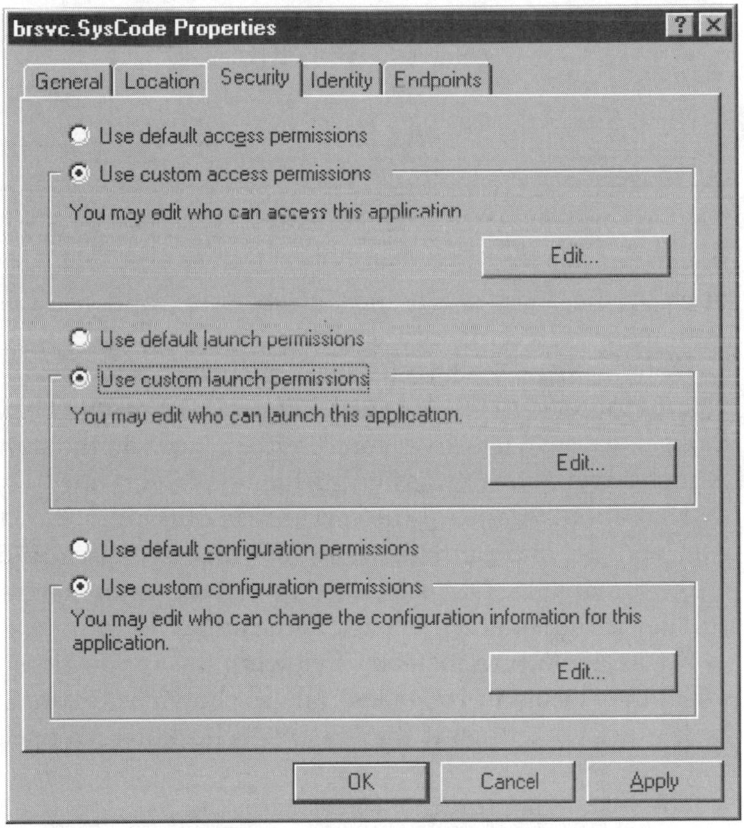

FIGURE 13-17 *Modifying access security.*

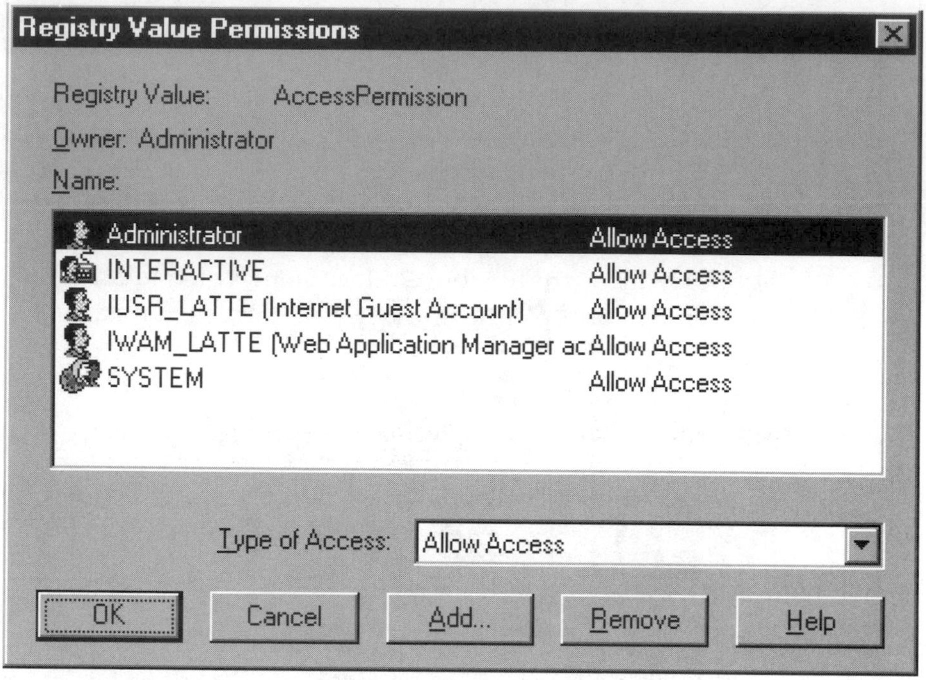

open up the doors to anyone. Select "Add," and you will be presented with what you see in Figure 13-18.

Double-click "Everyone" and then select "Add." This will add "Allow Access" to "Everyone." Figure 13-19 should be what the dialog looks like now with "Everyone" added. Now do the same thing for the launch permissions by assigning them to "Everyone."

That about wraps up the server side of things. The last thing I suggest you do, and perhaps many of you have already done this, it to make sure that DCOM is enabled on this server in the first place. We are still in the right place. Get back to the initial dcomcnfg window shown in Figure 13-15, and instead of viewing the applications on this server, select the "Default Properties" tab, as shown in Figure 13-20. It should look exactly like this. If the "Enable" checkbox isn't selected, then do so.

The installation on the server from the package we created should have registered everything for us. However, there will be times when

FIGURE 13-18 *Adding access to Everyone.*

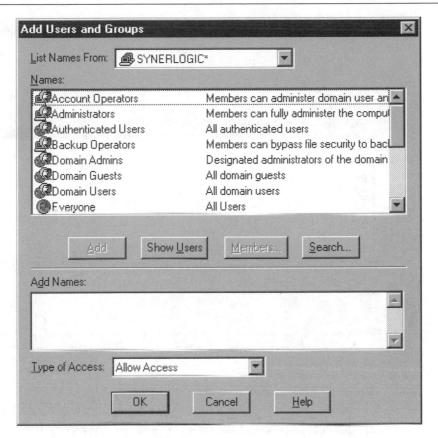

for one reason or another, we need to unregister either an ActiveX EXE or DLL. ActiveX EXEs are self-registering when they are loaded. Once the EXE is invoked, if it isn't registered then it registers itself. However, you can specifically request that it be registered or unregistered manually. This is done by entering the following from either a DOS window or by selecting "Start" then "Run":

- "activexserver.exe/register", where activexserver is your server name, such as brsvc.exe or

- "activexserver.exe/unregister", where activexserver is your server name, such as brsvc.exe.

FIGURE 13-19   *Access to Everyone added.*

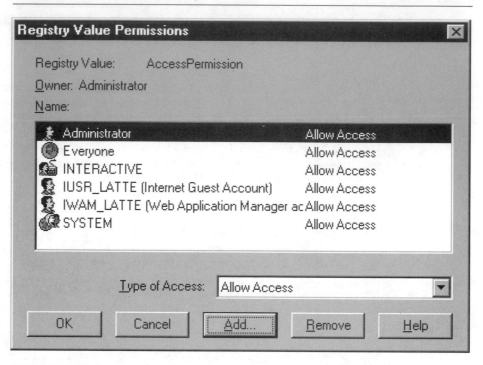

For DLLs, we have to jump through a little bit of a different hoop. Since these files are passive in that they don't do anything until some caller requests their services, they can't register themselves. To specifically request that a DLL register and unregister itself, do so by entering either:

- "regsvr32 activexserver.dll", where activexserver.dll is your server name, such as dasvc.dll or

- "regsvr32 /U activexserver.dll", where activexserver.dll is your server name, such as dasvc.dll.

The `regsvr32.exe` file is found in your \Windows\System directory on Windows 95/98 and \Windows\System32\ on Windows NT. Please pay special attention to the "/U" parameter and that it, strangely, precedes the DLL name. I can't tell you how many times I have really thought I was daft only to find out that I had kept putting the "/U" after the DLL's name.

FIGURE 13-20   *Enabling DCOM on the Default Properties tab.*

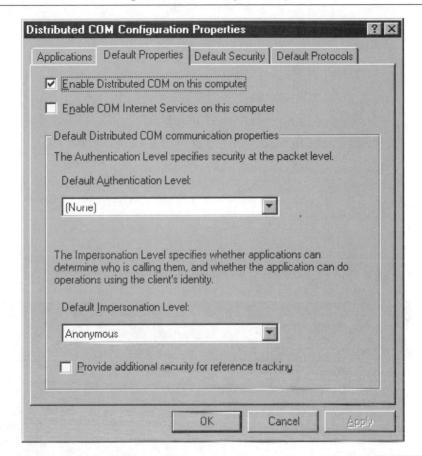

Construction—Getting the Client Ready to Test the DCOM Installation

Now that all is well on the server, we have to tweak a few things on our development machine to be able to talk to the remoted component layers on the Windows NT machine.

Remember, we said earlier that Remote Automation is an older technology, introduced in VB v4.0 to be exact, but it typically isn't utilized much any longer with the advent of DCOM. However, we are about to look at a tool that is a real workhorse to get the client in shape, but it still carries the "Remote Automation" stamp. The Remote Automation

Connection manager is similar in construct to what `dcomcnfg` shows us, but it provides us with the ability to change important information about class execution location information. To get to this tool on the client on which you are developing, do the following.

1. Select the "Start" button on the toolbar.

2. Select "Programs."

3. Select "Microsoft Visual Studio 6.0."

4. Select "Microsoft Visual Studio 6.0 Enterprise Tools."

5. Select "RemAuto Connection Manager."

You should see the Remote Automation Connection Manager dialog box, as shown in Figure 13-21.

FIGURE 13-21 *Remote Automation Connection Manager dialog box.*

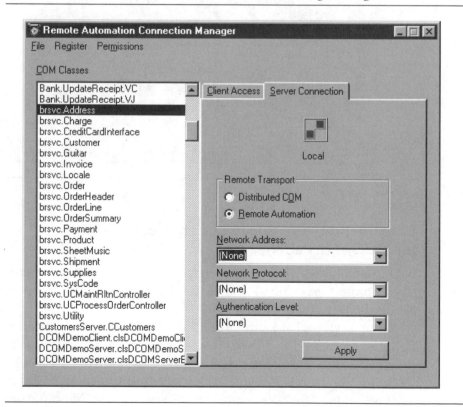

Notice that in the middle of the dialog box are all the classes for our `brsvc` component. On the right-hand side is an indication that this class is currently being accessed locally. The information below applies only if the `brsvc` component is remote. Let's tell all the classes for `brsvc` that we want them to be accessed remotely. If you are a real sadist, you could go through each class and set the remote properties. However, a little-known shortcut to set them all at once is as follows.

1. Click the first class in `brsvc`.
2. "Shift+Click" the last class in `brsvc`; they should all now be highlighted.
3. Select the "Distributed COM" radio button.
4. Enter the name of your Windows NT machine in the "Network Address" field (without slashes).
5. Select the menu item "Register."
6. Select the drop-down menu item "Remote."
7. As an alternative to the last two steps, you can right-click the selected classes and select "Remote" or just use the hot key sequence "Ctrl+R."
8. Click the "Apply" button.

Figure 13-22 is what you should end up with.

Notice that the information on the right-hand side of the dialog box now reflects that the classes are going to be using DCOM and the server that they are going to be placed after is called "Latte." If you haven't guessed by now, I only have one vice.

Believe it or not, you're done with the client changes and ready to test your remote components. Simply execute the EXE we created for the `uisvc` component and everything should work as planned. However, here are some errors you may encounter.

- Error 429 – Server Cannot Create Object

The most common cause for this error in a DCOM scenario is that the Class ID on your client machine doesn't match the Class ID in your remote DCOM server. This usually occurs because binary compatibility wasn't maintained. Someone perhaps recompiled the DCOM server

FIGURE 13-22   *Remote Automation Connection Manager with changes.*

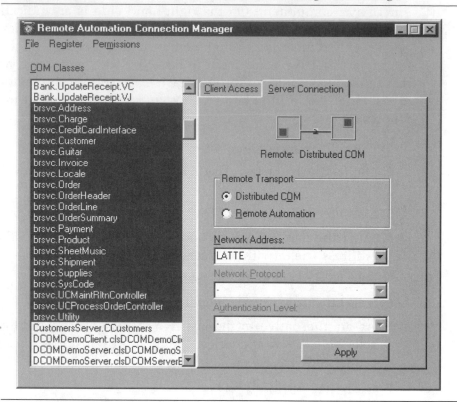

on the client development machine, changing its Class ID, and this doesn't match an older DCOM component on the server.

To fix this, unregister the DCOM server on the Windows NT machine, copy the new EXE over to the server, and then register the DCOM server. You should probably also rebuild your client install sets from scratch (covered next in this chapter).

This error can also arise because the user doesn't have "Access" and/or "Launch" privileges on the Windows NT server DCOM component. However, if you open access to "Everyone," this shouldn't arise.

Lastly, and unfortunately because of the fragile Registry, the DCOM server on the Windows NT machine may be fine, but the Registry entries may be referencing something else—yes, I know, even though you unregistered and reregistered the server. This will require that you hack into the Registry and remove two keys for each class (yuk!): one referenced by the class name and the other referenced by its Class ID. The last error shouldn't show up that often if you follow your procedures closely when installing and reinstalling components.

- Error 7 – Out of Memory

This is a bit vague, but usually it means that the DCOM server itself doesn't have proper access rights on the Windows NT server. This pertains to the "Identity" tab when running dcomcnfg on the server. The rights error referenced previously for the error 429 message concerns the settings under the "Security" tab, which we covered.

Lastly, I want to mention another really nice feature of our DCOM setup. Let's say you wanted, for some reason, to execute all the code as it currently resides on your development machine—in essence, not execute the remote components. Perhaps you want to step through the code and analyze some values. The only change you have to make is to do the reverse of what was shown in Figure 13-22. Simply highlight all the classes in the Remote Automation Connection Manager dialog box, and just change them to "Local" instead of "Remote." When you are ready to execute the remote versions, just repeat the process again but mark them as previously for "Remote" execution. No need to recompile anything.

However, be forewarned that if you recompile anything and it breaks your compatibility, you will get your old friend, the error 429, or, worse yet, a hard crash. Just because you have something marked as "binary compatibility" doesn't mean that the IDs won't change. Changing a class's interface (for example, a new operation, deleted operation, or changed signature) will generate new IDs even if you have "binary compatibility" selected. (See Appendix D.)

Construction—Creating a Client Install Package

Although everything mentioned previously will prove that things can be remoted and DCOM can communicate between client and server, it doesn't prepare the Remulak Productions application to be distributed to the masses. To do this, we will use the same packaging procedure used for the server install, but this time, we will point at the uisvc component instead of brsvc.

Execute the Package and Deployment Wizard as we did for the DCOM server previously, only this time navigate to the `uisvc.vbp` project file. Take all the defaults until you get to the Included Files dialog box, as shown in Figure 13-23.

Now, this may seem odd but we *don't* want the `brsvc.exe` component to be distributed with this package. This got included because there was a reference to it in the `uisvc` project. The `brsvc.exe` component will be running remotely on our server; we don't want it installed at all on our clients. The two files mentioned earlier in this chapter, the TLB and VBR files, now become very important. What we want to do is uncheck the `brsvc.exe` entry and add the `brsvc.tlb` and `brsvc.vbr` files. Remember, these can be found in the `brsvc` directory. They were created when we recompiled the `brsvc.exe` with the "Remote Server Files" option checked. If you select the VBR file first, it will automatically bring the TLB file in for you. You should have something that looks like Figure 13-24.

FIGURE 13-23 *Included Files dialog box for the client install package.*

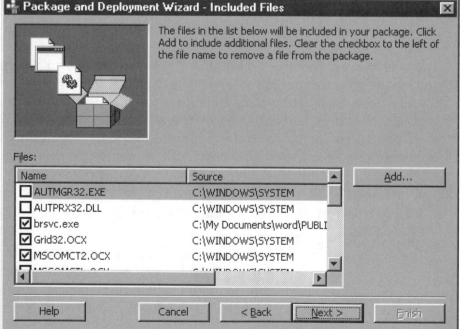

FIGURE 13-24   *Included Files dialog box with VBR files included.*

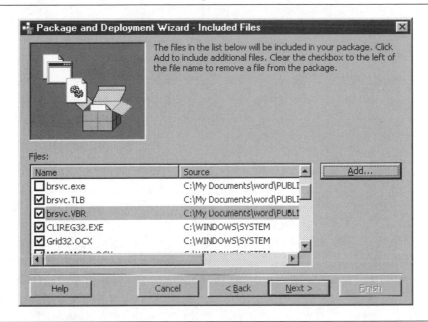

FIGURE 13-25   *Remote server inclusion using the Remote Servers dialog box.*

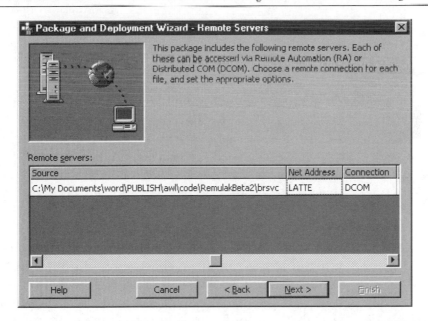

Continue on with selecting the defaults until you come to a prompt regarding Remote Servers, as shown in Figure 13-25.

This dialog box is telling us that it has determined that `brsvc` is remote because of the VBR and TLB additions that we made and asks what type of connection we want. The default is DCOM, but we need to fill in "Net Address" with our Windows NT server name.

Continue until the package is complete, just as was shown previously when we did the server. All that is necessary is to go to each client and install the package on the machine. They should then be able to also access our DCOM server.

That's it for our native DCOM adventure. Not too bad, but still a lot of work having to tweak this and that as well as making sure we don't get things crossed up along the way. However, if you need remote support and don't plan on using MTS, then once you have gone through the process of setting it up a few times, it will seem like a pretty mundane task. Besides, it is strongly rumored that when Windows 2000 (NT v5.0) is introduced and the new COM+ is implemented, the handholding we went through should get easier. The installation process should be very similar to what you will see next for MTS. Now, let's visit the same scenario as previously discussed, but implement the remote aspects of the application under MTS.

Remote Solutions—Microsoft Transaction Server

MTS started out with the code name "Viper" at Microsoft, a somewhat ominous name but right in line with names such as "Wolf Pack" (Microsoft Cluster Server). MTS, in a way, is like a snake in that it weaves together all the aspects of transaction management across heterogeneous database resources. For instance, it was next to impossible to have a client/server application that updated both an Oracle and Microsoft SQL Server database and then could issue just one "Commit" statement and have both different database environments remain in sync. There are some very expensive transaction monitor products on the market that can assist in this orchestration, but they are, in many cases, cost prohibitive. Enter MTS to make things a lot simpler.

In a previous chapter, we reviewed many of MTS's benefits. One of the biggest is that it affords the ability to manage transaction scope transparently regarding the actual physical DBMS resources involved. The reason is that every action taken, as to the objects in the application, does so under the same context. In MTS, this is done by communicating through its primary interface, `IObjectContext`.

For those interested in playing in the MTS sandbox, you can get to this interface by referencing the "Microsoft Transaction Server Type Library" in the References dialog for the project, as shown in Figure 13-26.

Construction—Getting to the Interface

Once the project reference is made, we can then get at the context for a transaction by issuing the message, `GetObjectContext()`.

```
Dim moObjectContext As ObjectContext
Set moObjectContext = GetObjectContext()
```

FIGURE 13-26 *Referencing the MTS type library.*

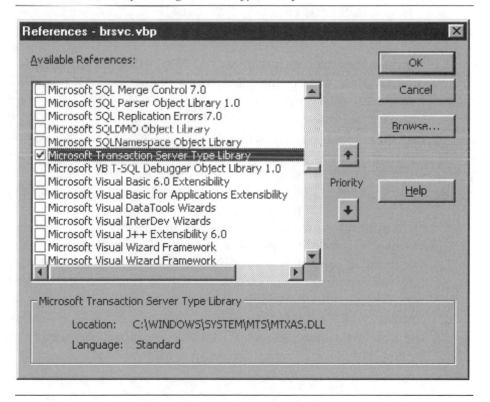

The `GetObjectContext` operation is defined in the MTS type library that we referenced for our project. Now, `moObjectContext` has a reference to the `IObjectContext` interface that is the gateway to communicating with MTS. Why would we want to communicate with the interface in the first place? One of the most important reasons is to tell MTS whether we are happy with the results of the transaction. Remember, transactions running under MTS can do lots of things, the biggest of which is updating databases. These databases may live on different platforms and come from different vendors. As long as the database vendor supports OLE transactions, then they can work under MTS's control in conjunction with other databases.

So, if we have made changes to, let's say, Oracle and Microsoft SQL Server databases in the scope of one transaction, we need to communicate only with `moObjectContext` and cast our vote of success or failure. This is done with `SetComplete` and `SetAbort` operations.

```
moObjectContext.SetComplete
moObjectContext.SetAbort
```

A message of `SetComplete` would commit all the work made against any database during this transaction. Furthermore, you don't have to issue individual `committrans` statements to each data source. Just one message does the trick. It would then stand to reason that there is no further need for any specific `begintrans` statements either. Don't be misled; the application still must get connections, open them, and close them. However, in our case, using ADO, there would no longer be a need to specifically begin and end a transaction. MTS is the engine that begins and ends the transaction. More on that later.

Another important feature of MTS, although not fully supported yet, is object pooling. Remember from Chapter 8, pooling makes for very efficient and highly scalable applications. Objects that are pooled have already been instantiated and can be reused to provide for even more throughput potential. To get to these pooling features, we must implement a special MTS interface, `ObjectControl`. We do this with the `Implement ObjectControl` statement, just like we did when we implemented the `ICrud` interface in the DT classes.

```
Implements ObjectControl
```

Once this is keyed into your class, click the "Object" drop-down and you will see `ObjectControl` listed; select it. Now click the "Procedure" drop-down and you will see three operations; the class (just like any interface) must implement all of them, as indicated next.

```
Private Sub ObjectControl_Activate()
    Set moInstanceInfo.objectContext = GetObjectContext()
End Sub
Private Function ObjectControl_CanBePooled() As Boolean
    ObjectControl_CanBePooled = True
End Function
Private Sub ObjectControl_Deactivate()
    Set moInstanceInfo.objectContext = Nothing
End Sub
```

The `activate` operation is sent to your class right before MTS sends it its first operation request. A class's `Initialize` event always happens prior to the `activate`. It is important to note that the class `initialize` event only happens once in its lifetime, while `activate` may be invoked many times as it is brought in and out of the pool. If an object needs to do any special things before being activated, you would add the code here. In our case, we want to create a new UDT and populate it with the `ObjectContext`. We will need this later if we want code that can live both in and out of MTS. The UDT is shown next and will be added to a new `PublicNotCreatable` class called `DictionaryMTS` that is shared by all the MTS-managed projects but that resides in `brsvc`.

```
'holds information about an object instance
Public Type InstanceUDT
    objectContext As objectContext
End Type
```

At the top of every class that is going to participate in MTS transactions, in the declarations section, the following line of code would have to be added:

```
Dim moInstanceInfo As InstanceUDT
```

The `canBePooled` operation is called immediately after the object is deactivated to see whether the object supports pooling. Although object pooling isn't currently supported by MTS, many developers are going ahead and adding the return value of `True` anyway. Be fore-warned that eventually you will have to come back and visit the ramifications of pooling on your objects. If an object is brought out of the pool and reactivated, the object's users must find the object in the same state as if it had just been created; no excess baggage can be hanging around. The `deactivate` operation is just like `activate` but would be called prior to the actual object's deactivation. In our implementation, we want to set the `ObjectContext` to `Nothing`. Think of deactivation like putting the object to sleep. In the future, when MTS supports object pooling, it is important to understand that in a single object's lifetime, it may have deactivate invoked many times as it is brought in and out of the pool.

It is important to note that this interface is optional; it isn't a required interface if you don't care to take advantage of any of these MTS-generated messages or object pooling. MTS isn't going to crash—nor will your application—if your objects don't support the interface. However, for the Remulak Productions application, it will be vital to have code that can run both with and without MTS.

Construction—Types of Transactions

In VB, classes are the granularity by which MTS creates transactions. When you add a component, an ActiveX DLL, you must tell MTS what kind of transaction manners each class will demonstrate. If you think about it, some classes in the Remulak Productions application, such as `Access` in `dasvc`, are really doing work on behalf of a larger whole. Other classes, such as `UCMaintRltnController`, are driver classes that orchestrate the entire pathway of a use case. With those distinctions in mind, let's review how classes in MTS can be categorized as to transaction support (see Table 13-1).

Let's review what these different levels can do for us.

Requires a Transaction: Indicates that this class must run inside of a transaction. If a context has already been established by some other class, which has instantiated this class, then it will run within the context of the initiating class. If there is no context already established, then it will start a new transaction.

TABLE 13-1   *Transaction Types as Expressed by MTS and VB Equivalents*

MTS Transaction Support Setting	VB's MTSTransactionMode
Requires a Transaction	`RequiresTransaction`
Requires a New Transaction	`RequiresNewTransaction`
Supports Transactions	`UsesTransaction`
Doesn't Support Transactions	`NoTransactions`
N/A	`NotAnMTSObject`

Requires a New Transaction: Indicates that this class must start a new transaction. This allows for nested transactions. An inner nested transaction can fail and call `SetAbort` without affecting the outer transaction's outcome.

Supports Transactions: If a class is instantiated and there is a context already established, then it will work within that context. If there is no context established, the object will be created without transaction support.

Doesn't Support Transactions: The object is created within MTS without any transaction support.

You can mark classes as to their transaction status in one of two ways. One is through VB during development time. The other is through the Transaction Server Explorer on the server that will be hosting the component. Figure 13-27 shows the properties dialog box in VB for the `UCMaintRltnController` class and its MTS setting.

We will look at the MTS method of setting this property later in the chapter during our tour of the MTS administration tools.

Construction—Remulak Productions Transaction Types

Because of the architecture that our application is designed around and the way we have utilized the UML and object-design principles, our transaction decisions are very simple. All of our classes will either be "Requires a New Transaction" or "Supports Transactions."

FIGURE 13-27 *Properties dialog box for MTS settings.*

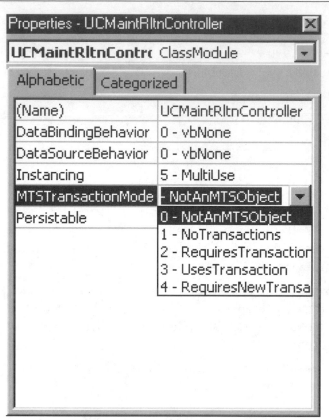

The design that we have followed places all the control of a transaction in the use case controller classes. Everything from the user interface funnels through these classes. Remember, each use case will have a use case controller class. So, all use case controller classes will be marked as "Requires a New Transaction." All the other classes will be marked as "Supports Transactions." Ultimately, when you think about our approach, all the other classes in all three components that will reside on the MTS server machine directly or indirectly do the bidding of the use case controller.

Unfortunately, there is a flaw in MTS's approach to transaction delegation. I personally think that its granularity is too coarse. When you think about a class and the operations that they support, there are two different categories. If we examine our `UCMaintRltnController` class, it has operations, such as `RltnInquiry`, which don't need a database transaction context from MTS at all (they still need ADO connections though, which is fine, but they don't need to update anything).

On the other hand, we have `saveCustomerRltn`, which does lots of inserts, updates, and deletes that must operate within a transaction context so that all the changes can be committed or rolled back together. This poses a dilemma for us. Since we have to mark the transaction status at the class level, all inquiry-oriented use case pathways are still going to create an MTS transaction context.

An often-used alternative approach is to split the use case controller classes into two types: update-oriented and read-oriented. This would work just fine because if a read-oriented pathway, such as `RltnInquiry`, which would reside in a class marked "Doesn't Support Transactions," used `Customer`, then since `Customer` is marked as "Supports Transactions" and since its owner doesn't have a context, it would be created without one. If `saveCustomerRltn` used `Customer`, then all of the classes would run under the context of the update-oriented use case class where `saveCustomerRltn` resides.

However, as you probably guessed, I don't like this alternative. It now artificially splits the controllers, which can cause problems for users of these controllers. They must decide which one to use for which pathway. A good case in point is the Customer Inquiry Screen. It would now have to use one use case controller for inquiry and a different one for update. This could be alleviated a bit by still having them talk to one class and then letting this use case broker class figure out which use case controller, read or update, to actually use. I still use just one controller class and have found the overhead to be unrecognizable. For larger applications that support very high rates of transactions, splitting the controller classes may be a design alternative to pursue.

Construction—MTS Administration

Before we begin modifying our Remulak Productions code to take advantage of MTS transactions, let's take a quick tour of MTS on the Windows NT server. Also, I will keep my promise by showing just how easy it is to deploy an application remotely, all under MTS, without giving any thought about transaction management or changing one line of our code.

When you see how easy this is, you may want to use MTS just to avoid some of the handholding that the native DCOM approach caused.

The primary management mechanism for MTS is the Transaction Server Explorer. If you have MTS installed on a Windows NT server, then you can get to it by doing the following.

1. Select "Start."

2. Select "Programs."

3. Select "Windows NT 4.0 Option Pack."

4. Select "Microsoft Transaction Server."

You should see the Microsoft Management Console splashscreen followed by the Transaction Server Explorer window, as shown in Figure 13-28.

We want to build a new MTS package, actually two of them, for our Remulak Productions application. If you double-click the "Packages Installed" folder, you should see something like Figure 13-29.

Packages are how components are managed in MTS. They contain classes, and the way that the classes get assigned is as easy as dragging and dropping an ActiveX DLL into the components folder. A package can have more than one DLL assigned to it. However, before you toss everything into one package, you have to think about deployment.

Just as with the DCOM solution, the only thing that the client-side software needed to be aware of was the ActiveX EXE server, `brsvc.exe`. The two other DLLs, `dtsvc` and `dasvc`, were just simply copied to the Windows NT machine and registered with `regsvr32`. We need to use the same thought process for MTS deployment. As a result, we will have two packages for Remulak Productions: one for `brsvc` and one for both `dtsvc` and `dasvc`.

In the MTS world, instead of using the Remote Automation Control Manager to tell the system where the classes live that the client needs to access, we "Export" the MTS package, which will create an install executable for the client. All we have to do to get the client to access MTS is to run this install program on the client. This executable will install the necessary client-side files, including type libraries and custom proxy-stub DLLs.

Let's first create two packages, install them with components, and then enable the client to access them under MTS. Keep in mind, we

FIGURE 13-28   *Transaction Server Explorer.*

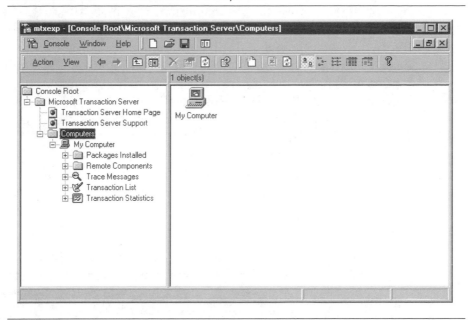

FIGURE 13-29   *MTS packages.*

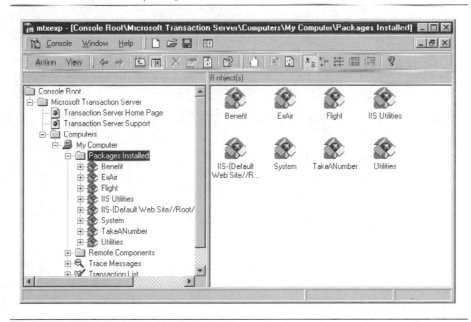

haven't done anything about modifying our software to take advantage of MTS's transaction management features. Although these features are our primary reason for using MTS, MTS is just as happy to run all of your components under its umbrella even if you don't choose its transaction services. You obviously must still manage your own transactions with `begintrans` and `committrans` statements.

Right-click the "Packages Installed" folder and select "New." You will then see the dialog for the Package Wizard for setting up the package, as shown in Figure 13-30.

Select the "Create an Empty Package" button. Let's give our package the name "remulakbrsvc" so that we know it is the Business Services layer. Your package names can be up to 500 bytes long, for those of you who are wordy.

FIGURE 13-30 *Creating a new MTS package.*

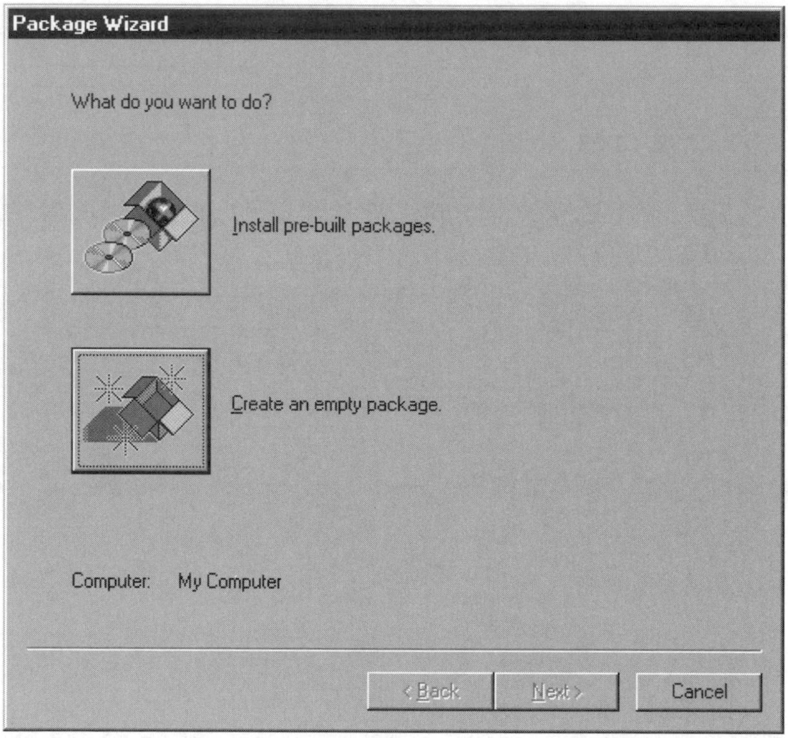

You will then be prompted with a screen to select the identity. Take the default, which is the interactive user. Select the "Finish" button, and your package is built. Next, we need to assign components to the package. You can right-click the Components tab and walk through a dialog box to specify a DLL, but I prefer to just use drag-and-drop.

Double-click the components folder so that you have an empty pane on the right-hand side of the Explorer. Now, open the Windows Explorer and navigate to your three DLLs, `brsvc`, `dtsvc`, and `dasvc`. You can go directly to the client machine where you built them or, before this step, copy them to a temporary folder in the Windows NT machine. You should have two windows open. To get them side-by-side without a lot of positioning on your part, right-click the taskbar at the bottom of the screen and select "Tile Vertically."

Next, grab `brsvc.dll` and drag it across to the Transaction Server Explorer's right-most component pane and drop it. After some work on MTS's part, you should see something like Figure 13-31.

The little marble-like icons with Xs each represent a class defined in the `brsvc` component. These icons will actually spin for us later to indicate that clients are accessing their services. That's not all. Let's look at what else we can see. If you right-click the `brsvc.Customer` marble and then select the "Transaction" tab, you will see the previously mentioned "other way" to set a class's transaction properties. This is shown in Figure 13-32.

Another very nice feature is to visit the interface(s) supported by a class. This can all be done in the Transaction Server Explorer. In the left pane of the explorer, do the following.

1. Select to expand the "Components" folder by clicking the "+".

2. Select to expand the "brsvc.Customer" entry by clicking the "+".

3. Select to expand the "Interfaces" folder by clicking the "+".

4. Select to expand the "_Customer" interface by clicking the "+".

5. Double-click "Methods," and you should see something like Figure 13-33.

Notice anything familiar? All of our Public operations such as `getInfo` and `setState` show up as little marbles with nuts and bolts next to them. You may also not recognize some of the operations, such as `GetIDsOfNames` and `QueryInterface`. These are standard COM

FIGURE 13-31 *Assigning components to a package.*

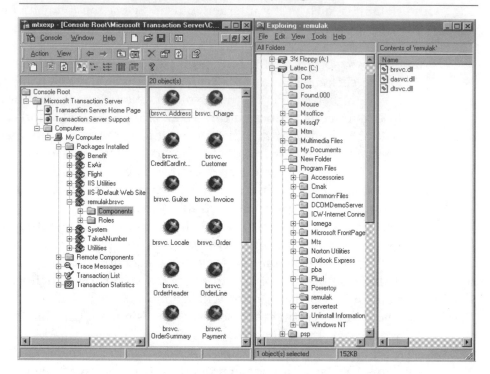

interfaces that every object must implement. VB does all of this for you behind the scenes; you never see it. However, since MTS can support any component that is an ActiveX DLL, regardless of language (that is, Java and C++), MTS shows you everything that it knows about the class.

Now, set up another package that supports both dtsvc and dasvc. Call the package "remulakdtdasvc." Drag both DLLs, at the same time if you wish, by Shift-clicking them, and drop them onto the components pane for this package. You should end up with something like Figure 13-34.

The next task will be to "Export" the package and create the necessary files so that we can tell any client-side application how to get to our MTS installed components. One question is, which package do we export? If you answered remulakbrsvc, you are right. Remember, just as with our DCOM solution, the client, uisvc.exe, doesn't know

FIGURE 13-32   *Transaction tab for the* Customer *class.*

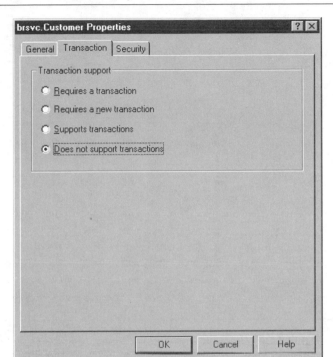

anything about the dtsvc and dasvc components. The only thing it needs routing information about is the brsvc component.

Right-click the remulakbrsvc package and select "Export." You should be presented with a dialog box like that shown in Figure 13-35.

The only thing necessary to specify is the location for the exported package. Just fully qualify the directory and give it a name; MTS will append the PAK at the end. Select "Export," and the results of the export will create what you see in Figure 13-36.

These files are all that is necessary to install the client-side components to access the MTS-managed Remulak Productions application. The remulakbrsvc.pak file is used to "Import" a package into another MTS installation, which we won't be doing.

In the "Clients" folder, you will find the executable remulakbrsvc. exe. It is this EXE that we need to execute on each client machine that

FIGURE 13-33 *Methods for the* Customer *class.*

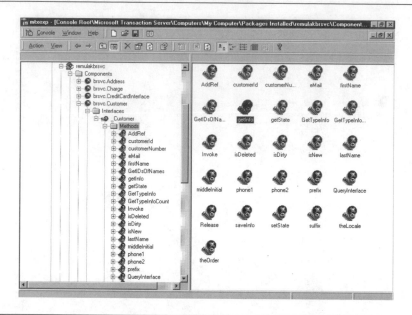

FIGURE 13-34 *Package for the* dtsvc *and* dasvc *components.*

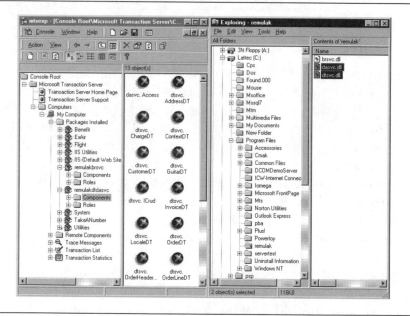

FIGURE 13-35 *Export Package dialog box for the* remulakbrsvc *package.*

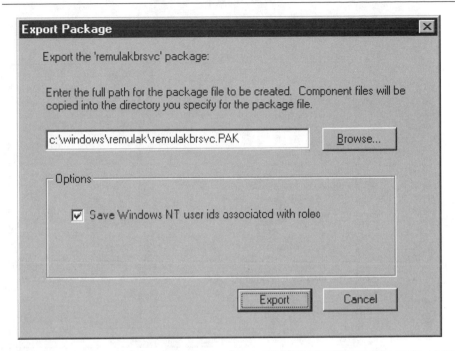

needs to access our MTS components. If you wanted to combine other things into the installation process, such as the uisvc.exe and any documentation such as readme files, you can do so by placing, into the "Clients" subdirectory, a clients.ini file. MTS will then consult that file to incorporate additional non-MTS components as part of the install. This can be further researched, if you're interested, by consulting the MTS documentation.

After the remulakbrsvc.exe is run, the client application will be able to access our MTS-managed components. I must admit, this was much easier than the DCOM approach. However, all we get from this so far is a really easy way to distribute our application. But our database code still is managing its own transactions with begintrans and committrans statements. Let's next explore how to modify our Remulak Productions application to take advantage of MTS's transaction management capabilities.

FIGURE 13-36   *Files resulting from the export.*

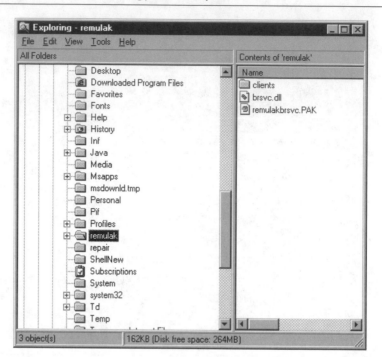

Construction—Modifying Remulak to Use MTS Transaction Management

Since we have already determined what MTS-defined transaction levels our classes will support, we must explore what changes are necessary to our code. It should be clear by now that we can run under MTS, just as an easier way to distribute our applications, without using its transaction processing abilities. But what about transactions?

The question that may be on the mind of many of you is, "How does MTS know that work done by one class should use the context of work done by another class?" For non-MTS transactions, it is easy because all update work is done against the same connection object. However, in MTS, if work is in-progress and something goes wrong, how does calling `SetAbort` on the `ObjectContext` identify all prior work since the start of the application pathway?

The answer lies in how we communicate to MTS when we create an object. It is important to understand that MTS, actually `mts.exe`, is the host for all the packages installed in the MTS environment. This is why our components must be DLLs, because `mts.exe` acts as the server (see Figure 13-37). When a client application requests a service of an MTS-managed component, control is passed to `mts.exe`, which activates the objects for us.

The three Remulak Productions components that will be managed by MTS are accessed by what MTS calls a base client. Our base client is `uisvc.exe`. A base client will activate our MTS-managed classes

FIGURE 13-37 *MTS execution environment.*

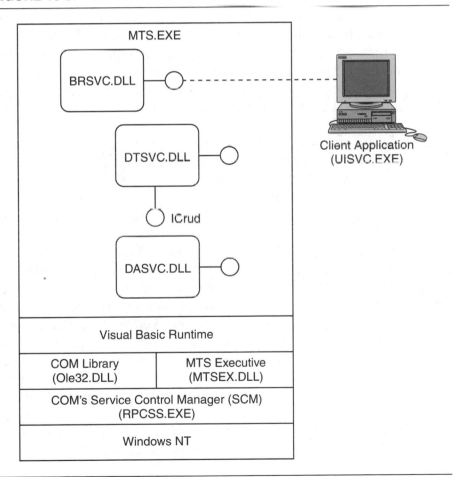

found in `brsvc.dll` when either the `New` or `CreateObject` keyword is used to create them. Now for some sleight of hand.

When our Remulak Productions components were originally installed in MTS, the Registry entries were changed by MTS to force all activation requests for classes to pass through a special MTS package first. It is actually MTS, not the client, that is activating the object. As soon as MTS gets a request to create, for instance, a new `UCMaintRltnController` class, the activation request goes through MTS and is then activated. This allows MTS to be very aware of not only what objects are being created, but also, as you shall see, how to string activation contexts together.

Every object managed by MTS, which our base client creates, will start what MTS calls a new activity (that is, if the class has been marked to use transactions). The first object created that uses transactions is called the root. In most cases, with the exception of nested transactions, which we won't discuss, all subsequent object activations need to be associated with this root. We associate these subsequent activations to the root activity via the `CreateInstance` operation. This operation is supported by the `ObjectContext` interface.

```
Dim moObjectContext As ObjectContext
Set moObjectContext = GetObjectContext()
Dim oCustomer As Customer
Set oCustomer = _
  moObjectContext.CreateIntance("brsvc.Customer")
```

If this code was in the `UCMaintRltnController` class, the `oCustomer` object would then be attached to the activity initially created when the base client, `uisvc.exe`, created the controller class. If you recall our conversation about transactions, `UCMaintRltnController` was marked as "Requires a New Transaction" and the `Customer` class was marked as "Supports Transactions." So, in this example, `UCMaintRltnController` is considered the root, with a new MTS transaction. `Customer` is merely carrying out additional work, as far as MTS transaction management is concerned, to be done in behalf of the root and will be attached to its activity. If the root now calls `setAbort`, then MTS knows what prior work was carried on within that activity and can deal with it accordingly.

What if the base client initiates a transaction via a New on our UCMaintRltnController class? Well, we know MTS will start a new transaction for it because of how we marked it in MTS, but what happens if we issue a CreateObject or a New on other classes after the transaction starts instead of using CreateInstance?

A call to CreateObject is just like a sending New or Create Object from the base client. This forces the request to go back through MTS, and what will happen depends on how the class is marked as to transactions.

```
Dim oCustomer As Customer
Set oCustomer = CreateObject("brsvc.Customer")
```

In our case, if we use the above code inside of UCMaintRltn Controller, some interesting things happen. Customer is marked as "Supports Transactions," which means that if there is a context already, it'll join in; otherwise, it won't create a transaction. Since this is being treated as a new MTS activation request and because we didn't use CreateInstance, we end up with no transaction at all. If Customer had been marked as "Requires Transactions," what would have been the result? You're right—we would have had a second transaction started because again, we didn't refer to the prior context by using CreateInstance.

Even worse things can happen when you use the New operator on an MTS object.

```
Set oCustomer = New brsvc.Customer
```

If you recall from Appendix D, the New operator can do some different things depending on where the components are in relation to each other. If UCMaintRltnController and Customer didn't live in the same DLL (but they do), then a New would behave just like CreateObject. However, since they live in the same DLL, neither COM's Service Control Manager (SCM) nor MTS gets involved. VB does all the activation internally. So, we don't even have a valid MTS object. The best practice to follow is to always create subsequent MTS-managed objects, once the root is established, with CreateInstance.

There is an exception to this advice (isn't there always!). There is no need to issue a CreateInstance on standard VB objects. This would include things such as collections, ADO, RDO, and DAO. You can continue to use New on these. However, anything installed into an MTS package that you or someone else built should use CreateInstance. The last bit of confusion is with the base client. The base client still treats the objects managed by MTS as it always has. A base client won't know anything about CreateInstance because it isn't referencing the MTS type library.

From this section, we can state the following facts that we will call our Round 1 changes necessary to the application as follows.

- All objects created, from the use case controllers forward, must be instantiated with the CreateInstance operation if and only if we are operating in an MTS environment.

- All classes should implement the pooling and activation features offered by the ObjectControl interface. The code reviewed previously that got the ObjectContext and placed it in a module-level UDT must be added to every class managed by MTS.

- Only the use case controller classes will be marked as "Requires a New Transaction."

- All other classes will be marked as "Supports Transactions."

Construction—Supporting the Right to Vote

Previously in this chapter we indicated that our programs would want to communicate with the ObjectContext, not only to create new objects attached to the root context but also to signal their disposition as to the success or failure of a transaction. Enter again the SetComplete and SetAbort operations.

As we did with the implementation of the Remulak Productions application that didn't use MTS transactions, we called an operation named DTSetContext to start a transaction and get a connection and DTSetComplete to commit a transaction (the operation names used in our non-MTS implementation closely parallel those of MTS; this was quite intentional). This was all done from the use case controller class, which is a root object as far as MTS is concerned. We also had an operation called DTSetAbort that issued an ADO rollback command if we weren't happy with the result.

We must change our architecture a bit to substitute what these DT operations do with MTS-compatible constructs. Actually, we will attempt to do more than that. It would be nice to have the Remulak Productions code be smart enough to know whether it is running under MTS and then act accordingly.

In Ted Pattison's classic, "Programming Distributed Applications with COM and Microsoft Visual Basic," he makes the statement, "An MTS transaction and the objects inside it should be flashes in the pan." To strive toward objects that do as much work in as little time as possible and then terminate themselves, we must follow some simple rules. We will call these rules our Round 2 changes, as follows.

- Each object should call the MTS SetComplete upon completion of its work. This not only signals that it was happy with its part of the transaction; it also deactivates the object and frees resources to the server. If the object is not happy with the result of its work, it should call the MTS SetAbort.

- The root object, our controller classes, must always call either the MTS SetComplete or SetAbort after its pathway is complete. If a child object called SetAbort, then the root should also call SetAbort. The same applies for SetComplete.

It is critical that the developer understand that calling SetComplete in a child object of the root does not commit the transaction. It does, however, allow the object and its resources to be deactivated. Only a call to SetComplete within the root commits a transaction.

Construction—Remulak Changes: Give and Take

Previously, in this chapter, we added some code that would enable us to perform certain transaction management tasks while at a minimum being able to determine if our application was running under MTS. Remember the code.

```
Implements ObjectControl
Dim moInstanceInfo As InstanceUDT

Private Sub ObjectControl_Activate()
    Set moInstanceInfo.objectContext = _
      GetObjectContext()
End Sub
Private Function ObjectControl_CanBePooled() As _
```

```
Boolean
    ObjectControl_CanBePooled = True
End Function
Private Sub ObjectControl_Deactivate()
    Set moInstanceInfo.objectContext = Nothing
End Sub
```

Having access to `moInstanceInfo.objectContext` will assist us in branching to specific MTS code, while at the same time, in the absence of MTS, we will be able to fall back to more traditional transaction management functionality such as the good old `begintrans` and `committrans` statements. The logic is straightforward: If `moInstanceInfo.objectContext` is `Nothing`, then we aren't running under MTS—that's it. If MTS isn't running, then the `ObjectControl_Activate` event will never be sent to our object in the first place, which means we won't have a context reference.

The next thing we must address is the stateful nature of some of our objects. As was alluded to in an earlier chapter, the concept of stateful and MTS have reached the comparative status of oil and vinegar. It's not that MTS dislikes stateful objects; it just can't scale to its ultimate potential with them, or so it is claimed. Although there is ample reason to strive toward the goal of statelessness, I have found a very worthy happy medium between statefull and stateless objects that scales quite nicely. It is necessary to distinguish between two kinds of stateful objects.

- **Long-lived**: These objects live as active references for long durations during the course of a transaction. Think back to our discussion in the chapter where we initially constructed the Customer Inquiry aspect of the system. At that time, I indicated a common design theme that showed up in many applications. It has to do with creating an object from the client, `Customer` perhaps, and interacting with that object while the user ponders its action of entering `Customer` information. The whole time, our object languishes within MTS, waiting to be told to update itself or forget the whole thing.

- **Short-lived**: These objects live for only a short period of time and contain absolutely no long-lived client-side interaction. This means that once the client has completed its work, the objects spring into action long enough to accomplish their missions and then disappear. During this interaction, many objects may collaborate and some objects may contain references to other objects, but they do so in such a short time-span that their mission is done almost as soon as it starts.

Long-lived, stateful objects should be avoided when deploying an application using MTS. However, short-lived stateful objects can function quite happily within MTS while still allowing the application to scale in size. In addition, the object design isn't compromised to satisfy the most current technology shift that happens to be in vogue. Certainly, one of the keys to transaction management in MTS is a very focused point of control that coordinates the activities of the other objects, and we have that with our use case controller classes.

One area that we can improve on in our current design, to be considered better citizens within MTS, is to see where we can further reduce stateful activity. Following is a list of changes that we need to make not only to provide dual-mode transaction support (MTS and no MTS), but also to further reduce statefulness within our design.

1. At present, when `DTSetContext` is called, it creates an instance of `Access`, as well as gets a database connection, `moConn`, which is kept within `Access`. This is still required in a non-MTS environment for update-oriented transactions so that we can issue a `begintrans` on the connection. However, this isn't necessary at all for MTS transactions. For MTS, we should explore ways to get the database connection when database access is required and not before.

2. At present, when `DTSetComplete` is called, either it will issue a `committrans` on the connection if it is update-oriented and close the connection or it will just close the connection. However, issuing a `committrans` isn't necessary at all for MTS-type transactions.

Let's call these modifications dealing with stateful objects our Round 3 changes. Let's now look at how we will implement all three rounds of changes.

MTS—Round 1 Changes

The changes in this round dealt with making our objects aware of whether we are running within MTS, as well as using `CreateInstance` to instantiate objects if MTS is running. The "MTS-awareness" logic was reviewed previously. This must be added to every class that we have in the `brsvc`, `dtsvc`, and `dasvc` components. Luckily, it is a small change. So, let's pick a class to show a sample, like the controller `UCMaintRltnController`.

In Figure 13-38, we add `Implements ObjectControl` to gain access to the three MTS messages that can be sent to our object. We also add the declaration for the `InstanceUDT` type declaration that was added to the `DictionaryMTS` class.

Figure 13-39 shows the implementation of the `ObjectControl` interface and its three operations. Notice that in the `Object Control_Deactivate`, we get the `ObjectContext` and set it to `Nothing`. Now our object has the ability to determine if it is running within MTS. This same small but broad change must be made to every class that we have whose "Instancing" property is set to "Multi-Use."

FIGURE 13-38 *Changes to* `UCMaintRltnController` *in support of MTS.*

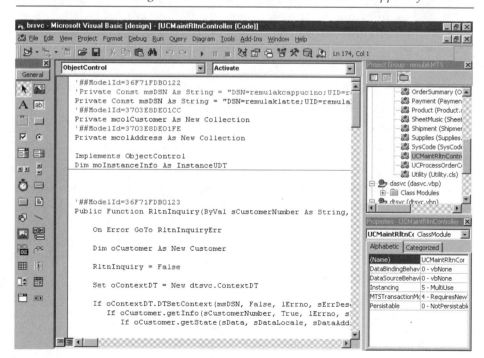

FIGURE 13-39 *Changes in* `UCMaintRltnController` *to support* `ObjectControl` *messages.*

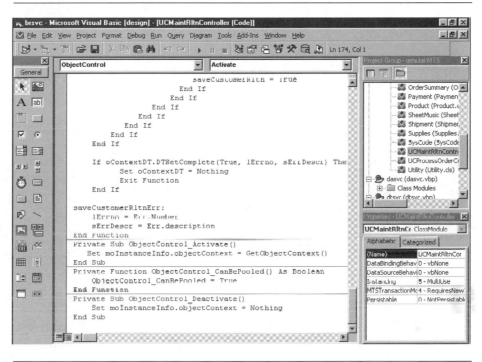

This would encompass all of our classes with the exception of the `Dictionary` and `DictionaryMTS` classes, which were defined as `PublicNotCreatable`.

The second part of our change deals with using `CreateInstance` to instantiate objects once the use case controller begins a pathway. This applies to every `New` or `CreateObject` that we may be using now. The only exceptions, again, are standard VB objects such as collections and our data management layer, which is ADO in our case. Also, don't forget that we must be able to live in a non-MTS world, so this must be conditional. Let's just randomly choose a class on which to demonstrate it. Following is the `Address` class and its `getInfo` operation.

```
Public Function getInfo(ByVal lAddressId As Long, _
    Optional lErrno As Long, Optional sErrDescr _
```

```
As String) As Boolean

    On Error GoTo getInfoErr
    Dim sData() As String
    Dim oICrud As ICrud

    getInfo = False

    If moInstanceInfo.objectContext Is Nothing _
      Then
         Set theAddressDT = New dtsvc.AddressDT
    Else
         Set theAddressDT = _
               moInstanceInfo.objectContext. _
            CreateInstance("dtsvc.AddressDT")
    End If

    'Talk to the DT interface
    Set oICrud = theAddressDT

    If oICrud.getInfo(CStr(lAddressId), sData, _
      lErrno, sErrDescr) Then
       If unPack(sData, giZERODIM, True) Then
          getInfo = True
          Exit Function
       End If
    End If
getInfoErr:
    lErrno = Err.Number
    sErrDescr = Err.description
End Function
```

The crucial code change here is the If..Then..Else block, which still uses New to create AddressDT if there is no valid ObjectContext. If there is a valid ObjectContext, we use the CreateInstance operation. This, too, is not a difficult change but still a rather broad one. Obviously, this change is dependent on Address's having made the prior change of implementing the ObjectControl interface and getting the reference to the ObjectContext.

The same applies to the use case controller UCMaintRltn Controller. At the top of the saveCustomerRltn operation, oCustomer, oLocale, and oAddress are defined. These classes will also need to conditionally check the status of MTS and instantiate accordingly.

The last change has to deal with marking our classes as to the type of transaction that they support. Every class should be marked as "Support Transactions" with the exception of our use case controller classes, which will be marked "Requires New Transaction." This is shown in either Figure 13-38 or 13-39.

MTS—Round 2 Changes

The changes in this round deal with using the SetComplete and SetAbort logic to inform MTS of our desire to either commit all the work begun on its root object or to cancel everything done since the start of the transaction. We will want to make these changes in two places in our code.

The first thing that we must address are our use case controller classes. If the work done within the pathway is successful, then we want to call the MTS SetComplete operation. If it isn't successful, we want to call the SetAbort operation.

The second thing that we need to address deals with the completion of every Public operation in most of our classes. Remember that calling SetComplete not only informs MTS that you are happy with the work done so far, but also performs the more important task of deactivating our object in MTS. If we didn't call SetComplete at the end of every Public operation in all of our classes, MTS would work just fine and our transaction integrity would remain intact, but all the objects used in that transaction wouldn't be deactivated until the root, UCMaintRltnController, called SetComplete. This change is more for getting the most out of MTS performance than to implement transaction support. Let's choose a class at random—why not the AddressDT class.

```
Private Function ICrud_getInfo(ByVal sQualifier As String, _
     ByRef sData() As String, Optional lErrNo As Long, _
        Optional sErrDescr As String) As Boolean

   Dim sQry As String
        ICrud_getInfo = False
```

```
'Build query string
sQry = gsSELECT
sQry = sQry & "maddressID" & gsCOMMASPACE
sQry = sQry & "maddressLine1" & gsCOMMASPACE
sQry = sQry & "maddressLine2" & gsCOMMASPACE
sQry = sQry & "maddressLine3" & gsCOMMASPACE
sQry = sQry & "mcity" & gsCOMMASPACE
sQry = sQry & "mstate" & gsCOMMASPACE
sQry = sQry & "mzip"
sQry = sQry & gsFROM
sQry = sQry & msAddress
sQry = sQry & gsWHERE
sQry = sQry & "maddressId" & gsEQUALS
sQry = sQry & CLng(sQualifier)

'Call the operation on the Access class
If goAccess.DARetrieve(sQry, sData, False, _
   lErrNo, sErrDescr) Then
      ICrud_getInfo = True
   End If
   SetStatus
End Function
```

Notice that there is a function, SetStatus, executed at the very end of the getInfo operation for AddressDT.

```
'If MTS is running, then call setComplete to
'Deactivate object
Private Sub SetStatus()
   If Not moInstanceInfo.objectContext Is Nothing Then
      moInstanceInfo.objectContext.SetComplete
   End If
End Sub
```

The SetStatus function simply checks to see if MTS is running, and if so, it calls SetComplete on the moInstanceInfo.objectContext. This will deactivate our object in the eyes of MTS. This won't affect our transaction status because we can still end up in the root of the transaction, UCMaintRltnController, and call SetAbort.

In what classes do we want to add this logic? This is a bit tricky. You have to think about which objects could be deactivated after every method call without affecting what other objects referencing them may need in the future. The answer is pretty easy if you think about it. The only short-lived stateful objects that we are going to have are just the entity classes. For instance, when we execute the use case pathway, `saveCustomerRltn`, we end up with a collection of objects before we finally persist them with `persistCustomerRltn`. So, all of the classes in `dtsvc` and `dasvc` can add this code to call `SetComplete` at the completion of every `Public` operation.

We should probably also look at how we will deal with the dual-environment support in the use case controller classes. For clarity, let's look only at the code that will change in the `saveCustomerRltn` operation in the `UCMaintRltnController` class. The following code would replace the current call to `DTSetComplete` on the completion of the use case pathway.

```
'if all went well '
If saveCustomerRltn Then
    'If MTS isn't running
    If moInstanceInfo.objectContext Is Nothing Then
        If oContextDT.DTSetComplete(True, lErrno, _
          sErrDescr) Then
           Set oContextDT = Nothing
           Exit Function
        Else
           saveCustomerRltn = False
        End If
    Else 'MTS is running
        moInstanceInfo.objectContext.SetComplete
        Exit Function
    End If
Else 'troubles ahead
    'If MTS isn't running
    If moInstanceInfo.objectContext Is Nothing Then
        If oContextDT.DTSetAbort(True, lErrno, _
          sErrDescr) Then
           Set oContextDT = Nothing
           Exit Function
```

```
    Else
        saveCustomerRltn = False
    End If
 Else 'MTS is running
    moInstanceInfo.objectContext.SetAbort
    Exit Function
 End If
    End If
```

Although this code has a rather lengthy closing process, it is simply checking to determine whether all the work so far has gone as planned. If so, and MTS isn't running, we do what we always have done. However, if MTS is running, we need to call `SetComplete`. The same sequence also occurs if things haven't gone as planned.

This type of closing logic in our root class should be added to all of our use case controller operations that are `Public`.

MTS—Round 3 Changes

The last set of changes are the most intense, although still not difficult. However, they should reap us the largest rewards as far as MTS is concerned because they will increase the number of classes that are stateless.

The changes that we will make fall into the following areas.

- We must modify `DTSetContext` to check whether MTS is running, and if it is, it should simply return. Remember, this operation, within the `ContextDT` class, will issue a `begintrans` on a connection, which we don't want to do in the MTS world but we do in a non-MTS environment.

- At present, in the `class_initialize` of the `Access` class, a new ADO connection is obtained and assigned to `moConn`, a module-level variable. This needs to change because in the MTS world, when pooling is supported someday, the object's initialize event will fire only once, but the connection will have been closed after the first time because we will have called `setComplete`. To remedy this and still provide the dual transaction-mode support, we will modify `DAConnect` to get a new ADO connection and assign it to `moConn` and then connect to the resource. Both the `DARetrieve` and `DAQuery` operations within `Access` need to call new `Private GetStatus` and `SetStatus` operations immediately before work begins in their respective operations and after completion of each operation. The `GetStatus` operation will determine if MTS is running, and if it is, it will message to its `DAConnect` operation and establish a connection. The `SetStatus` operation will be called at the end of the operation's work and if MTS is running, it will close the connection and call the MTS `SetComplete`.

- All the DT classes need to change in several ways, although the changes are minor. First, all calls to the `Access` class are currently going through a global variable, `goAccess`. This is found in the `dtBAS` module and is very necessary in a non-MTS environment because the commit and rollback scope must be performed on one connection. This should be changed to reference `theAccess`, which has always been defined in the DT classes but never used. We will see how we switch this in the next dialog box. Second, a call to a Private `GetStatus` operation needs to be added at the beginning of each operation in the DT classes. This operation will determine whether MTS is running and, if so, will instantiate a new `Access` object with `CreateInstance` and assign it to `theAccess`. If MTS isn't running, it will assign `goAccess` to `theAccess`. So, in a non-MTS environment, `theAccess` will be referring to an `Access` object that `DTSetContext` established at the beginning of the use case pathway; otherwise, it will be a new `Access` object for MTS.

- Lastly, the connection string must be passed in, optionally, from the use case controller all the way to the `Access` object. This will provide the ability for all the DT classes, with the exception of `ContextDT` and the `Access` class, to be completely stateless objects when running in the MTS environment.

Let's review a few of the more interesting coding changes that are required. Starting with the second previous one, here is the code for the `GetStatus` and `SetStatus` found in the `Access` class.

```
Private Function GetStatus(ByVal sConnect As String) _
  As Boolean
    GetStatus = False
```

```
    'MTS is Present
    If Not moInstanceInfo.objectContext Is Nothing _
      Then
        If DAConnect(sConnect) Then
           GetStatus = True
        End If
      Else
        GetStatus = True
      End If
End Function

Private Function SetStatus() As Boolean
    SetStatus = False
    If Not moInstanceInfo.objectContext Is Nothing _
      Then
        If DAClose() Then
           moInstanceInfo.objectContext.SetComplete
           SetStatus = True
        End If
      Else
         SetStatus = True
      End If
End Function
```

Notice that if MTS is not available, then both `GetStatus` and `Set Status` do nothing and return. If MTS is found to be running, then a connection is made, using the `sConnect` string passed in to either the `DARetrieve` or `DAQuery` operation. We also have the `SetComplete` being called if everything went well. This will cause this instance of `Access` to deactivate within MTS.

Let's look last at the ramifications of the third change to the code.

```
Private Sub GetStatus()
    If Not moInstanceInfo.objectContext Is Nothing _
      Then
        Set theAccess = moInstanceInfo.objectContext. _
          CreateInstance("dasvc.Access")
      Else
         Set theAccess = New Access
         Set theAccess = goAccess
```

```
    End If
End Sub
```

To not disturb the transaction thread created by a non-MTS transaction, we need a way to reference an existing connection through an existing `Access` object. Otherwise, in the MTS scenario, we will create a new `Access` object with `CreateInstance`.

Now that we have transaction support in place, we can monitor the transactions within MTS as they run. Figure 13-40 shows the MTS Transaction Statistics dialog box.

Construction—Transaction Management

You may have noticed a previous no-no in client/server development being acted out with the MTS solution. This is the continual opening and closing of connections. In fact, in most traditional client/server applications, the goal is to open one connection for read processing and

FIGURE 13-40   *MTS Transaction Statistics dialog box.*

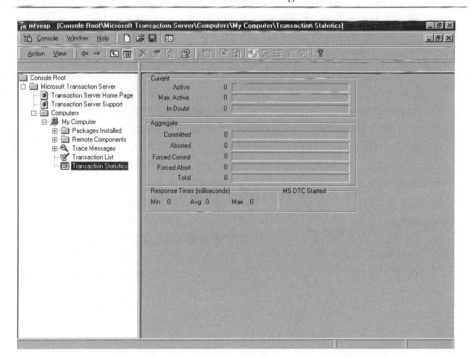

use it until the client closes the application. Establishing a database connection is slow and expensive. We have always been taught to keep them to a minimum but at the same time alive as long as possible.

This isn't the case with MTS, actually, with the design that we have put forth to handle dual-transaction support (MTS and no-MTS). The MTS solution will perform faster, when scaled, due to the concept of enlisted objects and their database connections. Remember that the root object is the controller. As each operation issues a database call in the MTS solution, the object is instantiated, a connection is obtained, the query is performed, and the connection is closed. This all happens within the lifecycle of just one object. Fortunately, MTS doesn't discard the database connection. It is kept in a pool, and this pool is available to other objects as well. As long as the connect string matches, it is usable.

As long as each object that opens a connection also closes it, then there should never have to be more than one physical connection used, regardless of how many different database calls are required. MTS makes database management and the touchy subject of precious and slow database connections much less of an issue than it is in traditional database-oriented client/server applications.

So, that's it for remote distribution scenarios. There are certainly two viable alternatives from which you can choose. DCOM is a little more bare bones but requires absolutely no changes to your code, with the exception of a few recompiles. MTS on the other hand provides a much broader, new solution to transaction management. However, fully taking advantage of MTS requires a serious reconsideration of how your physical application design is laid out. This is especially true if you attempt to make every method in every class completely stateless. The positive side of MTS is that it frees the developer from most transaction management responsibilities as well as provides a very easy mechanism to actually get the objects into MTS and make clients aware of them. Based on the efforts going into MTS at Microsoft and its incorporation into the core of Windows NT, I personally wouldn't be surprised if in the not too distant future, we see the native DCOM solution consciously put on the back shelf by Microsoft.

Checkpoint

Where We Have We Been

1. Distributing an application can provide many immediate benefits, the most important of which is the ability to easily modify the business logic and distribute it only to those servers that will house the logic. Smaller applications, having only a few active users, should perhaps not consider a distributed solution. The key to success is to follow a layered architecture so that at some point in the future the application can be distributed without a rewrite.

2. DCOM is currently one of two popular Microsoft solutions for distributing an application. DCOM requires more manual steps to actually attain a distributed platform architecture, but they are not so difficult that someone on the project team couldn't handle them.

3. MTS is Microsoft's flagship transaction monitor and is very much part of the Windows NT operating system. We saw that MTS can be used to very quickly distribute the application and without any lines of code being changed. However, to take advantage of MTS's transaction management features, we must mark classes for transaction support and properly create them—this is an extremely vital consideration.

Where We Are Going Next

In the next chapter, we:

1. Explore the changes and additions needed to support an Internet-enabled use case pathway.

2. Review the abilities of the Web, and especially Active Server Pages (ASP), to act as a doorway to our Remulak Productions application.

3. Explore the use of JavaScript and VBScript to automate some of the client-side Web editing.

CHAPTER 14

Alternative Interfaces: The Internet

The first release of the Remulak Productions application is constructed. The architecture is in place and the VB front-end forms provide an easy-to-use interface into the application. However, the owner of Remulak Productions, Jeffery Homes, isn't completely satisfied with everything. One of the requirements of the application was to provide order inquiry functionality for the application over the Internet.

In this chapter, we will build a Web front-end to provide inquiry access to orders. Anyone who has an Internet account can visit the Remulak Productions Web site, key in an order number, and get a brief display of who placed the order, the vital customer information and what was ordered, along with a total. That said, to perform this task will require some technology with an emphasis on Web integration. The Remulak Productions team will need to use HTML forms, ASP, JavaScript, and VBScript to get the job done. Fortunately, most of the behind-the-scenes, Remulak-specific work is already in place.

GOALS

⇨ Review the role of the Web in application development today.

⇨ Review the tools necessary to provide a Web front-end to the order inquiry use case pathway for Remulak Productions.

> ⮌ Explore any changes necessary to make this functionality viable given the prior work done for Remulak Productions.

Construction Phase

Synergy Process

This chapter adds Internet access features to the project.

Although the Construction phase considers several different areas as outlined in Figure 14-1, this chapter will focus on:

- The "Component Design/Build" block, in this chapter, will deal with creating the Internet aspects of the application.

The Role of the Web

In an earlier chapter, we reviewed the role of Microsoft's DNA strategy in application design and development. DNA not only espouses a component-building strategy but also categorizes applications by the way that they use the Internet and intranet environments. However, just as we alluded to in the prior chapter on building distributed applications, an Internet presence in the application must be based on a business need, and not on the fact that it is cool.

FIGURE 14-1 *Synergy process model and the Construction phase.*

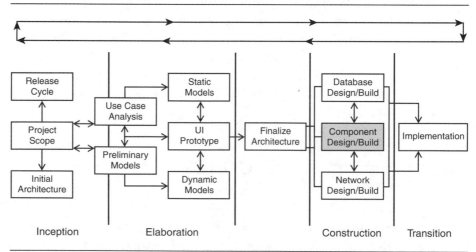

Many applications today assume that the entire set of process components will be run entirely on the Web. This can sometimes lead to undesirable results, particularly in the area of unique customer service needs and performance. However, we would be grossly underestimating the impact of the Web in application design and development if we didn't consider this. Remulak Productions is no exception; it can benefit greatly by initially allowing order inquiry through the Web, followed in future releases by perhaps online order entry. Remember, due to the unique nature of the products that they sell and the handholding that the customer requires, order entry over the Web is still on the drawing board.

Web Technologies

There are many Web technology choices today. These range from plain HTML-based advertisement forms (which I call virtual shingles) to interactive, dynamic Web applications using Dynamic HTML. In the case of Remulak Productions, we will need a technology mix that will allow a customer to inquire about an order and get some level of detail returned. Let's look at that technology mix, outlined in Figure 14-2.

In Remulak Productions's case, a client will invoke a Web page that will be served up by the Web server. The Web server, IIS, will reside on a Windows/NT machine. The Web server will also be required to take in a request, accept the parameters provided from a form, and act on them, hopefully producing the desired results.

Our previous exercises using DCOM and MTS will be leveraged here as well. IIS is just another host process that needs to request the services of our components. There is a change we must make, given our architecture of avoiding stateful objects, to manipulate information returned in a fashion similar to the way that VB forms have done up to this point. Remember, our forms were able to manipulate collections that contained UDTs for each class. That approach worked very well for just VB. But with the Web, we must make some adjustments because of the way that scripting languages deal with native data types such as String, Long, and Currency.

Component Reconfiguration

You may be wondering how we can manipulate the information found in the user interface controllers, such as `UIMaintRltnController` and `UIProcessOrderController`, if they are implemented in the

FIGURE 14-2   *The Remulak Productions Internet technology mix.*

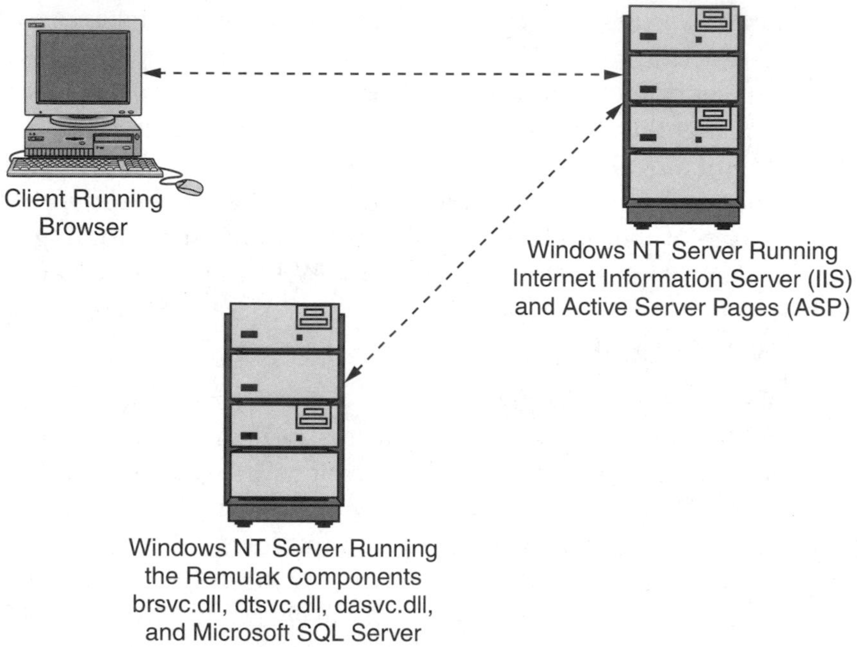

Client Running
Browser

Windows NT Server Running
Internet Information Server (IIS)
and Active Server Pages (ASP)

Windows NT Server Running
the Remulak Components
brsvc.dll, dtsvc.dll, dasvc.dll,
and Microsoft SQL Server

uisvc.exe component. Clearly, for VB forms, these controllers must be located on the client. They provide for a fast access mechanism to our information. However, in the case of the Internet, what is the client? The browser is one form of client, and it plays an active role in the Internet portion of Remulak Productions's solution. However, to our application as a whole, viewed from a component perspective, the client in our case is the ASP.

ASP acts as a surrogate between the browser population and the components of the application. What is needed is a way to use the user interface controllers found in uisvc.exe. However, the uisvc.exe has forms in it as well. A worthy solution to this dilemma is to create a new component, called inet.dll. This component will implement only the classes from the uisvc.exe component.

Before you flinch at the idea that we may be duplicating code and having it physically in two places, don't worry, we aren't. It is quite easy in VB to build a class and then use that class in more than one component. This is a good example of class reuse. We have actually been doing this all along with both the `Dictionary` and `DictionaryMTS` classes. However, they only contained UDTs and ENUMs.

We could also approach this challenge with a different solution, that is, permanently pull out the user interface controllers and leave them in their own ActiveX DLL. This same DLL would be used for both the VB forms and also the ASP. The only negative to this approach stems more from a potential for human error versus a technical one. It may confuse the implementers when they have to install the same DLL on the client, to act as a server to `uisvc.exe`, as well as register it on the Web server, to act as a server to the ASP.

Figure 14-3 is an overview of how ASP will interact with this new component and the other Remulak Productions components.

We need to implement this new component that will allow the ASP to interface with the other components with the same ease that the VB forms do. To do that, create a new project, call it `inet.vbp`, and add to it the following components from `uisvc.vbp`.

FIGURE 14-3 *ASP and the Remulak Productions components.*

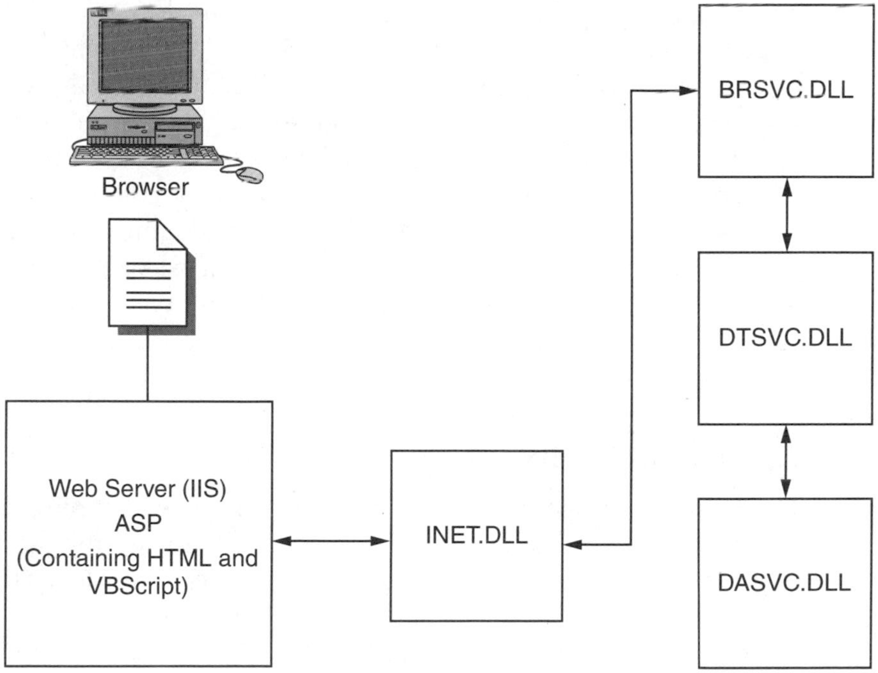

```
Dictionary.cls
UIMaintRltnController.cls
UIProcessOrderController.cls
Utility.cls
```

Mark this project as an ActiveX DLL. We also need to reference the `brsvc.dll` component in the "Project | References" dialog box. Once these two steps are completed, compile the project. Now we are set for the next phase, which is to build an HTML form and ASP to talk to the `inet.dll` component.

Crafting the Web Components

To get the Internet flavor of the order inquiry use case pathway off the ground, we need to construct only two Web components. The first one is an HTML page that can take as input an order number and an ASP that can receive the order number on the Web server and request information about it from our VB components. The HTML page is by far the most straightforward, so let's start with it.

There are many environments available today that make the act of building HTML pages almost a nonevent. I use both Microsoft's Front-Page as well as Microsoft's Visual InterDev. For the Remulak Productions project, we will use Visual InterDev because we have everything we need, in one package, to build and test our Web components. In the production environment, Remulak Productions will deploy its Web components on Microsoft's IIS. Visual InterDev comes with the Personal Web Server (PWS), which uses the same engine as IIS but doesn't support some of the peripheral components such as FTP. However, it is important to point out that to build both of these Web components, you could also get by with something as low technology as Microsoft's Notepad application.

Order Inquiry HTML Form

The HTML form that we will be using won't take too much technology. It must be able to allow for the entry of a text field and then submit that request to the ASP. Figure 14-4 is a picture of what our low-technology order inquiry HTML form will look like.

Let's look at what is behind this form from an HTML perspective and examine its components. Figure 14-5 is a snapshot of the Visual

FIGURE 14-4   *Order Inquiry HTML form running in a browser.*

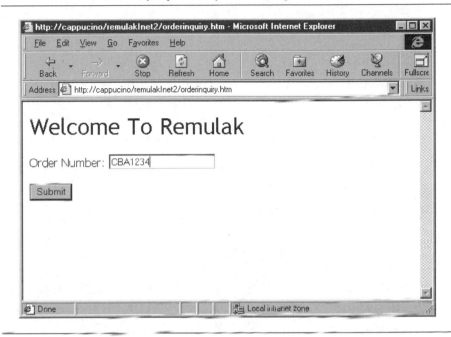

FIGURE 14-5   *Order inquiry HTML source.*

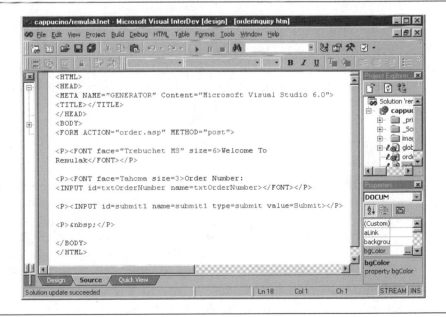

InterDev tool showing the HTML source code behind the form shown in Figure 14-4.

Microsoft's Visual InterDev allows drag-and-drop for placing controls on the HTML page. It is very similar to dropping controls on a VB form. I won't go into the Visual InterDev IDE or how to use it, but rest assured, using it can save you countless numbers of person hours. Our HTML page will be called `orderinquiry.htm`.

There are a few HTML tags that are important to point out. The first one deals with the text entry field for keying in the order number.

```
<P><FONT face=Tahoma size=3>Order Number:
<INPUT id=txtOrderNumber
name=txtOrderNumber></FONT></P>
```

The literal "Order Number:" that appears on the screen is shown in this code as enclosed within paragraph `<P>` tags and in a custom font of "Tahoma." The next line is what gives us the text entry field. The `<INPUT>` tag specifies that this is an input field. The `id=txtOrderNumber` will become important in the ASP because it allows for an easy way to grab values for this input field.

```
<P><INPUT id=submit1 name=submit1 type=submit
value=Submit></P>
```

This `INPUT` tag is a special one because of its type value. The value of `submit` tells the HTML page to transfer control to the `FORM ACTION` tag if there is one. This line is what makes the command button appear on the window. The next line was actually shown earlier in Figure 14-5.

```
<FORM ACTION="order.asp" METHOD="post">
```

This HTML line is our link from the browser to the Web server and the ASP. Notice the `ACTION=` tag and the fact that it is referencing a file called `order.asp`. This file is the name of the ASP that will be invoked by the Web server. The `Method` attribute deals with how information is sent back to the Web server. For our purposes, we will use `POST`.

So, when the "Submit" button is clicked on the HTML form, the form will gather up all the input fields, with the exception of the special `submit` type, and send them as a string back to the Web server that originally sent the initial page. Figure 14-6 is an overview of the interaction that takes place in our Remulak Productions configuration.

FIGURE 14-6   *Remulak Productions's browser and server interaction.*

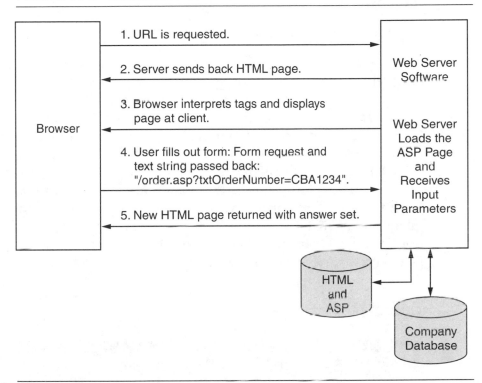

Notice the string that is returned to the Web server. If you have ever been surfing the Web and seen these long strings of characters in the display bar, now you know what they are. Every INPUT field that you specified will be separated by a "&" followed by its ID and the value from the form. There is no magic involved. It is actually a somewhat crude but effective way of getting information from the browser to the Web server. Now let's explore how we can get at these values once they get to the Web server.

Active Server Pages

So far we have laid the foundation for getting information from the browser sent to the Web server. We must now explore how the Web server can hand off control to something that can process the input. ASP pages are components that can be invoked by the Web server. As we saw previously, when the Web server gets this string sent back from the browser:

```
/order.asp?txtOrderNumber=CBA1234
```

IIS or the PWS will invoke the file `order.asp` and load it into memory and pass control to it. This is exactly how the older Common Gateway Interface (CGI) worked as well. Once the ASP page takes over, it can do anything it wants. In our case, we shall construct some output HTML to go back to the browser in tandem with accessing information from our VB components.

ASP pages can use different scripting languages. The two most popular are VBScript and JavaScript (sometimes called JScript; although JScript is the successor to JavaScript, they are still not the same language and neither one is Java). However, you can also use Perl. We will use VBScript in our ASP page. Figure 14-7 is a picture of Visual Inter-Dev with the ASP page, `order.asp`, in the script window.

FIGURE 14-7   *ASP page in Visual InterDev.*

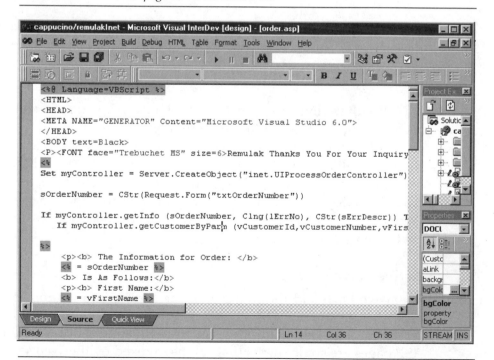

Before we take off on learning how to build the output in the ASP page to send back to the client, let's provide a glimpse of what that final output will look like. This is shown in Figure 14-8.

It takes a little while to get used to what an ASP page is doing. I don't mean from a technology perspective, but how the page is actually a combination of HTML being generated in preparation for a return trip to the client combined with a scripting language.

The scripting language is usually used to access some data repository in response to a browser query. To begin with, just as in VB, to use the scripting language to talk to a component, a reference to that component must be instantiated. In VBScript, as well as JavaScript, this is done with the `CreateObject` method.

FIGURE 14-8   *Browser display us a result of an order inquiry.*

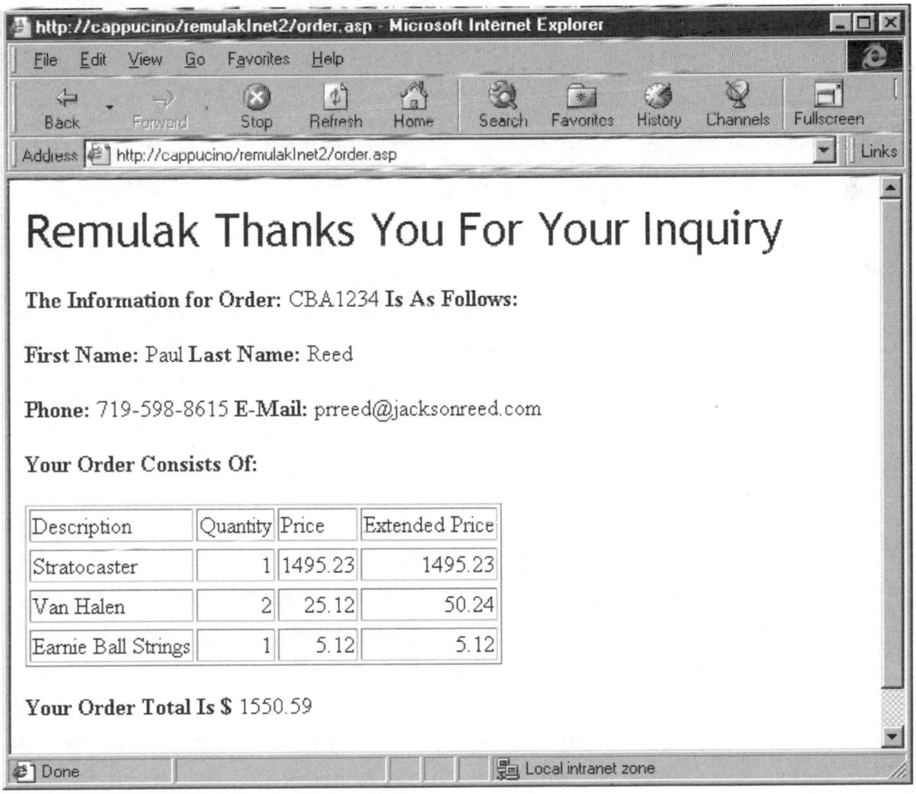

```
Set myController = Server.CreateObject _
   ("inet.UIProcessOrderController")
```

ASP offers five different objects that are available to every server-side ASP page:

- `Application`
- `Request`
- `Response`
- `Server`
- `Session`

We will use the `Request`, `Response`, and `Server` objects in our script. Notice that the `CreateObject` method is actually sent to the ASP `Server` object. This is for reasons similar to those for using the `ObjectContext` in MTS. It allows ASP to track our object as well as opens up access to other ASP features. So, `myController` is our reference to the `UIProcessOrderController` class that resides in the `inet.dll` component.

Remember that I said that the ID of an `INPUT` field defined on a form will become important to us later. Notice the following line of VBScript:

```
sOrderNumber = CStr(Request.Form("txtOrderNumber"))
```

The `Request.Form` takes as a parameter the ID of an attribute that came in from an HTML form. In this case, we are asking for the value of the `txtOrderNumber` field. If you had more than one field coming in, then there would be a request for each variable. We then convert it to a string and assign it to `sOrderNumber`. Notice that there are no `Dim` statements in the script. You can use `Option Explicit` in the script to force variable declaration. But you will have to get used to one thing: *All variables in VBScript are Variants.*

This brings us to a very important point that should be brought out. Any variables passed `ByVal` to an operation defined in an ActiveX component can be cast to any data type using any of the conversion functions (`CStr`, `CLng`, `CCur`). Actually, you would have to do this or you will get a "Type Mismatch" error because your operation signature data types won't match what you are sending it. Unfortunately, all variables passed `ByRef` must be passed as Variants. There are some exceptions if the components that you're talking to are written in C++, but if they are VB components, then they must be Variants.

More bad news is that ASP pages and VBScript don't understand UDTs. This is true whether you are returning them to the page as a result of an operation call or if you are reaching into the component to reference them. For instance, this line of code, which should be familiar, will generate a VBScript compile error:

```
MyController.mcolCustomer(1).firstName
```

Using this line of code is how we retrieved information from the user interface controllers when populating our VB forms, and it worked just fine. So, to alleviate this problem, there were some operations that we reviewed in a previous chapter that we said would come in handy in the future. They are basically operations that will retrieve the collections defined in the user interface controllers and return them as Variants. They all have a similar naming convention, getObjectByParm, where Object is the class you are after. So, getCustomerByParm will return to any scripting language the information kept in the user interface controller collection mcolCustomer.

For instance, the following function defined in the UIProcess OrderController class will return information from the mcolOrder collection found in that class. Much like we saw with the Customer Relationship Maintenance use case, these collections are populated by the getInfo operations that the clients using them request.

```
Public Function getOrderByParm(vOrderId As _
  Variant, vOrderNumber As Variant, _
    vInvoiceId As Variant, vCustomerId As Variant, _
      Optional vErrNo As Variant, Optional _
        vErrDescr As Variant) As Boolean
  On Error GoTo getOrderByParmErr
  getOrderByParm = False

  vOrderId = mcolOrder(1).orderId
  vOrderNumber = mcolOrder(1).orderNumber
  vInvoiceId = mcolOrder(1).invoiceId
  vCustomerId = mcolOrder(1).customerId

  getOrderByParm = True
    Exit Function
```

```
getOrderByParmErr:
    vErrNo = Err.Number
    vErrDescr = Err.description
End Function
```

The next few lines of VBScript code actually perform `getInfo` using the `txtOrderNumber` passed in to the ASP page from the HTML form. After that, a call is made to `getCustomerByParm` to get the customer information out of the `mcolCustomer` collection. These are passed `ByRef` as Variants to appease ASP's need for Variants.

```
If myController.getInfo (sOrderNumber, _
  Clng(lErrNo), CStr(sErrDescr)) Then
If myController.getCustomerByParm _
    (vCustomerId,vCustomerNumber,vFirstName, _
      vLastName,vMiddleInitial,vPrefix,vSuffix, _
        vPhone1,vPhone2,vEmail,vErrNo,vErrDescr) Then
```

You may have noticed the "<%" that begins a block of VBScript code and the "%>" that ends it. These are interspersed throughout our ASP page because wherever you see HTML tags such as <BODY>, these are being put into the HTML output buffer that will soon be sent back to the client. We need to distinguish code that needs to run on the server from HTML tags that need to get sent back to the client. What we will do next is dynamically build HTML tags as a result of communicating with our VB components.

The next block of ASP code builds HTML output for the top portion of what you saw displayed in Figure 14-8.

```
<p><b> The Information for Order: </b>
        <% = sOrderNumber %>
        <b> Is As Follows:</b>
        <p><b> First Name:</b>
        <% = vFirstName %>
        <b>Last Name:</b>
        <% = vLastName %>
        </p>
  <p><b> Phone:</b>
        <% = vPhone1 %>
```

```
<b>E-Mail:</b>
<% = vemail %>
```

To just take a sample, notice the = vFirstName parameter. This is saying to write the value of this variable after the preceding HTML code <p><b> First Name:</b>.

The next block of code sets up the table that you see holding the order information shown in Figure 14-8.

```
<table BORDER="1">
    <tr>
    <td>Description</td>
    <td>Quantity</td>
    <td>Price</td>
    <td>Extended Price</td>
    </tr>
```

This sets up the headings in the first row of the table.

The next piece of code actually loops through and retrieves from the UIProcessOrderController class both the OrderLine and Product collection information.

```
<%
For vIndex = 1 to myController.mcolOrderLine.Count
If myController.getOrderLineByParm (vIndex,vOrder _
  LineId,vOrderId, _
      vProductId,vQuantity,vDiscount,vUnitPrice, _
        vErrNo,vErrDescr) Then
  If myController.getProductByParm (vIndex, _
    vProductId,vDescription,vPrice, _
          vDiscount,vQuantityOnHand,vEoq, _
          vProductType,vErrNo,vErrDescr) Then
    Response.Write "<TR>"
    %>
    <tr>
     <%
    Response.Write "<TD> " & vDescription &
    "</TD>"
    Response.Write "<TD align=right> " &
    vQuantity & "</TD>"
```

```
      Response.Write "<TD align=right> " &
      vUnitPrice & "</TD>"
      Response.Write "<TD align=right> " &
      (vQuantity *  vUnitPrice)
      & "</TD>"
       Response.Write "</TR>"
       vTotal = (vQuantity * vUnitPrice) + vTotal
    End If
  End If
Next
Set myController = Nothing
%>
```

The key statements here are the `Response.Write` operation calls. These stick whatever we tell them into the output buffer for the return trip to the client. Notice that when we are done looping through the collection, we set the `myController` object to `Nothing`.

The remaining piece of the ASP puzzle is to close our table definition and then to display a total message.

```
</tr>
</table>
</p>
<p><b> Your Order Total Is $ </b>
        <% = vTotal %>
<%End If
End If
%>
<P> </P>
</BODY>
</HTML>
```

Notice that the total was accumulated as we looped through the `OrderLine` items.

The result of this ASP page will be sent to the output buffer from the Web server back to the requesting client. What we will see is what is shown in Figure 14-8. The beauty of using ASP pages is that they leverage the Microsoft tool set without putting demands on the browser technology. This means that the Web server infrastructure can be very

Microsoft, while the browser could be Netscape or Internet Explorer running on any operating system (for example, UNIX or Macintosh).

A More Dynamic Client with JavaScript

An area of our Web design that could use some enhancement is the HTML form that requests an order. As it is presently coded, if no one enters an order number and just clicks "Submit," then a trip will still be made to the Web server. It's better if you catch this at the client before it ever gets to the Web server in the first place without an order number. This is where client-side scripting comes in very handy.

As stated in the section that discussed ASP, both VBScript and JavaScript are likely candidates. Although it would be nice to leverage our VBScript knowledge and code this client-side edit in that language, we would be reducing the number of potential users of our order inquiry function. This is because VBScript is not supported by the Netscape browser (note that a special plug-in can be installed to remedy this problem). A more resilient solution is to use JavaScript, as it is the most common client-side scripting language today and is supported by the greatest number of browsers (both Microsoft and Netscape browsers support it and combined they have over 90% of the browser market).

The changes to the HTML form are quite small. First, we need to tell the form to invoke some edit routine once the user clicks the "Submit" button on the form. We do this by adding some information to the <FORM> tag in our HTML. We want to invoke an edit routine right before the form is submitted, and if the order number hasn't been provided, we will tell the user about it and give the user another try. The following modified <FORM> tag needs to replace our existing one:

```
<FORM NAME="orderInquiry" ACTION="order.asp"
METHOD="post"
onSubmit="return editSubmit()">
```

We have added a NAME attribute to the <FORM> tag so that we can address one of its contained elements. We have also added an onSubmit attribute and given it the name of the function that we want to invoke, editSubmit(). Notice, by our saying return editSubmit(), the value returned from the function will either let the form continue with the submission or block it.

Now we need to add some JavaScript code that will implement the editSubmit() function. You can add this block of code after the <BODY> tag in the HTML (you can put it anywhere but functions are usually defined at the top of the HTML as a standard).

```
<SCRIPT LANGUAGE=javascript>
<!—
function editSubmit(){
   if (document.orderInquiry.txtOrderNumber.value
     == "") {
         window.alert("Enter a Valid Order
         Number")
         return false
      }
      else {
         return true
      }
}
//—>
</SCRIPT>
```

Just as we saw with the ASP, when the browser encounters the <SCRIPT LANGUAGE=javascript> tag it knows to load the JavaScript interpreter located within the browser. The difference again between this script tag and the one used for the ASP is that in this tag, we used JavaScript.

The previous code will check to see if there is anything in the txtOrderNumber text field on the form, and if not, it will use the JavaScript Alert method to pop up a window and ask the user to enter an order number. Figure 14-9 is what will be shown to users if they don't use the form correctly.

Other Possibilities

The Internet portion of the Remulak Productions application, once you get used to HTML and ASP, is surprisingly simple. There are many other opportunities available to the Remulak Productions team to stretch their hard work into other areas.

FIGURE 14-9   *JavaScript order number edit in the HTML form.*

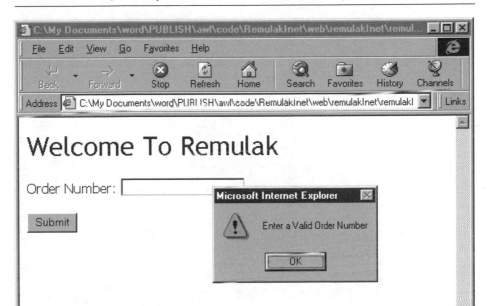

One is to use Microsoft Word to generate customized thank you letters. Using VBA, an order number could be requested and the identical operations called to populate the HTML form could be called, but instead they would populate bookmarks identified in a Word template.

Another is to use Excel to analyze sales order trends. Again, using the same VBA technology, you can have the objects interfaced and the cells populated. Figure 14-10 is a snapshot of the VBA environment with some code set up to access the `brsvc.dll` component.

The beauty of building an object with COM as the plumbing is that almost anything can interface to it. Actually, we could even publish these COM components and then other language environments could talk to them, such as Visual C++ or even competing products to Microsoft's, such as PowerBuilder.

FIGURE 14-10 *Excel and a Remulak Productions interface.*

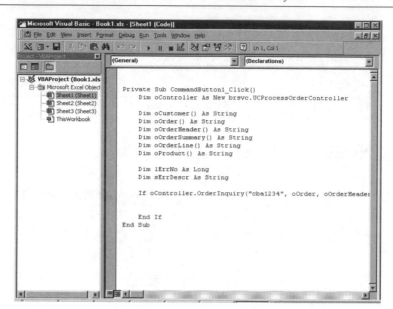

Checkpoint

Where We Have Been

1. Interfacing to the Internet provides many opportunities for an organization to reach customers that they never dreamed of reaching. In addition, it can maintain the existing customer base by providing better customer service. However, every perceived need for the Internet must be accompanied by a business justification for addressing it.

2. ASP is a Microsoft technology that provides for a very elegant mechanism to interact with HTML form-driven technology. The browser base can be from any vendor and run on any operating system.

3. VBScript is a popular scripting language for building ASP pages. VBScript is used to instantiate objects, built in VB, and then provides the procedural framework to dynamically build pages of responses to the inquiry.

4. ASP can't deal with `ByRef` variables unless they are typed as Variants. However, parameters passed `ByVal` can be of any type.

Estimating Projects Using Use Cases

Countless times I have heard presenters and consultants alike dodge the issue of estimating person-hours and completion dates for project deliverables. Unfortunately, estimating project deliverable timelines isn't an easy proposition. Most of us, myself included, typically use our own personal "rule of thumb" approaches to come up with estimates. The more software development one does, the more accurate the latter approach works. Regardless of the level of skill, a better approach is necessary to account for personal biases as well as those projects that don't have a staff with a wealth of experience.

Rational Software acquired Ivar Jacobson's Objectory AB in 1995. Along with that purchase came the excellent research conducted by Gustav Karner, then of Objectory AB, in estimating person-hours for software projects based on use cases. Although this work was based on earlier work by Albrecht that involved using function point analysis, it brought unique insight by using artifacts that were directly derived from the use case.

The process involves four separate inputs based on the following:

- Weighting of actors
- Weighting of use cases
- Weighting of technical factors
- Weighting of project participants

Actors

Karner's work initially begins by with the weighting of actors. The rating is based on whether or not the actor is ranked as being *simple, average,* or *complex.*

Simple actors are those actors that fall into the category introduced in this text as "external systems." In the case of Remulak Productions, a good example would be the interface to either the accounting system or the credit card system. These types of actors have a well-defined interface and are very predictable as to their reactions to the output that the system in question provides or the input that it receives from the interface.

Average actors are those actors that fall into the category introduced in this text as "hardware devices," as well as those actors labeled as "timers." In the case of Remulak Productions, a good example would be the timer necessary to kick off given reports as well as the timer necessary to instigate the interface to the accounting system. Although these actors are predictable, they require more effort to control them and are usually more prone to errors.

Complex actors are those actors that fall into the category introduced in this text as "humans." In the case of Remulak Productions, a good example would be the majority of actors, for example, the Customer Service Clerk, the Supplier, and the Billing Clerk. These types of actors are the most difficult to control and are totally unpredictable. Although a GUI or even a text-based interface can enforce edits and controls, there is more complexity involved when working with an unknown actor that maintains its own free will to do as it pleases.

For Remulak Productions, we rate the actors involved as follows:

Customer—Complex

Order Clerk—Complex

Customer Service Clerk—Complex

Manager— Complex

Time—Average

Billing Clerk—Complex

Accounting System—Simple

Credit Card System—Simple

Shipping Clerk—Complex

Packaging Clerk—Complex

Supplier—Complex

Table A-1 lists the weighting factors that are input to the estimating process.

TABLE A-1   *Weighting Factors for Actors*

Type of Actor	Description	Factor
Simple	External systems	1
Average	Hardware or timers	2
Complex	Humans	3

These factors lead us to deduce the following about Remulak Productions:

2 Simple * 1 = 2

1 Average * 2 = 2

8 Complex * 3 = 24

This gives Remulak Productions an actor weight of 28 (2 + 2 + 24).

Use Cases

It is now time to consider the use cases. The primary aspect of the use cases that we judge are their pathways. The number of pathways determines the weighting factor. The pathways consist of both the happy path as well as the alternative pathways through the use case. If there are a large number of primary exception pathways, then these should also be included. If the exceptions are incidental or simple error situations, then don't consider them. Remember the story that I gave in the chapter on use cases: For some applications, errors are more important than the happy path.

One area where I modify the approach used by Karner is the inclusion of *includes*, *extends*, and *generalize* extensions on the use case diagram. Karner elects not to include these; however, this is a concern, as many of these use cases are very robust and are much more than an alternative path (as is outlined by extends, for instance). In the text of this book, I refer to many of the includes and extends use cases as shadow use cases. So, include all use cases, regardless of their types.

Another consideration to be aware of is that the granularity of "what is a use case" can be a bit subjective. Some analysts tend to materialize use cases that are more coarse-grained, while others make them more fine-grained. This leveling issue can also influence the weighting that you end up with.

Table A-2 is used along with the weighting factor to aid in the estimating process.

TABLE A-2   *Weighting Factors for Use Cases*

Type of Use Case	Description	Factor
Simple	3 or fewer pathways	5
Average	4 to 7 pathways	10
Complex	More than 7 pathways	15

For Remulak Productions, we rate the use cases involved as follows:

Maintain Orders—12 pathways—Complex

Process Orders—7 pathways—Average

Maintain Relationships—4 pathways—Average

Decision Support—11 pathways—Complex

Invoicing—3 pathways—Simple

Shipping—6 pathways—Average

Maintain Inventory—6 pathways—Average

Security—5 pathways—Average

Application Infrastructure—5 pathways—Average

These factors lead us to deduce the following about Remulak Productions:

1 Simple * 5 = 5

6 Average * 10 = 60

2 Complex * 15 = 30

This gives Remulak Productions a use case weight of 85 (5 + 60 + 30).

Now we need to add the actor total to the use case total to get what is called the unadjusted use case points (UUCP). Later, this number will be further adjusted based on both the technical and project team characteristics.

These factors lead us to the following UUCP for Remulak Productions:

UUCP = 28 (actor weight) + 95 (use case weight)

UUCP = 123

Technical Factors

The next step in our estimating process is to consider the technical factors of the project. To do this, we use the Table A-3 and assign a rating between 0 and 5 for each topic. Zero means that the factor is irrelevant, and 5 means that it is essential. After rating each topic, we then multiply the weight by the rating for an extended weight. Table A-3 is the table with the weights and ratings for Remulak Productions.

TABLE A-3   *Weighting Factors for Technical Complexity*

Technical Factor	Weight	Rating 0-5	Extended Weight	Reason
Distributed system	2	3	6	System must be able to scale.
Response or throughput performance objectives	1	2	2	Although response times aren't "hard," they must be tolerable.
End-user efficiency (online)	1	3	3	System must be easy to comprehend.
Complex internal processing	1	1	1	There is very little complex processing.
Reusable code	1	3	3	The code must be extensible to add future functionality.
Easy installation	.5	2	1	Installation will be minimal to two different sites.

(continued)

TABLE A-3 *(continued)*

Technical Factor	Weight	Rating 0-5	Extended Weight	Reason
Easy to use	.5	4	2	System must be easy to use.
Portable	2	0	0	There are no portability requirements.
Easy to change	1	3	3	The system must be changeable as the needs of Remulak Productions evolve.
Concurrent	1	1	1	At present, concurrency issues are low.
Special security features	1	2	2	There will be security requirements in future releases, but they are basic.
Direct access for third parties	1	2	2	There are Internet access requirements for order inquiry.
Special user training required	1	0	0	There are no special training requirements.
T Factor			26	

Now that we have the T Factor, we plug that into the formula to obtain the Technical Complexity Factor (TCF), which is calculated as $(0.6 + (0.01 * \text{T Factor}))$.

TCF = $(0.6 + (0.01 * 26))$

TCF = 0.86

Project Participants

The last factor to consider deals with the experience levels of the project team members. This is called the environmental factor (EF). Take each factor in Table A-4 and assign it a rating between 0 through 5. Consider the following context.:

- For the first four factors, 0 means no experience in the subject, 3 means average, and 5 means expert.

- For the fifth factor, 0 means no motivation for the project, 3 means average, and 5 means high motivation.
- For the sixth factor, 0 means extremely unstable requirements, 3 means average, and 5 means unchanging requirements.
- For the seventh factor, 0 means no part-time technical staff, 3 means average, and 5 means all part time technical staff.
- For the eighth factor, 0 means easy-to-use programming language, 3 means average, and 5 means a very difficult programming language.

TABLE A-4 *Weighting Factors for Project Participants*

Environmental Factor	Weight	Rating 0-5	Extended Weight	Reason
Using a formal process	1.5	3	4.5	Using the Synergy process with average experience.
Application experience	.5	5	2.5	Users are very knowledgeable of Remulak Productions' needs.
Object-oriented experience	1	0	0	Development team and users have virtually no knowledge of object-oriented concepts.
Lead analyst capability	.5	5	2.5	Very competent.
Motivation	1	5	5	High motivation to get the project up and running.
Stable requirements	2	5	10	Requirements are unchanging.
Part-time workers	-1	0	0	No part-time staff.
Difficult programming language	-1	3	-3	VB is very easy to learn and apply, but the staff isn't that familiar with it.
E Factor			21.5	

Now that we have the E Factor, we plug that into the formula to obtain the Environmental Factor (EF), which is calculated as (1.4 + (-0.03 * E Factor)).

EF = (1.4 + (-0.03 * 21.5))

EF = 0.755

Use Case Points

Now that we have our three components, UUCP, TCF, and EF, we are ready to proceed with getting to a bottom-line number called use case points (UCP). UCP is calculated as UUCP * TCF * EF. So, the UCP for Remulak Productions is as follows:

UCP = 123 * .86 * .755

UCP = 79.86

The Project Estimate

Karner, in his research, applies 20 person-hours for each UCP. Using this, we would end up with a (20 * 79.86) = **1597.20** person-hours for the Remulak Productions project. Using a 32 hour-per-week schedule, this would be approximately 50 person-weeks with one person doing the work.

Since there are five people working on this project, we should allow about 10 weeks to finish the job. However, after considering time for unproductive meetings, communication issues, and show-and-tell sessions (you know, the ones that are never scheduled but you find yourself doing a lot of), we will add 4 additional weeks to the schedule. This makes the project 14 weeks in duration.

Although the approach by Karner isn't cast in stone, and it doesn't profess to provide the magical number, it is an excellent approximation. Others have suggested areas for improvement. Geri Schneider, in her excellent book *Applying Use Cases* (Addison-Wesley, 1998), suggests that care should be given to the Environmental Factor (EF). She suggests counting the number of 1-6 factors that are rated (not extended weight) below 3 and how many 7 and 8 factors are above 3. If the total is 2 or fewer, use 20 person-hours per UCP. If the total is 3 or 4, use 28 person-hours per UCP. She goes on to indicate that if the total is 5 or more, then some attention is needed because the risk for failure is very high. Using her criteria, we are still in good shape with 20 person-hours per UCP.

Use Karner's heuristics; they are the best that I have seen to-date for estimating projects using the artifacts from the UML (primarily the use case). Make your own tweaks where necessary, but it certainly attempts to rid us of those sometimes dangerous rules-of-thumb estimates that we are so quick to provide but quite often overrun and regret.

APPENDIX B *Adding Additional Functionality to Rational Rose Data Definition Language Capability*

In the chapter that deals with the database design, there was an additional shortcoming in Rational Rose that we wanted to get around by using the Rational Rose Extensibility Interface (REI). Remember from that chapter that the REI allows for Rational Rose to be extended from a functionality perspective. Not only can the scripts be changed that generate the DDL (along with many other areas within Rational Rose), but we can add entirely new sets of functionality. The user interface can also be enhanced as well to support this new functionality.

Enhancements—Persistent and Transient Attributes

One area of concern pointed out in the database chapter was the inability to mark attributes within the class diagram as either persistent or transient. Rose allows us to mark an entire class as persistent or transient, and the `ddlgen.ebs` script correctly identifies those and excludes them from the generation process. However, there are several attributes that we utilize that are used only during the runtime execution of our application. Most of these deal with the determination of an object's state. The attributes used are `isDirty`, `isNew`, and `isDeleted`. These attributes are examined at runtime to determine what to do with a given object once we are done with it. These attributes also enforce our framework approach of software architecture by providing a common set of properties, across many of our classes, to make interacting with them consistent as well as to extend their abilities should the need arise.

Some may think that this is a bit of overkill. Why not just create the DDL and then hand edit the resulting script, deleting those attributes that shouldn't be persisted? The reason is that the more that we have to "touch-up" our deliverables, the more error-prone they become (because we make a mistake or just plain forget to do something). Besides, Rational provides us a great start; all we have to do is tweak it a bit. So, what we need is the ability to do the following.

1. Add a model property, called "Persistent," to the "DDL" tab of an attribute.

2. Default the value of this new property to "True." This default value is chosen because most attributes of a class are persistent; the ones we are identifying are the minority.

3. Allow only a Boolean choice of "True" or "False" for the new attribute property.

4. Modify the DDL generation script, `ddlgen.ebs`, to recognize the new property and act accordingly.

We shall see that Rational Rose makes this task incredibly easy. With a little effort on our part and some help from REI, our solution is a few steps away.

Modifying Rational Rose—Persistent Attribute Setup

The first thing that we need to do is to define the new property for the attribute. The scripting command to do this is called `AddDefault Property`, and it takes several parameters as input. A template for this command takes the following form.

```
IsAdded = theProperties.AddDefaultProperty _
   (theClassName, theToolName,
theSetName, thePropName, thePropType, theValue)
```

In our case, we need to substitute the template with our own values. To start this process of modifying our Rational Rose model, do the following.

1. Open the Rational Rose Model for Remulak Productions.

2. Select "Tools" from the menu.

3. Select "New Script" from the Tools menu.

You are now in edit mode on a new script file that looks like Figure B-1.

We now need to add the code to add the property, using the template syntax outlined previously. Figure B-2 is the script code that we need to enter into the window.

Let's discuss what this script is going to do for us, as well as some of the other scripting commands.

1. A working variable called `defProps` is defined and is of type `DefaultModelProperties`. This gives us a variable to hold our `DefaultModelProperties` object.

2. A working variable called `worked` is defined and is of type Boolean. This will allow us to test our return from the property addition.

3. Next we open an instance of the `Viewport` object. This will allow us to view the results of our work as the commands execute.

FIGURE B-1   *New Rose script window.*

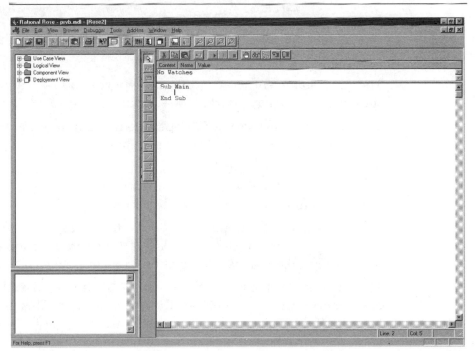

FIGURE B-2   *New Rose script window with new definitions.*

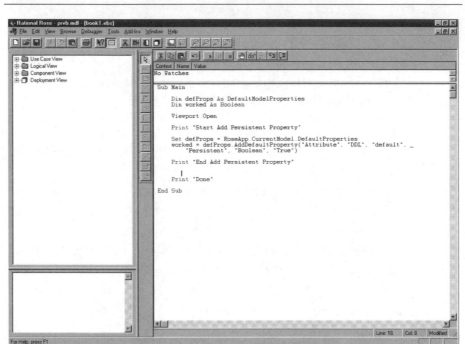

4. The print statement writes to the viewport window. This line is showing that we have started the scripting process.

5. The next line assigns to `defProps`, the model that we are working with, which happens to be the one that is opened.

6. Now the work actually happens. The `AddDefaultProperty` method is called on the model pointed to by `defProps`. The following essential values are passed into the method.

7. The "classname" being passed in is set to `attribute`. Rational Rose supports many different classes that can be augmented, such as class, operations, and relations, to name a few.

8. The "tool name" being passed is set to `DDL`. In our case, the tool name maps to the tab name for the attribute class. This is where Rose is really powerful. If you specify a tool name that doesn't exist, there will be a new tab added for you for that specific class.

   For instance, a client of mine once wanted to generate DDL for both Informix and DB2, which, at the time, had a restriction of 18 bytes for table, view, and column names. Rather than make the attribute and class names conform to the DDL restrictions, we first added a new property called DDL Name to the DDL tool for attributes (the DDL tool previously existed). Next, we added two properties, DDL Name and View Name, to a new tool, called DDL, and associated it to a class (there was no previous DDL tool tab for classes).

9. Rational Rose allows for multiple "property sets" for each class (note that class here means the class of the Rational Rose object, not a class in the object sense). Here we specify default to have it added to the default set.

10. The "property name" is being set to "Persistent." This is what will show up in the DDL tool for attributes.

11. The "property type" is being set to "Boolean." The answer can be either True or False.

12. The "default value" is being set to True. Remember from our previous discussion that the majority of attributes will be persisted, so to cut down on the amount of typing, we set all attributes to default to True.

13. The last two lines simply print out additional information messages to the viewport.

Modifying Rational Rose—Running the Definition Script

Now let's run the script to add the property to the attribute class. To do this, simply execute the script by doing the following.

1. Select "Debugger" from the menu.

2. Select "Go" from the Debugger menu.

Figure B-3 is what you should see when the script completes its execution.

If you have made it this far, then we are in good shape. Let's go see if in fact there is now a property associated with the attribute's DDL tool called "Persistent." To find this property, do the following.

1. Double-click the Customer Class (any class will do).

FIGURE B-3   *BasicScript viewport.*

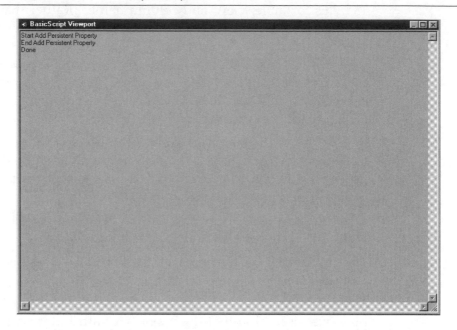

2. Select the "Attributes" tab from the Class specification for Customer.

3. Double-click the "isDirty" attribute displayed in the list of attributes (any attribute would do).

4. Select the "DDL" tab from the Attribute specification for the "isDirty" attribute.

5. Select the value field for the new "Persistent" property.

Notice that the dialog box will let you change the default value, which is True, to False. In this case, we want this attribute's "Persistence" property to be set to False. Figure B-4 shows what the dialog box should look like.

Modifying Rational Rose—Changing the Script to Recognize the Attribute

So far we have succeeded in just planting the seed of customization. This new property, "Persistent," won't do us a bit of good if we don't

FIGURE B-4   *Modified attribute specification dialog box.*

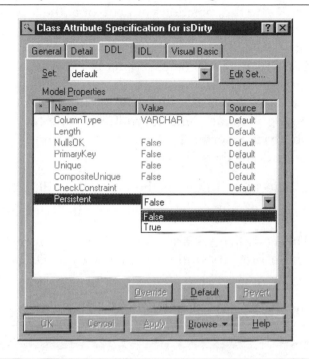

modify the script, `ddlgen.ebs`, that builds the DDL to look for this new model property and act accordingly.

Using Rational Rose, we can edit the script that generates the DDL. It is located in the "Scripts" subdirectory. To perform this task, do the following.

1. Open the Rational Rose Model for Remulak Productions.

2. Select the Customer Class.

3. Select "Tools" from the menu.

4. Select "Open Script" from the Tools menu.

5. From the File Open Dialog, double-click the "scripts" subdirectory.

6. Select the file "DDLGEN.EBS."

You are now in edit mode on the script that generates DDL. If you applied any of the changes that were outlined in the chapter on database design and construction, then this change will be in addition to those. From this point, we need to make a change to the generation script. To do this, position your cursor at the top of the script where the variable declarations are located, as shown in Figure B-5, and then add the line of code that is highlighted.

This attribute will be used later to extract from the model the value during execution of the script. The next challenge is to use this constant in our code. As was found in the database chapter, the code that needs changing is in the same subroutine as the code that we fixed for the attribute length error. To make the change, find the subroutine that is at issue by doing the following.

1. Select Edit | Find on the subroutine "PUTATTR."

2. Add the code that is highlighted in Figure B-6.

This code that we are adding simply retrieves the new "Persistent" attribute property and checks to see if it is False. If it is, then we

FIGURE B-5 *Adding the "Persistent" attribute as a declaration.*

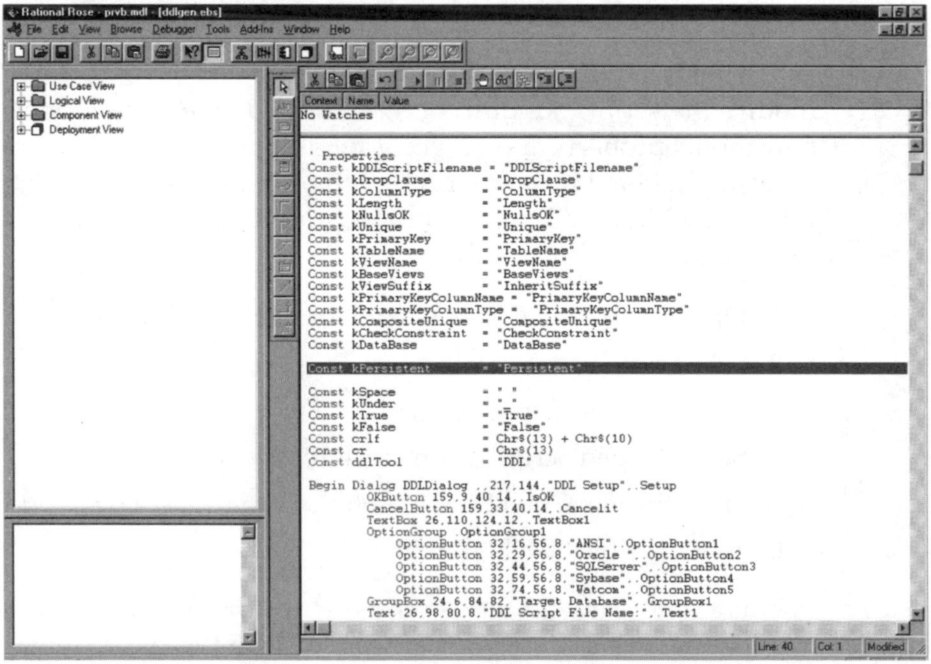

FIGURE B-6   *Script modification for the "Persistent" attribute.*

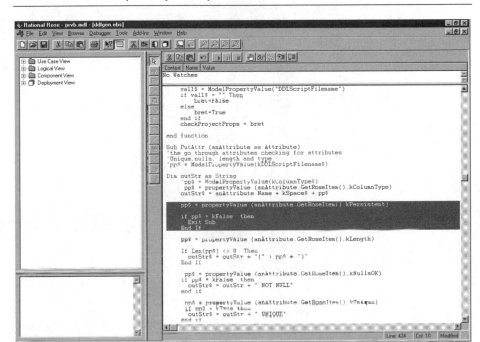

bypass this attribute and get the next one from the class. Notice that the four lines of script after this are the changes made during the database chapter.

There is one more place within the script that requires some attention. The same essential check needs to happen when a view is being created. To find the place to add the addition scripting, do the following.

1. Select Edit | Find on the subroutine "getviewinfo."

2. Add the code that is highlighted in Figure B-7.

Now all the changes have been made. You can test the changes by running the script in place, and you shouldn't see any column definitions for attributes that are marked as "Persistent."

To permanently make this script part of the runtime environment, it needs to be compiled into an "ebx" file. To compile the DDLGEN.EBS into an "ebx," do the following.

FIGURE B-7   *Script modification for the "Persistent" attribute.*

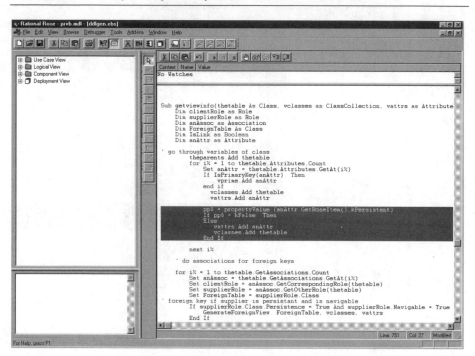

1. Select "Debugger" from the menu.

2. Select "Compile" from the Debugger menu.

3. Replace the "DDLGEN.EBX" file that is found in the Rational root directory.

Other Areas of Change

This is really just the beginning of the changes that can be made to the DDL generation process. Other changes that I have made include the following.

1. Add an attribute model property to the DDL tab called "Alternate Key." This would create a "Create Index" DDL statement for this attribute/column name. Although Rose will do the same thing by adding a qualifier between two classes, this solution is much cleaner and doesn't clutter the class diagram.

2. Add an attribute model property to the DDL table called "Cascade Foreign." This was necessary for a client who didn't want the primary key to cascade as a foreign key to a related table.

3. Add additional database support. This would allow for the selection of additional DBMSs to generate DDL from the initial prompt screen.

Don't be bashful in enhancing your modeling tool. My compliments to Rational Software for selling not only a great tool but also one that is easily extensible should the project require unique functionality.

An Object-Oriented Primer

This appendix deals with the concept of object-oriented in the large. Object-oriented thought and concepts have been around since the mid-1970s. Initially popular only in the academic setting, it wasn't until the early emergence of formal language constructs, which offered object abilities, that the mass appeal for the approach really took off.

What Does Object-Oriented Mean?

I once taught a five-day UML course at a large organization and began the session with an enthusiastic crowd, all of whom were supposed to have had some basic object knowledge. The class was going well and during my first break, a lady came up to me and very politely asked, "So, what is this object-oriented thing anyway?" Feeling a bit like someone who was well into the theory of flight dynamics, only to have someone ask me, "What is flight," I began to launch into my standard spiel about encapsulation, inheritance, and polymorphism. I then quickly realized that this answer was only going to confuse her even more. What follows is a synopsis of the dialog that ensued, and I have used it ever since as a means to explain object-oriented in very easy and simple terms.

Object-Oriented—Right in Your Own Backyard

Object-oriented is all about categorizing and abstracting things. It also has to do with organization and placing rigor into how we categorize things. Abstract thinking is initially very difficult. Just the name itself, abstract, is a fuzzy, produce-nothing-sounding term. However, in our everyday lives, we are all pretty good at categorizing and abstracting.

Take anyone's kitchen. I wager I could go into your kitchen and quickly understand how you have categorized things in your domain. I would also bet that behind every cupboard door, there are artifacts that are seemingly related. Take the dish cabinet. Opening this door would reveal plates and saucers on the bottom shelf, maybe glasses on the second shelf and on the less-used upper shelf, the larger platters. These eating things all represent categories because you consciously organized them based on some conception that you have about them. The same story replays itself for the refrigerator, spice cabinet, and so on.

These common objects that we categorize in our everyday world are called classes in the object-oriented context. A class is a categorization, something of concrete importance to the problem domain. A class maintains two important elements: structure and behavior. Structure represents the attributes that describe the class. Behavior represents the services that the class supports.

In the case of our kitchen, a blue plate can be categorized into a class. The class would be plate. Each plate has structure, such as color, size, and texture. Each plate also has behavior, such as stack, sort, remove, and break. An object, on the other hand, is a specific instance or occurrence of a class. So, the third blue plate would be considered an object of class plate.

This is how we approach the object-oriented project domain. We initially must categorize and abstract the elements in the system to provide some level of order. These abstractions many times are the part of the project that yield the largest fruit, although sometimes they are the hardest to grasp.

Some practitioners use the notion of inheritance, encapsulation, and polymorphism as their definitions of what object-oriented represents. Although this line of thought is not fundamentally incorrect, they have missed the larger view of object-oriented and rushed to embrace what are merely by-products of what good abstraction and categorization can yield. Let's examine some of those by-products.

By-Products of Object-Oriented

Some powerful by-products of object-oriented are based on the premise of three key concepts:

- Inheritance
- Encapsulation
- Polymorphism

Inheritance

Inheritance allows you to implement the functionality that is unique to your class and borrow the rest of the structure and behavior from higher-level classes. For instance, all boats will have attributes such as weight, draught, and beam. However, only sailboats will have attributes such as jib, mainsail, and spinnaker. Inheritance allows developers to leverage the power of the class hierarchy by building new objects without having to redevelop them from scratch (see Figure C-1).

A similar example that we are all familiar with is the relationship that we might have with a bank. Banks offer products to all of their customers. However, these products vary in both the structure and behavior that define them. Some are deposit products, while some are loan products. Each product is unique, but they also all share some commonality, such as account numbers, current balance, and customer relationship information. The goal is to package the products in such a way as to leverage their common aspects, while keeping their individuality intact. This notion of inheritance would also allow the bank in the future, as the business evolves, to offer new types of products, while at the same time using much of the common structure and behavior that has already been defined at the overall product level.

FIGURE C-1   *Boat objects.*

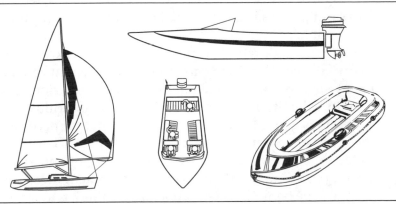

Encapsulation

This concept is sometimes called "information hiding." It maintains that each object contains all the necessary implementation details about how it functions and hides all internal details about the way it carries out services or manages its internal structure. This notion of encapsulation supports the premise that an object should do one thing and one thing well. If I send the "Accelerate" message to a powerboat by increasing the throttle, the boat knows what to do. The driver doesn't know or care how it works. The biggest benefit from encapsulation is that the interface of the class can stay the same, while its implementation can vary over time.

Let's revisit our banking example. The operation that accumulates the dollar value of all accounts that a person may have must hide from the outside world how it carries out its task. The reason is that what makes up the account relationships, over time, may change. We always want the outside world to be able to continue to ask the customer what his or her balance is without worrying about how the account calculates it. That is the responsibility of the account.

Polymorphism

This big word means "many forms." In the object-oriented world, it is important to be able to send the same message to different objects and have them respond accordingly. Again, the concept of polymorphism is assured through encapsulation and is also the primary benefit of inheritance.

You can send the "Turn" message to each boat-like object, and each will behave in different ways to accomplish your request. What provides uniqueness is the combination of the message and the object that is receiving it.

Our banking example can again be used to explain polymorphism. Every customer has many accounts. Each account can have a very different structure and behavior. One of the behaviors is that it knows how to value itself. The complexity of the algorithm to value a stock portfolio is going to be quite different from that necessary to calculate the value of a simple interest-bearing savings account. The important aspect is that each and every unique account can support the same operation, `value()`. Each class will implement a `value()` operation, but the code behind the operation, the method, may vary considerably.

In a traditional language such as COBOL, two subroutines of the same name would generate a compile error. In object-oriented languages, it is often quite common, and is especially good, if you find classes that can all implement the same interface or operations.

No Silver Bullet

This short primer must emphasize that there is no silver bullet or free ride with object-oriented. The biggest mistake you can make is assuming that object-oriented, in and of itself, will solve all your present and future data processing problems. This couldn't be further from the truth.

To be a success with this approach requires a sound project plan, excellent analysis, and, above all, a very clear understanding of what the expectations of the user community are regarding the features and functionality of the application. Putting the technology, object-oriented, ahead of the business purpose and requirements is a certain road to failure for any project.

Component Object Model and COM+

This appendix will briefly cover the Component Object Model (COM) as it relates to its utilization in VB. It will also address what happens when certain aspects of COM are used by VB and what impact those will have on the application. For a more complete review, I highly recommend the book, referenced in both the Bibliography and Suggested Readings, by Ted Pattison entitled, *Programming Distributed Applications with COM and Microsoft VB*, published by Microsoft Press, 1998.

Lastly, this appendix will provide a review of what the next generation of COM, called COM+, will supposedly bring to the development environment. This functionality will be delivered with Windows 2000.

COM—The Plumbing

Component Object Model (COM) is Microsoft's middleware plumbing that allows components to communicate. It is not general knowledge that COM reaches out further than the Windows platform. COM has been ported to different flavors of the UNIX operating system as well. Unfortunately, enhancements to COM and its distributed flavor, DCOM, are not always released in unison to all platforms. This makes for a difficult integration strategy at best. The good news is that most of you reading this text are using COM and DCOM in Microsoft operating system solutions only.

COM/DCOM is thus an integral part of VB. Luckily, much of the COM infrastructure is hidden from the VB developer. In most cases, VB doesn't provide direct access to some of the COM interfaces, such as `IDispatch` and `IUnknown`. These interfaces though are an integral part of, let's say, a Visual C++ programmer's knowledge base. In all but a few cases, this doesn't pose any restrictions on the VB programmer.

COM—Infrastructure

COM is actually implemented as a group of DLLs and EXEs. These automatically get set up during the installation of either Windows 95, 98, or NT. The primary COM API interface is packaged in the file `OLE32.DLL`. VB shields the developer from this API and makes the calls for you. In the case of C++ developers, they call directly into this DLL.

Most components built with VB implement many classes and/or interfaces. For instance, in our `BRSVC.DLL` component, which was built to contain the business rules for Remulak Productions, we implemented such classes as `Customer` and `Product`. In the `DTSVC.DLL` component built to contain the SQL code to service the needs of the business layer, we implemented classes such as `CustomerDT` and `ProductDT`, as well as an interface, `ICrud`.

For components to be accessible through the COM infrastructure, there must be a way for a client process to instantiate and gain access to class properties and methods. Also, since COM components can be built in many different languages (for example, VB, C++, and Java), there needs to be some common map of just what classes and interfaces a given component supports. This is done through an Interface Definition Language, better known as IDL.

The information in the IDL is like a language-neutral menu of services that a component supports. VB ActiveX components have their IDL information bundled in with the EXE or DLL that you "make" from within the VB IDE. The exception to this, if you remember from our chapter on DCOM, is that when the component is accessed remotely, then a separate type library (.TLB) file is created when you check the "remote server files" option under the "Component" tab on the Project Properties windows (see Figure D-2).

So just what does this type library have in it? Figure D-1 is a view of what the type library contains as viewed using a tool available with VB called OLE View (`oleview.exe`).

OLE View is available off of the Visual Studio Tools menu option For most users of VB, it isn't that beneficial, but it is an excellent learning tool to understand how COM works. The view in Figure D-1 happens to be looking at the `Order` class within `brsvc.dll`.

Every class defined in a COM component implements at least one interface. That interface is the default interface, and it is hidden. It is made up of all the methods and properties that the class supports. It is aptly named `_Classname`. In our case, with `Order`, the default interface is `_Order`.

FIGURE D-1   *OLE View rendering of the* `brsvc.dll` *component.*

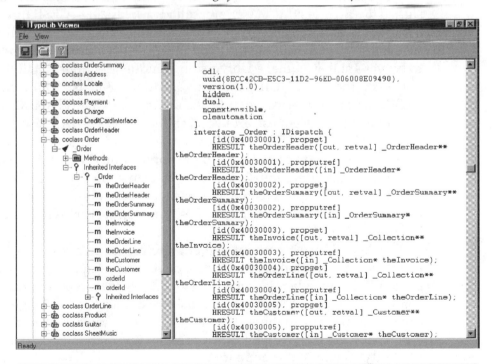

We need to learn some more COM terms before we go any further. Each class implemented within a COM component, such as the `Customer` class found in `brsvc.dll`, is called as a coclass. A coclass represents the COM implementation plumbing surrounding the class. How does a client gain access to a class to instantiate it? There must be some mechanism to identify a class or an interface that would allow the client to compile a reference to it in its own load module. This is where the infamous Globally Unique Identifier (GUID) comes into play.

The GUID (pronounced *goowee id*) is a 128-bit integer that is created when a COM component is compiled (many may be created at once if your component supports more than one class or interface). These GUIDs are then physically implanted within the type library information. These values are created based on information from either your network interface card (NIC) or your system clock.

Every class or interface that your component implements is assigned a unique GUID. The type library for the component also gets a GUID. GUIDs are not reused and are unique across time and space. The VB IDE does all of the GUID generation behind the scenes. GUIDs assigned to a coclass (a class) are called a Class ID (CLSID). GUIDs assigned to an interface are called an Interface ID (IID). To really confuse things, if you examine the IDL in Figure D-1, these two are referred to by yet another name, a Universally Unique Identifier (UUID). So, if you hear the term UUID, the conversation could be about either a CLSID or an IID. A competing technology to COM/DCOM, called Common Object Request Broker Architecture (CORBA), also calls its unique identifiers UUIDs.

These GUIDs are compiled into the applications binary (that is, DLL or EXE) when the component is built using "make." Furthermore, when a client compiles its binary image, any COM server components it references (via that server's GUIDs) has that server's GUIDs placed into its DLL or EXE.

This last discussion about a client's reference to a server's GUIDs should start to crystallize the concept of version compatibility. Just how does VB know when a client's reference to a server interface has changed? Simple: A GUID previously referenced is no longer valid because something in the server that you were using changed, thus creating a new GUID. We will talk more about this in the VB Version Compatibility section in this appendix.

COM at Work

If COM is the communication plumbing between components, then what within the Windows operating systems makes the plumbing work? The real workhorse in the COM world is the SCM (Service Control Manager). This service is implemented by `RPCSS.EXE`. All access to the SCM (sometimes called the "scum") is made through the API published in `OLE32.DLL`.

Remember from before that the VB runtime engine makes the calls through the COM API, which in turn works with the SCM. So, in VB, when we do something such as

```
Set MyCustomer = New Customer
```

here is what happens under the covers.

1. VB calls the `coCreateInstance` method within the `OLE32.DLL` and passes the SCM the CLSID of the coclass and the IID of the interface used to connect to the object (in most cases, this will be the GUID for the default interface for the class `_classname`).

2. The SCM locates the server component from entries found in the client's Registry.

3. The SCM calls into the server component (`QueryInterface`) and passes in the CLSID and the IID (both of which are GUIDs as well as UUIDs!!!).

4. The server creates an object in the image of the class (CLSID).

5. The server returns an interface reference of the type specified by the IID to the SCM.

6. The SCM forwards the interface reference back to the client.

The client is now bound to the object and can now invoke methods on the object.

The previous example illustrates the concept of early binding. That is to say, the concrete class, `Customer` in our case, was known in advance and all the GUIDs representing all the coclasses and interfaces are referenced in the client's binary image.

However, what happens when you don't know the class you need to instantiate at compile time? This is, of course, handled by VB and is known as late binding. Late binding is always slower than early binding and should be avoided at all costs. Assume we have the following:

```
Dim myCustomer As Object
Set myCustomer = CreateObject("brsvc.Customer")
MyCustomer.getInfo(-,-,-)
```

For late binding to work, our nice clean six-step process defined previously must be enhanced. A special COM interface called `IDispatch` is called by the VB runtime service and assigned to the `myCustomer` variable declared as type `Object`. Since the client doesn't know anything about the server component, it must ask the `IDispatch` interface if it knows anything about the method `getInfo`. It does this by calling the method `GetIDsOfNames` of the `IDispatch` interface. This method within COM will look for the method requested by the client, and if it is found, it returns a DISPID (an integer representing an offset to the object's method) reference to that method.

Next, the `Invoke` COM method is called using the DISPID returned to actually invoke the method. So, at a minimum, there will be two additional COM method calls for every late bound object-method request. In summary, early bound clients can expect their method calls (just the time that it takes to invoke an object's method) to be about 500 to 1,000 times faster than a late bound method request.

Another type of binding that is sometimes considered early binding but technically is its own category is vtable (virtual table) binding. vtable binding is the fastest form of binding. This type of binding allows the client to directly invoke methods with the least amount of COM intervention. A vtable is a pointer structure that statically defines entry points for each method supported by an interface. There will be one vtable for every interface supported by a component. So, for our `brsvc.dll` component, there will be a vtable for every class that it implements (remember, each class has a default interface such as `_Customer`, `_Order`, and so on). VB will always use vtable binding if the following conditions are met.

1. The client project contains a reference to the type library of the server component.

2. The reference is typed to an interface or a creatable class (the default interface such as `_Customer`).

3. The object exposes vtables (all of your VB-created components expose them by default). However, some components purchased from third-party vendors may not. A good way to tell is to snoop around using OLE View.

Visual Basic—Version Compatibility

Many consider the version compatibility options in VB confusing to say the least. Now that we have a fundamental baseline understanding of what is going on inside of COM when an object is activated, let's examine some of the unique aspects as they pertain to VB's version compatibility dialog.

Every ActiveX component that we build in VB is marked with a default level of compatibility, which happens to be "project compatibility" (discussed later in this appendix). Think of this compatibility as the status or state of the component and the contract that it promises to honor to any client wanting to use its services. Figure D-2 is a snapshot

FIGURE D-2   *Project Properties dialog box for* BRSVC.DLL.

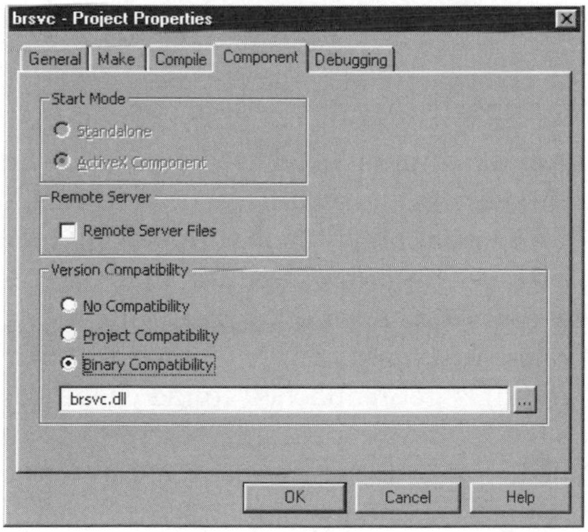

of the "Project Properties" dialog box for our `brsvc.dll` component. This is found under the "Component Tab."

Remember from the discussion about COM and GUIDs that each time an ActiveX component is compiled, the version compatibility setting of that component will influence how that component's GUIDs are dealt with (each class and interface implemented by the component will get a unique GUID).

A component's interface, which is composed of all public attributes and operations, is like a contract to any potential consumer of the component. To help ensure that the contract is maintained, COM tries to control when and how a component's GUIDs can change. VB offers three levels of compatibility, with "Project Compatibility" being the default for new components. Let's review each level.

No Compatibility

If a component is marked with no compatibility, VB will generate a new collection of GUIDs for all the classes (CLSIDs) and interfaces (IIDs), as well as for the type library, every time the component is compiled. This level of compatibility is probably the least used as well as the most problematic. It virtually disables the components used by external clients because the GUIDs are in a constant state of flux. Also, when users want to use the component from within the VB IDE, they will find that their reference is "missing," thereby requiring the component to be rereferenced (this is because the type library is getting assigned a new GUID).

Project Compatibility

This is the most common level used during the development phase of a server component. The key difference between this level of compatibility and "no compatibility" is that the GUID for the type library stays constant. This is important because while in the VB IDE, it is disconcerting to continually have a server's reference "missing" from the client's "references" dialog. When working within the IDE, all the new CLSIDs and IIDs get reattached to the client anyway. However, if the GUID for the server's type library changes, then the client gets really excited and acts as if the server has disappeared entirely (that is until it is re-referenced, as described previously).

The GUIDs representing both the CLSIDs and IIDs will change with each compile (actually, in VB v6, CLSIDs will remain constant across builds) within "project compatibility" mode (assuming nothing changes in the component). However, this is good news only if you're using the server from within the IDE. Any client that has performed a "make" against this server will now be broken.

Binary Compatibility

This mode should be called "production compatibility" or something of that nature. The reason is that this is the equivalent of saying that I am releasing this for all to consume and I will abide by the contract I am publishing (read: I won't change my GUIDs). This option should be selected only once your server component is in a very stable state because VB will do its best to preserve all the GUIDs for your component.

It is important to point out that even with "binary compatibility" selected, certain changes that you make will still generate new GUIDs, including the following:

- Modifying a public property/method signature on a public class
- Removing a public class
- Removing a public property/method from a public class
- Changing the composition of an ENUM block
- Changing the default method of the class

Remember that you can change the implementation, that is, the "body" code of the method, all day long. It is the signature that is the contract to the outside client, and not its implementation. This is the whole message behind encapsulation and the feature that enables polymorphism. When using "binary compatibility," you can add new methods anytime that you wish. VB will actually create a new interface (an IID) that consists of the old methods plus the new one. However, any clients that are bound to the prior version will still work.

COM+

The next generation of COM, which will be released with Windows 2000, is called COM+. COM+ will add some additional features that will make it not only more robust in its implementation but also much easier to use, especially for server components that are distributed on other machines.

The key new features that will be found in COM+ are the following:

- An in-memory database
- An eventing service
- Queued components
- A load balancing service

The in-memory database will provide for much faster creation of objects and access to their properties and methods. Today, COM doesn't cache such things as DISPIDs—this can tend to slow down COM performance.

The eventing service will be a formal acknowledgement of the need for a callback-like service but within COM. Callbacks are not new, but what has been lacking is a publish and subscribe model for events. A client can register with a server regarding its desire to be notified when a given event takes place.

Queued components will allow COM objects to transparently use Microsoft's Message Queue (MSMQ) technology as their transport. For instance, a COM component could be instantiated from a client and sent messages. However, these would use the services of MSMQ to potentially allow asynchronous processing of those requests. This also opens up the door for transaction prioritization (things that developers using MQSeries, CICS, and IMS/DC have had for years).

The load balancing service will provide the much needed support of pooled server resources and the ability to dynamically adjust execution loads based on the load of the servers. Today, load balancing logic, that is, the ability to shuttle object activation and servicing among a pool of servers, requires custom code on the part of the development team. Load balancing will allow servers to occasionally report their load status to a router agent, which will dynamically shift processing in the case that a server is bogged down or perhaps has disappeared.

Perhaps the biggest improvement will be the convergence of COM and MTS as one unified whole. Prior to COM+, MTS and COM used two different security models. In addition, object instantiation has to be done with a special method, `CreateInstance`, which has MTS creating the component for you. This makes for a very confusing programming model. A developer can quickly get into trouble in the way they create instances of classes when running under MTS. What works without MTS may be disastrous when running under MTS. The need for special code that works in and out of MTS, as was introduced in this book, will be eliminated.

Another big benefit, which I alluded to in the book, is that distributing components using the MTS infrastructure is almost child's play compared to the native DCOM distribution mechanism. This will become the de facto approach for distributing applications under COM+. Application distribution using the MTS package will be the preferred approach and will alleviate many of the Registry problems that can occur when manually registering components.

My only pet issue, which I would love to see addressed, is the granularity of transaction assignment within MTS. Transaction status is assigned at the class level. This is a shame, as most classes have operations that require transaction support (for example, `Create`, `Delete`, and `Update`) as well as those that don't (for example, `getInfo`). To get around establishing the transaction overhead for read-only methods, the class must be broken into two separate objects, one that will ask for transaction services and the other that won't. By dropping transaction assignment down to the method level, MTS would be more in line with object-oriented design techniques. This enhancement would also align MTS with their biggest competitor, Enterprise Java Beans (EJB), who did it correctly. EJBs can assign transaction characteristics at both the class and the operation level.

Object-Oriented Project Plan

I have stressed in this book the importance of a sound project plan. Actually, I went so far to say that without a sound lifecycle process and accompanying project plan, YOU WILL FAIL. This appendix presents a project plan, given in Table E-1, that I have found invaluable. By working on real projects, I have made it better over the years.

It initially started out as a plan for only client/server-based projects, regardless of methodology. It has been through the paces, and the good part is that it is meant as a baseline on which to build your own plan. I wouldn't expect that you would follow every task in the plan. The plan must be molded for your own project needs.

A few items are worth pointing out.

1. Every high-level task, such as "Inception—Project Scope," will always be composed of the same task sections, as follows.

   - **Management Tasks**: These tasks are usually administrative in nature but also are very focused and strategic.

   - **Execution Tasks**: These tasks are what I call "doer" tasks. They represent the prime work necessary to produce the bulk of the deliverables that will be delivered to the project sponsor.

   - **Education Tasks**: These tasks represent the educational steps necessary for certain team members to be successful on the project.

2. The timeline is moot in that given each project's unique characteristics, the composition of the project along with the required effort to complete the work will vary. For estimating projects, see Appendix A that covers the project estimates for Remulak Productions.

3. On the Web site that is pointed out at the end of the book, where all the source code for this book is available, you will find a copy of this project plan. It is in Microsoft Project 98 format. I have also included a copy of it in HTML format.

The Plan

TABLE E-1   *Synergy Process Model and the Elaboration Phase*

#		Task
1		⊟ **Inception - Project Scope**
2		⊟ **Management Tasks**
3	✓	Identify Business Unit Sponsor
4		Define Roles and Responsibilities
5		Establish Business Objectives
6	▦	Assign Project Team
7		Assess Project Risks
8		Establish Risk Assessment/Mitigation Procedures
9		Establish Problem Resolution Procedures
10		Establish Change Control Procedures
11		Refine Business Objectives
12		Establish Preliminary Project Releases
13		Estimate Preliminary Project Releases
14		Prepare Project Charter
15		Kickoff Initial Increment
16		⊟ **Execution Tasks**
17		⊟ **Scoping - Iter#1**
18		Assess/select CASE Toolkit
19		Identify Project Features
20		Identify Actors
21		Identify Events
22		Create Event Table
23		⊟ **Scoping - Iteration#2**

24		Identify Use Cases from Events Table
25		Identify Happy Path (Basic Course of Events) - name only
26		Identify Alternate Course of Events - name only
27		Identify Exceptions - name only
28		Identify Shadow Use Cases- name only
29		Prioritize Basic and Alternate Course of Events
30		⊟ **Scoping - Iteration#3**
31		Create Happy Path Activity Detail
32		Assess Network Impact
33		Assess Operations Impact
34		Assess Preliminary Execution Architecture
35		⊟ **Education Tasks**
36		Prepare/Analyze Skills Assessment
37		Prepare Training Plan
38		Conduct Basic Object Training
39		⊟ **Elaboration - Requirements Gathering - Cycle1**
40		⊟ **Management Tasks**
41		Monitor Project Plan
42		Monitor Politics
43		Monitor Expectations
44		Assess Project Plan
45		Assess Project Risks
46		Re-affirm Release Cycles/Dates
47		Assess Change Control
48		⊟ **Execution Tasks**
49		Document Repository Standards
50		Identify Modeling Standards
51		Create Preliminary Test Cases from Course of Events
52		⊟ **Requirements Gathering - Iter#1**
53		Create Course of Event Detail for Alternate Paths
54		Create Course of Event Detail for Exception Paths
55		Identify/Categorize Business Rules
56		Brainstorm Classes (nouns)
57		Filter Classes
58		⊟ **Requirements Gathering - Iter#2**
59		Class Associations and Multiplicity
60		Create Initial Class Diagram
61		⊟ **Requirements Gathering - Iter#3**
62		Add any known attributes/operations
63		⊟ **Education Tasks**
64		Conduct UI Prototype Training
65		Conduct Database Training
66		Conduct Object Construction Training
67		⊟ **Elaboration - Requirements Gathering - Cycle2**
68		⊟ **Management Tasks**
69		Monitor Project Plan

70		Monitor Politics
71		Monitor Expectations
72		Assess Project Plan
73		Assess Project Risks
74		Assess Change Control
75		⊟ **Execution Tasks**
76		⊟ **User Interface Prototype - Iter#1**
77		Select UI Prototyping Tool
78		Build/Buy UI Standards Tool
79		Create UI Structure Charts from Use Case Paths
80		Identify UI objects from Use Cases
81		Validate UI Structure Chart
82		Build Prototype
83		Validate UI Prototype Functionality
84		Validate UI Prototype Usability
85		⊟ **Requirements Gathering - Iter#2**
86		Create Sequence Diagram-Happy Path
87		Create Sequence Diagram-Alternate Paths
88		Create Collaboration Diagrams (where appropriate)
89		Update Class Diagram-Attributes/Operations
90		⊟ **Requirements Gathering - Iter#3**
91		Identify Classes with Dynamic Behavior
92		Create State Diagrams for Classes
93		Update Class Diagram-Attributes/Operations
94		Create Activity Diagrams
95		⊟ **Requirements Gathering - Iter#4**
96		Object/Location Matrix
97		Object/Volume Matrix
98		Event/Frequency Matrix
99		Assess Network/Operations Impact
100		⊟ **Education Tasks**
101		Conduct UI Prototype Training
102		Conduct Database Training
103		Conduct Object Construction Training
104		⊟ **Elaboration - Execution Architecture - Cycle3**
105		⊟ **Management Tasks**
106		Monitor Project Plan
107		Monitor Politics
108		Monitor Expectations
109		Assess Project Plan for Design
110		Assess Project Risks
111		⊟ **Execution Tasks**
112		Assess Operations Impact
113	·	Assess Network Impact
114		Update Test Plans
115		⊟ **Technology Architecture**

116		Select Database Technology
117		Select Hardware Platform
118		Select Network Infrastructure
119		Select Construction Tools
120		Select Support and Implementation tools
121		⊟ **Application Architecture**
122		Determine Build/Buy Strategy
123		Establish security requirements
124		Select Internet Tools
125		Select Partitioning Models
126		Map Tools to Partitioning Models
127		Select Application Component Interfaces
128		⊟ **Data Access Architecture**
129		Establish Data Stewards
130		Select Data Access APIs
131		Assess Data Distribution Requirements
132		Assess Data Synchronization Requirements
133		Assess Replication Technology
134		⊟ **Education Tasks**
135		Architecture Awareness Training
136		Client/Server & Object Tools Awareness Training
137		Component Building and Language Training
138		⊟ **Construction-Database-Cycle 1**
139		⊟ **Management Tasks**
140		Monitor Project Plan
141		Monitor Politics
142		Monitor Expectations
143		Assess Project Plan for Construction
144		Assess Project Risks
145		⊟ **Execution Tasks**
146		Assess Operations Impact
147		Assess Network Impact
148		⊟ **Database Design - Iter#1**
149		Assess Object Impact on Relational Design
150		Verify Data Distribution Scenarios
151		Verify Usage Matrix Accuracy
152		Apply DBMS Transform Rules to ERD
153		Validate Physical Design
154		Denormalize Physical Design
155		⊟ **Build Database Environment - Iter#2**
156		Create Tables
157		Create Indexes
158		Create Views
159		Establish Locking Standards
160		Establish Recovery Standards
161		Establish Disk Storage Management Standards

162		Validate Server Selection
163		Formalize Database Stress Test Plans
164		⊟ **Education Tasks**
165		Configuration Management Training
166		Debugging Techniques Training
167		⊟ **Construction - Component - Cycle 2**
168		⊟ **Management Tasks**
169		Monitor Project Plan
170		Monitor Politics
171		Monitor Expectations
172		Assess Project Plan for Construction
173		Assess Project Risks
174		⊟ **Execution Tasks**
175		Assess Operations Impact
176		Assess Network Impact
177		⊟ **Component Design - Iter#1**
178		Assess Object Impact to Component Strategy
179		Verify Process Distribution Scenarios
180		Verify Usage Matrix Accuracy
181		Apply UML Artifacts to Partitioning Model
182		Allocate Client Tasks
183		Allocate Server Tasks
184		Design Process Components
185		Create Component/Deployment Diagrams
186		Finalize Design Model
187		⊟ **Component Build - Iter#2**
188		Code Process Components
189		Reassess UI Screen Dialogues
190		Code UI Screen Dialogs
191		Identify Batch Streams
192		Code Batch Streams
193		Formalize component Stress Test Plans
194		⊟ **Education Tasks**
195		Configuration Management Training
196		Debugging Techniques Training
197		⊟ **Construction - Network - Cycle 3**
198		⊟ **Management Tasks**
199		Monitor Project Plan
200		Monitor Politics
201		Monitor Expectations
202		Assess Project Plan for Construction
203		Assess Project Risks
204		⊟ **Execution Tasks**
205		Assess Operations Impact
206		Assess Network Impact
207		Establish Existing Network Baseline

208		Validate Unique Network Requirements
209		Update Physical CRUD with Network Parameters
210		Simulate Network Load
211		Validate Network Load Against Baseline
212		Formalize Network Stress Test Plans
213		⊟ **Education Tasks**
214		Configuration Management Training
215		Debugging Techniques Training
216		⊟ **Transition**
217		⊟ **Management Tasks**
218		Monitor Project Plan
219		Monitor Politics
220		Monitor Expectations
221		Assess Project Plan for Construction
222		Assess Project Risks
223		Allocate Resources for Beta and Maintenance Support
224		Formulate Production Handover Strategy
225		Establish Final Acceptance Criteria for Handoff
226		Conduct Beta Post-Mortem
227		Conduct Production Post-Mortem
228		Conduct Maintenance Handoff Post-Mortem
229		⊟ **Execution Tasks**
230		⊟ **Deployment Beta - Iter#1**
231		Select Software Distribution Tool
232		Create install sets and deployment plans
233		Create database creation and build scripts
234		Create Beta Test Directory Structures
235		Create Beta Environment
236		Execute Install Set
237		Assess Beta Results and Track Trouble Reports
238		Prioritize and Implement Changes
239		⊟ **Deployment Production - Iter#2**
240		Create install sets and deployment plans
241		Create database creation and build scripts
242		Create Production Directory Structures
243		Create Production Environment
244		Execute Install Set
245		⊟ **Deployment Maintenance - Iter#3**
246		Create post-delivery maintenance plans
247		Accept Production System
248		Establish Trouble Reporting and Help Desk Integration Strategy
249		Establish Service Pack Release Strategy
250		⊟ **Education Tasks**
251		Software Distribution Tool Training
252		Help Desk Support Training

Sample Project Output

In the body of this book, we used several examples to demonstrate the deliverables of the project as we moved through the phases. During their introductions, we referred to the appendix for a more detailed set of examples. This appendix presents those examples.

Use Cases—Use Case Details for Increment I

If you recall from Chapter 3, "Getting the Project Started: Project Charter," many use cases were defined and then assigned to one of three Remulak Productions project increments. To provide a more informed estimate while still early in the project requires an in-depth fly-by of all the project's use cases. At a minimum, prior to estimating a project, the following must be done.

1. Identify events.
2. Identify use cases.
3. Assign events to use cases.
4. Identify happy paths for all use cases.
5. Identify alternative pathways for all use cases.
6. Produce detailed task steps for all use case happy paths.

7. Assign use cases to project increments. This may include both use cases and pathways, as they may be split across increments.

8. Detail all use case pathways for the project's first increment.

Steps 1 through 5 were completed in the book, primarily in Chapter 3, "Getting the Project Started: Project Charter." This portion of the appendix contains the completed use case templates for all of Increment 1, as well as the detailed task steps for the happy paths.

Use Case Definition—Process Orders

Use Case Name:	Process Orders
Use Case Description:	This use case starts when an order is either initiated or inquired about. This use case handles all aspects of the initial definition and authorization of an order. The use case ends when the Order Clerk completes a session with a customer.
Use Case Authors:	Rene Becnel
Actors:	Order Clerk
Locations:	New Port Hills, Washington
Status:	Pathways defined.
Priority:	1
Assumptions:	Orders will be taken by the Order Clerk until such time that the customer base is comfortable with the specialized services being provided now.
Preconditions:	Order Clerk has logged onto the system.
Postconditions:	- Order is placed. - Inventory is reduced.
Primary Pathway:	Customer calls in and orders a guitar and supplies and pays with a credit card.
Alternative Pathway(s):	- Customer calls in and orders a guitar and pays with a P. O. - Customer calls in and orders a guitar on the Remulak Productions easy finance plan.

	- Customer calls in and orders an organ using a credit card. - Customer calls in and orders an organ and pays with a P. O.
Exception Pathway(s):	- Customer calls in to place an order with a credit card and the card is invalid. - Customer calls in with a P. O. and has not been approved to use the P. O. method - Customer calls in to place an order and the items desired are not in stock

Use Case Definition—Maintain Orders

Use Case Name:	Maintain Orders
Use Case Description:	This use case starts when an order is modified in any way. This use case handles all aspects of the order modification. The use case ends when the Order Clerk completes the order modification session.
Use Case Authors:	Rene Becnel
Actors:	Order Clerk
Locations:	New Port Hills, Washington
Status:	Pathways defined.
Priority:	1
Assumptions:	Orders will be modified by the Order Clerk.
Preconditions:	Order Clerk has logged onto the system.
Postconditions:	- Order is modified. - Inventory is reduced or increased.
Primary Pathway:	Customer calls in to inquire on an order's status.
Alternative Pathway(s):	- Customer calls in to change a product quantity for one order item on the order. - Customer calls in to cancel an order. - Customer calls in to add a new order item to the order.

- Customer calls in to delete an order item from the order.
- Customer calls in to change the shipping terms of an order.
- Customer buys an extended warranty on an order item.
- Customer calls in to change the billing method.

Exception Pathway(s):   - Customer calls in to cancel an order and it isn't found in the system.
- Customer calls in to add a warranty to an item that is no longer eligible based on the existing time of ownership.
- Customer calls in to change an order and the product to be added is not found in the system.

Use Case Definition—Maintain Inventory

Use Case Name: Maintain Inventory

Use Case Description: This use case starts when product is ordered and/or added to stock. This use case handles all aspects of inventory management. The use case ends when either new stock is ordered or new stock has been accounted for in inventory.

Use Case Authors: Rene Becnel

Actors: Supplier

Locations: New Port Hills, Washington

Status: Pathways defined.

Priority: 1

Assumptions: Only products carried by Remulak Productions are ordered or processed into inventory (that is, unauthorized products are not sold).

Preconditions: Replenished products have product numbers assigned.

Postconditions: - Product is ordered.
- Product is checked into inventory.

Primary Pathway: Product arrives into the warehouse with a copy of the P. O. attached.

Alternative Pathway(s):   - Product arrives in the warehouse with a P. O. attached but incomplete as to products ordered.
- Product is ordered to replenish stock on hand.
- Product is ordered to fulfill a special order.
- Product is ordered to fulfill a backordered item.
- Products are accounted for through a physical inventory count.

Exception Pathway(s):   - Product arrives with no attached P. O. or bill-of-lading.

Use Case Definition—Shipping

Use Case Name: Shipping

Use Case Description: This use case starts when an order is either completely ready or partially ready for shipment. This use case handles all aspects of shipping. The use case ends when the order is shipped and is either partially fulfilled or completely fulfilled.

Use Case Authors: Rene Becnel

Actors: Packaging Clerk, Shipping Clerk

Locations: New Port Hills, Washington

Status: Pathways defined.

Priority: 1

Assumptions: For an order to be partially fulfilled, the customer must have authorized partial shipments.

Preconditions: Packaging Clerk and Shipping Clerk have valid access to the system and are logged on.

Postconditions: Order is shipped.

Primary Pathway: An entire order is shipped from stock on hand to a customer.

Alternative Pathway(s):	- A partial order is shipped from stock on hand to a customer. - An entire order is shipped to a customer directly from a third-party supplier.
Exception Pathway(s):	Order is ready to ship and has no shipping address.

Use Case Definition—Invoicing

Use Case Name:	Invoicing
Use Case Description:	This use case starts when an order is invoiced to a customer. This use case handles all aspects of invoicing. The use case ends when the order is invoiced and payment is received.
Use Case Authors:	Rene Becnel
Actors:	Accounting System and Billing Clerk
Locations:	New Port Hills, Washington
Status:	Pathways defined.
Priority:	1
Assumptions:	- For an invoice to be produced, there must be a valid order. - An order can have more than one invoice (to accommodate authorized partial shipments). - The invoicing interface to accounting happens nightly.
Preconditions:	Billing Clerk has valid access to the system and is logged on.
Postconditions:	- Order is invoiced and/or funds are collected. - The accounting system is updated as to the invoiced orders.
Primary Pathway:	- An order is invoiced and sent to the customer indicating that payment was satisfied by credit card billing.
Alternative Pathway(s):	- An overdue notice is sent to a customer for a past-due account.

- Interface of subledger transactions to the accounting system.

Exception Pathway(s):   - None.

Use Case Definition—Maintain Relationships

Use Case Name: Maintain Relationships

Use Case Description: This use case starts when a relationship with a customer or supplier requires attention. This use case handles all aspects of Remulak Productions's relationships with its customers and suppliers. The use case ends when a relationship is either created or maintained for a customer or supplier.

Use Case Authors: Rene Becnel

Actors: Customer Service Clerk

Locations: New Port Hills, Washington

Status: Pathways defined.

Priority: 1

Assumptions: For a customer to order product or a supplier to ship products, their relationships must be established.

Preconditions: Customer Clerk has valid access to the system and is logged on.

Postconditions: Relationship is either created or maintained.

Primary Pathway: Customer calls in to change its mailing address.

Alternative Pathway(s): - Customer calls in to change its default payment terms and payment method.
                        - New customer is added to the system.
                        - Prospective customer is added to the system.
                        - New supplier is added to the system.
                        - Supplier calls in to change its billing address.

Exception Pathway(s):   - None.

Use Case Definition—Decision Support

Use Case Name:	Decision Support
Use Case Description:	This use case starts when a predefined or undefined request for information is made. This use case handles all aspects of the decision support effort. The use case ends when a reply is formulated for the inquiry.
Use Case Authors:	Rene Becnel
Actors:	Manager
Locations:	New Port Hills, Washington
Status:	Pathways defined.
Priority:	1
Assumptions:	None.
Preconditions:	Manager has valid access to the system and is logged on.
Postconditions:	Reply is formulated for request.
Primary Pathway:	Manager requests backorder status report.
Alternative Pathway(s):	Time to print backorder report created.
Exception Pathway(s):	None.

Use Cases—Happy Path Task Steps

This section contains the detailed task steps for all of the use case happy paths.

Process Orders (Customer Calls In and Orders a Guitar and Supplies and Pays with a Credit Card)

1. Customer supplies customer number.
2. Customer is acknowledged as being current.
3. For each product that the customer desires:
   3.1 Request product ID or description.
   3.2 Resolve description to ID if necessary.

    3.3 Request quantity.

    3.4 Item price is calculated.

4. Extended order total is calculated.

5. Tax is applied.

6. Shipping charges are applied.

7. Extended price is supplied to the customer.

8. Customer supplies credit card number.

9. Customer credit card is validated.

10. Inventory is reduced.

11. Sale is finalized and completed.

Maintain Orders (Customer Calls In to Inquire on an Order's Status)

1. Customer supplies order number.

2. Order number is acknowledged as being correct.

3. Order header information is supplied, along with key customer information for verification.

4. For each Order Line that the Order contains:

    4.1 Provide product description.

    4.2 Provide quantity ordered.

    4.3 Provide product price.

    4.4 Provide extended product price.

    4.5 Provide estimated shipping date.

5. Extended order total is calculated.

6. Tax is applied.

7. Shipping charges are applied.

8. Extended order total is supplied to the customer.

Maintain Inventory (Product Arrives in the Warehouse with a Copy of the P.O. Attached)

1. P. O. is verified for validity.

2. Accompanying P. O. is compared with the actual product shipment received.

3. Shipment items received are acknowledged as matching the P. O.

4. Product's quantity on hand is updated, reflecting new inventory amount.

5. For each Order Line that is backordered that matches the product received:

   5.1 Allocate inventory.

   5.2 Assign inventory to Order Line.

Shipping (An Entire Order Is Shipped from Stock on Hand to a Customer)

1. Order is assigned to a shipping clerk.

2. Order is assigned to a packaging clerk.

3. Order is pulled from stock by a packaging clerk.

4. Order Line items are packaged for shipment.

5. Shipping clerk verifies shipping method and cost.

6. Order is shipped.

Invoicing (An Order Is Invoiced and Sent to the Customer Indicating Payment Satisfied by Credit Card Billing)

1. Order number is validated as to existence.

2. For customers authorizing partial shipments:

   2.1. For each Order Line with product in stock:

   2.2 Mark the product as drawn down.

   2.3 Generate an invoice line item.

Maintain Relationships (Customer Calls in to Change Its Mailing Address)

1. Customer number is validated.

2. Customer's addresses are returned.

3. Customer Service Clerk accepts address changes to mailing address.

Decision Support (Manager Requests Backorder Status Report)

1. Print each order that has a line item that is presently backordered.

Database Support

This section of deliverables deals with the DDL (Data Definition Language) statements necessary to support Microsoft or Sybase SQL Server as well as Oracle. In most cases, the differences between SQL Server and the Oracle DDL, at least for the data types used in the Remulak Productions project, are restricted to simple formatting issues and the use of DateTime in SQL Server versus Date in Oracle.

It is important to point out that the VB code written for the Remulak Productions project and the accessing SQL statements found in the DT modules will work on both platforms unmodified. Because of the layered architecture used and the ability of ADO to deal with the back-end in an abstract fashion, the physical DBMS utilized is completely transparent.

Microsoft SQLServer v7.0

```
CREATE TABLE T_Address (
        maddressLine1 varchar (30) NOT NULL ,
        maddressLine2 varchar (30) NOT NULL ,
        maddressLine3 varchar (30) NOT NULL ,
        mcity varchar (30) NOT NULL ,
        mstate char (2) NOT NULL ,
        mzip varchar (15) NOT NULL ,
        maddressId int NOT NULL
)
GO

CREATE TABLE T_Customer (
        mcustomerId int NOT NULL ,
        mcustomerNumber char (14) NOT NULL ,
        mfirstName char (20) NOT NULL ,
        mlastName char (20) NOT NULL ,
```

```
                mmiddleInitial char (10) NOT NULL ,
                mprefix char (4) NOT NULL ,
                msuffix char (4) NOT NULL ,
                mphone1 char (15) NOT NULL ,
                mphone2 char (15) NOT NULL ,
                meMail varchar (30) NOT NULL
)
GO

CREATE TABLE T_Guitar (
                mstringCount int NOT NULL ,
                mright char (5) NOT NULL ,
                mfretLess char (5) NOT NULL ,
                mmake varchar (20) NOT NULL ,
                mmodel varchar (20) NOT NULL ,
                mage int NOT NULL ,
                mproductId int NOT NULL ,
                mguitarId int NOT NULL
)
GO

CREATE TABLE T_Invoice (
                minvoiceNumber int NOT NULL ,
                minvoiceId int NOT NULL ,
                minvoiceAmount decimal(17,2) NOT NULL ,
                minvoiceDate datetime NOT NULL
)
GO

CREATE TABLE T_Locale (
                mrole int NOT NULL ,
                mlocaleId int NOT NULL ,
                maddressId int NOT NULL ,
                mcustomerId int NOT NULL
)
GO

CREATE TABLE T_Order (
                morderId int NOT NULL ,
                minvoiceId int NULL ,
```

```
          mcustomerId int NOT NULL ,
          morderNumber char (10) NOT NULL,
          morderdatetime datetime NOT NULL ,
          mterms varchar (30) NOT NULL ,
          msalesPerson varchar (20) NOT NULL ,
          mdiscount decimal(17, 2) NOT NULL ,
          mcourtesyMessage varchar (50) NOT NULL
)
GO

CREATE TABLE T_OrderLine (
          mquantity int NOT NULL ,
          mdiscount decimal(17, 2) NOT NULL ,
          mextendedUnitPrice decimal(17, 2) NOT NULL
          ,
          morderLineId int NOT NULL ,
          mproductId int NOT NULL ,
          morderId int NOT NULL
) ON PRIMARY
GO

CREATE TABLE T_Payment (
          mpaymentId int NOT NULL ,
          mpaymentAmount decimal(17, 2) NOT NULL ,
          mpaymentDate datetime NOT NULL
)
GO

CREATE TABLE T_Product (
          mproductId int NOT NULL ,
          mdescription varchar (50) NOT NULL ,
          mprice decimal(17, 2) NOT NULL ,
          mdiscount decimal(17, 2) NOT NULL ,
          mquantityOnHand int NOT NULL ,
          meoq int NOT NULL ,
          mrefproductId int NULL ,
          mproductType int NULL
)
GO
```

```
CREATE TABLE T_SheetMusic (
        msheetId int NOT NULL ,
        mpages int NOT NULL ,
        mproductId int NOT NULL
)
GO

CREATE TABLE T_Shipment (
        mshipmentId int NOT NULL ,
        mshipmentdatetime datetime NOT NULL
)
GO

CREATE TABLE T_Supplies (
        msupplyId int NOT NULL ,
        mindependent char (5) NOT NULL ,
        mproductId int NOT NULL
)
GO

CREATE TABLE T_SysCode (
        msysCodeId int NOT NULL ,
        mname char (12) NOT NULL ,
        mcode char (4) NOT NULL ,
        description varchar (20) NOT NULL
)
GO

CREATE VIEW Guitar_V(
    mstringCount,
    mright,
    mfretLess,
    mmake,
    mmodel,
    mage,
    mguitarId,
    mproductId,
    mdescription,
    mprice,
    mdiscount,
```

```
    mquantityOnHand,
    meoq,
    mproductType)

    AS SELECT
    T_Guitar.mstringCount,
    T_Guitar.mright,
    T_Guitar.mfretLess,
    T_Guitar.mmake,
    T_Guitar.mmodel,
    T_Guitar.mage,
    T_Guitar.mguitarId,
    T_Product.mproductId,
    T_Product.mdescription,
    T_Product.mprice,
    T_Product.mdiscount,
    T_Product.mquantityOnHand,
    T_Product.meoq,
    T_Product.mproductType

    FROM T_Guitar,T_Product
    WHERE T_Guitar.mproductId=T_Product.mproductId
GO

CREATE VIEW SheetMusic_V(
    mpages,
    msheetId,
    mproductId,
    mdescription,
    mprice,
    mdiscount,
    mquantityOnHand,
    meoq,
    mproductType)

    AS SELECT
    T_SheetMusic.mpages,
    T_SheetMusic.msheetId,
    T_Product.mproductId,
    T_Product.mdescription,
```

```
    T_Product.mprice,
    T_Product.mdiscount,
    T_Product.mquantityOnHand,
    T_Product.meoq,
    T_Product.mproductType


    FROM T_SheetMusic,T_Product
    WHERE T_SheetMusic.mproductId=T_Product.mproductId
GO

CREATE VIEW Supplies_V(
    mindependent,
    msupplyId,
    mproductId,
    mdescription,
    mprice,
    mdiscount,
    mquantityOnHand,
    meoq,
    mproductType)

    AS SELECT

    T_Supplies.mindependent,
    T_Supplies.msupplyId,
    T_Product.mproductId,
    T_Product.mdescription,
    T_Product.mprice,
    T_Product.mdiscount,
    T_Product.mquantityOnHand,
    T_Product.meoq,
    T_Product.mproductType


    FROM T_Supplies,T_Product
    WHERE T_Supplies.mproductId=T_Product.mproductId
GO
```

Data Definition Language for Oracle (v7.3.2)

```
CREATE TABLE T_Address (
        maddressLine1 varchar (30) NOT NULL ,
        maddressLine2 varchar (30) NOT NULL ,
        maddressLine3 varchar (30) NOT NULL ,
        mcity varchar (30) NOT NULL ,
        mstate char (2) NOT NULL ,
        mzip varchar (15) NOT NULL ,
        maddressId int NOT NULL)

CREATE TABLE    T_Customer  (
        mcustomerId   int  NOT NULL ,
        mcustomerNumber   char  (14) NOT NULL ,
        mfirstName   char  (20) NOT NULL ,
        mlastName   char  (20) NOT NULL ,
        mmiddleInitial   char  (10) NOT NULL ,
        mprefix   char  (4) NOT NULL ,
        msuffix   char  (4) NOT NULL ,
        mphone1   char  (15) NOT NULL ,
        mphone2   char  (15) NOT NULL ,
        meMail   varchar  (30) NOT NULL)

CREATE TABLE    T_Guitar  (
        mstringCount   int  NOT NULL ,
        mright   char  (5) NOT NULL ,
        mfretLess   char  (5) NOT NULL ,
        mmake   varchar  (20) NOT NULL ,
        mmodel   varchar  (20) NOT NULL ,
        mage   int  NOT NULL ,
        mproductId   int  NOT NULL ,
        mguitarId   int  NOT NULL )

CREATE TABLE    T_Invoice  (
        minvoiceNumber   int  NOT NULL ,
        minvoiceId   int  NOT NULL ,
        minvoiceAmount   decimal (17, 2) NOT NULL
        ,
        minvoiceDate   date NOT NULL)
```

```
CREATE TABLE    T_Locale  (
        mrole   int  NOT NULL ,
        mlocaleId   int  NOT NULL ,
        maddressId   int  NOT NULL ,
        mcustomerId   int  NOT NULL )

CREATE TABLE    T_Order  (
        morderId   int  NOT NULL ,
        minvoiceId   int  NULL ,
        mcustomerId   int  NOT NULL ,
        morderNumber   char  (10) NOT NULL,
        morderdatetime   date  NOT NULL ,
        mterms   varchar  (30) NOT NULL ,
        msalesPerson   varchar  (20) NOT NULL ,
        mdiscount   decimal (17, 2) NOT NULL ,
        mcourtesyMessage   varchar  (50) NOT NULL
        )

CREATE TABLE    T_OrderLine  (
        mquantity   int  NOT NULL ,
        mdiscount   decimal (17, 2) NOT NULL ,
        mextendedUnitPrice   decimal (17, 2) NOT
        NULL ,
        morderLineId   int  NOT NULL ,
        mproductId   int  NOT NULL ,
        morderId   int  NOT NULL )

CREATE TABLE    T_Payment  (
        mpaymentId   int  NOT NULL ,
        mpaymentAmount   decimal (17, 2) NOT
        NULL,
        mpaymentDate   date NOT NULL)

  CREATE TABLE    T_Product  (
        mproductId   int  NOT NULL ,
        mdescription   varchar  (50) NOT NULL ,
        mprice   decimal (17, 2) NOT NULL ,
        mdiscount   decimal (17, 2) NOT NULL ,
        mquantityOnHand   int  NOT NULL ,
        meoq   int  NOT NULL ,
```

```
            mrefproductId   int  NULL ,
            mproductType   int  NULL )

CREATE TABLE     T_SheetMusic (
            msheetId   int  NOT NULL ,
            mpages   int  NOT NULL ,
            mproductId   int  NOT NULL )

CREATE TABLE     T_Shipment  (
            mshipmentId   int  NOT NULL ,
            mshipmentdatetime   date  NOT NULL )

CREATE TABLE     T_Supplies  (
            msupplyId   int  NOT NULL ,
            mindependent   char  (5) NOT NULL ,
            mproductId   int  NOT NULL )

CREATE TABLE     T_SysCode  (
            msysCodeId   int  NOT NULL ,
            mname   char  (12) NOT NULL ,
            mcode   char  (4) NOT NULL ,
            mdescription   varchar  (20) NOT NULL )

CREATE VIEW Guitar_V(
    mstringCount,
    mright,
    mfretLess,
    mmake,
    mmodel,
    mage,
    mguitarId,
    mproductId,
    mdescription,
    mprice,
    mdiscount,
    mquantityOnHand,
    meoq,
    mproductType)

    AS SELECT
    T_Guitar.mstringCount,
```

```
        T_Guitar.mright,
        T_Guitar.mfretLess,
        T_Guitar.mmake,
        T_Guitar.mmodel,
        T_Guitar.mage,
        T_Guitar.mguitarId,
        T_Product.mproductId,
        T_Product.mdescription,
        T_Product.mprice,
        T_Product.mdiscount,
        T_Product.mquantityOnHand,
        T_Product.meoq,
        T_Product.mproductType

        FROM T_Guitar,T_Product
        WHERE T_Guitar.mproductId=T_Product.mproductId

    CREATE VIEW SheetMusic_V(
        mpages,
        msheetId,
        mproductId,
        mdescription,
        mprice,
        mdiscount,
        mquantityOnHand,
        meoq,
        mproductType)

        AS SELECT
        T_SheetMusic.mpages,
        T_SheetMusic.msheetId,
        T_Product.mproductId,
        T_Product.mdescription,
        T_Product.mprice,
        T_Product.mdiscount,
        T_Product.mquantityOnHand,
        T_Product.meoq,
        T_Product.mproductType
```

```
    FROM T_SheetMusic,T_Product
    WHERE T_SheetMusic.mproductId=T_Product.
    mproductId

CREATE VIEW Supplies_V(
    mindependent,
    msupplyId,
    mproductId,
    mdescription,
    mprice,
    mdiscount,
    mquantityOnHand,
    meoq,
    mproductType)

    AS SELECT

    T_Supplies.mindependent,
    T_Supplies.msupplyId,
    T_Product.mproductId,
    T_Product.mdescription,
    T_Product.mprice,
    T_Product.mdiscount,
    T_Product.mquantityOnHand,
    T_Product.meoq,
    T_Product.mproductType

    FROM T_Supplies,T_Product
    WHERE T_Supplies.mproductId=T_Product.
    mproductId
```

Bibliography

There are many books that have influenced my thought and approach on this project. Some of these are duplicated again in the Suggested Readings appendix. Anyone who considers writing today must have fuel for the mind, and these provided me with quite a bit of power.

Chapter 1

1. Booch, Grady, James Rumbaugh, and Ivar Jacobson. *The Unified Modeling Language User Guide*. Addison Wesley Longman, Inc., October 1998, Reading, Mass.

2. Jacobson, Ivar, Grady Booch, and James Rumbaugh. *The Unified Software Development Process*. Addison Wesley Longman, Inc., January 1999, Reading, Mass.

3. Quatrani, Terry. *Visual Modeling with Rational Rose and UML*. Addison Wesley Longman, Inc., January 1998, Reading, Mass.

4. Rumbaugh, James. *OMT Insights*. SIGS Publishing, 1996.

5. Rumbaugh, James, Grady Booch, and Ivar Jacobson. *The Unified Modeling Language Reference Manual*. Addison Wesley Longman, Inc., December 1998, Reading, Mass.

Chapter 4

1. Jacobson, Ivar. *Object-Oriented Software Engineering*. Addison Wesley Longman, Inc., March 1994, Reading, Mass.

2. Karner, Gustav. *Resource Estimation for Objectory Projects*. Rational Software Corporation, September 1993. Used with permission.

3. *Using Legacy Models in CBD (Component Based Development)*. Component Strategies, November 1998.

Chapter 5

1. Jacobson, Ivar. *Object-Oriented Software Engineering*. Addison Wesley Longman, Inc., March 1994, Reading, Mass.

Chapter 6

1. Gottesdiener, Ellen. *Object-Oriented Analysis and Design Using the UML* (seminar material). EBG Consulting, Carmel, Indiana, 1995-1999.

2. Tasker, Dan. *The Problem Space—Practical Techniques for Gathering and Specifying Requirements using Objects, Events, Rules, Participants, and Locations*. Published electronically; no longer available, 1993.

Chapter 8

1. Reed, Paul R., Jr., and Steven H. Jackson. *An Introduction to Client/Server and Internet Computing* (Seminar Material). Jackson-Reed, Inc., Colorado Springs, 1992-1999.

2. Reed, Paul R., Jr., and Steven H. Jackson. *Analysis and Design of Client/Server Systems* (Seminar Material). Jackson-Reed, Inc., Colorado Springs, 1992-1999.

Chapter 11

1. Lhotka, Rockford. *Professional Visual Basic 5.0 Business Objects*. Wrox Press, November 1997, Chicago.

Chapter 13

1. Gray, Stephen, Rick A. Lievano, and Robert Jennings. *Microsoft Transaction Server 2.0*. SAMS Publishing, December 1997. Indianapolis.

2. Pattison, Ted. *Programming Distributed Applications with COM and Microsoft Visual Basic 6.0*. Microsoft Press, March 1999, Redmond, Washington.

Appendix A

1. Karner, Gustav. *Resource Estimation for Objectory Projects*. Rational Software Corporation, September 1993. Used with permission.

Suggested Readings

There are just too many books out on the market today. In our busy schedules, we never get enough time to read about topics that interest us, let alone those that would help out our jobs and careers. I have the wonderful opportunity to teach and consult on a worldwide basis and over the years have collected a laundry list of books that have been recommended to me by my associates, along with my personal favorites. I would recommend all of these as being an excellent addition to your personal libraries.

- Bellin, David and Susan Suchman-Simone. 1997. *CRC Card Book*. Addison-Wesley Publishing Co.

  These authors provide excellent insight into the uses of the Classes, Responsibilities, Collaborations technique for uncovering object-based classes and their relationships. A must read for anyone involved in object projects that require a level of brainstorming to quickly set the foundation of a project.

- Booch, Grady. 1994. *Object Oriented Analysis and Design with Applications*. Addison-Wesley Publishing Co.

  Includes five complete application design projects using C++, Smalltalk, Object Pascal, the Common Lisp Object System, and Ada.

- Booch, Grady. 1999. *The Unified Modeling Language User Guide*. Addison-Wesley Publishing Co.

This is one of the three books to come from the "three amigos" (Jacobson, Booch, and Rumbaugh) written since the introduction of the Unified Modeling Language.

- Budd, Timothy. 1991. *An Introduction to Object-Oriented Programming*. Addison-Wesley Publishing Co.

  A lucid introduction to the concepts of object-oriented programming. Concepts are presented in a language-independent way, but the book does assumes a knowledge of conventional programming.

- Davis, Alan M. 1995. *201 Principles of Software Development*. IEEE Computer Society.

  Many software projects are late and over budget because software managers are untrained in the principles of software development. Here's the first guide that gathers together all the principles necessary to enhance quality and productivity.

- Derfler, F. J., Jr. 1995. *PC Magazine Guide to Connectivity, Third Edition*. Ziff-Davis Press.

  Covers all the bases with PC Magazine's most up-to-date product information and a special section on modems and modem communications. In addition, the author delivers lab-tested product comparisons, practical advice, and two disks with the latest in network utilities.

- Ericksson, Hans-Erik. 1998. *UML Toolkit*. John Wiley and Sons.

  One of the first texts out on the Unified Modeling Language. Excellent example of the entire process of analyzing and designing an object-based application. An example library system is presented along with sample source code on a companion CD-ROM.

- Fowler, Martin. 1997. *UML Distilled*. Addison-Wesley Publishing Co.

  One of the initial texts on the Unified Modeling Language. Provides several practical guidelines and insights into this emerging modeling notation.

- Gamma, Erich, Richard Helm, Ralph Johnson, and John Vlissides. 1995. *Design Patterns—Elements of Reusable Object-oriented Software*. Addison-Wesley Publishing Co.

  A must for anyone serious about doing object-oriented development. The "gang of four" have collected and formalized all the many software patterns that are consistently found time and time again in object-oriented design. This text can provide an immense jump-start to any design effort.

- Gilly, D. 1992. *UNIX In A Nutshell*. O'Reilly & Associates.

    A complete UNIX reference containing all commands and options, plus generous descriptions and examples that put the commands in context.

- Guengerich, Steven and BSG. 1992. *Downsizing Information Systems— Proven Methods for Reengineering Complex Information Systems*. SAMS Publishing.

    Discusses business opportunity and organization suggestions that help you decide when downsizing is necessary. Includes problem-solving answers and advice to help you plan, design, and implement your changes. Perfect for the corporate information systems strategist faced with the right sizing question.

- Hackathorn, Richard, D. 1993. *Enterprise Database Connectivity*. John Wiley and Sons.

    A must for people wanting to know more about database connectivity across the Wide Area Network. Dr. Hackathorn, original founder of Micro Decisionware, Inc., (purchased by Sybase, Inc., in 1994) does a great job taking you through the subtleties of the many issues and technologies that facilitate enterprise connectivity.

- Jacobson, Ivar. 1995. *Object-Oriented Software Engineering: A Use Case Driven Approach*. Addison-Wesley Publishing Co.

    This book is one of the pillars of object-oriented thought today. Its main focus is the concept of use case-driven development. Jacobson has contributed his use case concept to what has become the Unified Modeling Language.

- Jacobson, Ivar. 1999. *The Unified Software Development Process*. Addison-Wesley Publishing Co.

    This is one of the three books to come from the "three amigos" (Jacobson, Booch, and Rumbaugh) written since the introduction of the Unified Modeling Language.

- Jennings, Roger. 1997. *Microsoft Transaction Server 2.0*. Coriolis.

    This book is one of the first complete references on the Microsoft Transaction Server technology. Examples are given using Visual Basic and C++.

- Kimball, Ralph. 1996. *The Data Warehouse Toolkit*. John Wiley and Sons.
  Excellent book on the fundamentals of data warehouse design. Emphasis on multidimensional databases. Lots of case scenarios on various design approaches based on industry sectors.

- Larman, Craig. 1997. *Applying UML and Patterns: An Introduction to Object-Oriented Analysis and Design*. Prentice Hall.
  Written for the developer with previous programming and design experience. Combines Unified Modeling Language, software patterns, and Java to illustrate the author's own design strategy. Though author Craig Larman sometimes relies heavily on the jargon of software engineering, there's no doubt that his book contains some immediately useful ideas on software design using the latest and greatest in software-engineering research.

- Lee. 1993. *Object-Oriented GUI Application Development*. Prentice Hall.
  Presents an object-oriented life-cycle approach that integrates the process of developing an application with the development of the application's graphical user interface.

- Maguire, Stephen A. 1993. *Writing Solid Code*. Microsoft Press.
  Provides practical approaches to the prevention and automatic detection of bugs. Throughout draws candidly on the history of application development at Microsoft for cases in point—both good and bad—and shows you how to use proven programming techniques to produce solid code.

- McConnell, Steven C. 1993. *Code Complete*. Microsoft Press.
  This ingeniously organized handbook contains state-of-the-art information that can help you write better programs in less time with fewer headaches. It is not a panacea, but it is an encyclopedic treatment of software construction, which is a critical part of the software-development life cycle. It contains some five hundred examples of code (good and bad) and includes ready-to-use checklists to help you assess your architecture, design approach, and module and routine quality.

- Naughton, Patrick. 1996. *The Java Handbook*. Osborne-McGraw Hill.
  An excellent book on the fundamentals of Java programming. Well written and easy to understand.

- Negroponte, Nicholas. 1996. *Being Digital*. Vintage Books.

  Decodes the mysteries and debunks the hype surrounding bandwidth, multimedia, virtual reality, and the Internet.

- Orfali, Robert and Dan Harkey. 1997. *Client/Server Programming with Java and CORBA*. Wiley Computer Publishing.

  Excellent book on building CORBA applications using Java. There is also an excellent review and comparison of DCOM, Microsoft's competing distributed infrastructure.

- Orfali, Robert, Dan Harkey, and Jeri Edwards. 1996. *Essential Client/Server Survival Guide*. John Wiley and Sons.

  Distributed objects and components are a revolution in the making. The authors combine detailed technical explanations with their unique brand of offbeat humor. Zog Lives!

- Pattison, Ted. 1999. *Programming Distributed Applications with COM and Microsoft Visual Basic*. Microsoft Press.

  This book is on its way to being in the "bible" category. Although there is a lot more C++ code in the book than you would expect based on the title, Ted does the best job I've seen to date on explaining COM and DCOM in terms that are digestible by the common man. A must have.

- Ross, Ron. 1997. *The Business Rule Book: Classifying, Defining and Modeling Rules*. Database Research Group.

  Excellent review of how to categorize business rules and provide accountability for the implementation.

- Rumbaugh, James. 1991. *Object-Oriented Modeling and Design*. Prentice Hall.

  The classic text from the developer of the Object Modeling Technique methodology. This technique has been one of the most utilized object methodologies in existence today.

- Rumbaugh, James. 1999. *The Unified Modeling Language Reference Manual*. Addison-Wesley Publishing Co.

  This is one of the three books to come from the "three amigos" (Jacobson, Booch, and Rumbaugh) written since the introduction of the Unified Modeling Language.

- Salemi, J. 1993. *PC Magazine Guide to Client/Server Databases*. Ziff-Davis Press.

  Covers all major client/server systems on all major platforms and includes a client/server vendor directory.

- Schnaidt, Patricia. 1992. *Enterprise-Wide Networking*. SAMS Publishing.

  This is a good primer on the ins and outs of networking as it relates to the enterprise. New technology such as Frame Relay and Asynchronous Transfer Mode (ATM) are reviewed.

- Smith, Patrick and BSG. 1992. *Client/Server Computing*. SAMS Publishing.

  An all-in-one reference for total systems development that includes an in-depth analysis of information processing, expert design and procedure tips, and a focus on building systems development environments.

- Taylor, David. 1998. *Object Technology: A Manager's Guide*. Addison-Wesley Publishing Co.

  An excellent introduction to object-oriented technology for "those who are afraid to ask." Covers all the basic concepts without being intimidating. A quick read.

- Tyma, Paul, Gabriel Torok, and Douglas Downing. 1996. *Java Primer Plus*. Waite Group Press.

  Brings the novice and the experienced programmer up to speed on creating Java-based Web pages with multimedia and interactive trimmings. CD-ROM includes the Java 1 compiler for Windows 95, Windows NT, and Solaris.

Index

Object Solutions
Managing the Object-Oriented Project
Grady Booch
Addison-Wesley Object Technology Series

Object Solutions is a direct outgrowth of Grady Booch's experience with object-oriented projects in development around the world. This book focuses on the development process and is the perfect resource for developers and managers who want to implement object technologies for the first time or refine their existing object-oriented development practice. Drawing upon his knowledge of strategies used in both successful and unsuccessful projects, the author offers pragmatic advice for applying object technologies and controlling projects effectively.

0-8053-0594-7 • Paperback • 336 pages • ©1996

The Unified Modeling Language User Guide
Grady Booch, James Rumbaugh, and Ivar Jacobson
Addison-Wesley Object Technology Series

The Unified Modeling Language User Guide is a two-color introduction to the core eighty percent of the Unified Modeling Language, approaching it in a layered fashion and showing the application of the UML to modeling problems across a wide variety of application domains. This landmark book is suitable for developers unfamiliar with the UML or modeling in general, and will also be useful to experienced developers who wish to learn how to apply the UML to advanced problems.

0-201-57168-4 • Hardcover • 512 pages • ©1999

Surviving Object-Oriented Projects
A Manager's Guide
Alistair Cockburn
Addison-Wesley Object Technology Series

This book allows you to survive, and ultimately succeed with, an object-oriented project. Alistair Cockburn draws on his personal experience and extensive knowledge to provide the information that managers need to combat the unforeseen challenges that await them during project implementation. *Surviving Object-Oriented Projects* supports its key points through short case studies taken from real object-oriented projects. An appendix collects these guidelines and solutions into brief "crib sheets" —ideal for handy reference.

0-201-49834-0 • Paperback • 272 pages • ©1998

Real-Time UML, Second Edition
Developing Efficient Objects for Embedded Systems
Bruce Powel Douglass
Addison-Wesley Object Technology Series

The Unified Modeling Language is particularly suited to modeling real-time and embedded systems. *Real-Time UML, Second Edition,* is the completely updated and UML 1.3–compliant introduction that developers of real-time systems need to make the transition to object-oriented analysis and design with UML. The book covers the important features of the UML and shows how to effectively use these features to model real-time systems. Special in-depth discussions of finite state machines, object identification strategies, and real-time design patterns to help beginning and experienced developers alike are also included.

0-201-65784-8 • Paperback • 368 pages • ©2000

Analysis Patterns
Reusable Object Models
Martin Fowler
Addison-Wesley Object Technology Series

Martin Fowler shares with you his wealth of object modeling experience and his keen eye for solving repeating problems and transforming the solutions into reusable models. *Analysis Patterns* provides a catalog of patterns that have emerged in a wide range of domains, including trading, measurement, accounting, and organizational relationships.

0-201-89542-0 • Hardcover • 384 pages • ©1997

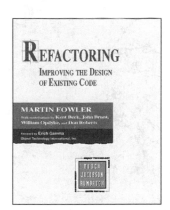

Refactoring
Improving the Design of Existing Code
Martin Fowler with contributions by Kent Beck, John Brant, William Opdyke, and Don Roberts
Addison-Wesley Object Technology Series

In this book, Martin Fowler, well-known author of *Analysis Patterns*, breaks new ground again with the first focused introduction to the process of refactoring. Formerly a tool employed by expert programmers only, refactoring is a method of reworking an existing bad design into a good one. Each refactoring step is simple—seemingly too simple to be worth doing. Refactoring may involve moving a field from one class to another, or pulling some code out of a method to turn it into its own method, or even pushing some code up or down a hierarchy. While these individual steps may seem elementary, the cumulative effect of such small changes can radically improve the existing design and is a proven way to prevent software decay.

0-201-48567-2 • Hardcover • 464 pages • ©1999

UML Distilled, Second Edition
A Brief Guide to the Standard Object Modeling Language
Martin Fowler with Kendall Scott
Addison-Wesley Object Technology Series

Thoroughly revised and updated, this best-selling book is a concise overview that introduces you to the Unified Modeling Language, highlighting the key elements of the standard modeling language's notation, semantics, and processes. Included is a brief explanation of UML's history, development, and rationale, as well as discussions on how UML can be integrated into the object-oriented development process. The book also profiles various modeling techniques associated with UML—use cases, CRC cards, design by contract, dynamic classification, interfaces, and abstract classes. The first edition of this classic work was the recipient of *Software Development* magazine's 1997 Productivity Award.

0-201-65783-X • Paperback • 224 pages • ©2000

Software Reuse
Architecture, Process and Organization for Business Success
Ivar Jacobson, Martin Griss, and Patrik Jonsson
Addison-Wesley Object Technology Series

This book brings software engineers, designers, programmers, and their managers a giant step closer to a future in which object-oriented component-based software engineering is the norm. Jacobson, Griss, and Jonsson develop a coherent model and set of guidelines for ensuring success with large-scale, systematic, object-oriented reuse. Their framework, referred to as "Reuse-Driven Software Engineering Business" (Reuse Business) deals systematically with the key business process, architecture, and organization issues that hinder success with reuse.

0-201-92476-5 • Hardcover • 528 pages • ©1997

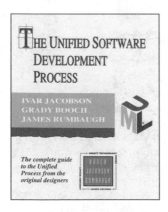

The Unified Software Development Process
Ivar Jacobson, Grady Booch, and James Rumbaugh
Addison-Wesley Object Technology Series

The Unified Software Development Process goes beyond other object-oriented analysis and design methods by detailing a family of processes that incorporate the complete lifecycle of software development. This new book, representing the collaboration of Ivar Jacobson, Grady Booch, and James Rumbaugh, clearly describes the different higher-level constructs—notation as well as semantics—used in the models. Thus stereotypes such as use cases and actors, packages, classes, interfaces, active classes, processes and threads, nodes, and most relations are described intuitively in the context of a model.

0-201-57169-2 • Hardcover • 512 pages • ©1999

The Rational Unified Process

An Introduction
Philippe Kruchten
Addison-Wesley Object Technology Series

This concise book offers a quick introduction to the concepts, structure, content, and motivation of the Rational Unified Process. This revolutionary software development process provides a disciplined approach to assigning, managing, and completing tasks within a software development organization and is the first development process to exploit the full capabilities of the industry-standard Unified Modeling Language. *The Rational Unified Process* is unique in that it captures many of the proven best practices in modern software development and presents them in a form that can be tailored to a wide range of projects and organizations.

0-201-60459-0 • Paperback • 272 pages • ©1999

Enterprise Modeling with UML

Designing Successful Software through Business Analysis
Chris Marshall
Addison-Wesley Object Technology Series

In this groundbreaking book, the author fuses object technology, workflow, data warehousing, and distributed systems concepts into a single coherent system model that has been successfully implemented worldwide. He describes specific methods for modeling large, complex, and adaptable enterprises, using the Unified Modeling Language (UML) for designing model components. The accompanying CD-ROM contains Java and XML implementations of many of the ideas and models in the book, demonstrating how software components are created to reflect business specifications.

0-201-43313-3 • Paperback with CD-ROM • 288 pages • ©2000

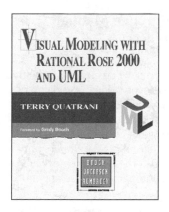

Visual Modeling with Rational Rose 2000 and UML

Terry Quatrani
Addison-Wesley Object Technology Series

Terry Quatrani, the Rose Evangelist from Rational Software Corporation, uses a simplified case study to teach readers how to analyze and design an application using UML and how to implement the application using Rational Rose 2000. With the practical direction offered in this updated book, you will be able to specify, visualize, document, and create software solutions. Highlights include an examination of system behavior from a use case approach, a discussion of the concepts and notations used for finding objects and classes, an introduction to the notation needed to create and document a system's architecture, and a review of the iteration planning process.

0-201-69961-3 • Paperback • 256 pages • ©2000

Use Case Driven Object Modeling with UML

A Practical Approach
Doug Rosenberg with Kendall Scott
Addison-Wesley Object Technology Series

This book presents a streamlined approach to UML modeling that includes a minimal but sufficient set of diagrams and techniques you can use to get from use cases to code quickly and efficiently. *Use Case Driven Object Modeling with UML* provides practical guidance that shows developers how to produce UML models with minimal startup time, while maintaining traceability from user requirements through detailed design and coding. The authors draw upon their extensive industry experience to present proven methods for driving the object modeling process forward from use cases in a simple and straightforward manner.

0-201-43289-7 • Paperback • 192 pages • ©1999

Software Project Management

A Unified Framework
Walker Royce
Addison-Wesley Object Technology Series

This book presents a new management framework uniquely suited to the complexities of modern software development. Walker Royce's pragmatic perspective exposes the shortcomings of many well-accepted management priorities and equips software professionals with state-of-the-art knowledge derived from his twenty years of successful from-the-trenches management experience. In short, the book provides the software industry with field-proven benchmarks for making tactical decisions and strategic choices that will enhance an organization's probability of success.

0-201-30958-0 • Hardcover • 448 pages • ©1998

The Unified Modeling Language Reference Manual

James Rumbaugh, Ivar Jacobson, and Grady Booch
Addison-Wesley Object Technology Series

James Rumbaugh, Ivar Jacobson, and Grady Booch have created the definitive reference to the UML. This two-color book covers every aspect and detail of the UML and presents the modeling language in a useful reference format that serious software architects or programmers should have on their bookshelf. The book is organized by topic and designed for quick access. The authors also provide the necessary information to enable existing OMT, Booch, and OOSE notation users to make the transition to UML. The book provides an overview of the semantic foundation of the UML through a concise appendix.

0-201-30998-X • Hardcover with CD-ROM • 576 pages • ©1999

Applying Use Cases
A Practical Guide
Geri Schneider and Jason P. Winters
Addison-Wesley Object Technology Series

Applying Use Cases provides a practical and clear introduction to developing use cases, demonstrating their use via a continuing case study. Using the Unified Software Development Process as a framework and the Unified Modeling Language as a notation, the authors step the reader through applying use cases in the different phases of the process, focusing on where and how use cases are best applied. The book also offers insight into the common mistakes and pitfalls that can plague an object-oriented project.

0-201-30981-5 • Paperback • 208 pages • ©1998

Enterprise Computing with Objects
From Client/Server Environments to the Internet
Yen-Ping Shan and Ralph H. Earle
Addison-Wesley Object Technology Series

This book helps you place rapidly evolving technologies—such as the Internet, the World Wide Web, distributed computing, object technology, and client/server systems—in their appropriate contexts when preparing for the development, deployment, and maintenance of information systems. The authors distinguish what is essential from what is incidental, while imparting a clear understanding of how the underlying technologies fit together. The book examines essential topics, including data persistence, security, performance, scalability, and development tools.

0-201-32566-7 • Paperback • 448 pages • ©1998

The Object Constraint Language
Precise Modeling with UML
Jos Warmer and Anneke Kleppe
Addison-Wesley Object Technology Series

The Object Constraint Language is a new notational language, a subset of the Unified Modeling Language, that allows software developers to express a set of rules that govern very specific aspects of an object in object-oriented applications. With the OCL, developers are able to more easily express unique limitations and write the fine print that is often necessary in complex software designs. The authors' pragmatic approach and illustrative use of examples will help application developers to quickly get up to speed.

0-201-37940-6 • Paperback • 144 pages • ©1999

Addison-Wesley Computer and Engineering Publishing Group

How to Interact with Us

1. Visit our Web site

http://www.awl.com/cseng

When you think you've read enough, there's always more content for you at Addison-Wesley's web site. Our web site contains a directory of complete product information including:

- Chapters
- Exclusive author interviews
- Links to authors' pages
- Tables of contents
- Source code

You can also discover what tradeshows and conferences Addison-Wesley will be attending, read what others are saying about our titles, and find out where and when you can meet our authors and have them sign your book.

2. Subscribe to Our Email Mailing Lists

Subscribe to our electronic mailing lists and be the first to know when new books are publishing. Here's how it works: Sign up for our electronic mailing at **http://www.awl.com/cseng/mailinglists.html**. Just select the subject areas that interest you and you will receive notification via email when we publish a book in that area.

3. Contact Us via Email

cepubprof@awl.com
Ask general questions about our books.
Sign up for our electronic mailing lists.
Submit corrections for our web site.

bexpress@awl.com
Request an Addison-Wesley catalog.
Get answers to questions regarding your order or our products.

innovations@awl.com
Request a current Innovations Newsletter.

webmaster@awl.com
Send comments about our web site.

jcs@awl.com
Submit a book proposal.
Send errata for an Addison-Wesley book.

cepubpublicity@awl.com
Request a review copy for a member of the media interested in reviewing new Addison-Wesley titles.

We encourage you to patronize the many fine retailers who stock Addison-Wesley titles. Visit our online directory to find stores near you or visit our online store: **http://store.awl.com/** or call 800-824-7799.

Addison Wesley Longman
Computer and Engineering Publishing Group
One Jacob Way, Reading, Massachusetts 01867 USA
TEL 781-944-3700 • FAX 781-942-3076